Building Database Applications on the Web Using

PHP3

Building Database Applications on the Web Using
PHP3

Complete with Step-by-Step Demonstrations

Craig Hilton
Jeff Willis

ADDISON-WESLEY

An imprint of Addison Wesley Longman, Inc.

Reading, Massachusetts • Harlow, England • Menlo Park, California
Berkeley, California • Don Mills, Ontario • Sydney
Bonn • Amsterdam • Tokyo • Mexico City

The publisher offers discounts on this book when ordered in quantity for special sales. For more information, please contact:

Pearson Education Corporate Sales Division
One Lake Street
Upper Saddle River, NJ 07458
(800) 382-3419

Visit AW on the Web: www.awl.com/cseng/

Library of Congress Cataloging-in-Publication Data
Hilton, Craig, 1949–
    Building database applications on the web using PHP3 / Craig Hilton, Jeff Willis.
        p. cm.
    Includes bibliographical references and index.
    ISBN 0-201-65771-6 (alk. paper)
    1. Database design. 2. PHP (Computer program language) 3. World Wide Web
(Information retrieval system) I. Willis, Jeff. II. Title

    QA76.9.D26 H56 2000
    005.2'762—dc21

                                                                                99-049969

Executive Editor: Paul Becker
Editorial Assistant: Ross Venables
Production Manager: Sarah Weaver
Project Management: Diane Freed
Cover Design: Simone R. Payment
Compositor: Stratford Publishing Services, Inc.

ISBN 0-201-65771-6
Text printed on recycled and acid-free paper.
1 2 3 4 5 6 7 8 9 10—CRS—0302010099
First printing, December 1999

Contents

Preface

A good beginning makes a good ending.
—English proverb

We began developing Internet database applications several years ago. We tried most of the commercial database products. We found that the learning curve, coupled with seemingly endless product upgrades, worked together to discourage our efforts. (Just keeping our network running was hard enough, let alone trying to juggle an off-site database development environment!)

Within a week of discovering PHP3, we were converts. Could anything really work this well? We found the learning curve to be gradual. The performance statistics were comparable to everything else we were using. And it is open source!

As the proverb suggests, "a good beginning" does indeed make for a "good ending." The robust syntax of PHP3, its broad database connectivity, and the worldwide user support base were strong factors in our adoption of PHP as one of our development standards.

To see for yourself, take a 30-minute "test drive" by logging onto *www.php123.com*. You will need the ID available on the CD. Turn to Chapter 3 in the book and type in "Example 1." Then run your example. Your real-world application example is worth ten thousand words. We think you will be as pleased as we were with what you find. No excuses, jump to *www.php123.com* now!

For readers who are already PHP3 users, we hope you will find this book useful as a comprehensive reference guide. We included virtually every important function, with sections on syntax and user functions. We omitted detailed examples on certain arcane or highly specialized functions that we felt would not be useful in the average development effort. For the most part, the Language and Function Reference contains examples the authors have developed to demonstrate actual working snippets of logic. *These examples are not a reprinting of the on-line technical documentation!*

The book emphasizes applications using PostgresSQL and MySQL, two powerful database management systems. This is not to say that PHP3 can't use Oracle, Sybase, Informix, and Microsoft SQL Server—quite the contrary, all are supported at the native access levels by PHP3. We had only so many pages to work with, and since all database functions are similar, we have not included detailed examples of these in this book. Examples are found on the Readers Only web site.

Suggestions or additions? We welcome and encourage your feedback. PHP3 is a collective effort and this is a collective book. The acknowledgment section gives lists of people whose collective efforts have built and continue to maintain PHP3, and of others who have been so helpful in this book's preparation and development.

So, what is PHP3 anyway? In short, *PHP3 is a server-side programming environment that lets you mix HTML and script code.* The scripting language resembles C and Perl. Because PHP3 was specifically designed to be a server-side scripting language for web servers, it offers a vast array of functions and behind-the-scenes magic to make common tasks easy. Read on.

Acknowledgments

The authors would like to gratefully acknowledge and thank several of our numerous friends, colleagues, and industry professionals who directly or indirectly helped bring this book to press.

Our reviewers, Bruce Momjian, Randy Cosby, Eric Raymond, Jon Forrest, Jonathan Stigelman, and Michael A. Smith, for their helpful suggestions and professional analysis.

Our friends and colleagues George W. Lackamy, Joan Burnett, Sheri Smith, and Jenny Ho for their daily encouragement and support.

Rasmus Lerdorf for the little CGI wrapper written in Perl that has grown into PHP as we know it today. All of the countless others who have improved PHP. Linus Torvalds for Linux.

W. Richard Stevens for his excellent text on UNIX system programming, *Advance Programming in the Unix Environment*. He passed away on September 1, 1999, and will be missed.

Eric Steven Raymond for helping the world understand the economics and dynamics of Open Source and other collaborative development efforts such as PHP, Linux, and Apache.

Our editor, Paul Becker, and his assistant, Ross Venables, for their encouragement, support and guidance.

Diane Freed, for getting this manuscript into its final form.

Craig's wife, Peggy, and the kids, for putting up with all the late nights and early mornings.

Introduction

This book describes how to build web-based database applications using PHP3. If you want to build real-world, industrial-strength database applications for use on the web, this is the book for you. It's all about building web sites with content that changes.

PHP3 is both intuitive and easy to use, providing a robust platform that the authors have used to build and host dozens of major projects. It prototypes quickly. It demos well. It's fast. It's easy to maintain. And it scales easily to full production.

We weren't surprised to learn that over 1 million web sites are being built using PHP3 (Netcraft's November 1999 Server Survey, *http://www.netcraft. com*). We *were* surprised at what a well-kept secret it is. When we began looking for printed documentation, we found virtually nothing. So, we've included a comprehensive Language and Function Reference with real-world examples. This is *not* just another copy of the on-line technical docs—rather, these are real-world examples that we've written based on the latest function releases. We've also provided a step-by-step tutorial about getting the combination to work for you.

According to columnist Graeme Merrall, PHP3 and MySQL are the "world's best combination for creating data-driven sites." The combination was awarded Database of the Year at Webcon98. So you are reading the right book.

In addition to being free, PHP3 is also portable, which means you can develop on Windows and serve on a UNIX or Mac platform, or vice versa. For you more savvy users, PHP3 can be run as an external CGI process, a stand-alone script interpreter, or an embedded Apache module.

PHP3 supports a host of other features right at the technological edge of web development. These include user authentication, XML, dynamic image creation, and dynamic PDF document creation. Not enough? If you're programming-savvy, PHP3 is also easy to extend, so you can expand the function library to suit your own unique requirements.

We've also included a 400-page comprehensive Language and Function Reference covering virtually all of PHP3's hundreds of functions. Most have examples directly from the authors' development lab, so the reader can cut and paste them directly into real-time applications.

The attached CD-ROM provides everything you need to install PHP3 under Red-Hat Linux. Or, if you really want to get up and running quickly, use our Readers Only web site at *www.php123.com.* Just connect to the web and begin building all the applications in the book.

You do not need to install *any* software to build live, real-world database applications on the Internet. *Everything* is included at *http://www.php123. com.* Use the attached CD-ROM only if you need to put PHP3 on your local computer.

Who Is This Book For?

This book is for anyone who wants to

- build a web site with active content
- build web-based (Intranet or Internet) applications
- develop web-based applications that access new or existing SQL databases

This book is for the novice and almost-expert alike. Whether you make a living supporting interactive database applications or you just want to build a counter for your personal web page, you will find this book both a step-by-step teaching guide and a comprehensive technical resource. (If you are already writing custom PHP3 functions and classes, this may not be the book for you.)

We've divided the book up into "fundamental" and "advanced" sections. If you have *never* built a database application, this book will teach you *fundamentals* and guide you through building seven applications, from a simple page counter to an interactive e-mail server. We have included special fundamental sections, indicated by the abacus icon (shown at left), that we hope will tie some of the important concepts into a clearer perspective.

On the other hand, if you are already adept at active-content web-based development but are looking for a more robust solution, you will also find what you need in this book. We have included working examples of important language functions, along with syntax and grammar overviews. We've also included a few advanced sections, indicated by the calculator icon (shown at left), that are just for you.

What prior experience is necessary?

- It will help if you have some experience creating web pages using HTML. Don't have any? You'll learn along the way.

- It will help if you have some basic experience with programming logic and syntax. But if you've never programmed "Hello World" before, this book will teach you how.
- It will help if you have some basic experience with database concepts. Don't have any? Just follow the examples carefully and you'll learn how to create maintainable databases in SQL (Structured Query Language).

PHP3 and PostgreSQL combine two powerful UNIX-based capabilities: a strong scripting language (PHP) and a transaction-oriented database management system (PostgreSQL) into a single integrated development environment. PHP3 has recently been extended to accommodate an expanded function library, plus various maintenance and installation scripts. PHP3 also provides the capacity for your applications to read and write many popular databases (including Oracle, dBase, Informix, and even Microsoft Access).

The combination of capabilities gives you, the developer, a diversity of tools and procedures that has been likened to a "Swiss army knife" of Internet database development. PHP3 not only provides a broad tools collection, but, more importantly, insures a robust and industrial-strength environment on which to build real-world applications.

You may be a seasoned programmer looking for a "better way." Or you may be planning to develop your first application. We'll try and provide both of you with a step-by-step guide to building powerful database applications on the Internet or your company intranet (well, for that matter, they will run just fine on your local network, too).

Do you need a college degree in computer science? Of course not. Look around at the people building the "next generation" computer applications. Who are they? They are very often people with experience in areas outside computer technology who bring their experience to bear on technology issues.

One of the authors taught college-level computer science full-time for several years and discovered an amazing fact: Regardless of a student's education level or background, *any* student with time and interest could become proficient at building computer applications—not just learning to use a computer, but developing meaningful and unique applications. The authors firmly believe this even more today, having watched hundreds of people learn the basics of application development and then jump into building applications that use the experiences they have gleaned in their chosen professions.

So who is this book for? If you want to build an application for public use that can be accessed by anyone in the world on the Internet (or on a local area network, or even for use on your own personal computer), then you will want to consider using PHP3.

Chapter by Chapter

The book has six sections:

- Overview
- Background
- Applications
- Technical Notes
- Language and Function Reference
- Appendices

Overview (Chapter 1) deals with how best to use this book. Here you will find the how-to's of installing the CD-ROM, accessing the Readers Only web site, and the like.

Background (Chapters 2–11) focuses on issues, techniques, and concepts important for any user of web-based technologies. Topics covered include TCP/IP, the web, UNIX, PHP, PostgreSQL, and MySQL. This section lays the foundation for understanding the interrelationships of PHP3 and database-development tools on the web.

Applications (Chapter 12) leads the reader through the step-by-step building of seven PHP3 applications. The first two involve basic techniques, the third uses the language to build run-time generated graphics, the fourth and fifth focus on database integration and design, and the sixth and seventh provide a working example of login authentication.

Technical Notes (Chapter 13) digs deeper into selected topics.

The **Language and Function Reference** is a comprehensive reference of the syntax, grammar and functions of PHP3. All functions are listed alphabetically within their respective category. A categorical index of all functions in the Reference Section precedes the listings. The examples that make up this section come directly from the authors' development lab. We hope they provide sufficient depth to be useful in your real-world applications. The Reference Section is divided into seven primary categories:

- Expressions
- Data-related functions
- Network-related functions
- Process-related functions
- Database-related functions
- Graphics-related functions
- File-related functions

Appendix 1 covers variables provided to PHP3 scripts, and **Appendix 2** discusses PostgreSQL and fsync().

There is both a **comprehensive index** for the entire book and a **function index** that alphabetically lists all of the functions covered in the book.

If you have a strong database programming background and want to see PHP3 in action, jump to the Reference Section.

If you are a neophyte, then start at the beginning. Work the examples. Pay particular attention to the beginner-level sections, which are there just for you. Plan on finishing the seven applications in about 10 hours if you use our free on-line development site. The best place to start will be the Background sections.

Chapter 1

Getting Started

1.1 Getting the Most from This Book

You will need access to a computer.

If you plan on building your first applications on the *www.php123.com* Readers Only web site, you will need access to the Internet (of course!). Don't have it? We've included on the CD-ROM several national providers that offer special dial-up access rates.

 Some of you might wonder just how much "computer" it takes to access the Internet. Not much. Actually, almost any computer will do. The important part is the modem. You will want the fastest modem you can get. We suggest 56Kb-V.90-compatible. (Most computer shops will install a 56Kb-V.90-compatible modem and connect you to the Internet for under $100.) Those of you with much higher-speed ISDN, DSL, or cable-modem Internet connections will really experience the full power of PHP3. The faster your Internet connection, the faster PHP3 will appear to work on your computer.

If you will be installing the CD-ROM on your local computer, we suggest a Pentium-class or better processor with at least 32 Mb of RAM.

If you will be installing Linux for the first time, you will need about 200 Mb of hard drive space in a separate partition. If you already have Linux, then 50 Mb of space will do.

 RedHat Linux is also available for DEC Alpha and Sun Sparc systems, if you prefer.

How-to instructions on partitioning your hard drive are included in the install package that comes with Linux.

If you are planning on installing PHP3 on your Web server, you will need 50 Mb of hard-drive space. No additional RAM is required. However, you will find database applications run much faster when you have more memory.

1.2 What You'll Need to Know

What background do you need? Not much. We'll cover (albeit briefly) most of what you need to know to build a PHP3 database application on the Internet. However, this book is not meant as a beginner's tutorial. (Neither is it intended to supplement a Ph.D. dissertation!) We suggest you have some knowledge of basic computer programming, database design and manipulation, and Web page development with HTML. However, this book does *not* require advanced skills in these areas.

The stronger your computer application development background, the faster PHP3 will impress you.

1.3 Online Web Site—http://www.php123.com

If you don't already know: When you bought the book, you received free access to our Readers Only web site for PHP3 development. We think it will be easier to test your first few applications on-line before having to install the software contained on the attached CD-ROM.

Why did we include an on-line web site with this book? We have always been a little surprised that people learning a new computer language are forced to spend hours of often frustrating complexity to assemble the framework to develop an application. Why not just provide a site where all the development framework setup has already been done and the reader need only test it out? Isn't that what the Internet is all about—access from anywhere, anytime? We decided to incorporate that capability into our book. So (drum rolling), as an added benefit to having purchased the book, you have a web site dedicated to helping you learn to build database applications on the Internet using PHP3 (as well as a couple of spiffy database management systems).

There is absolutely nothing to install on your end. All you need is Internet access through a provider.

We are providing two database management systems (DBMSs) for your use on the site: PostgreSQL and MySQL, both powerful, full-function relational DBMSs. Though we cover MySQL in the Reference section, the focus of this book is on PostgreSQL. Why? No particular reason, really. Database development is nearly identical from one DBMS to another. PostgreSQL is, perhaps, the more "industrial-strength" of the two. It contains a few more features. However, MySQL is faster. So, if speed is what you want, use MySQL as your DBMS. If "object-relational" features are what you want, then use PostgreSQL. In any event, the web site (*http://www.php123.com/*) contains them both, so the choice is all yours!

Do you have to use our web site? Of course not. The attached CD-ROM has everything necessary to build your own PHP3 and SQL server. We have enclosed a multi-user copy of one of the most powerful relational database management systems in the world, PostgreSQL. Configure away.

Use *www.php123.com* or configure your own web server—which do we suggest? You may find it much faster to get the feel of PHP3 by building the simple applications contained in this book using the web site. Then, if you choose, create your own PHP3 and SQL servers.

1.4 The "Big Picture" in Pictures

For readers who prefer a graphic representation of the environments covered here, we include a few diagrams. The diagrams are not comprehensive but are meant to demonstrate the interrelationships between systems and subsystems (see Figures 1.1, 1.2, and 1.3).

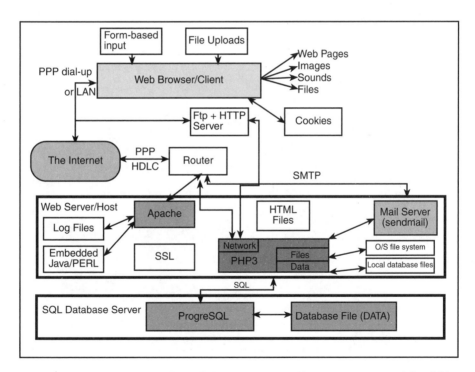

Figure 1.1 How PHP integrates with the web client, the web server, and the SQL database server.

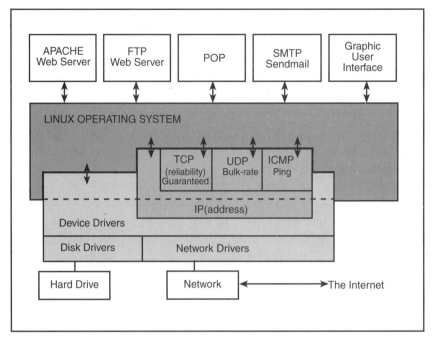

Figure 1.2 The Linux environment: How the Linux operating system integrates its component features.

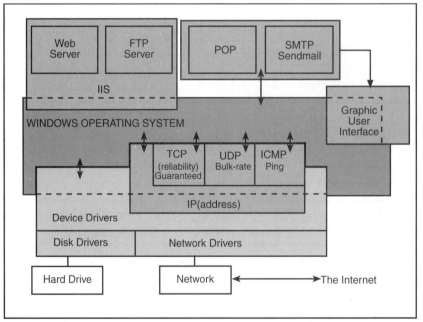

Figure 1.3 The Windows environment: How the Microsoft Windows operating system integrates its component features.

1.5 Getting Up and Running

This is *not* meant to be a tutorial on Linux or Apache. If you would rather not install the CD-ROM, you may choose to work the examples directly on the Readers Only web site (*www.php123.com*).

Using the Readers Only Web Site—*www.php123.com*

Jump to *http://www.php123.com* using your favorite web browser. Purchasers of the book may use this site *100% free* for three months from date of first login.

Each time you enter the site, you will be asked for a login ID.

Once you have successfully logged in (using PHP3 login authentication—which you will be learning how to do in this book), a personal application development directory will be created for you on our server. It's all yours, for three months. You will be required, of course, to abide by our Acceptable Use Policy (*http://www.php123.com/about.html*).

Your account will allow you to build the various applications in this book, on-line. You can work on these anytime you like. You will, of course, be limited in the size of the databases you can build (2.5 Mb of total disk space), but you will be free to customize any aspect of your applications. (You may continue to use the site after three months subject to the conditions listed at *http://www.php123.com/continue.html*.)

Which web browser should you be using? Any browser will work; however, we strongly suggest using a version that is no more than six months old. Want to upgrade your browser? It takes about 30 minutes with a 56Kb connection and it's free. Check out our free download site at *http://www.php123.com/downloads.html*.

 If you don't have an Internet connection or a web browser, hook up to one of the national Internet Service Providers (ISPs) contained on the attached CD-ROM. As you install their service, a web browser will automatically be installed on your computer.

What's There? Once you have logged in, you will be presented with five selections:

1) Your personal application area

2) Up-to-the-minute updates and changes to the book

3) Code snippets and examples of PHP3 code organized by category

4) Links to important PHP3 sites

5) Technical chat

The site is written entirely in PHP3 and MySQL.

Take some time to look around. Have we missed something? Should we add another link? Let us know.

1.6 Using a Local Computer

Installing the CD-ROM

The authors suggest than new users of PHP3 spend some time on the Readers Only web site and build several of the practice applications *before* installing the CD-ROM.

What's There?

- PHP 3.0.12 (latest version) source
- PHP 3.0.11 Win32 binary
- PostgreSQL 6.5.3. (latest version) source
- MySQL GPL 3.20.32a (latest version released under the GPL) source
- All code built in this book
- Expanded function set

Computer Prerequisites. You'll need a PC. You'll need at least 8M of memory and at least a 486 processor. If you've got a Mac or another UNIX-like box, visit *http://www.php123.com/* and download whatever you need from there. Actually, almost any UNIX-like system with a C-compiler will work. If you are running a version of Windows on your machine, you will need to partition the disk to accommodate a UNIX (i.e., Linux) partition. It's not too hard. Just follow the instructions that come with the Red Hat package on the enclosed CD-ROM or visit Red Hat's site directly at *www.redhat.com.*

Apache is not required to make things work. Any good web server (e.g., NCSA, Netscape) will do. But, because PHP3 runs as a module inside Apache, you'll get optimal performance using Apache.

Installing PHP3. If you just want to get PHP3 up and running on your computer, you will need to first install Linux.

During the Red Hat install, you need to select to install "mod_php3" in the list of packages at the beginning of the install. PHP3 is installed automatically.

Or you can install or upgrade PHP3 simply by typing the command rpm -U mod_php3*.rpm from the command line, in the directory in which you have the updated rpm files stored. You will need to get the latest copy of the **rpm** files from *http://www.php123.com/*.

Administering PHP

If you see the source to your PHP program rather than its execution output, then check to see if you have the line below somewhere in /etc/httpd/srm. conf:

```
AddType application/x-httpd-php3 .php3
```

Also, the two lines below should be somewhere in your /etc/httpd/httpd. conf:

```
LoadModule php3_module lib/apache/libphp3.so
AddModule mod_php3.c
```

The above lines tell Apache not to blindly send out files that end in .php3, but to send them to the PHP3 interpreter instead.

Adding Libraries to PHP3

Now, suppose you want to extend the default PHP. Why would you do this? You may want to add features to the default PHP3 library, such as PDF, XML, and other databases. You will first need to download the individual source package (from *http://www.php123.com/*). Next, you will need to compile these packages using your built-in C-compiler. It's not too hard. First you download the modules. Then you uncompress them (tar -xvf php3.*. tar.gz). Now you change to the directory you've just created. Then you type ./configure *options you need (this builds the configuration file). Then you type make, and finally make install. That's it. The packages will compile into the PHP3 library. (If there are errors, read the manual.) Confused? Read the detailed instruction at *http://www.php123.com/*.

Installing PostgreSQL. Just as with PHP, you'll find that during the Red Hat install, you need to select all of the "PostgreSQL" options at the beginning of the install process:

- postgresql
- postgresql-clients
- postgresql-data

PostgreSQL is installed automatically.

Or, you can install or upgrade PostgreSQL simply by typing the command "rpm -U postgresql*.rpm from the command line, from the directory in which you have the updated rmp files stored. Why would you do this? To upgrade to a newer version. Remember, you will first need to download the individual source package (from *http://www.php123.com/*). ▬▬▬▬

Administering PostgreSQL. This section discusses how to start PostgreSQL and set up your own environment. We assume PostgreSQL has already been successfully installed.

Some of the steps listed here apply to all PostgreSQL users, and some apply primarily to the site database administrator. This site administrator is the person who installed the software, created the database directories, and started the **Postmaster** process. This person need not be the UNIX super-user, "root," or the computer system administrator.

Setting Up Your Environment. For simplicity, we assume that PostgreSQL has been installed in the directory /var/lib/pgsql. Therefore, wherever you see the directory /var/lib/pgsql you should substitute the name of the directory where PostgreSQL is actually installed on your system.

Starting the Postmaster. The Postmaster process must be running before anything will work. Why? The Postmaster handles incoming connections and initiates processes to handle the actual database work. If you are running Red Hat Linux, you will find the Postmaster is automatically started at boot. If not, then type

```
/etc/rc.d/init.d/PostgreSQL start
```

Otherwise, you can start the Postmaster as follows:

```
% postmaster &
```

The & puts the process in the background so you get your command prompt back. If you don't see your command prompt, Ctrl-C and start over. ▬▬▬▬

There is one important option that allows connections from other hosts to the database. Why would you need to do this? If you are running your database server on one machine and a client is coming from another, you need to initiate the Postmaster like this:

```
% postmaster -i &
```

Adding and Deleting Users. The createuser command enables specific users to access PostgreSQL. The destroyuser command removes users and prevents them from accessing PostgreSQL. These commands affect users only with respect to PostgreSQL; they have no effect on the administration of users that the operating system manages.

For example, to add Craig Jones (account name: cjones), you type the following:

```
createuser cjones.
```

cjones is now a user. But cjones can't create, modify, or delete database—permission to do these things must be individually granted.

Starting Applications. Assuming Postmaster has been initiated and you are authorized to access a database, you (as a user) may begin to start up applications. If you get the following error message from a PostgreSQL command (such as psql or createdb):

```
connectDB() failed: Is the postmaster running at
  'localhost' on port '5432'?
```

it is usually because (1) the Postmaster is not running, or (2) you are attempting to connect to the wrong server host. The following error message:

```
FATAL 1:Jan 1 20:12:22:process userid (1234) != database
  owner (678)
```

means that the site administrator started the Postmaster as the wrong user. Tell him or her to restart it as the PostgreSQL superuser.

Chapter 2

PHP3

2.1 Why PHP?

There are many ways to create web-based active content, including Perl,
UNIX shell scripts, C (with and without CGI libraries), Cold Fusion, Interbase, JavaScript, and Java. Each has its benefits and drawbacks. We've found
PHP3 competitive with, and often better than, these other languages. Many
of the best interactive catalog sites on the Internet are built with PHP.

PHP3 is *independent* of the operating system, the web server, HTML, and
the database system. With paradigm shifts at the hardware and operating
system levels occurring constantly (or so it seems!), PHP3 isolates your
development efforts from unforeseen changes in equipment, browsers, and
operating environments.

PHP3 has borrowed some of the best capabilities and functions from C,
Java, Perl, and UNIX shell. In fact, PHP3 shares many of the same language
constructs as C, so any experience with C can be useful. (Many PHP3 functions are simply wrappers for the underlying functions written in the C programming language.) For the most part, the most important of over 500
PHP3 functions are documented with examples in the accompanying Reference section.

Tight integration with HTML and HTTP is a big advantage. PHP3 is not
simply another add-on to an existing language, such as a library, but, rather,
it is embedded directly in the HTML code. Unwieldy print statements aren't
required to generate HTML output. PHP3 allows standard HTML documentation, with embedded scripting using special tags (<?PHP … ?>) to mark
where the scripting starts and ends. (This contrasts with the complexity of
embedded SQL (i.e., Oracle's Pro*C™), where SQL statements are dropped as
needed into the C code. C and embedded SQL data type incompatibilities
are often cantankerous, a problem avoided by PHP3.)

PHP3 is an interpreted language. Interpreted languages provide rapid turnaround during application development by eliminating compile time at the expense of a slower execution time. PHP3 has a tightly integrated relationship with many system components, such as mail servers, C libraries, regular expression libraries, and many different database systems. In most cases, PHP3 builds upon time-proven components, and capabilities rather than reinventing methods and procedures. Also, because PHP3 scripts are interpreted, they can typically be moved among systems without modification or recompilation. (Those of us who remember spending hours tweaking C programs to port them to a new system much appreciate this feature.)

Large systems are typically divided into layers (also called tiers). In our model, the top layer is the web browser, next the web server, next the PHP interpreter, and finally the database. Web browsers, web servers, and database systems are all fairly mature products. However, the middle layer, where PHP resides, is undergoing what seems to be a continuous rapid evolution. The main purpose of this layer is to connect the web servers to the data, and the requirements imposed upon this layer are becoming increasingly more complex. PHP is a natural choice, as a fast-evolving scripted language, for making this connection. PHP can talk to many different data sources and provide a unified interface to these different systems. For a large organization, PHP can be the *perfect* choice to unify many different systems under a single web interface.

One of the original names given to this middle layer was "application switching," and the name "middleware" has recently come into vogue. A name that the authors believe applies is "data hub." PHP can act as the hub to interconnect all of your systems connected via TCP/IP (whether over a private network or the public Internet). This "hub" can support the following:

- Many clients using one server
- Many clients using many servers
- One client using many servers

PHP can make these potentially complex relationships invisible to the end user.

PHP scripts are executed on the server. Server-side processing is nothing new. Businesses have relied on mainframes and client/server DBMS for years. The advantages of keeping the processing on the server side include:

- **Security of data/procedures**: By leaving the application and the data on the server, access can be more tightly controlled. No client is able to look at the program(s) that read and manipulate your data.
- **Communication security**: When used with SSL or HTTPS, PHP can make all network traffic safe from eavesdropping. This is very important if you use a public network, like the Internet, to get to servers.

Deciding to use a thicker client, like a Java application using JDBC or a Visual Basic application using ODBC to connect to the database server, will unencrypt network traffic.

- **Manageability**: Server-side applications are typically easier to monitor and update. There is only one machine to oversee, not potentially thousands of clients. The larger the organization or the larger the customer base, the more important this becomes.

- **Performance**: Database-intensive applications typically perform better when they are run closer to the DBMS. Local network speeds are typically on the order of a 100 Mbps versus WAN speeds on the order of hundreds of Kbps, or less. Having PHP handle all of the communication to your database servers can save on expensive WAN bandwidth. Also, using pooled database connections can increase performance and increase the number of clients a DBMS can support. For example, a web server executing PHP scripts may be able to support hundreds of clients with only a few tens of concurrent database connections by multiplexing its individual persistent connections. PHP's support of persistent database connections does away with the costly build-up and tear-down of DBMS connections that would happen otherwise.

- **Reliability**: How much more reliable is a UNIX web server than a Windows client machine? Enough said.

 As is typical of interpreted languages, PHP3 does not have strong data types. The variable type is decided at run time by PHP3 depending on the context in which a variable is used. The automatic conversion makes programming much faster, easier, and less error-prone. Under Apache, the PHP3 interpreter is a web-server module that is significantly faster than running an external process to interpret the code. This contrasts with many other interpreted languages where the entire interpreter is loaded, executed, then terminated every time a browser accesses a web page containing the code on the server. Of course, one has the option of running PHP3 as a stand-alone CGI program or even as a stand-alone interpreter from the UNIX shell. This makes PHP3 essentially a *run-anywhere system*.   ▬▬▬▬

The PHP3 feature set is continually growing and evolving. We will be covering the topic in much greater detail, but if you want to move on quickly, here's a short list:

- PHP3 is not limited to creating HTML output. It can also create binary output, including JPEG, PNG, and GIF graphics. For example, you can create on-the-fly clickable buttons with dynamically generated text.
- PHP3 can be used to generate PDF files, so that you can make ready-to-print forms.
- HTTP authentication password-protects your web pages.

- HTTP file upload support (as described by RFC-1867) allows the uploading of both binary and text files. For example, users can place their images directly into the PostgreSQL database for use in an on-line catalog.
- PHP3 supports reading and setting HTTP cookies. Cookies are a mechanism for storing data in the remote browser and thus tracking or identifying return users.
- Simple Network Management Protocol (SNMP) functions to monitor many different devices from routers to hubs to servers.
- PHP3 supports many standards, including but not limited to HTML, LDAP, SMTP, SNMP, POP, and IMAP.
- PHP3 has regular expressions for complex string manipulation.
- PHP provides a nice, color-coded source viewer.
- PHP gives you an integrated debugger.

PHP3 is Open Source™. Open Source software is inherently peer-reviewed.

2.2 History

PHP3 was developed late in 1994 by Rasmus Lerdorf to keep track of visitors to his on-line resume. The first public version, available in early 1995, was known as the *Personal Home Page Tools* (PHP Tools). It consisted of a simple interpreter engine that understood a few special macros and a number of common utilities, such as a guestbook and a built-in counter.

The interpreter was rewritten in mid-1995 and named *PHP/FI Version 2*. The *FI* came from the Form Interpreter, another package Rasmus had written that interpreted HTML form data. He combined the *Personal Home Page Tools* scripts with *FI*, added mSQL support, and *PHP/FI* was born. *PHP/FI* use grew quickly, and the user community began contributing code to it. Though early statistics are hard to come by, it has been estimated that by late 1996 *PHP/FI* was in use on at least 15,000 web sites worldwide. One year later, this number had grown to over 50,000.

In 1997, PHP3 changed from Rasmus's personal project to an Open Source development. The interpreter engine was completely rewritten (from scratch) by Zeev Suraski and Andi Gutmans. This all-new interpreter formed the basis for *PHP3 Version 3* (PHP3). Though some of the utility code from *PHP/FI* was ported over to PHP3, much of it was completely rewritten to take advantage of the new interpreter logic. Today, the PHP3 library of functions numbers over 480. PHP4 is anticipated in 2000, and the beta-test version has been released as of this printing (look for details on *www.php123. com*). Zend, a new compiler for PHP3, will be available in late 1999, and its beta-test version has been released as of this printing (look for details on *www.php123.com*).

Today PHP3 ships with a number of commercial products (C2's Strong-Hold web server and RedHat Linux). NetCraft has estimated current use to be somewhere over 500,000 sites worldwide and growing quickly. To put this number in perspective, it is nearly *twice* the number of sites that run Netscape's flagship Enterprise Server on the Internet.

Open Source

PHP3 is open source. Open source is software that is inherently peer-reviewed. *http://www.opensource.org/* describes itself best: "The basic idea behind open source is very simple. When programmers on the Internet can read, redistribute, and modify the source for a piece of software, it evolves. People improve it, people adapt it, people fix bugs. And this can happen at a speed that, if one is used to the slow pace of conventional software development, seems astonishing. We in the open-source community have learned that this rapid evolutionary process produces better software than the traditional closed model, in which only a very few programmers can see source and everybody else must blindly use an opaque block of bits."

We do not attempt to review the issue of private versus public development of software; however, we note that open source systems have demonstrated increasingly positive gains against privately developed systems. Why? Eric Raymond expressed it as follows: "Engineers build bridges with independent peer-review. We don't expect bridges to crash. Perhaps software developers can learn from engineers." Perhaps.

2.3 What PHP3 *Doesn't* Do

Taken as a whole, PHP3 is today a robust and powerful scripting capability. But like any language, PHP3 has its shortcomings; most of them listed below are included simply as food for thought, not as a serious complaint about the features and capabilities of PHP.

1. **Because PHP3 is an interpreted language, PHP3 scripts do not execute as quickly as a compiled program.** However, with Zend, PHP3 will have a partial compiler and execution speed should begin to rival native languages.

2. **PHP3 does not handle bit-level manipulations** (easily).

3. **PHP3 does not support pointers.** Neither does Java. Not having pointers greatly simplifies the maintainability and comprehensibility of the program. The authors do not perceive this lack of pointer support as a liability, but rather as an asset.

4. **CORBA.** There is no support for CORBA (Common Object Request Broker Architecture). With CORBA support, PHP could pull data from

existing client/server systems. PHP could be a practical and powerful method to add a web interface to existing enterprise-scale CORBA applications.

5. **Queuing support**. There are major advantages to being able to queue processes and actions. A few of the advantages to a queued environment might be:

   a) **Overload protection**: Sometimes your PHP scripts can feed data faster to another system than it can can process it. The usual analogy here is putting water in a bucket faster than it can flow out of a hole in the bottom. If you pour too fast, you spill some water.

   b) **Limited availability**: If one has limited Internet bandwidth between two sites, after-hours queueing can save valuable bandwidth during the day.

   d) **Increased robustness**: If an update fails, following internal policies, it can be attempted again later.

   e) **Prioritization scheduling**: If you have a queue, then it can be prioritized and scheduled.

6. **Transaction system**. Even if your database systems supports transactions, they are not useful if all of the data to be updated is not on the same DBMS server. It would be nice if PHP had a method of making all of the updates in a single PHP execution into a transaction. This could help greatly with data integrity between database systems, and it could help database systems that do not support transactions, like MySQL.

7. **fprintf()**. There's no fprintf() function as in C. This is a curious omission considering the strong influence of C in PHP's design. For example, the gymnastics shown below are required when using PHP:

```
fputs($fp, sprintf("HTTP_USER_AGENT:%s\n",
   getenv("http_user_agent")));
```

The above could be expressed in C without the call to sprintf() to create a string containing the formatted data as:

```
fprintf(fp, "HTTP_USER_AGENT:%s\n",
   getenv("http_user_agent"));
```

Because the second line is less complicated, there should be less chance of an accidental error in coding it.

8. **STDIN**. There is no stdin as in C. This lack makes it harder to use PHP as a replacement for UNIX shell or Perl scripts used for system administration. Typically, on a complicated site, an admin may have to write web applications in PHP and other scripts with the UNIX shell. Rather than learning two very different scripting languages, it would be nice if PHP were stronger in this regard. On Linux, at any rate, the lack of a stdin can be worked around by opening a device file with:

```
...
$fp = fopen("/dev/stdin", "r");
...
```

To execute your new "console" PHP script you would do something like:

```
/usr/local/bin/php -q /tmp/script_name.php3
```

The -q option supresses the HTTP header output. The above line could be placed in /etc/crontab so that it could be scheduled to run every so often. Because of its lack of strong typing and compile-time checks, PHP does not make a great systems language, but it is often a better choice for novice admins than learning another language.

9. **PHP needs more database independence.** Most PHP database functions are simply wrappers for the supported database C API. This means that working with each database requires different functions and methods, making it more complicated than necessary to use PHP as a "data hub" to pull data from multiple different data sources. Also, it makes it harder to switch database systems. For example, if you decide transactions are a requirement, then you must move from MySQL to PostgreSQL. This can involve changing a large portion of your application.

10. **Sun RPC (remote procedure calls) would help build distributed applications.** This feature could help with scalability, and help companies with existing distributed applications either create web interfaces or integrate other systems with their existing apps. Again, PHP would act as a "data hub." CORBA support may render this request obsolete.

11. **Tighter integration with Perl modules would be nice.** Dozens of useful and unique PERL libraries are available from CPAN (Comprehensive Perl Archive Network), an archive of Perl source code with thousands of modules and scripts—see *www.cpan.org*. One notable example is the dynamic update DNS libraries. It would be nice to call

a Perl library function directly from PHP. This will be inefficient, because the Perl interpreter would have to start up to process for each function call, but it might be better than rewriting the code in PHP. It might be possible to interface with the **mod_perl**, the persistent Perl interpreter that runs as an Apache module, to avoid this start-up time.

12. **State**. HTTP is a stateless protocol. CGI programs and PHP scripts are transient. They run once, then quit. This necessitates a unique mark or signature for clients to use to distinguish themselves. Cookies are the standard method of keeping up with a unique ID. Combined with this unique ID should be a method for storing data. Also, this ID should be difficult to spoof. PHP includes an **md5()** function that could easily be used to generate a hard-to-guess pattern of IDs. An easy method in PHP of storing a set of variables and restoring them would be nice. This state information must be stored somewhere; the obvious choice with PHP would be an SQL database. The workaround for this lack could be a complicated library.

13. **Regression test**. Used by many large software vendors to provide an automated testing and quality-control of software developments, regression tests use the power of the computer to validate the correctness of a program. Regression testing provides a confidence factor that cannot be easily duplicated by human trial and error.

14. **Data reference identifiers**. A method of assigning unique IDs to updates as they are passed around between systems would be nice. This could help track the flow of data in a system. For example, this ID could tag an order from the web browser, to the order database, to the credit-card transaction, to the boxing, and finally to shipping. With PHP, this feature may be easier to implement in an include file, with some extra programming at each db update, than as a core feature. It's mentioned here more as a suggestion to track data updates.

Some of the items listed in this section could be added to a DBMS system. However, most DBMSs are relatively mature products. If a DBMS doesn't have a particular feature by now, it is probably not going to be added.

Chapter 3

Databases

The value of information is not in the individual data element, but in the structure. A database requires that structure be assigned to data. A database management system (DBMS) provides a framework for creating and maintaining structure for data. This framework usually includes the capability to access structured data by way of queries. Structured Query Language (SQL) (coming up next) is an example of one such query capability. It is important that the packaging of data be independent of the technology used to access the data. PHP3 accommodates interfaces to many different (heterogeneous) access technologies, many in native access mode.

Though the examples in this book focus on PostgreSQL, the basic concepts of database design and programming apply to all supported DBMSs. The Reference Section includes functions related to each of these RDBMSs. In addition, we have included functions relating to "flat-file" data access as well as xBase (e.g., Foxpro ®, dBase®, Clipper®) data.

Refer to the web site *http://www.php123.com/* for on-line examples of interfacing with other DMBS.

3.1 Databases 101

 A database is simply a method of storing and retrieving data. Data are chunks of information. Unorganized data has very limited usefulness—like a filing cabinet piled high with random papers. Organization is the key to making data useful and usable. A database provides an organizational framework for data—just as a filing cabinet provides organization for papers that are arranged alphabetically.

There are many kinds of databases. Any organization of data is, by definition, a database.

A simple list of phone numbers is a database. To find a phone number in an unorganized list, we start scanning from the top to the bottom until we find the desired data. As the list becomes longer or we begin to store more information that just a phone number, it becomes more and more difficult to find the data we seek.

Imagine a phone directory with absolutely no organization. Each time someone's number must be found, one must literally scan every entry from top to bottom. (Actually, it makes no difference if you start at the top, or the middle, or go from top to bottom—statistically, it still takes the same amount of time to find the sought-after number.)

Database management systems (DBMSs) are applications that provide a consistent framework under which to organize data and retrieve it quickly. Alphabetizing our phone list is an example of a time-saving DMBS framework.

There are many types of DBMS methodologies, including "flat-file," "relational," and "object-oriented." Conveniently, PHP3 provides direct interfaces to each of these, so we are not particularly limited to which kind of DBMS we choose to work with. Each type of DBMS provides methods to organize, store, and retrieve data. These methods vary based on the amount of data we are concerned with, efficacy of the storage media, and query requirements.

Is there a best DBMS methodology? Each DBMS has specific capabilities that make it unique to a particular data requirement. We will focus the examples in this book on the most popular type of DBMS, relational DBMS—or RDBMS.

Relational databases provide for the aggregate grouping of data based on simple logical relationships that exist between the data. These "relationships" are based on boolean algebra. (Interested in reading more? Check out the Reading List at the back of this book.)

For example, one number is bigger than another $(a > b)$. The "greater than" symbol > represents a simple relationship between two items. Armed with the concept, we can easily compare any two items: "Elm Tree" > "Sunflower". Get the idea?

Some important relational symbols include:

>	← greater than
<	← less than
<> -or- !=	← not equal to
! -or- NOT	← not
&& -or- AND	← and
‖ -or- OR	← or

By combining relations and using parentheses to group relations together, we can express very complex ideas. Here is a simple example:

```
(This tree > That tree ) AND ( This flower < That flower).
```

Relational logic can express complex organizations of data using relational logic. For example, a number larger than 10 and not equal to 5 can be conveniently expressed as:

```
(a > 10 AND a <> 5).
```

Relational syntax is used to express these relationships. A relational database management system provides for the ordering and retrieval of data based on these "relations" between various data elements.

3.2 SQL and PHP

Structured Query Language (SQL) is the "language" spoken by many relational database management systems. Why? Because SQL provides a logical framework for organizing and retrieving data. As you will see, SQL has a handy and commonsensible syntax. Because we tend to think in terms of stereotypes, conceptualization of data plays a key part in the development of successful database applications. SQL has evolved to become a standard access language for many important database management systems; indeed, it is the most popular and widely used database query language in the world.

SQL is a data retrieval language. If the information is buried somewhere in the data, SQL provides an intuitive method for extracting it. Whether one is dealing with a single row of data or hundreds of thousands of rows, **Select** statements provide a framework for extracting data, by way of queries.

However, SQL is weak in presenting the resulting data sets to the user. SQL inherently supports neither print nor screen-formatted reporting. These weaknesses in SQL are complemented by PHP3. PHP3 generates dynamic HTML that gives the developer total control over the display of the SQL query result. This combination of PHP3 and SQL provides optimal functionality in applications involving web-based database developments.

Persistent Database Connections and PHP

Persistent connections are database links that do not close when the execution of a PHP3 script ends. In some cases, and when properly used, a persistent database connection can result in a substantial savings in processing overhead.

When a persistent connection is requested, PHP3 checks whether there is already a preexisting data link. If one exists, the preexisting connection is used. If one does not exist, PHP3 creates the link. An identical persistent connection is one that was opened to the same host, with the same user name and the same password (where applicable).

Persistent connections do *not* provide any faster data transfer speeds than nonpersistent links. They do, however, often provide faster DBMS connect times. Why? Let's look at two methods by which a web server can utilize PHP3 to generate web pages.

The first method is to use PHP3 as a CGI "wrapper." When run this way, a separate instance of the PHP3 interpreter is created and destroyed for *every* PHP3 page request to the web server. Because the instance is destroyed after every request, all allocated resources, such as a link to a server, are closed. If PHP3 is used as a CGI wrapper, then there is no gain from a persistent connection—since no connection persists once the script has finished.

The second method is to run PHP3 as a *module in a multiprocess web server* (MPWS), which currently only includes Apache. A multiprocess server typically has one process (the parent) that coordinates a set of subordinate processes (children) that actually perform the work of serving web pages. When a request from a client is received by the MPWS, it is routed to one of the child connections that is not already serving another client. Obviously, when the same client makes a second request to the server, it may be serviced by a different child process from the first time. In this case, the persistent database connection provides for reuse of a child connection already established and in use by another child. Persistent connections provide efficiency and increased throughput when used in a multiprocess web server.

Persistent connections are particularly useful if there is a significant overhead in creating a link to your database server. Connection overhead can be affected by factors such as transaction rollback and triggers. In addition, DBMS connection overhead depends on many other factors, including the type of database, the indexing methodology, the physical location of the DBMS, the caching paradigm, and the loading of the DMBS processor.

If connection overhead is high, a persistent connection improves throughput considerably. A child process needs to connect only once for the lifespan of the DBMS link, rather than reconnecting each time a database request is processed from a script.

Persistent connections are designed to have one-to-one mapping to pre-existing connections. This insures that a persistent connection can be replaced with a nonpersistent connection without affecting the script behavior.

Chapter 4

PostgreSQL

4.1 Description

PostgreSQL is a sophisticated object-relational DBMS that supports almost all SQL constructs, including subselects, transactions, and user-defined types and functions. The "object" in object-relational reflects the extended ability of PostgreSQL to define data objects with inheritance and extensibilty.

PostgreSQL supports a large subset of the SQL/92 standard. PostgreSQL provides strong transaction processing.

 Need something a bit "simpler"? Something that is faster, but with somewhat fewer features? Try MySQL. We have them both working on *www. php123.com*, so you can try them out to determine which is best for you.

4.2 History

PostgreSQL began in 1986 as a DBMS research project by Michael Stonebraker at the University of California at Berkeley. His original database project, called Ingres, was publicly available in 1985. University Ingres is no longer maintained but is still freely available.

Stonebraker's followup project was Postgres (as in "*after* Ingres"), which used a new query language, POSTQUEL. In 1987, Postgres introduced rules, procedures, and extensible types with indices and object-relational concepts. Postgres was commercialized to become Illustria, which was later purchased by Informix and integrated into Informix's Universal Server.

Postgres Version 3, appearing in 1991, added support for multiple storage managers, an improved query executor, and a revised rewrite-rule system.

For the most part, releases since then have focused on portability and reliability. Postgres has been used in a diverse range of research and production applications, and is also used as an educational tool at several universities. Stonebraker's project officially ended with Version 4.2. Two members of Stonebraker's lab, chief programmer Andrew Yu and Ph.D. student Jolly Chen, rewrote PostgreSQL, replacing POSTQUEL with an extended subset of SQL. This was released in 1995 as PostgreSQL95 and the development was taken over by the Open Source community in 1996. PostgreSQL95 has developed into what is now PostgreSQL. Ongoing PostgreSQL development is performed by a team using Open Source methods over the Internet. The current system coordinator is Marc Fournier (*scrappy@PostgreSQL.org*). This team is responsible for all core development of PostgreSQL.

The core code of PostgreSQL is entirely ANSI C. In 1998, the code size was trimmed by 25% and many algorithms were rewritten. Internal core changes have *significantly* improved performance and code maintainability. PostgreSQL now runs about 30% faster on the Wisconsin Benchmark than its previous version.

4.3 Overview

Traditional relational database management systems (RDBMSs) support a data model consisting of a collection of relations, each containing attributes of a specific type. These attribute types usually include floating-point numbers, integers, character strings, money, dates, and large binary objects (BLOBs). The relational model successfully replaced previous models in part because of its inherent simplicity and extensibility.

PostgreSQL incorporates four extensions:

- Classes
- Inheritance
- Types
- Functions

Although we will review these extensions briefly in this book, we suggest that the reader interested in digging deeper into these topics survey some of the excellent sources in the Reading List.

4.4 Comparison (Feature) Chart

So, how does PostgreSQL stack up to the competition? The chart that follows (from *www.postgresql.com*) lets you judge for yourself. Of course, each DBMS is designed to meet particular data-handling requirements that may not be reflected in this comparison.

Area	PostgreSQL 6.4.2	Oracle 8	Sybase 11	MiniSQL 2.0
Overall				
Free Source	✓			
Any Source	✓			✓
On-line Documentation	✓	✓	✓	✓
Features				
Client-server	✓	✓	✓	✓
Multithreaded		✓	✓	
Shared SQL cache		✓		
Row-level locking		✓		
On-line backup	✓	✓	✓	
On-line recovery		✓		
Parallel query		✓	✓	
Read-only databases		✓	✓	
Multiple index types (B-tree, hash, etc.)	✓	✓		
Unique indexes	✓	✓	✓	✓
Multicolumn indexes	✓	✓	✓	✓
Standards				
ANSI/ISO SQL92 entry-level	Partial	✓	✓	
ODBC level 1	✓	✓	✓	
Supported Programming Languages				
C	✓	✓	✓	✓
C++	✓	✓		✓
Java	✓	✓	✓	✓
Perl 4	✓	✓	✓	
Perl5 OO	✓	✓	✓	✓
Python	✓	✓		✓
Tcl	✓			
Supported Operating Systems				
FreeBSD, NetBSD	✓			✓
Linux x86	✓	✓	✓	✓
Linux Alpha	✓			
Linux Sparc				
SGI Irix 5.3	✓	✓		
Solaris Sparc	✓	✓	✓	✓
Solaris x86	✓	✓	(client only)	
SunOS 4 (Sparc)	✓			✓
HP/UX	✓	✓	✓	✓
BSDI	✓			
DG-UX	✓	✓		
IBM AIX	✓	✓	✓	
Nextstep	✓			✓
Ultrix 4	✓			

(continued)

Area	PostgreSQL 6.4.2	Oracle 8	Sybase 11	MiniSQL 2.0
OSF/1 Alpha Digital Unix	✓	✓	✓	
System V R4.2	✓			
SCO Open Server		✓		✓
OS/2		✓		
Windows 95/98	(client only)	✓	✓	
Windows NT	(client only)	✓	✓	
Novell Netware		✓	✓	
Macintosh	(client only)	✓		

4.5 Performance and Processes

PostgreSQL has a supervisor program that manages incoming connects and spawns copies of the database to handle database queries. For example, on our test machine, the table below shows three active connections:

```
4742 ?    S    0:00 /usr/bin/postmaster -S -D/var/lib/pgsql -o -F
4755 ?    S    0:00 /usr/bin/postgres localhost postgres test idle
4758 ?    S    0:00 /usr/bin/postgres localhost postgres test
4761 ?    S    0:00 /usr/bin/postgres localhost postgres test
```

Postmaster is the "supervisor" and postgres is the database server; the leftmost column is the PID (process ID). Each copy of postgres is independent of the others. Because we are dealing with separate process (as with sendmail or Apache), adding more processors, generally speaking, linearly increases the performance. So, having a four-processor PostgreSQL server should, theoretically, handle four times the number of connections while still providing the same performance (ignoring disk I/O and network bandwidth issues).

4.6 OIDs: Inversion Large Objects

An OID is a integer value that is used as a pointer to a file with large blocks of data divided up into smaller pieces and a tree structure that stores the structure of the interleaved blocks. For those of us who have worked with dBase files, it is reminiscent of a memo file. The OID (the integer stored in the database) is a pointer to a particular inversion large object. The Large Object is the data that is referenced by the OID.

To store more than 4096 characters in a single field with PostgreSQL, you must use Inversion Large Objects. They break up large objects into "chunks," smaller pieces that are stored in the database. This is useful, for example, for storing images, complete web pages, PDF documents, and data entered into large text-area boxes on HTML forms. Assume that we want to create a table with an ID #, an employee's name, and a picture of the employee. In PostgresSQL, we could type:

```
CREATE TABLE employees (id varchar(8), name char(50),
  picture oid);
```

To insert an employee's information, you could type:

```
INSERT INTO employees (id, name, picture) VALUES ('1234',
  'Joe Smith',
lo_import('/tmp/1234.gif'));
```

This would place the contents of the file /tmp/1234.gif into the database. To extract the image, you could type:

```
SELECT lo_export(picture, '/tmp/1234.gif') FROM employees
  WHERE id='1234';
```

This would place a copy of the stored image into the file /tmp/1234.gif. Combine this feature with PHP and you could display the employee's picture on a web browser, along with other relevant information.

Now we will create PHP programs to place the data into the database from a file-upload form and display it on the web browser. Below is the form to feed the image to our PHP program:

```
<FORM ENCTYPE="multipart/form-data" ACTION="logo_save.php3"
  METHOD=POST>
  <INPUT TYPE=TEXT NAME=ID VALUE="1234"><BR>
  <INPUT TYPE=HIDDEN NAME="MAX_FILE_SIZE" VALUE="100000">
  Send this file: <INPUT NAME="userfile" TYPE="file"><BR>
  <INPUT TYPE=SUBMIT NAME=SUBMIT VALUE="Send File">
</FORM>
```

Below is the PHP program that places the uploaded file into a large object in the PostgreSQL database:

```
<?PHP
$conn = pg_Connect("dbname=test port=5432");
if(!$conn) {
  print "Error: Could not connect to database.<br>\n";
  exit;
}

pg_Exec($conn, "BEGIN");
```

```
$oid = pg_locreate($conn);
$handle = pg_loopen($conn, $oid, "w");
pg_lowrite($handle, $userfile);

pg_loclose($handle);

pg_Exec($conn, "INSERT INTO employees (id, picture) VALUES
   ($id, $oid)");
pg_Exec($conn, "COMMIT");

pg_close($conn);
?>
```

Now we will create a PHP program to display the picture in a web browser:

```
<?PHP
Header("Content-type: image/gif");

$conn = pg_Connect("dbname=test port=5432");
if(!$conn) {
  print "Error: Could not connect to database.<br>\n";
  exit;
}

$result = pg_Exec($conn, "SELECT picture FROM employees
  WHERE id=$id");
$oid =  pg_Result($result, 0, "picture");
$handle = pg_loopen($conn, $oid, "r");
pg_loreadall($handle);

pg_close($conn);
?>
```

To call the above program, you can use a URL that looks like:

```
http://hostname/script_name.php3?id=1234
```

Here is a portion of a web page that could use the above program:

```
...
<?PHP
echo "Employee ID #: "$id."<BR>";
echo "Name: ".$name."<BR>";
?>
```

```
<IMG SRC="script_name.php3?id=1234"><BR>
...
```

For more information on the PostgreSQL library functions used, see the Language and Function Reference Section.

4.7 Advanced Features

Several important features distinguish PostgreSQL from many other conventional RDBMs, including inheritance and non-atomic data values (array- and set-valued attributes).

Inheritance

To demonstrate inheritance, we create two classes (or tables). For our example, we let the **Cities** class inherit from the **People** class.

First we create the **People** class.

```
CREATE TABLE PEOPLE (
    name          char(40),
    age           int,
    balance_hi    real
);
```

The **People** class contains the following instances:

Name	Age	Balance_hi
Craig Jones	42	145.50
Sally Jones	31	200.00
Joe Henry	25	175.00

```
CREATE TABLE Cities (
    city           char(30),
    population     int,
    altitude       int,
    date_entered   date,
    state          char(2)

) INHERITS (People);
```

The **Cities** class has been created with the following structure:

```
Table    = cities
+------------------+------------------+--------+
| Field            | Type             | Length |
+------------------+------------------+--------+
| name             | char()           |     10 |
| age              | int4             |      4 |
| balance_hi       | float8           |      8 |
| city             | char()           |     10 |
| altitude         | int4             |      4 |
| date_entered     | date             |      4 |
| state            | char()           |      2 |
+------------------+------------------+--------+
```

The **Cities** class contains the following instances:

City	Population	Altitude	Date_Entered	State
Mariposa	20,100	2175	1-1-1990	CA
Mariposa	21,200	2175	10-10-1999	CA
Greenville	68,933	1011	1-1-1990	SC
Spartanburg	47,611	1140	1-1-1990	SC

In this case, an instance of **Cities** inherits all attributes (or fields, i.e., **name, balance_hi**, and **age**) from its parent, **People**.

The attribute **name** has a data type of varchar (text), a built-in PostgreSQL type for variable-length ASCII strings. The type of the attribute **balance_hi** is float4, a built-in type for double-precision floating-point numbers.

Cities has several new attributes, such as City, Population, Altitude, Date_Entered and State.

A class can inherit other classes. For example, we could create yet another class called **State** that would inherit all attributes from **Cities**, which in turn inherited all attributes from **People**.

A query can reference either all instances of a class or all instances of a class plus all of its descendants. To find the names of all cities, using our attribute **City**, that are located at an altitude over 500 feet, the query is:

```
SELECT c.name, c.altitude, d.city
FROM People* c,  cities* d
WHERE c.altitude > 500;
```

which returns:

c.Name	c.Altitude	d.City
Craig Jones	2175	Mariposa
Sally Jones	1011	Greenville

Here the asterisk (*) after **cities** indicates that the query should be run over cities and all classes below cities in the inheritance hierarchy. Many of the SQL commands that have been discussed, including **select, update,** and **delete**, support this asterisk notation, as do many others, such as the **alter** command.

Non-Atomic Values

One of the tenets of the relational model is that the *attributes* of a relation are discrete, in other words, indivisible. PostgreSQL does not have this restriction; attributes can themselves contain subvalues that can be accessed from the query language. This is a powerful extension that allows, for example, attributes that are arrays of SQL base types.

```
SELECT name, balance_hi
FROM People
WHERE name = substr(1,1)='J';
```

Name	Balance_hi
Craig Jones	145.50
Sally Jones	200.00

Arrays

PostgreSQL allows attributes of an instance to be defined as fixed-length or variable-length *multidimensional arrays*. Arrays of any SQL base type or user-defined type can be created. Where would you use a user-defined type? Geographic information systems might create a type representing latitude/longitude/altitude factors.

For our example, we first create a class with scalar arrays (arrays that contain a *single* value in each array element) of SQL base types. (Thanks to *http://www.postgresql.org/* for this example.)

```
CREATE TABLE PEOPLE (
    name            char(20),
    pay_by_quarter  int4[],
    schedule        char16[][]
);
```

The previous query creates a class named PEOPLE with a text string (name), a one-dimensional array of integers (pay_by_quarter), which represents the employee's salary by quarter, and a two-dimensional array of characters (schedule), which represents the employee's weekly schedule.

Now we INSERT some data into the table. (Note that when appending to an array, the values are enclosed within braces and separated by commas, similar to array initialization notation in C.)

```
INSERT INTO PEOPLE
   VALUES ('Jeff',
      '{5000, 6000, 7000, 8000}',
      '{{"meeting", "lunch"}, {"swimming", "beach"}}');

INSERT INTO PEOPLE
   VALUES ('Jane',
      '{5000, 4000, 5000, 5000}',
      '{{"talk", "consult"}, {"meeting"}}');
```

By default, PostgreSQL uses the "one-based" numbering convention for arrays—that is, an array of n elements starts with array[1] and ends with array[n] (unlike array indexes that start at zero, as in PHP3 or C).

Now, we run some queries on PEOPLE. First, we show how to access one single element of an array at a time. This query retrieves the names of the employees whose pay changed in the second quarter:

```
SELECT name
FROM PEOPLE
WHERE PEOPLE.pay_by_quarter[1] <> PEOPLE.pay_by_quarter[2];
```

Name
Carol

We can also access arbitrary slices of an array, or subarrays. This is useful when we want to view only a particular part of a general query. The following query retrieves the first item on Jeff's schedule for the first two days of the week:

```
SELECT PEOPLE.schedule[1:2][1:1]
FROM PEOPLE
WHERE PEOPLE.name = 'Jeff';
```

The results show us only the first element of the array contained in the schedule field—just as we expected:

Schedule

{{"lunch"},{"swimming"}}

You may ask whether it would be just as easy to restructure the table to accommodate this capability? Perhaps.

4.8 What PostgreSQL *Won't* Do

Like any DBMS, PostgreSQL has its weaknesses:

- Subqueries (which can be imitated with user-defined SQL functions) are not supported.
- Compared to commercial products such as Oracle and Sybase, PostgreSQL supports a smaller subset of the SQL/92 standard.
- Compared to speed-enhanced DBMSs (e.g., MySQL), the feature-rich PostgreSQL is somewhat slower with databases of less than 10 Mb.

The newest version (6.5) at the time of writing now includes NUMERIC data types. However, the CD-ROM has an older version of PostgreSQL that does not contain the NUMERIC type.

Chapter 5

MySQL

MySQL is a small, compact database server ideal for many on-line database applications. It supports standard SQL (ANSI), though not as complete a subset of the standard as PostgreSQL.

MySQL compiles on a number of platforms and has multithreading abilities on UNIX servers. In non-UNIX environments, MySQL can be run as a service on Windows NT and as a normal process in Windows 95/98 machines. MySQL is a privately maintained RDBMS. It is a multi-user, multithreaded SQL relational DBMS server. MySQL is a client/server implementation that consists of a server daemon and many different client programs and libraries.

MySQL was originally developed in 1996 to provide a SQL server that could handle transactions in very large databases at high speed. Today, MySQL applications are reported that contain 10,000 tables, of which more than 500 have more than 7 million rows (about 100 gigabytes of data).

MySQL can be downloaded at no cost from *www.mysql.com*. We maintain a MySQL server running at *http://www.php123.com/*.

5.1 Comparison of MySQL and PostgreSQL

Claims that MySQL is "... 40 times faster" than Oracle and "10,000 times faster" than Microsoft (Sybase) SQL required us to compile and test the latest version of MySQL (version 3.23b3) and race it against the latest version of PostgreSQL (version 6.3.5).

Well? MySQL is *fast!*

PostgreSQL by default waits until each transaction has been committed to disk before continuing to the next queued item. This feature can be disabled. So, for purposes of this test, we compared PostgreSQL with the feature (fsync()) enabled, as well as disabled. According to the SQL spec, transaction (e.g., update, insert) commands shouldn't return until they are committed to disk. For example, when you do an UPDATE, the command doesn't return (PHP3 waits) until the updated data is actually on the disk. Disabling this synchronization using fsync() made writes with PostgreSQL 5 to 20 times faster. (See Appendix 2 for the actual timings.)

MySQL is *considerably* faster than PostgreSQL. The question you as the developer need to ask is whether the increase in performance is worth the loss of a few features. Remember, PostgreSQL provides support for stored procedures, transaction processing (where partial updates to a record are never done), field-level locking, and a more robust ANSI-SQL subset.

For the same database, MySQL used only about 80% of the space that PostgreSQL did. This is important for performance, because a larger percentage of a database can stay in the cache. 200,000 records with two 50-character fields created 20 Mb worth of files for MySQL and 24 Mb worth for PostgreSQL. This would be more important if one is creating large databases. For example, a colleague of the authors' switched from Oracle to MySQL simply because he could get their database of astronomy data to fit in less than 500 Gb, whereas Oracle recommended they have 8000 Gb of hard-drive space as a minimum (which they obviously couldn't do).

Each PostgreSQL connection used a total of 5 Mb of RAM with 1.5 Mb actually used (Linux uses a lazy allocator so that the 5 Mbytes the program requested isn't actually allocated until it is needed, if ever; the 1.5 Mb is the important number for performance and RAM size, and the 5 Mb number is important for sizing the swap partition). MySQL used about 10 Mb of RAM with 0.5 Mb actually used. MySQL's lower RAM usage is important if one is going to have many (say, more than 50 concurrent) users using the database server. However, where database connections last on a very short period of time, this is not really an issue.

Handling multiple users with different privilege levels is well documented for MySQL. The documentation is excellent. Take a look: *http://www.mysql. com/Manual_chapter/manual_Privilege_system.html#Privilege_system.*

Chapter 6

Other SQL Databases

6.1 Proprietary SQL Databases

If you prefer using a proprietary (non-Open Source) SQL database, perhaps due to company policies or a requirement for commercial support, PHP3 supports many excellent commercial alternatives.

Supported proprietary DBMSs include any database with an ODBC interface (if you aren't terribly concerned about performance), and:

- Oracle (*http://www.oracle.com/*)
- Solid (*http://www.solidtech.com/*)
- Informix (*http://www.informix.com/*)
- Empress (*http://www.empress.com/*)
- Sybase (*http://www.sybase.com/*)
- Informx (*http://www.informix.com/*)
- MySQL (*http://www.tcx.se/*)
- mSQL (*http://www.hughes.com.au/*)

mSQL (*http://www.Hughes.com.au/*)

mSQL, or MiniSQL, is a privately maintained RDBMS. It uses a lightweight database engine designed to provide fast access to stored data with low memory requirements. As its name implies, mSQL offers a *subset* of the ANSI SQL standard as its query interface.

Mini SQL 2.0, introduced in 1998, is the second generation of the mSQL database system. The product was built around a baseline goal of performing 100 basic operations per second on an average UNIX workstation with small data sets using very few system resources (memory and CPU cycles). Successive versions of the product continue to meet this requirement while adding further functionality as outlined in the ANSI SQL specification.

Today, mSQL applications are reported that contain up to 1 million rows of data.

MSQL can be downloaded from *http://www.hughes.com.au*.

Microsoft Access (*www.microsoft.com*)

Often touted as the most popular desktop DBMS, Access provides a robust development environment through Visual Basic for Applications (VBA). VBA is ubiquitous, widely understood, and has an intuitive object model. Hyperlinks can be used in databases to link other parts of the database, other Microsoft Office documents, and to web sites. Tables, forms, reports, and queries can be saved in HTML format.

Access is a component of Microsoft Office Professional Edition, and can also be purchased as a stand-alone product from Microsoft at *http://www. . microsoft.com*.

6.2 Nonnative Database Connection Standards

At times one may wish to connect to a database for which there is no built-in direct support. PHP3 supports built-in direct (or native) connection to many databases, such as those outlined above.

For completeness, we include a brief overview of two of the more common access standards that accommodate reading data from heterogeneous databases.

ODBC, its precursor, Embedded SQL, and several other methods are included in this book for completeness; ODBC is *not* considered by the authors to be an *optimal* method of data access. It is best utilized when heterogeneous (dissimilar) databases must be accessed and direct calls cannot be made to the database back ends. Whenever possible, data is best stored and accessed using direct (native) access. PHP3 supports a number of native accesses for a wide range of DBMSs.

Java Database Connector (JDBC)

JDBC is based on the Sun JAVA specification. It is generally faster than ODBC (see next page), and many of the latest software packages have integrated support for it. JDBC can be an order of magnitude faster than ODBC. Check out *www.sun.com/java/* for more information.

Embedded SQL

As RDBMSs became increasingly popular in the late 1980s, the only portable interface for applications was Embedded SQL. There was no common API (Application Programming Interface) methodology for communicating with database servers, nor was there a standard programming or data-access language (called a "fourth-generation language," or 4GL).

Embedded SQL uses a language-specific pre-compiler. SQL commands are embedded in a host programming language, such as C or COBOL. The pre-compiler translates the embedded commands into host language statements that use the native API of the database.

Open DataBase Connectivity (ODBC)

ODBC is a standardized API that provides portable database connectivity. It is a set of function calls based on the SQL Access Group (SAG) function set for utilizing a SQL-based DBMS. The target DBMS is referred to as the back-end system. The SAG function set implements the basic functionality of Dynamic SQL. PHP3 commands can be translated to call ODBC.

Several companies sell ODBC drivers for a wide variety of operating systems. But, as is the case in the Windows operating environment (for which it was initially written), most of these implementations lack speed and (in some cases) tend to be periodically unreliable. ODBC, though, is generally portable among many SQL databases. This portability generally means that more time is required to establish and maintain database connectivity and processing.

Applications access ODBC functions through the ODBC Driver Manager that dynamically links to the appropriate ODBC driver. ODBC drivers translate ODBC requests to native format for a specific data source. The data source may be a complete relational database system like PostgreSQL, or it may be a simple file format, like dBase.

PHP3 provides a complete set of functions for access through ODBC to a database. Because ODBC is controlled by a single vendor, Microsoft, they alone define the specification of the API and supply the basic driver-manager software used on Microsoft operating systems. This control obviously will determine the future portability and extension of the specification.

Chapter 7

Why UNIX? (Why Not Windows?)

We include this brief discussion for those of our readers who have not already made up their minds. As readers may have noticed, PHP3 and the several SQL servers covered by this book run optimally under a UNIX environment. So, those of you who are asking "why UNIX?" may find this chapter revealing.

7.1 Brief Overview of UNIX

Perhaps UNIX versus Windows will be one of the significant implementation issues of the next five years. In particular, which operating system offers the best cost benefits, Microsoft Windows NT (soon to be Windows 2000) or UNIX?

Of course, UNIX is not a single operating system. Developed in the early 1970s by AT&T, it was not intended for beginners. Built for computer professionals who were comfortable with programming and software architectures, the early UNIX soon migrated to the university community, running on a wide variety of platforms. Today, UNIX is a family of operating systems including AIX, Digital UNIX, FreeBSD, HP-UX, IRIX, Linux, NetBSD, OpenBSD, Pyramid, SCO, Solaris, and SunOS.

Although we will not explore why Microsoft Windows NT was supported in over 80 million licensed client and server copies in late 1998 (according to International Data Corporation in Framingham, MA), we will explore the tradeoffs between the two environments. One of the most concise comparisons between the Microsoft and UNIX environments has been coordinated by John Kirch, whose site (*http://www.unix-vs-nt.org/kirch/*) is a wealth of up-to-date information on the subject. This comparison relies heavily on Kirch's analytical data.

Is NT Server worth the price? Maggie Biggs, a senior analyst who specializes in database technology and deployment, in a 1997 *InfoWorld* article compared Windows NT 4.0 to Red Hat's commercial Linux system; the Linux solution had a 100:1 price advantage ($4,636 for NT 4.0, $50 for Red Hat Linux). Even more cost-conscious versions of UNIX would include Linux, FreeBSD, NetBSD, or OpenBSD, all offered free for the downloading.

Windows NT is often considered a "multi-user" operating system, but this is very misleading. An NT server will validate a user, but once logged onto the NT network, the user can access only files and printers. The NT user cannot run any application on an NT server, but is rather limited to running applications that have been written in two pieces: a client and a server section.

On the other hand, when a user logs in to a UNIX server, any application can be run provided the user is authorized to do so. This allows moving the application processing off the client workstation, effectively moving the processing requirements to the server.

D.H. Brown's Scorecard (*http://www.dhbrown.com/dhbrown/OpSys ScoreCard.cfm*), shown in the figure that follows, is often cited as an excellent summary of the comparison.

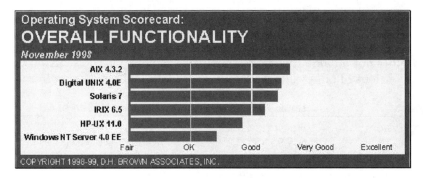

7.2 Why Linux?

Historically, large corporations have steered clear of "free" software. However, recent shifts in supportability and adoption by major software and hardware firms are changing corporate acceptance of the Open-Source™ model. As Robert W. Lucky wrote in *IEEE Spectrum* in May, 1999, ". . . we have an operating system, Linux, developed by some 40,000 volunteers, and given away freely. Some even say Linux is better than Windows. I won't take sides, but the idea that a bunch of relatively unorganized volunteers can compete with a giant corporation (Microsoft) by giving away an equivalent product has to be an intriguing example of how value is created in the Information Age."

Linux, the most popular of the "Open Source" UNIX flavors, runs on a wide range of hardware: Sun, Intel, DEC Alpha, PowerPC, and PowerMac. Paul Krill's recent article in *InfoWorld* ("Linux picking up steam and Linux supporters rally around freeware OS") focuses on the increasing support of major vendors and future plans for added functionality. Today, Linux is perhaps the fastest-growing operating system in the world.

Two factors have weakened corporate objections to Linux. One is the documented performance achieved in several recent academic and military projects. In particular, a 1997 NASA initiative sponsored by the High Performance Computing Systems group of the Jet Propulsion Laboratory in Pasadena, California used Linux to integrate a cluster of 16 PCs costing less than $50,000 that sustained a 1.25 gigaflop performance rate. The second factor has been the adoption of Linux by commercial vendors pursuing a new business model. Red Hat Software, Caldera Systems, and VA Research are among distributors that have chosen to distribute Linux free and collect fees for documentation and support.

7.3 A Comparison: Linux versus Windows

Let's look at Windows NT with Linux on Intel hardware using John Kirch's comparison chart (*http://www.unix-vs-nt.org/kirch/*), updated May 1999. (Note: Only the items/features that actually ship with each operating system are listed here. Perl 5.0, for instance, is available for all platforms, but Microsoft does not provide it with its operating systems. On the same note, most distributions of Linux ship with only about four GUIs to choose from.)

Component	Linux	Windows NT Server 4.0
Operating System	Free, or around $49.95 for a CD-ROM distribution	Five-user version $809 10-user version $1129 EE 25-user version $3,999
Free online technical support	Yes, Linux Online or Redhat	No
Kernel source code	Yes	No
Web server	Apache	IIS
FTP server	Yes	Yes
Telnet server	Yes	Yes (optional)
SMTP/POP3 server	Yes	Yes (optional)
DNS	Yes	Yes
Networking	TCP/IP, IPv6, NFS, SMB, IX/SPX, NCP Server (NetWare Server), AppleTalk, plus many other protocols	TCP/IP, SMB, IPX/SPX, AppleTalk, plus many other protocols

(continued on next page)

Component	Linux	Windows NT Server 4.0
X Window server (for running remote GUI-based applications)	Yes	Yes (in Windows 2000)
Remote management tools	Yes, all tools	Web Administrator 2.0 (a recent addition) offers a large, but still not complete, set of tools
News server	Yes	No
C and C++ compilers	Yes	No
Perl 5.0	Yes	No
PostgreSQL	Yes	No
PHP3	Yes	No
Revision control	Yes, RCS	No
Number of file systems supported	32+	3
Disk quotas support	Yes	No
Number of GUIs (window managers) to choose from	Many	1

Chapter 8

Internet Basics

8.1 Internet 101

 So how does a computer translate a web address anyway? Every computer with TCP/IP (if your computer is connected to the Internet, it has TCP/IP installed in it) has a unique Internet Protocol (IP) address. That address is unique to your computer. Sometimes that address is assigned "on the fly" when you connect to the Internet and is not permanent—but the essential thing is that your computer is *uniquely* defined.

When someone wants to contact your computer, they use your (unique) IP address. Information is "packetized"—subdivided into packets of data. Each packet is enclosed in a standard "package" that includes the sender's (unique) IP address and the recipient's (unique) IP address as well as an identifier of what piece of the entire package the packet represents. The packet is then sent out over a network. The size and complexity of the network is immaterial. The larger the network, the more "routing" that must be done to read the destination, but, conceptually, the delivery of the packet using TCP/IP is exactly the same.

Packets are transmitted across networks by way of the "IP" (Internet Protocol) part of TCP/IP. The "TCP" (Transport Control Protocol) adds a layer of reliability to the IP logic though such features as flow control. Any network relying on TCP/IP protocols can be referred to as an IP network, and vice versa.

A network can be as large or small as you like. You can have an IP network that is as small as two computers connected together with a phone line or as large as every computer (well, virtually every computer, 2^{32} addresses minus a few reserved blocks) on earth connected by the Internet.

In any event, when a packet enters a network, routers along the way decipher where the packet is headed and "route" it along the way based on the recipient's IP address contained in the packet header. When a packet arrives at its intended destination, it is acted upon by the client computer. If either the server or the network in between do not support large packets, then packets are stored and assembled into the complete packet when enough arrive at the client.

What happens if a packet doesn't make it—say, the network connection dies? Well, the packet is returned to the sender—and you get a message on your computer something like "Unable to Connect to. . .". What makes the TCP/IP methodology so powerful is that individual packets don't have to travel along the same path. One packet may go via Miami, whereas another may go up through Chicago. But they all end up in Greenville, South Carolina and are assembled on your computer.

Of course people don't do particularly well remembering long numbers, like an IP address of 126.222.2.52. So the Domain Name System (DNS) was introduced in 1984. (Prior to DNS, Unix provided a file called /etc/hosts that contained hostnames and their IP addresses. DNS, though merely a newer conversion method, has been credited with much of the explosive growth of the Internet.) This allows us to type in a *name* instead of the long IP address number. *www.Upstate.net* is the domain name that represents the IP address 126.254.2.2. When someone types in *www.Upstate.net*, the domain name is translated by a name server into its IP address, which is what is actually used in transmitting the packet. Of course, if you really like long numbers, you can always use the raw IP address. For example, typing in 126.254.2.2 will connect you just as readily to *www.Upstate.net* as typing in the domain name.

There you have it.

For a detailed overview of Internet (TCP/IP) technology, see the Reading List.

8.2 Browsers 101

 Where does your browser fit into all this?

Browsers are programs for interpreting HTML code. Browsers are used for "browsing" the World Wide Web, the graphic component of the Internet. In addition to their ability to display graphics (not *every* browser supports graphics) and animations, browsers can also perform several nongraphic functions, including file transfer protocol (FTP)—transferring data files from one computer to another—and electronic mail.

The first browsers, Viola and Midas, were released in 1993 for UNIX-based machines running X-Windows. The first popular browser, NCSA Mosaic, supported only HTML 1.0 and was released for all common platforms (UNIX X-Windows, MS Windows, Macintosh) in September 1993.

Marc Andreessen, the "under-20" developer of Mosaic, cofounded the company Mosaic Communications Corp. (now called Netscape, a subsidiary of AOL). He rewrote Mosaic and released it under the name Netscape Navigator. The product soon was in use by 70% of the browser market. Microsoft, recognizing the groundswell of interest in the Internet and the pivotal importance of the browser, soon released its own browser, MS Internet Explorer. Traditionally, browsers are given away at no charge. In 1998, Netscape released the source code to Navigator, which is now being developed open source. To learn more, stop by *http://www.mozilla.org/*.

When Internet Explorer 2.0 came out, it supported a few things the Navigator browser didn't, for example, the scrolling text (marquee) function, background sounds, and table cell backgrounds. Netscape, not to be outdone, added a few features not included in Microsoft's product, among them "frames," which allow splitting a browser window into different sections, and a "tables" function for creating partitioned scrollable areas on web pages called "tables." The competition among the browsers (so-called browser wars) has resulted in disturbingly different browser implementations. Increasingly, developers are forced either to settle for a reduced set of capabilities shared by both major browsers or to support a single browser platform.

PHP3 is browser-independent and supports all HTML standards (including the XML standard).

Chapter 9

HTML and PHP

9.1 HTML 101

All WWW pages are written in HTML. Although some files may have different file extensions (such as .html, .php3, .php, .cfm or .asp), their output is still HTML. HTML is always the medium that is sent to the web browser, whether the page is static, a script (like PHP), or is generated with CGI.

HTML is not a bit-level language such as C++ or Pascal. It is, rather, a markup language for describing documents. We refer to HTML as the actual coding of an HTML document. A WWW browser interprets the HTML and displays it on your monitor.

HTML is a simplified version of SGML (Standardized Generalized Markup Language), which is a language for exchanging data. HTML code is written in ASCII-format. ASCII-format is often referred to as "text." Simple text is easy to understand and many times easier to modify than, let's say, a proprietary word-processing language. This is a tremendous advantage to portability, because ASCII can be read by about any platform (IBM, Macintosh, UNIX, . . .), therefore making an HTML document usable for any platform through a "viewing" program such as a browser.

The current standard defined by the W3 Consortium is HTML 4.

History

Originally, there was no official standard describing HTML; HTML 1.0 was simply what Mosaic, the first popular browser, could do. The first official version of HTML was 2.0, defined in RFC (Request for Comment) 1866. You should consider HTML 2.0 the baseline to design for if you want your documents to be read on as many different platforms as possible. Later HTML standards have been released by the W3 Consortium. The HTML 3.2

specification, available from *http://www.w3.org/*, adds many new features, the most important of which is support for tables, superscripts, and subscripts. You will find, as you present data pulled from a database, that tables are an important presentation and organization tool. The W3C's newest specification for HTML is 4.0, which, most importantly, adds support for cascading stylesheets (CSS). CSS helps to return HTML to its original intention as a language in which to structure information rather than a layout language (like a word processor).

9.2 The PHP3 Script

A Five-Minute Example

PHP3 is browser-independent and supports all HTML standards. PHP3 lets you mix HTML and PHP-script code. So, what does this look like in practice? Let's consider the following code:

```
<TITLE>Sample PHP3 script</TITLE>
<H1>Date sample</H1>
<?PHP
   $today = date("Y-m-d");
   echo "Today's date is $today.n";
?>
```

As you can see, we start out with some standard HTML code. We provide a title for the page and a heading:

```
<TITLE>Sample PHP3script</TITLE>
<H1>Date sample</H1>
```

Then we encounter the section of the document enclosed within `"<?PHP"` and `"?>"`. These are technically called SGML processing tags and are how we tell the Web server where there's code that we wish to run. For the web server to recognize the `<?PHP ... ?>` SGML processing tags, it must have PHP3 installed on it. So, you may either use our free Readers Only web site (*http://www.php123.com*) or install it yourself using the enclosed CD-ROM.

Back to what's going on. First, our example calls the **date()** function with some parameters about how we would like the current date formatted. (Several hundred of the important PHP3 built-in functions are covered in the Reference Section.) The result of date() is assigned to variable $today and on the next line we print the result. When run on a PHP3-enabled web server, the output would look something like this:

```
Date Sample
Today's date is 99-6-19.
```

Getting to Your PHP3 Script

Somewhere (on your desktop or local web server, if you've installed the CD-ROM, or at our facility in South Carolina if you're using *www.php123.com*) there is a web server running the PHP3 interpreter. You write a web page called *test.php3* containing the PHP3 script

```
<TITLE>Sample PHP3 script</TITLE>
<H1>Date sample</H1>
<?PHP
   $today = date("Y-m-d");
   echo "Today's date is $today.n";
?>
```

and send your page to a PHP3-enabled web server. There your PHP3 script sits until someone asks to retrieve the page and view it on a browser. Let's say your web page is located at *http://www.php123.com/* (this is its URL—Uniform Resource Locator). The request `http://www.php123.com/test.php3` is forwarded to *www.php123.com* using the protocol HTTP. The page **test.php3** is located and executed by the PHP3 web server. The PHP3 interpreter in the PHP3 web server parses the page and dynamically creates an HTML document containing your scripted instructions (in this case printing "Today's date is . . ." on the screen) and returns it to the requestor.

PHP3 is browser-independent and supports all HTML standards (including the newest XML standard). The script that you create in your HTML is independent of the version of HTML (or XML) you are using. Your pages can incorporate Java, JavaScript, or any other programming language or tool, as well as exploit the full capabilities of PHP3.

How PHP3 Is Interpreted

The PHP3-enabled server scans the requested web page and determines whether there are any PHP3 scripts embedded in the document. PHP3—that is, the portion of PHP3 that interprets the meaning of the PHP3 script—then processes the PHP3 script. If the script requires an output of some type (it often does), PHP3 builds "dynamic" (or "on-the-fly") output. This dynamic quality of PHP3 is its most important feature.

PHP3 is not case-sensitive. This means that you may call a PHP3 function, let's say SUBSTR(), by writing it any way you choose—Substr(...) or SUBSTR(...) or SubStr(...). You cannot add or remove letters to or from the name of a function. PHP3 is, however, *very very* sensitive to the case of the variables you use in your application. A variable **$ABD** is totally different from variable $Abc.

Execution Speed

One might assume the execution speed of "dynamic" PHP3 would be quite slow, because each script command must be individually interpreted. Actually, it's suprisingly fast. PHP3 has been optimized to parse (or analyze) a document very quickly.

Two things you can do to improve the execution speed of your application are:

- Place logical blocks as close together as possible.
- Do not include in your application user-defined functions that will not be used.

If the application requires database connectivity, which database management system you select will greatly impact the speed of your application. Some DBMSs are faster than others.

9.3 PHP and JAVA

Java

Java is a general-purpose language, like C and Pascal. Java "executables," which are actually a form of a system-independent interpreted byte-code, are downloaded by the browser.

Java and JavaScript are two very different things. Netscape did the industry a disservice in naming its unrelated language JavaScript. (In 1998, Netscape renamed JavaScript to LiveScript.) At the programming level, the code of Java and JavaScript looks somewhat alike. However, both are entirely different languages used for two different purposes: Java was designed to be a general-purpose language, whereas JavaScript (JS) is a special-purpose scripting language that is tightly integrated with the browser.

Java is from Sun and JS is from Netscape. JavaScript code is included in a web page and is interpreted directly by the browser. Thus, the client sees the JavaScript source. On the other hand, Java is called from the browser and executed as a discrete process. Thus, the client never sees the Java source.

Any PHP3 script can call a Java program.

```
<?PHP
  $UserName = "Jeff Smith";
  echo '
```

```
    <applet archive="application.jar"
      code="php123.applet.Example.class" width=0 height=0>
      <param name=username value="$UserName">
      <param name=rows value="24">
    </applet>';
  ?>
```

The HTML code provides a pointer to the location of the JAVA program, and the web browser downloads and executes the program on the client machine.

JavaScript

JavaScript is a scripting language that is embedded directly in HTML documents. The HTML tag

```
<SCRIPT LANGUAGE="JavaScript">
  <?PHP
  echo 'history.back()';
  ?>
</SCRIPT>
```

is used as a container for the JavaScript code. JavaScript is tightly integrated with the browser and is interpreted by the browser. Typically, this scripting language is used to change the appearance of pages and to validate form elements.

HTML includes the ability to specify applications to run directly from the browser to be executed on the client machine. They are typically small applications, hence the name applet. The HTML tag `<APPLET CODE="">` can be used to specify a Java program for the browser to download and execute. Java applications can be compiled once and run on a wide range of browsers and operating systems.

In contrast to Java and JavaScript, server-side scripts (like embedded Perl, server-side Java, and PHP) and CGI programs are executed on the web server. Their output is HTML that is displayed by the web browser.

Any PHP3 script can output JavaScript to be executed by the browser.

Chapter 10

The PHP3 Language

10.1 Basics

"Programming language constructs" are the *rules* by which a computer programming language is used. As in to speaking the English language, the order and logic, or *syntax*, of the programming language construct are important. "Jane programs" has an entirely different meaning than "Program Jane." The PHP3 language is straightforward and based on standard programming syntax. There should be nothing odd or confusing about the language.

PHP's rules involve **expressions** and **functions**. We cover each in turn.

PHP3 is composed of a large number of sophisticated, simple, special-purpose functions, many of which are covered individually in the Reference section. Functions simplify many tedious and redundant tasks.

PHP3 also provides a method for creating user-defined functions. The function libraries for PHP3 are constantly growing as Open Source PHP3 contributors continue to expand the language.

10.2 The Language Construct

A computer language is a medium in which you, the programmer, can tell the computer which actions should be performed and in what order. Most modern computers use serial processing, that is, they process one instruction at a time.

The **syntax** (or language construct) determines how the program is interpreted. *Expressions* provide a logical layer to the program. *Functions* perform discrete tasks—or functions—generally involving several commands in a logical framework that often incorporates expressions. A function is interpreted by the syntax that surrounds it. **Instructions** are discrete operations that are terminated in PHP3 by a semicolon.

The total language **program** (or **script**) can be likened to a written paragraph. Just as a poorly written paragraph may be unintelligible, so a poorly written program will generally not accomplish the intent of its author.

10.3 Syntax

Syntax determines how a program is interpreted. Proper syntax is critical in the accurate execution of a PHP3 program.

PHP3 requires a uniform and structured layout. You can't GOTO (or jump to) some place in a program and then RETURN back where you came from. Program statements are executed sequentially, one after another, except in specific, well-defined control structures. Each expression in PHP3 must be logical and follow explicit rules. This structured layout is helpful in keeping program development logical and easy to understand.

10.4 Encapsulating PHP3 and HTML

There are four PHP3 **segment identifiers** that indicate where a PHP3 programming segment begins and ends in an HTML document. These identifiers are called **opening tags** and **closing tags**. There are four ways of moving between HTML and PHP: Method 1 is preferred. Method 4 may be necessary if you use tools such as FrontPage that have parsers with built-in identifiers to delimit executable scripts. (This is important to FrontPage users!)

Method 1 (preferred)

```
<H3>Outside PHP</H3>
<?PHP
Echo "Inside PHP";
?>
```

Method 2: Short tags

```
<H3>Outside PHP</H3>
<?
Echo "Inside PHP";
?>
```

Method 3: Script identifiers

```
<H3>Outside PHP</H3>
<SCRIPT LANGUAGE="PHP">
Echo "Inside PHP";
</SCRIPT>
```

Method 4: ASP-style tags

```
<H3>Outside PHP</H3>
<%
Echo "Inside PHP";
%>
```

Whatever is contained between the segment identifiers must be syntactically correct PHP3 code. Unlike HTML, which is quite forgiving of many programming errors, PHP3 displays an error message and stops the script execution if the syntax is not correct.

We will use Method 1 for most of the examples in this book, and it is always the preferred method. Note that PHP does not support the second or fourth methods by default: it must be configured to support them at compile time. For those of you using FrontPage, remember that you may need to use Method 4! Does one identifier work "faster" than another? No.

10.5 Statement Separation

Statements are terminated just as in C or PERL (unlike the separation in Pascal). Each statement is terminated with a semicolon.

```
<?PHP
    echo "This is a test";
?>
```

10.6 Comments

PHP supports C, C++, and UNIX-style comments. Comments are a powerful programming tool in documenting a program inside the program. They are like "REM" (remarks) in BASIC. Comments are free-form text and are not executed by the PHP interpreter.

C-style comments start with the characters '/*' and end with '*/'. For example:

```
<?PHP
    /* Print out the total amount of the order including:
    equipment
    shipping
    tax
    */
echo "Total: ".$total_amount;
?>
```

As you can see, the comment spans multiple lines. C++ and UNIX-style comments span only a single line. C++ comments start with '//' and UNIX-style comments begin with a '#'. These comments extend only to the end of the current line. For example:

```
<?PHP
  echo $equipment;   // Output the cost of the equipment
  echo $shipping;    # Output the cost to ship the equipment
?>
```

10.7 Variables

A **variable** is used to store a piece of data temporarily when you don't know what it will be ahead of time.

Variable names are always preceded by a dollar sign $. A variable can be any letter or number combination (including the special character '_') up to 32 characters in length. It may begin with either a letter or underscore, but not a number. Variable names longer than 32 characters will have any excess discarded by the parser.
For example:

```
<?PHP
$name = "Craig";   //here we are assigning a value to the
                        variable $Name
echo $name;        //here we have the variable echo'd to the
                        screen
?>
```

Output

```
Craig
```

Variable Types

PHP3 supports the following variable types:

- integer
- double
- string
- array
- object

For completeness when working with PDF, if you have compiled in PDF support, two additional variable types will be available:

- Pdfdoc
- Pdfinfo

The *type* of a variable is usually decided at run time by PHP3 depending on the context in which that variable is used. If you need to force a variable to be converted to a certain **type**, you may either cast the variable or use the **settype()** function on it.

Of course, a variable can behave in different manners depending on what type of variable it is at the time. For more information, see the Type Determination section (page 63).

Creating Variables. A variable does not need to be declared before it can be used. Some programming languages (C, Pascal, Java) require each variable to be declared before it can be used. However, PHP3 automatically creates the correct type of variable based on the type of data that is put in it. For example: `$i = "ABC"` results in a *string* variable, whereas, `$i = 1.234` results in a *double* variable.

To create a variable in PHP, you simply assign a value to it. For most types, this is straightforward. Arrays and objects, however, can use slightly different mechanisms, as discussed in the next two sections.

Creating Arrays. An array may be initialized in one of two ways:

1) sequential assigning of values

2) using the **array()** construct

To sequentially add values to an array, assign to the array variable using an empty subscript. The value is automatically added as the last element of the array.

```
$people[] = "Craig";
$people[] = "Jane";
```

is equivalent to:

```
$names[0] = "Craig"
$names[1] = "Jane"
```

As in C, array elements are numbered starting with 0, not 1.

Initializing Objects

To initialize an object, use the **new** statement to instantiate the object to a variable. The word instantiate means to *create* and *initialize* an object.

```
class suitcase {
  function close() {
     echo "Suitcase is closed. Let's go.";
  }
}

$trip = new suitcase;
$trip -> close();
```

Scope of Variables

The **scope** of a variable is the context within which the variable is defined. Generally, all PHP3 variables have a single scope. However, in user-defined functions a **local function scope** is introduced. Any variable used *inside* a function is by default limited to the local function scope, and in addition it is not available outside the local function.

For example:

```
$a = 1;      //global scope because it is outside of the
                 function

Function Test () {
   echo $a;  //references local scope variable
}

Test ();
```

This script will *not* produce any output because the echo statement refers to a **local** version of the $a variable, and it has not been assigned a value *within this scope*. (This differs from the C language in that global variables in C are automatically available to functions unless specifically overridden by a local definition.) The example above is contrived, however, because one should never create global variables inside a function.

In PHP, **global** variables must be declared global *inside* a user-defined function if they are going to be used in a global context outside of the function. For example:

```
$a1 = 2;
$b1 = 4;

Function Sum () {
   global $a1, $b1;
   $b = $a1 + $b1;
}
```

```
Sum ();
echo $b;
```

The previous script will output "6." By declaring $a and $b global within the user-defined function, all references to either variable will refer to the global version. There is no limit to the number of global variables that can be manipulated by a function.

A second method to access global variables is to use the special PHP-defined $GLOBALS array. Using the $GLOBALS array, the above example can be rewritten as follows, and also outputs "6."

```
$a1 = "2";
$b1 = "4";

Function Sum () {
   $GLOBALS["b"] = $GLOBALS["a1"] + $GLOBALS["b1"];
}

Sum();
echo $b;
```

The $GLOBALS array is an associative array (in which each value in the array is defined with a name rather than a subscript number) with the name of the global variable being the key and the contents of that variable being the value of the array element.

Another important feature is the **static variable**. A static variable exists only in a local user-defined function scope. A static variable does not lose its value when program execution leaves this scope, exactly as in C. Consider the following example:

```
Function Counter () {
   $a1 = 0;
   echo $a1;
   $a1++;
}
```

This function is useless. Every time this function is called, **$a1** is set to 0 and echoes "0" to the screen. The $a1++, which increments the variable, serves no purpose because as soon as the function exits the $a1 variable disappears.

To make a useful counting function that does not lose track of the current count, the **$a** variable is declared **static**:

```
Function Counter2() {
   static $a1 = 0;
```

```
    echo $a1;
    $a1++;
}
```

Now every time the Counter2() function is called it prints the value of $a1 and increments it. Remember, the variable $a1 is not available outside the function, because it has not been declared as a global variable.

Static variables are also essential when functions are called recursively. A **recursive function** is one that calls itself. Be careful when writing a recursive function, because it is possible to make a function call itself indefinitely. Always create an adequate way of terminating the recursion.

The following simple example counts recursively to 100:

```
Function Counter3() {
    static $count = 0;

    $count++;
    echo $count;
    if ($count < 100):
        Counter3();
        else:
        break;
        endif;
}
```

Variables of Variables

Sometimes it is very convenient to have variables based on other variable names, often refered to as "macros." xBase's popularity has often been traced to this capability.

A "variable of variable" is a variable name that can be set and used dynamically. For example, a normal variable is set with a statement such as:

```
$a = "Craig";
```

A **variable variable** takes the value of a variable and uses it as the name of a variable.

In the previous example, the value **Craig**, now contained in **$a**, can be used as the name of a variable by using two dollar signs. For example:

```
$$a = "Jones";
```

or, in other words, the **variable of the variable** Craig.

At this point two variables have been defined and stored:

- **$a** with contents "Craig"
- `$Craig` (or, if you please, `$$a`) with contents " Jones"

Now either of these statements:

```
echo "$a". "${$a}";
echo "$a  ${$a}";
```

produces exactly the same output as:

```
echo "$a". "$Craig";
```

That is, they both produce: "Craig Jones".

Resolving the inherent ambiguity of *variable variables* with arrays is tricky. `$$a[1]` is ambiguous to the PHP3 interpreter. Is `$a[1]` meant to be a *variable*, or is **$$a** supposed to be the variable and then the **[1]** index from that array variable?

The syntax you should use to resolve this ambiguity is:

```
${$a[1]} when $a[1] is a variable, and
${$a}[1] when $$a is supposed to be the variable.    ▬▬▬▬▬
```

External Variables

HTML Forms (GET and POST). When a FORM is submitted to a PHP3 script, any variables from the form are created automatically. For example:

```
<FORM METHOD=POST ACTION="example_post.php3">
E-Mail Address: <INPUT TYPE=TEXT NAME="email_address"><BR>
Phone Number:   <INPUT TYPE=TEXT NAME="phone_number"><BR>
    <INPUT TYPE=SUBMIT NAME=SUBMIT>
  </FORM>
```

When the user hits the submit button, the web browser sends the form contents to example_post.php3, and it executes. The variable $email_address contains whatever the user typed into that text box, and $phone_number contains whatever the user typed into that text box. For example, a (very) simple program to display what the user entered into the two boxes is:

```
<?PHP
  echo $email_address."\n";
  echo $phone_number."\n";
?>
```

For (the rather uncommon) multiple SELECT elements, PHP places the values in an array. This is necessary because in this case a single form element has multiple possible values. Here is an example form of this type:

```
<FORM METHOD=POST ACTION="multiple_select.php3">
I like the following foods (select all that apply):<br>
<SELECT MULTIPLE NAME="food[]">
<OPTION VALUE="pizza˅>Pizza
<OPTION VALUE="hamburgers">Hamburgers
<OPTION VALUE="steak">Steak
<OPTION VALUE="ice_cream">Ice Cream
<OPTION VALUE="apple_pie">Apple Pie
</SELECT><BR>
    <INPUT TYPE=SUBMIT NAME=SUBMIT>
  </FORM>
  >
```

Note the brackets [] in the name of the form element. They tell PHP to place the values in an array. This simple program displays the selections:

```
<?PHP
  for ($x = 0; $x < count($food); $x++)
    echo $food[$x]."<br>";
?>
```

GET vs. POST Form Methods. Web browsers have two different methods for sending form data back to the web server, the GET and POST methods. The author of the web page or PHP script selects the most appropriate method to use and specifies it at the start of a form by:

```
<FORM METHOD=POST ACTION="example.php3">
<FORM METHOD=GET ACTION="example.php3">
```

Each method has it advantages and disadvantages.

GET Method. With the GET method, the form data is placed at the end of the URL that the web browser requests from the server. The web server sends the form data to the PHP interpreter or to a CGI program in an environment variable named QUERY_STRING. Because the data is passed in the URL and later an environment variable, there is a limit to how much data can be handled using this method. Any amount of data larger than 1K can be problematic for some web browsers. Therefore, you would not want to use a GET method with a TEXTAREA form element. The form data is encoded in the URL as follows:

```
example.php3?name1=value1&name2=value2&name3=value3
```

The question mark (?) denotes the start of the form data, the ampersand (&) separates the name/value pairs, and the equal signs (=) separate the names from the values. Because the data is passed in a URL, it must be URL-encoded. PHP includes the **urlencode()** function to URL-encode strings. Note that you don't want to encode the entire query string, because that will replace the equal signs and ampersands. You need to use the function on each individual element. The query string above creates the following PHP variables:

```
$name1 = 'value1';
$name2 = 'value2';
$name3 = 'value3';
```

The GET method is most useful when you want a link to take the place of an entire form. For example, the program name button.php3 generates a graphical button with the specified text. In our web page, we would place the line:

```
<IMG SRC="button.php3?string=Click+Here">
```

When the web client parses the page, the button.php3 will be executed with the specified parameters. If everything goes well, the PHP program will send back a graphical button.

POST Method. The POST method is the preferred way to send lengthy form data. The web server sends the form data to the PHP interpreter or a CGI program via STDIN. This allows for a virtually unlimited amount of data to be transferred.

PHP handles both form types transparently, so you don't have to worry about most of the details. PHP's tight integration with processing form input and magically creating variables with the appropriate names and values is a great asset that can greatly speed up and simplify development.

IMAGE SUBMIT Variable Names. When submitting a form, it is possible to use an image instead of the standard submit button by using a tag such as:

```
<input type=image src="image.gif" name="img">
```

When the user clicks somewhere on the image, the accompanying form is transmitted to the server with two additional variables, sub_x and sub_y, that contain the coordinates of the user click within the image. This is useful in designing a sophisticated submit button that takes different actions depending on where the user clicks.

HTTP Cookies. PHP3 supports HTTP cookies as defined by the Netscape Specification. Cookies are a mechanism for storing data in a browser that are often used in tracking or identifying return users. For an excellent intro-duction to cookies and where and when to use them, check out *http://www.netscape.com/newsref/std/cookie_spec.html* or click on the link from the *http://www.php123.com/* site.

HTTP is a *stateless* protocol. One result of this statelessness is that one web page cannot inherently pass information to another web page. Cookies are a method of passing information between stateless web pages. This is done when the "cookie" information is written onto the client computer, where subsequent pages can read and interact with the data. Cookies expire from the local computer either at a predetermined time (e.g., 20 years in the future) or at the end of the session (i.e., when you quit your web browser).

Cookies are set using the SetCookie() function. Because cookies are part of the HTTP header, the SetCookie function must be called *before* any output is sent to the browser:

```
<?PHP
SetCookie("Who_Is_This_Cookie", "Craig Jones");
?>
<html>
  <body>
    ...
  </body>
</html>
```

Any cookies sent to a server from the client are automatically turned into a PHP3 variable, just like GET and POST method data. For example,

```
<?PHP SetCookie("Who_Is_This_Cookie", "Craig Jones"); ?>
```

becomes the PHP3 variable $Who_Is_This_Cookie with a value of "Craig Jones" when read from a client script.

To assign multiple values to a single cookie, simply use the **add []** function to add to the cookie name. For example:

```
SetCookie ("Who_Is_This_Cookie[]", "Craig", "Jones", "South
   Carolina");
```

Of course, it is often easier simply to set multiple single-value cookies.

Note that a cookie replaces a previous cookie of the same name in the client browser unless the path is different. For applications where it is important to carry data from one page to another, try the following:

```
$item = "Potted Plant";
$Count++;
SetCookie ("Cart[$Count]", $item, time()+3600);
```

Environment Variables. PHP3 automatically makes **environment variables** available as normal PHP3 variables. Thus

```
echo $HOME;   //shows the HOME environment variable, if set
```

yields

```
/home/cjones
```

Since information coming in via GET, POST, and Cookie methods also automatically creates PHP3 variables, it is sometimes best to explicitly read a variable from the environment to make sure that you are getting the right version. The getenv() function can be used for this. You can also set an environment variable with the putenv() function.

Thus, in the example above, suppose we had set $HOME as a variable in the form. The form variable takes precedence over the environment variable. The code

```
...
<input type=text name=HOME>
...
user type in ABC in this field
...

echo $HOME;
echo getenv("HOME");
```

yields

```
 ABC
/home/cjones
```

Now we give a more useful real-world example. The code below uses environment variables that the web server provides to all CGI programs to determine the remote client's IP address and the web browser they are using.

```
<?PHP
  $message = "The user's IP address is ";
  $message .= getenv("remote_addr").".\n";
  $message .= "The user is running the web browser ";
  $message .= getenv("http_user_agent").".\n";
  echo $message;
?>
```

yields

```
The user's IP address is 127.0.0.1.
The user is running the web browser Mozilla/4.0
(compatible: MSIE 5.0; Windows 98; DigExt).
```

Type Determination

PHP3 neither supports nor requires explicit type definition in variable declaration. A variable's type is determined by the *context* in which that variable is used. If a string value is assigned to variable $str, then $str becomes a string. If an integer value is then assigned to the variable $str, then $str becomes an integer. This contrasts with most compiled programming languages (like C or Pascal) where you must define the type of the variable before it is used.

An example of PHP's automatic type conversion is the addition operator '+'. If any of the operands is a double, then all operands are evaluated as doubles, and the result is a double. Otherwise, the operands are interpreted as integers, and the result is also an integer. Note that this does *not* change the types of the operands themselves; the only change is in how the operands are evaluated.

```
$a1 = "0";
// $a1 is a string

$a1 += 1;
/* $a1 is now an integer because we have used the addition
   operator */

$a1 = $a1 + 1.3;
/* $a1 is now a double (3.3) */

$a1 = 5 + "Craig";
/* $a1 is an integer (5) because the type casting of an
   integer overrides a string */

$a1 = 5 + "10 Craigs";
/* $a1 is an integer (15) because it parsed the value 10
   out of "10 Craigs" and cast it as an integer
*/
```

To force a variable to be evaluated as a certain type, see the Type Casting section. To change the type of a variable, see **settype()** in the Reference Section.

Determining Variable Types. Because PHP3 determines the types of variables and converts them as needed, the type of a given variable at any particular time not always obvious. PHP3 includes several functions that determine a variable type. These are found in the Reference Section.

Type Casting. Type casting in PHP3 works just as it does in C. The name of the desired type is written in parentheses before the variable that is to be cast.

```
$a1 = 100;
// $a1 is an integer

$b1 = (double) $a1;
// $b1 is a double
```

The following casts are allowed:

- `(integer)` → cast to integer
- `(real)`, `(double)`, `(float)` → cast to double
- `(string)` → cast to string
- `(array)` → cast to array
- `(object)` → cast to object

String Conversion. When a string is evaluated as a numeric value, it evaluates as a double if it contains any of the characters '.' (decimal point), 'e', or 'E'. Otherwise, the string evaluates as an integer.

The value is given by the first characters of the string. When a string begins with valid numeric data, this data is the value used. Otherwise, the value is set to zero. Valid numeric data may also contain an optional value sign, followed by one or more digits with (or without) a decimal point, followed by a exponent. The exponent is an 'e' or 'E' followed by one or more digits. For example:

```
$a1 = 1 + "100.5";
//$a1 is double (101.5)

$a1 = 1 + "-1.3e3";
// $a1 is double (-1299)

$a1 =  1 + "Find 10 in here"
/* $a1 is integer 1 -- evaluates the string to 0 because
   the number does not lead off the string. */

$a1 = 1 + "10 in here";
// $a1 is integer (11)
```

```
$a1 = "10.7 in here " + 1;
// $a1 is integer (11)

$a1 = "10.7 in here " + 1.0;
// $a1 is double (11)

$a1 = "10.7 in here" + 1.5;
//$a1 is double (11.5) -- the string always evaluates to an
integer.
```

The type of the variable is set based on the final value added to the string, when the initiating value is a string.

Arrays

PHP3 supports both **scalar** and **associative arrays**. Actually, there is no *functional* difference between these two types of arrays: the difference is in how one accesses the individual elements. A scalar array uses a *numeric* subscript, whereas an associative array using a *string* subscript.

An array can be created using the list() or array() functions, or one can explicitly set each array element value.

```
$a[0] = "ONE";
$a[1] = "TWO";
```

An array can also be created by simply adding values to the array:

```
$a[] = "THREE";   // $a[2] == "THREE"
$a[] = "FOUR";    // $a[3] == "FOUR"
```

Arrays may be sorted, counted or traversed using a variety of built-in functions (see the Reference Section).

Constants

PHP3 defines a few **predefined global constants**. PHP3 also provides a mechanism for creating user-defined constants at run time. Constants are much like read-only variables, but they have a slightly different syntax.

The predefined constants are __FILE__ and __LINE__, which correspond to the file name and line number being processed when the constants are encountered. When writing a web application, these two constants are often useful in debugging. For example, you can output to STDERR so that you can read the location in the web server's log file. Typically, this file is in /var/log/httpd/error_log.

```
<?PHP
function report_error($file, $line, $message) {
   echo "An error occurred in $file on line $line: $message.";
}

report_error(__FILE__,__LINE__, "Something went wrong!");
?>
```

User-defined constants can be defined at run time using the **define()** function:

```
<?PHP
define("CONSTANT", "ABC  123");
echo CONSTANT;
?>
```

yields

```
ABC 123
```

10.8 Expressions

PHP3 provides a full and powerful implementation of **expressions**. Expressions are critical structures in virtually all programming languages. Almost every script you program in PHP3 will contain an expression. The simplest, yet most accurate way to define an expressions is to say that it is "anything that has a value."

Two examples of expressions are constants and variables. When one types '$a = 5', the integer 5 is assigned into the variable $a. $a=5; is an expression. The implicit logic of an expression should be expressed consistently throughout the language. Based on our example, one would expect the value of variable $a to be 5, regardless of how the variable was used. Thus, $b = $a should assign the value of 5 to the new variable $b, which is exactly what happens.

Slightly more sophisticated examples of expressions are **functions**. For instance, consider the following function:

```
function Plant () {
   return "tree";
}
```

Underlying each function is an assumption that typing $c = Plant() is essentially like typing $c="tree". Functions are expressions that are the value of their return value. Because Plant() returns "tree", the value of the expression 'Plant()' is "tree".

PHP3 supports three scalar value types: integer values, floating-point values, and string values (scalar values are values that you can't break down into smaller pieces, unlike arrays, for instance).

PHP3 also supports two composite (nonscalar—values that can be broken down into smaller pieces) types: arrays and objects. Each of these types can be assigned into variables or returned from functions.

PHP3 is an *expression-oriented language,* in the sense that almost everything is an expression. Consider the example we've already dealt with, **$a = 5**. It's easy to see that there are two values involved here, the value of the integer constant 5 and the value of **$a**, which is being updated to 5.

In practice, this means that $a = 5, regardless of what it does, is an expression with the implicit assignment of an integer value of 5. So, writing something like $b = ($a = 5) is the same as writing $a = 5; $b = 5;.

A common group of expressions is *comparison expressions*. These expressions evaluate to either 0 or not 0 (where not 0 = TRUE and 0 = FALSE). Remember that TRUE can be any value other than 0—not necessarily 1 (the values –5 and 3,532 are both examples of evaluations of TRUE). TRUE is any value that is not FALSE.

PHP3 supports:

>	greater than
>= '	greater than or equal to
==	equal
<	less than
<=	less than or equal to
!=	not equal to

These expressions are most commonly used inside **conditional expressions**, such as IF statements. For example:

```
If ($t1 >= 100):
   Echo "$t1 is > or = 100";
Endif;
```

or, if you prefer,

```
If ($t1 >= 100) {
   Echo "$t1 is > or = 100";
}
```

Combined Operator-Assignment Expressions. If you want to increment **$a** by **1**, you can type '$a++' or '++$a'. But suppose you want to add 5 to $a and then put the result back into $a. Of course, you could (inefficiently) write '$a++' five times. A much more common practice, however, is to write $a = $a + 5. $a + 5 evaluates to the value of $a plus 5, and is assigned back into **$a**, which results in incrementing **$a** by 5.

In PHP, as in languages like C, you can write this in a more compact notation. Adding 5 to the current value of **$a** can also be written $a += 5. This evaluates to taking the value of $a, adding 5 to it, and assigning it back into $a. In addition to being shorter and clearer, this also results in greater execution speed. The value of $a += 5, like the value of a regular assignment, is the assigned value. Notice that it is not 5, but rather the combined value of $a plus 5 (this is the value that's assigned into $a).

Any *binary operator* can be used in this operator-assignment mode. For example:

```
$a -= 5 (subtract 5 from the value of $a)
$b *= 5 (multiply the value of $b by 5)
```

Ternary Conditional Operator Expression

```
$first ? $second : $third
```

You may find, as we have, that this expression is difficult to interpret quickly. We avoid it. But for completeness, we note that if the value of the first subexpression is TRUE (non-zero), then the second subexpression is evaluated, and that is the result of the conditional expression. Otherwise, the third subexpression is evaluated, and that is the value. For example:

```
$A = 1;
$A ? echo "YES" : echo "NO";
```

yields

```
YES
```

Truth Value. In many events, especially in conditional execution and loops, one is interested only in whether the expression evaluates to TRUE or FALSE. (PHP3 doesn't yet have a dedicated boolean type. C doesn't either.)

The *truth value* of expressions in PHP3 is calculated in a similar way to C or PERL. Any numeric non-zero numeric value is TRUE; zero is always FALSE. Note that negative values are not zero and are thus considered TRUE. The empty string and the string "0" are FALSE; all other strings are TRUE.

10.9 Functions

A *function* is a programming construct that provides a method for accomplishing a particular task. Once a function has been written, it can be called to perform the intended task any number of times. Functions are obviously important to all programming languages.

Functions take a complex activity (say, finding a particular character in a string) and build a method to accomplish the task. Once written, the function can be used (or called) anywhere in a program. If you need to do something more than once in the same project, then the function needs only be written a single time.

A function is defined using syntax such as the following:

```
function one ($arg_1, $arg_2, ..., $arg_n) {
   echo "Example function.\n";
   return $returnval;
}
```

Any valid PHP3 code may appear inside a function, even other functions and class definitions.

There are two types of functions; built-in functions (see the Reference Section) and user-defined functions, as defined in the example syntax above.

 We do not discuss of functions that can be added to the built-in core libraries. These additions can be done in any compiled language, usually C. Look for details on adding built-in functions at *www.php123.com*.

Returning Values. Values are returned from functions by using the optional **return statement**. Any data type may be returned, including lists and objects.

```
function Double ($num) {
   return $num * $num;
}

echo Double(4);
```

Output

```
16
```

Multiple values cannot be returned. However, the same effect can be achieved by returning a list of the return values as follows:

```
function MyFunction() {
   return array ("apples", "oranges", 3);
}

list ($zero, $one, $two) = MyFunction();
```

Output

```
$zero = "apples", $one = "oranges", $two = 3
```

Arguments. Data can be passed to functions by way of the **argument list**, which is a comma-delimited list of variables and/or constants.

PHP3 defaults to passing function arguments by value.

```
function MyFunction($input) {
   $a1 = $input
   return $a1;
}

$b1 = "ABC";
$c = MyFunction( $b1);
```

Output

```
ABC
```

Arguments can also be passed by reference or by default argument values. When a parameter is passed to a function as a **value**, the value itself can be modified without changing the value of the parameter in the outside scope, whereas the value of the parameter passed to a function by **reference** in the outside scope can be changed inside the function.

Variable-length argument lists are not supported. However, a similar effect may be achieved by passing arrays:

```
function accept_array($input) {
   echo "$input[0] + $input[1] = ", $input[0]+$input[1];
}
```

Passing by Reference. By default, function arguments are passed by **value**. However, if you wish to allow a function to modify its arguments, you may pass them by reference.

The ampersand (&) preceding the variable name denotes that the parameter is passed by reference. This reference is based on the notion of pointers to the memory location containing the parameter. However, with pass-by-value the interpreter makes another copy of the variable contents and then discards it when the function ends.

If you require that a function's argument be passed by reference, insert an ampersand (&) at the beginning of the argument name in the function definition:

```
function MyFunction( &$bar ) {
   $bar .= ' and more here.';
}

$str = 'This is a string, ';
MyFunction ($str);
echo $str;
```

Output

```
This is a string and more here.
```

This feature is useful when a function is required to change the value of a parameter.

If you wish to pass a variable by reference to a function, you can add an ampersand to the beginning of an argument name in the call to the function.

```
function MyFunction ($bar) {
   $bar = ' and more.';
}

$str = 'This is a string, ';
MyFunction($str);
echo $str;
```

Output

```
This is a string,
```

```
MyFunction (&$str);
echo $str;
```

Output

```
This is a string, and more.
```

Default Values. Default values are like a shorthand. If you decide ahead of time that a particular value is an acceptable default, then the default will be automatically substituted if you don't specify the value.

Default values, which do not occur in C, are a powerful construct in PHP. A function may define C++-style default values for scalar arguments.

```
function TreeType($type = "Pine") {
   echo "This is a $type tree.\n";
}
```

```
echo TreeType();
echo TreeType("Elm");
```

Output

```
This is a Pine tree.
This is an Elm tree.
```

The default value must be a constant expression, not a variable or class member.

Note that any default arguments should be on the right side of any non-default arguments; otherwise things will not work as expected. Consider the following code snippet:

```
function Tree ($type = "Pine", $size) {
   return "The $type tree has $size leaves.\n";
}

echo Tree ("Elm");
```

Output

```
Warning: Missing argument 2 in call to Tree() in
/home/httpd/htdocs/php3test/test001.html on line 8
The tree has leaves.
```

Now, compare the above with this:

```
function Tree($size,  $type = "Pine") {
   return "The $type tree has $size leaves.\n";
}

echo Tree ("big");    // works as expected
```

Output

```
The Pine tree has big leaves.
```

The most important built-in functions are found in the Language and Function Reference Section.

10.10 Statements

A program is composed of statements. Statements are the smallest unit of code that accomplishes something.

Include. The INCLUDE statement includes the file specified in the **include()** argument.

Include() differs from **require()** in that the include statement is re-evaluated *each* time it is encountered. The require() statement is replaced by the required file when it is *first* encountered.

Looking for a reason to make it a habit to use C-style `if-then-else` conditional statements in your PHP3 scripts? (one of the authors does, the other doesn't)? You must enclose include() within a statement block if it is inside a conditional block.

```
// This does not work
if ($condition)
   include($file);
else
   include($other);

// This works great
if ($condition) {
   include($file);
} else {
   include($other);
}
```

Whenever you include a file, make certain that your include file has the PHP3 start and end tags (`<?PHP… ?>`). When the file is evaluated, the parser begins in "HTML-mode" and will not recognize the PHP3 script, thinking it is HTML script.

10.11 Classes

A class is a collection of data and the operations that act upon that data. A class is defined using the following syntax:

```
<?PHP
class class_name {

   // variables
   var $var1;
   var $var2;

   // Constructor
   function class_name(){
   }

   // Function
```

```
      function func_name() {
      }
  }
  ?>
```

The best way to explain classes is to show them in action. In this example, we create a class that represents a suitcase. When we open the suitcase,
we want to automatically throw in our shaving kit. Also, we need a method
of adding shirts to the suitcase. (Note that this is just an example. When you
pack a suitcase in the real world, we suggest that you also pack socks, shoes,
and pants.) When we finish packing, our suitcase needs to be closed, so we
need a method of checking to see if we put too much in the suitcase.
    Here is the complete example:

```
<?PHP

class suitcase {
var $items;        // # of items in suitcase
var $shirts;       // # of shirts
var $shaving_kit;  // # of shaving kits

function add_item($item) {
  if($item == 'shirt') {
    $this->shirts++;
  }
  $this->items++;
}

function close_suitcase() {
  if($this->items > 3)
    echo "WARNING: The suitcase will not close.\n";
  else
    echo "Suitcase will close.\n";
}

// The constructor
function suitcase() {
  $this->items++;
  $this->shaving_kit++;
}

}

$trip = new suitcase;
$trip->add_item("shirt");
```

```
$trip->add_item("shirt");
$trip->add_item("shirt");
$trip->close_suitcase();

echo "\nThere are ".$trip->items." item(s) in the
   suitcase.\n";
echo "\nItems in suitcase:\n".$trip->shirts." shirt(s)\n";
echo $trip->shaving_kit." shaving kit(s)\n";
?>
```

Output

```
WARNING: The suitcase will not close.

There are 4 item(s) in the suitcase.

Items in suitcase:
3 shirt(s)
1 shaving kit(s)
```

Now we give a more in-depth explanation. The line

```
$trip = new suitcase;
```

creates a new instance of a suitcase. The creation of the instance represents opening the suitcase. Constructors are functions that are automatically called when a new instance is created. A class has a constructor if a function in the class has the same name as the class. When the line above is executed, the function below is automatically called, because it has the same name as the class:

```
function suitcase() {
   $this->items++;
   $this->shaving_kit++;
}
```

This function automatically places the shaving kit into the suitcase.
    Next, we add three shirts to the suitcase:

```
$trip->add_item("shirt");
$trip->add_item("shirt");
$trip->add_item("shirt");
```

Finally, we attempt to close the suitcase.

```
$trip->close_suitcase();
```

That's all there is to it.

Derived Classes. Now we need to pack our carry-on bag. We also automatically pack a shaving kit in this bag just in case the airline loses our suitcase. The difference between the carry-on bag and the suitcase is that the carry-on bag doesn't hold as many items. We build the **carry_on_bag** class by **extending** the suitcase class. We could create an entirely new class for the carry-on bag, but that would require more work. An extended (or derived) class has all of the variables and functions of the original (base) class, and whatever new variables and classes we wish to add.

A derived class is denoted by the **extends** keyword. The derived class to represent our carry-on bag is:

```
class carry_on_bag extends suitcase {
  function close_carry_on_bag() {
    if($this->items > 2)
      echo "WARNING: The carry-on bag will not close.\n";
    else
      echo "Carry-on bag will close.\n";
  }
}
```

Chapter 11

Databases and SQL

11.1 Database Building Blocks

First, let's make certain we agree on a couple of important definitions that relate to databases. This short overview relates to the tables represented below.

The database EARTH contains the following tables:

Table Name: PEOPLE

Name	Age	Birthdate	Balance_hi	Balance_lo
Peggy Jenkins	38	Dec 11	5000.00	1005.00
Trevor Williams	18	March 12	25.00	1.25
Jeff Jenkins	25	October 28	1000.00	100.00
Craig Jones	40	June 14	100.00	40.00
Sally Jones	38	April 19	505.00	100.00

Table Name: PLANTS

Name	Description	Flowering?	Preferred_temp
Daisy	White flower	Yes	36
Pine	Evergreen tree	No	25

Table Name: ANIMALS

Name	Description	Weight	Eye_color
Dolphin	Underwater mammal	875 kilos	Brown
Black Labrador	Super dog	78 kilos	Brown

A **field** is a piece of data about an item or object. For example, "**Name**" is a field of "**PEOPLE**".

Name

Peggy Jenkins
Trevor Williams
Jeff Jenkins
Craig Jones
Sally Jones

Other fields in the table PEOPLE are Age, Birthdate, Balance_hi, and Balance_lo.

Each collection of *all* the fields (Name, Age, Birthdate, Balance_hi, Balance_lo) in a row is called a **record**. A single record in the table PEOPLE is:

| Sally Jones | 38 | April 19 | 505.00 | 100.00 |

One way of looking at a record is that it contains a group of information about one entity or item. In the authors' opinion, it is logical to group related information about Sally Jones into a single record. Thus, Sally Jones has an age, a birthdate, and bank balances. It might not be logical to put today's temperature in this table, as it has nothing to do with the entity Sally Jones. (As the reader intuits, database design is, in fact, based on the assumptions of the developer. It is quite possible that another developer just might consider today's temperature to belong in this table.)

A **table** is made up of a collection of records (instances). All the records are a table. The table PEOPLE on page 77 is made up of five records.

A **database** is made up of a collection of tables. A database generally contains a collection of tables. For example, our database EARTH is made up of three separate tables:

Table Name: PEOPLE

Name	Age	Birthdate	Balance_hi	Balance_lo

Table Name: PLANTS

Name	Description	Flowering?	Preferred_temp

Table Name: ANIMALS

Name	Description	Weight	Eye_color

Taken individually, each of these tables represents a distinct logical grouping of data. Again, as with all database design, categorization of data into tables is often based on the developer's own perspective on the data. For example, one developer might include a table about WEATHER in the database EARTH. Database design is a critical—and often underappreciated—step in designing any meaningful database application.

The analogy of a filing cabinet is often helpful in understanding database terminology. A **field** is a single piece of information on a single form—for example, the name of a particular person. A **record** is the form containing all the information about that particular person (name, address, phone, age, and the like). A **table** is a collection of all the same type of forms about all the people contained in an entire filing cabinet (A–Z). A **database** is a collection of a group of individual filing cabinets, each of which contain separate forms. **Database management systems** (DBMSs) are methods of storing information.

As we have discussed, there are many types of DBMSs, including flat files, relational, and object-oriented. The simplest of these is the so-called "flat file." Flat files are simply ordered lists of data that can be searched. Relational and object-oriented database management systems are often known by their initials: RDBMS and OODBMS.

Many PHP3 functions deal directly with accessing and manipulating data contained in database management systems. We do not concern ourselves in this book with the logic and methodologies behind access rules; however, it's important to remember that however data is stored, it is basically accessed and manipulated using similar concepts. So, whether you are using PostgreSQL, MySQL, or Oracle8, the techniques to open, access, insert, modify, delete, and query (retrieve) your data will be very similar. Each DBMS may, of course, have several unique capabilities, in the form of functions, that highlight its unique characteristics.

An **index** is a method for accessing data in a particular order. There are many types of indexes. Indexes can often significantly decrease the time it takes to access information in a database and can be particularly useful in accessing databases that contain many records. However, SQL provides mechanisms that sort and group result sets, so indexes are primarily used to optimize retrieval speed.

11.2 Native versus Generic Database Access

Native database interfaces are significantly faster at retrieving data than generic database interfaces such as OBDC or JDBC. Why? The generic method is forced to spend an extra step or two creating the specialized syntax necessary to open and access a generic database. On the other hand, the advantage to using a generic method, like JDBC, is that your program can be database-independent. In other words, you can change platforms and database systems without modifying your PHP programs. Even considering this great advantage, we believe that most database systems do not support generic interfaces nearly as well and as consistently as they support their own proprietary methods, and that therefore the path of least resistance is just to use their proprietary methods.

PHP3 supports both native and generic database interfaces. The authors prefer using native methods because of the substantial difference in performance. However, where you are required to use more than one type of database management system (in a heterogeneous environment), you may find that you must use a generic interface such as JDBC.

11.3 Database Design

We will not spend much time reviewing database design. To dig deeper, check out some of the fine books on the subject in the Reading List.

A well-designed database makes all the difference in building a real-world application. Most developers find that a database design evolves over time. As we actually use data to accomplish tasks, the logical interrelationships become more clear. There is probably no more important step in building database applications than to clearly and concisely group the data to be used. It is vastly simpler to begin with a strong database design than to come back and attempt to alter the interaction of illogical data elements and scripting processes.

The Problem

How do we create a collection of tables to reflect the requirements of a particular information system? First we need to understand

1) what data we want to store in a database,

2) how that data should be divided up into tables, and

3) how that data is interrelated.

These processes, taken together, are referred to as **normalization**. For many people, the easiest way to create a data dictionary is to begin by reducing the process involving the data to a form or series of forms. One can normalize the data associated with virtually any project or process. We will be normalizing a CD-ROM library.

Normalizing the Data

Normalizing data is the process of removing duplicate fields and reconciling shared fields in a database. We suggest that you give your fields names that clearly reflect what the data represents. Don't name fields with numbers or other arcane naming conventions—stick to labels that identify what is contained in the field. Different DBMSs have varying naming requirements. PostgreSQL allows you to use up to 32 letters and numbers.

The hardest part of database design is determining how to organize the data into tables and columns. If you do this properly, adding to, changing, or deleting data in the table should not create problems with inconsistent data. For example, assume you design a database to store items that have been sold. You could make a table like:

Customer ID #	Item	Price	Weight
1	shirt	100	5
1	coat	40	1
2	socks	5	1

In the above example, customer 1 has bought two items and customer 2 has bought one item. There are problems here. For example, assume customer 1 goes out of business and you remove it from the database. This is bad, because it also removes the fact that a shirt costs $100. This problem is called a *deletion anomaly:* By deleting one fact, you inadvertently delete another fact.

This problem can be solved by separating the data into two different tables: one for items and another for customers. The one for orders could become:

Customer ID #	Item
1	shirt
1	coat
2	socks

The one for items could become:

Item	Price	Weight
shirt	100	5
coat	40	1
socks	5	1

The core of the problem is that the first table dealt with more than one common idea. Normalization is this process of breaking up a table into multiple tables, each of which contains a single idea.

Obviously, linking multiple tables together using this methodology allows very complex data pictures to be created. And this is what database management systems do best—link data together into formats that can be easily accessed and queried.

Building a Data Dictionary

A **data dictionary** is the group of all database and tables involved in an application. Building a data dictionary in most DBMSs is a fairly straightforward process. Building one in PostgreSQL is no different. First, your data should be organized into a database containing one or more tables. Then you should understand the interrelationship of the data elements, and finally decide on a standard methodology for naming your fields.

Now it's time to build our database. This is done in the PostgreSQL world by using the interactive SQL monitor for PostgreSQL and opening an interactive session.

The database is first created, then each of the tables is created. If indexes are used, they are created either when the tables are created or following table creation. Tables can be modified or deleted as required. Remember, it is much easier to build a useful database the first time than to attempt to modify one already created.

11.4 Using Other Databases

xBase DBMSs (e.g., dBase®)

We've included xBase in this book because of the ubiquitous dbf database file. The dbf file is found virtually everywhere in the world and encased in many important vertical applications, so most developers will eventually encounter a requirement to access a dbf file.

Initially based on a Jet Propulsion Laboratory public-domain database development in the 1970s and popularized by the saxophone-playing Philippe Kahn of Borland fame, dBase rapidly became one of the most popular desktop DBMSs. Several flavors quickly developed, including FoxBase and Clipper, providing varying levels of performance optimization and compilation strategies.

The inherently straightforward data model, coupled with a powerful and intuitive language set plus command-line control of tables and queries, quickly created a large user community. It is still hard to find a faster DBMS for small applications. Collectively, the group of dBase-like DBMSs came to be referred to as x-Base.

Why is xBase so popular? Randy Solton, the architect of dBASE on Windows, perhaps said it best: "dBASE is the only language that lets a developer create an application without having to be concerned about what's going on under the hood. It's the only language in which an attorney can write the application he needs himself."

xBase products eventually adapted to the SQL paradigm. Virtually every flavor supports nominal support of the ANSI-SQL query model.

PHP3 provides comprehensive tools to access dbf files in their native format. However, neither indexes nor memo files are supported.

PostgreSQL

Overview. The PostgreSQL query language is a variant of ANSI SQL92. However, several important features of PostgreSQL are *not* part of the ANSI standard, such as very large binary objects.

PostgreSQL has many extensions such as an extensible type system, inheritance, functions, and production rules. Those are features carried over from the original PostgreSQL query language, POSTQUEL.

This section provides an overview of how to use PostgreSQL SQL to perform simple operations. It is intended only to give the reader an overview and is in no way a complete SQL tutorial.

PostgreSQL and Data. The fundamental notion in PostgreSQL (and in all other relational database management systems) is that of a **table**, which is a collection of **records**. Each individual record has the same collection of data **fields**. Each data field is a specific **type**.

In **object-speak** this can be restated as: The fundamental notion in PostgreSQL is that of a **class**, which is a named collection of object **instances**. Each instance has the same collection of named **attributes**, and each attribute is of a specific **type**. Furthermore, each instance has a permanent object identifier (OID) that is unique throughout the installation.

Thus, here is the object-speak "Rosetta Stone":

Standard		Object-speak
Database	=	Database
Table	=	Class
Column	=	Attribute
Field	=	Attribute
Record	=	Instance or Tuple
Row	=	Instance or Tuple

Because SQL syntax refers to **tables**, we use the terms **table** and **class** interchangeably. Likewise, a **row** is an instance and **columns** are attributes. As previously discussed, classes are grouped into databases, and a collection of databases managed by a single postmaster process constitutes an installation or site. ▬▬▬

For those of you coming from a languages background: Tables have an instance or "is-a" relationship to schema elements, whereas the relationship between tables and records is a "has-a" relationship, like array or set membership. Of course, the previous analogy greatly oversimplifies the concept of objects. ▬▬▬

Creating a Database. Let's say you want to create a database named **MyDB**. You can do this with the following command:

```
createdb MyDB
```

PostgreSQL allows you to create any number of databases. As the creator of the database, you automatically become its database administrator. Database names must have an alphabetic first character and are limited to 16 characters. For example,

MyDB is a valid name.
MyDB_anything is a valid name.
MyDB_anything_else_here is not a valid name—it's too long.
1MyDB is not a valid name—it begins with a number.

Not every user has authorization to create databases. If PostgreSQL refuses to create databases for you, then someone needs to grant you permission to create databases. If you are the "someone," then you will need to grant yourself permission to create databases while you are the PostgreSQL superuser.

Getting to (or Accessing) a Database. Once you have created your database, you can access it by either:

1) running the PostgreSQL terminal monitor programs (monitor or PSQL), which allows you to interactively enter, edit, and execute SQL commands, or

2) writing a C program using the LIBPQ subroutine library. This allows you to submit SQL commands from a C program and get answers and status messages back. This interface is not discussed in this book. Typically, this method is far more complex than using PHP3, so, in the authors' opinion, don't waste your time here.

For purposes of following this section, we suggest you start up **PSQL**. If you are using *http://www.php123.com/*, you can use *http://www.php123. com/psql/* front-end to execute any of the supported SQL commands—just as if you were at the psql command prompt.

Building Database Applications on the Web using PHP3
Addison-Welsley's Reader's Only Web Site

1) Your personal application area
2) Up-to-the-minute updates and changes to the book
3) Code snippets and examples of PHP3 code organized by category
4) Links to important PHP3 sites.
5) Technical chat

You are the **1,493,485** visitor since Jan '98   Copyright (c)
Central Data Corp 1999.   About   Feedback

Otherwise, enter the command psql at the command prompt in your shell, as shown below.

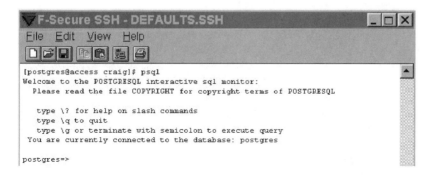

PSQL is an interactive SQL monitor that lets you interact directly with PostgreSQL. It's a great way to learn SQL and practice the examples in the book. Of course, anything you can do from PSQL you can do from PHP3.

PSQL (or *http://www.php123.com/psql/*) gives the developer complete access to all aspects of the data. No programs to write—type in the command to create a database and it's done. Create a table. Delete a table. Modify a table. Query your data. Change your data. The PSQL interactive monitor is an excellent tool.

The PSQL command set is shown as follows:

\?	—help
\a	—toggle field-alignment (default is on)
\C [<captn>]	—sets HTML version 3 caption (default is off)
\connect <dbname|-> <user>	—connect to new database (default is PostgreSQL)
\copy table {from | to} <fname>	
\d [<table>]	—list tables and indices, columns in <table>, or * for all
\da	—list aggregates
\dd [<object>]	—list comment for table, field, type, function, or operator
\df	—list functions
\di	—list indices
\do	—list operators
\ds	—list sequences
\dS	—list system tables and indexes
\dt	—list tables
\dT	—list types
\e [<fname>]	—edit the current query buffer or <fname>

\E [<fname>]	—edit the current query buffer or <fname>, and execute
\f [<sep>]	—change field separater (currently '|')
\g [<fname>] [|<cmd>]	—send query to backend [and results in <fname> or pipe]
\h [<cmd>]	—help on syntax of sql commands, * for all commands
\H	—toggle html3 output (default is off)
\i <fname>	—read and execute queries from filename
\l	—list all databases
\m	—toggle monitor-like table display (default is off)
\o [<fname>] [|<cmd>]	—send all query results to stdout, <fname>, or pipe
\p	—print the current query buffer
\q	—quit
\r	—reset(clear) the query buffer
\s [<fname>]	—print history or save it in <fname>
\t	—toggle table headings and row count (default is on)
\T [<html>]	—set html3.0 <table ...> options (default ")
\x	—toggle expanded output (default is off)
\z	—list current grant/revoke permissions
\! [<cmd>]	—shell escape or command

We discuss only a few of these commands.

Initially we want to access the MyDB database. This is done by typing in the command:

```
% psql MyDB
```

If you have forgotten your database name, you can get a complete list of all databases that belong to you by typing in:

```
% psql /i
```

You will be greeted with the following message:

```
Welcome to the POSTGRESQL95 interactive sql monitor:
  type \? for help on slash commands
  type \q to quit
  type \g or terminate with semicolon to execute query
  You are currently connected to the database: mydb

MyDB=>
```

The **MyDB=>** prompt indicates that the interactive terminal monitor (PSQL) is waiting for a command to be typed. The PSQL monitor responds to escape codes that begin with the backslash character, "\". (We assume the user is in the interactive PSQL monitor and connected to his or her database.) You can get help on the syntax of various POSTGRESQL SQL commands by typing:

```
mydb=> \h
```

(You actually type the **\h**—the **mydb=>** is the PSQL prompt.)
To exit PSQL and return to UNIX, type

```
mydb=> \q
```

PSQL will terminate and return you to your command shell.

White space (spaces, tabs, and newlines) may be used freely in SQL queries. Comments are denoted by --. Everything after the dashes up to the end of the line is ignored.

This will display help on the token you type in:

```
Mybd=>   \h token
```

This will display the structure of whatever tablename you request:

```
Mydb=> \d tablename
```

This will display all tables available in the current database (including indexes):

```
Mydb=> \d
```

Destroying a Database. If you are the owner (or database administrator) for the database MyDB, you can destroy it with the following command:

```
Destroydb  MyDB;
```

This action physically removes all of the files associated with the database and *can't* be undone, so *be careful* before issuing this command.

Building (or Creating) the Tables (Classes). You create a new class by specifying the class name, along with all attribute names and their types:

```
CREATE TABLE people (
   Name            varchar(50),
   Phone           char(20),
   Prefix          char(3),
   Balance_hi      real,
```

```
    Balance_lo        real,
    Age               smallint,
    Personal_info     oid,
    Birthdate         date
);
```

Note that SQL keywords (e.g., **CREATE TABLE**) are case-insensitive (Cre-aTE works just as well) but attribute names are case-sensitive ("**NAME**" is different from "**Name**").

PostgreSQL supports the usual SQL types int, float, real, smallint, char(N), varchar(N), date, and time. Several types are presently not supported, including boolean. The **varchar()** and **char()** type is limited to 4K of data contained in the actual data record. On the other hand, an OID is a pointer to a large object, which can be very large.

PostgreSQL can be customized with an arbitrary number of user-defined data types.

PostgreSQL classes have properties that are extensions of the relational model. This is why PostgreSQL is called an "object-relational database management system."

Building Indexes. Indexes allow a DBMS to access data orders of magnitude faster than when indexes aren't used. Where indexes are available, the DBMS creates an internal data structure (the index) that tells the DBMS where a certain row is in the table given an indexed-column value, much as a book index tells you on what page a given word appears. There are several types of indexes. Most indexes rely on sophisticated tree-based algorithms to determine the location of records based on some criterion. An in-depth discussion of indexes is beyond the scope of this book.

When a tree-based index exceeds the cache size, a search with a non-tree-based index (typically accessed in a more sequential pattern) may be faster than a tree-based search against the same index, since the latter may require disk searches rather than sequential reads to refresh the cache. Also, if you update the data often, the gain in update speed is often lost when indexes must also be updated. So, consider (and test) whether indexes are warranted in your application.

To create an index for the table PEOPLE based on the field NAME, we issue the following SQL command:

```
CREATE INDEX People_name ON PEOPLE (NAME);
```

This command causes PostgreSQL to create an alphabetical index in which the individual NAME fields for each record appear (their location is not actually changed in the database) to progress from A → Z. Searches of the data by the name criterion will be much faster. For example, the query:

```
SELECT * FROM people WHERE NAME = 'Craig';
```

uses the index People_name to optimize the search, whereas the query

```
SELECT * FROM people WHERE age > 20;
```

cannot use any index and must sequentially scan the entire table(s) to return the result set.

Ordering the Result Set. If all you want to do is "sort" the entire result set returned from a query against the table **People**, you can avoid using any indexes by using the ORDER BY syntax as follows:

```
SELECT * FROM People ORDER BY Name;
```

You'll get a result set sorted alphabetically by Name.

An index provides a mechanism to locate records and has nothing to do with displaying the result set. So, a query

```
SELECT * FROM People WHERE name = 'Craig'
```

returns a result set in unsorted order. To be sure, this query would execute faster. However, to return data in a particular sorted order, you need to use the ORDER BY qualifier, as follows:

```
SELECT * FROM People WHERE name = 'Craig' ORDER BY Name
```

Compound Indexes. A slightly more complex index in which we first index on AGE and then on NAME would give us a different view of the data. This would create an index where for each AGE group (1, 2, 3 ... 55) each NAME is subindexed by alphabetical order:

```
CREATE INDEX AGE_NAME_IDX ON PEOPLE (AGE, NAME);
```

Primary Unique Keys. Another type of index serves a purpose other than speeding up data access: a "Primary Unique Key" index. This index requires a unique value for the field(s) being indexed. That is, if you have an Unique Key index on the field name and already have a record with the Name field = "Craig", no other record with the name of "Craig" will be accepted. Sometimes this capability is very useful, but use it carefully.

To create a Primary Unique Key, type

```
CREATE UNIQUE INDEX NAME_IDX ON PEOPLE (NAME);
```

Dropping an Index. To get rid of an index, just drop it:

```
DROP INDEX AGE_NAME_IDX;
```

Adding Data to a Table. The INSERT statement is used to add individual records to a table. For example:

```
INSERT INTO people (name, age, GPA, Birthdate )
   VALUES ('Jane Smith',  27,  3.98, '6/14/49'  )
```

Records are added to the physical end of the table.

 Using the COPY Command. You can also use the copy command to load large amounts of data from flat (ASCII) files. Remember, this command only works for PostgreSQL and is not part of the SQL standard.

1) Create an text file containing the data you want to load. (For example, you have a dBase file called DATA.DBF with the following fields you want to extract: name - char(50), age - num(2,0), phone - char(20). Issue the dBase command:

```
copy fields name,age,phone from DATA into c:\temp\ABC.
   txt delimited with '|'.
```

    Then upload the resulting file to the location of your SQL server. If you are using *www.php123.com*, upload it to your personal directory.

2) Issue this PostgreSQL command from PSQL:

```
COPY E from '/home/Myarea/ABC.txt' using delimeters '|';
```

3) Or, create the following PHP3 script:

```
<?PHP
...
pg_Exec($conn, "Copy E from '/home/Myarea/ABC.txt' using
   delimiters '|'");
?>
```

11.5 Queries Using the SQL SELECT Statement

Obviously, getting the data out of a DBMS is as important as putting it in. The old adage "garbage in, garbage out" stresses the importance of accurate data going in.

Although most of what we will present applies generically to all SQL servers, several features unique to PostgreSQL are also introduced and we highlight a feature that is unique to PostgreSQL.

What's a Query?

A query retrieves information contained in one or more tables. A query can be very simple—"How many records are in the entire table?"—or very complex. SQL provides a syntax that allows us to access data with minimal effort.

A Query Example. The People table can be queried using the SQL SELECT statement. The SQL SELECT statement is divided into a target list (the part that lists the attributes to be returned) and a qualification (the part that specifies any restrictions). For example, to retrieve all the records (or rows) of People you type:

```
SELECT * FROM People;
```

Notice the semicolon at the end of every statement. That tells the parser that it has reached the end of the SQL statement.

And, based on the hypothetical data in the table, the output should include *every* field (or attribute) of *every* record (or instance) contained in the table PEOPLE, as follows:

Name	Phone	Balance_hi	Balance_lo	Age	Prefix	Birthdate
Jane Doe	555-1234	1000.00	25.00	30	555	6-14-1960
Sally Doe	222-1277	500.00	150.00	50	222	12-10-1979
John Doe	555-1234	1500.00	1000.00	40	555	7-12-1950

Case Sensitivity

Though SQL keywords are not case sensitive, it is best to assume case sensitivity in all queries. Many developers choose to make all keywords uppercase as in the following examples:

```
SELECT * FROM people
SELECT name,phone FROM people
```

However, individual SQL Servers may or may not support case sensitivity within target lists and qualification syntax. It is best to assume case sensitivity in all queries.

For example, PostgreSQL is not case sensitive in either the target list or the qualification. These queries will all obtain the same results:

```
SeleCT name,PHONE from PEOple
SELect NAME,phoNE from peopLE
```

However, MySQL is case sensitive in the qualification syntax, but not in the target list.

```
SELECT name,PHONE from people      //runs
select NAme,PHone from people      //runs
SELECT name,phone from PEOple      //fails
```

Fields in the Target List

You can specify specific fields (or attributes) in your target list. For example,

```
SELECT Name, Balance_hi, Balance_lo, Age FROM people;
```

would return on the specified fields from the PEOPLE table:

Name	Balance_hi	Balance_lo	Age
Jane Doe	1000.00	25.00	30
Sally Doe	500.00	150.00	50
John Doe	1500.00	1000.00	40

Arbitrary Expressions

You may specify any aribitrary expressions in the target list. For example:

```
SELECT name, (Balance_hi + Balance_lo)/2 AS Avg_Balance,
   Birthdate
FROM people
WHERE age > 30 ;
```

This will return the specified fields, plus a temporary field to be called `Avg_Balance` that is composed of `(balance_hi + balance_lo)/2` from the People database. The WHERE clause further qualifies the target list (or result set) to return only those records that match the qualification criterion—that the field AGE has a value greater than 30.

Name	Avg_Balance	Birthdate
Sally Doe	325	7-12-1950
John Doe	1250	12-10-1979

Arbitrary Logical Operators

Arbitrary logical (boolean) operators (and, or, and not) are allowed in the qualification of any query. For example,

```
SELECT Name, Age, Birthdate
   FROM people
```

```
WHERE Age > 35
   and Name = 'John Doe';
```

This produces the table below:

Name	Age	Birthdate
John Doe	40	12-10-1979

You must include every field that you use in your qualifications in your field list. For example, if you are qualifying your query to only Name = 'Doe', then the field Name must be in the target list:

```
SELECT Name FROM people WHERE Name = 'Doe';
```

You can specify the order of the returned results of a SELECT statement by using the ORDER BY qualifier as follows:

```
SELECT name, age
   FROM people
   ORDER BY Name;
```

Name	Age
Jane Doe	30
John Doe	40
Sally Doe	50

or, with duplicate instances removed:

```
SELECT DISTINCT phone, name, age
   FROM people
   ORDER BY Name;
```

Phone	Name	Age
555-1234	Jane Doe	30
555-1277	Sally Doe	50

Redirecting SELECT Queries

Any query can be redirected to a new table:

```
SELECT * INTO temp FROME People;
```

This syntax generates an implicit **create table** command that creates a new table TEMP with all the attributes of the parent table PEOPLE. Operations can then be performed on the resulting table.

We could just as easily perform the same redirection on a subset of the table, like this:

```
SELECT name,age, birthdate into Temp
   FROM people
   WHERE age > 30;
```

We would end up with the following:

Name	Age	Birthdate
Sally Doe	50	12-10-1979
John Doe	40	7-12-1950

Updating Tables

You can update any data contained in any table. Suppose all the individual records in the table People just attended the 1999 Walk-a-thon, and you want to enter that in their "Personal_info" field. You update the table like this:

```
UPDATE people
   SET Personal_info = "Participated in the 1999 Walk-a-thon";
```

This modifies the Personal_info field in *every* record in the People table.

This command modifies an OID field that is used for storing large amounts of information.

You can update existing records using the update command. Suppose the phone number and balance information changes for everyone named Doe. You update the data like this:

```
UPDATE People
   SET phone = '555-0000',  Balance_lo = 125.00
   WHERE Name = '%doe';
```

Be wary of UPDATE commands that are not limited by the WHERE clause! Obviously you could accidentally alter every single record in an entire table when you really just wanted to update a single record. *(Now who hasn't done that once or twice!)*

Deleting from Tables

Deletions are performed using the delete command:

```
DELETE FROM people WHERE name = '%doe';
```

All instances where the field Name = "Doe" are removed.

Technically, the data has been removed, but the space taken up by the data has not been reclaimed. Reclaiming deleted space is accomplished using the **vacuum** command.

A query against the database would now return the following results:

Name	Phone	Balance_hi	Balance_lo	Age	Personal_info	Birthdate

One should be *very* careful of queries of the form

```
DELETE FROM classname;
```

Without a qualification, the delete command simply deletes *all records* of the table, leaving it empty. The system does not request confirmation before doing this! There is no going back once the delete command has been issued to your SQL server—so be certain of what you are doing.

Using Transactions

Transactions are one of the main tools SQL provides for maintaining the integrity of your data.

A transaction is a collection of all of the SQL commands used to complete an action on your database. Typically, you want the series of commands to:

- do each operation exactly once, *and*
- do all or none (but not some) of the set of updates.

If something goes wrong during an update, all of the changes in the current set are undone. A few of the many things that can go wrong are running out of hard-drive room, program crashes, network problems, client machines locking up, servers running out of memory, programmer errors, and so forth. Typically, the process of not completing a set of operations is called "backing out." You don't really undo work, you simply don't complete it.

The SQL command **BEGIN WORK** is used to denote the start of a transaction. To end the transaction, the SQL command **END WORK** is used. If the program crashes before the **END WORK** command is reached, then the updates after the **BEGIN WORK** statement are not done. Also, the SQL command **ROLLBACK** can be used to cause a set of updates not to be done.

For example:

```
...
pg_Exec($conn, "BEGIN WORK");
pg_Exec($conn, "INSERT INTO mydb (name, age) values
('Craig', 85)");
if ($bad_condition) {
  pg_Exec($conn, "ROLLBACK");
  exit;
}
else {
  pg_Exec($conn, "COMMIT);
}
```

Vacuuming a Database (Housekeeping)

Most DBMS have a built-in method of removing space taken up by deleted records. PostgreSQL uses the **vacuum** command. You should issue the vacuum command periodically, from a command line (whether from the console or over telnet).

```
psql MyDatabase
vacuum
```

That's all there is to it. Depending on the size of your database, the process may consume a few minutes. When the space has been reoptimized, you are returned to the prompt. This reclaims and reoptimizes all deleted space. This action will *significantly* improve performance in databases where the data is being modified and deleted often.

To vacuum a database automatically every Saturday, you just add the following line to /etc/crontab:

```
3 3 * * sat PostgreSQL /usr/bin/psql -c "vacuum" dbname
```

This command vacuums the database dbname every Saturday at 3:03 AM.

Using Aggregate Functions

One meaning of the word aggregate is "a collection of items formed into a whole mass or sum." An example might be a rock formed by a collection of individual smaller rocks. This word is used to describe a group of SQL functions, because they take a collection of rows and form a result of a single row. SQL includes aggregate functions to find the maximum, minimum, sum, average, and count of rows in a result. Specifically, the functions are:

Function	Description
Count()	This function returns how many rows are in the result.
Avg()	This function returns the average of the values in the specified column.
Max()	This function returns the maximum value in the specified column.
Min()	This function returns the minimum value in the specified column. Note: NULLs are not treated as 0s.
Sum()	This function returns the sum of all of the values in the column.

Here's an example of how to use these functions in a real-world application. Consider the table below showing items in an order:

Item	Shipping weight	Price	Quantity
Coat	5	100	1
Shirt	2	40	1
Socks	1	5	2
Hangers		0	10

With MySQL, we can create a table to store the previous data as follows:

```
mysql> CREATE TABLE order (item varchar(20) NOT NULL,
weight int4, price int4, quantity int4);
```

The table created is:

```
mysql> DESCRIBE order;
```

which returns

```
+----------+------------+-------+-----+---------+-------+
| Field    | Type       | Null  | Key | Default | Extra |
+----------+------------+-------+-----+---------+-------+
| item     | varchar(20)|       |     |         |       |
| weight   | int(11)    | YES   |     | NULL    |       |
| price    | int(11)    | YES   |     | NULL    |       |
| quantity | int(11)    | YES   |     | NULL    |       |
+----------+------------+-------+-----+---------+-------+
```

First, we determine the heaviest item in the shipment. To do this, we use the **max()** function:

```
mysql> SELECT max(weight) FROM order;
```

which returns

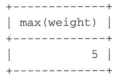

The heaviest item weighs 5 pounds. And now we want to determine the lightest item:

```
mysql> SELECT min(weight) FROM order;
```

which returns

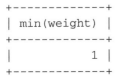

Note that this item is 1 pound. It is not 0 or NULL, even though the hangers have no weight specified, because the **min()** function does not treat NULL values as zeros.

Now we want to know the total price of the order:

```
mysql> SELECT sum(price*quantity) FROM order;
```

which returns

```
+------------+
| sum(price) |
+------------+
|        150 |
+------------+
```

It is $150.

Finally, we determine the number of items in the order:

```
mysql> SELECT count(item) FROM order;
```

which returns

```
+------------+
| count(item) |
+------------+
|          4 |
+------------+
```

Chapter 12

Applications

Why do the applications? If you want to learn how to program database applications on the web using PHP3 and PostgreSQL, then we strongly suggest you take two to three hours and build these sample applications. If you bought this book only for its Reference Section, then skip this.

These applications are meant to be neither sophisticated nor complex. We've tried to explain some of the rationale behind the underlying script code. We hope that, when you've finished Application 7, you will have a clearer appreciation of why PHP3 is so powerful. Of course, these applications are meant to serve as basic examples only. To continue learning PHP3, you should move on to studying the examples contained in the Reference section.

Note: We refer to functions used in the examples in the format **function()**.

There is *no easier way* to learn PHP3 than to type in these examples on the Readers Only Web site, *www.php123.com*.

12.1 Application 1—Hello World

This application is for those of you just beginning your web-based programming experience. Those of you with a bit more experience may want to skim through this example, as we cover several important topics including the basics of creating, uploading, and running the application.

Here's what we're going to do:

1) build a simple web page

2) write a PHP3 script that displays "Hello World" on the screen.

Writing It

Before we begin writing our code, we need to decide how we will be creating our web page. People have their own preferred methods of generating web pages. Because the first step in most PHP3 applications is to create a web page, we'll look at three methods:

- using www.php123.com
- using a text editor like NotePad (Windows) or Joe (UNIX)
- using Netscape's Composer, Microsoft's® Front Page™, or other WYSIWYG (What You See Is What You Get) HTML editor

Each has its advantages. We will assume you're using NotePad or some other familiar text processor that generates ASCII-text documents. However, we'll look spend a couple of pages reviewing how to use each in building a PHP3 application.

What's the difference between a text processor such as NotePad and Word-Perfect? Most full-featured word processors, such as WordPerfect or Microsoft Word, embed control characters to represent changes in fonts, bolding, and the like. These control characters, though hidden to you, are very much present when a computer program such as a PHP script parser tries to read them. Instead of seeing

```
<?PHP
```

the parser would see an indecipherable mishmash of characters like

```
fj☐⌐●☐˅php
```

Text processors do not embed special control characters in the text.

To be fair, most word processors have a text output capability. If you want to use your favorite word processor to build your applications, check that the output is for text-only.

Using www.php123.com. This couldn't be easier. Just type whatever code you want directly into the CODE window on the main form. Follow the on-line instructions.

Using Joe (UNIX). This is a "raw" method of creating an web page from a UNIX (specifically Linux) environment. We write everything by hand, and position items on our page by trial and error. Make no mistake: There are many developers who prefer this level of control.

Joe will generate an ASCII-text document, that is, a document that does not contain any hidden or embedded control characters. What you type is exactly what is saved. If you are familiar with the old WordStar command set (also used by Borland's editors), then there is no learning curve.

Here are some useful commands (^ means Control). Check out the help screen for the rest.

^K ^H = display a help screen
^K ^D = save
^K ^F = find
^K ^Q = quit

Using NotePad (Windows). This is another "raw" method of creating a web page from a Microsoft Windows environment. We write everything by hand, and position items on our page by trial and error. Again, many developers prefer this level of control.

NotePad will generate an ASCII-text document, that is, a document that does not contain any hidden or embedded control characters. What you type is exactly what is saved. Just open up Notepad from `Windows → Programs → Applications → Notepad`. (You can use WordPad also, just make *certain* you save your work as a **text** file [not the default Word document].)

To create a document, simply begin typing. When you want to save your work, click on **File → Save As**. Type in the name you want to call the document. Once you have named your document, simply click on **File → Save** to save any changes you have made. To exit, click on **File → Exit**.

Using WYSIWYG HTML Generators. A number of products build an HTML document in a WYSIWYG environment. Many users prefer the simplicity and functionality provided by these applications. For the most part, however, they are not free. There is also usually a short learning curve.

All the generators work in nearly the same manner. The user "draws" a web page, layering text, graphics, animations, and the like onto a template. When finished, the template is converted into HTML code. Because the converter is hidden from the user, there is usually little or no contact with the actual code underlying the page. Almost always, the HTML code generated is bloated and non-portable. It is almost always much harder to modify a page generated with a WYSIWYG tool than a page generated by hand. To add PHP scripts, you will have to modify the HTML by hand.

This can be a significant disadvantage for PHP3 developers. PHP3 scripts must be transposed into HTML code. There is no automatic generator to perform these actions. The developer is responsible for programming whatever interaction is expected from the web page. Thus, a user who has relied on a WYSIWIG HTML generator to build web pages will find a learning curve involved in the migration to fluency in HTML coding and syntax.

Netscape Composer (Windows). First, build your page using Composer. Create whatever forms and tables you will require. Then go to **View→Page** Source and pull up the entire source code for the page you have created. Place your PHP3 script code wherever required in the document. When finished, don't forget to save your changes.

We don't suggest trying to use the **Insert→HTML** tag onto a particular object. PHP3 is sensitive to the location of PHP3 code, so this will not work well.

FrontPage (Windows). First, build your page using FrontPage. Create whatever forms and tables you will require. Then go to **View→Page** source and pull up the entire source code for the page you have created. Place your PHP3 code wherever required in the document. When finished, don't forget to save your changes.

We don't suggest attempting to use the **Insert→HTML** code onto a particular object. PHP3 is sensitive to the location of PHP3 code, so this will not work well.

The Complete Code

```
<html>
<head>
  <title>PHP3 Application #1</title>
</head>
<body>
  <?PHP
  Echo "Hello World";
  ?>
</body>
</html>
```

Step By Step

1) We need to build a web page containing this code. First, decide which method to use to create your HTML document for this application. Create an HTML document called **hiworld.html**.

   Some environments will not let you save a four-letter extension such as **html**. In that case, save your work with the three-letter extension **htm**. Whenever you type in your web document name, make certain you change it to htm.

   If you are using *www.php123.com* to build your application(s), the extension html is *automatically* appended to each of the files you create.

   Now we build the basic wrapper that surrounds every web page. HTML commands are always enclosed in braces. Most begin with an HTML token and end with the same token preceded by /. For example: <html> begins an HTML page and </html> ends an HTML page.

   Each HTML page is broken into two distinct areas: the <head> and the <body>. Basically, things that relate to the formatting and information of the page and are not seen by the end user are contained in the <head> portion. The <body> contains those portions that are displayed to the user and with which the end user interacts. Notice that the <head> section ends with </head>, as does <body>.

```
<html>
<head>
  stuff here …
</head>
<body>
  more stuff here …
</body>
</html>
```

2) Now we put in the PHP3 code that writes "Hello World."

a) PHP3 can be placed anywhere in an HTML document. In fact, it can be placed before the <html>. However, for this application, we place our script in the <body> section.

```
<body>
  → your script will be going here ..
</body>
```

b) PHP3 script must be identified so the PHP3 interpreter can identify what belongs to PHP3 and what doesn't. Let's open a PHP3 section in the document:

```
<body>
<?PHP
  → your stuff here…
?>
</body>
```

One can also indicate a PHP3 code section as follows:

```
<body>
<%
  → your Stuff here …
%>
</body>
```

However, the new HTML specifications reserve the use of <?, so we strongly suggest you use the <?PHP format.

c) Now we put in the actual PHP3 script that instructs the screen to display "Hello World."

```
<body>
<?PHP
```

```
    Echo "Hello World";
  ?>
  </body>
```

echo is a function. Every important function in PHP3 is included in the Language and Function Reference Section in this book. There are over 500 PHP3 functions, and more are added every month. To understand more about functions, see the overview found in Section 10.9. You can even build your own functions and include them wherever you like.

Now, you might ask, is there any other way of writing "Hello World" to the screen? Of course. There are many. For example, this also works very well:

```
<body>
<?PHP
  Printf("%s", "Hello World");
?>
</body>
```

This is another example of a new function **Printf()**. This one is a bit more sophisticated because it lets us format what we want to print.
   Or how about this?

```
<body>
<?PHP
  Print( "Hello World\n");
?>
</body>
```

This code does the same thing. The \n adds a line feed after the Hello World.

Uploading It

Once you have created your HTML document, it needs to be in a place where the script can pass through the PHP3 interpreter so you can view it from a browser.

Using www.php123.com. If you're using *www.php123.com* to build this application, simply press the **SUBMIT** key. Your program will be uploaded automatically. That's all there is to it.

Using a Local Computer to Execute PHP Scripts. If you are working on your own machine and are planning on running PHP3 and PostgreSQL from there, things will be fairly simple. We assume you have correctly installed PHP3 and PostgreSQL. Since you have already saved your work in a directory, you've already "uploaded" your application to your web server. You're all set.

Using a Nonlocal Computer to Execute PHP Scripts. Save your work in a directory that can be accessed by your web server (e.g., */home/httpd/html* or *~username/public_html*).

If you need to **ftp** (file transfer protocol) your script to a URL, this is can be done in a couple of easy ways. If you are running any version of Windows or Linux:

a)   At the DOS prompt, while in the directory containing your PHP3 script program, type

```
FTP yourserver.com <return>
```

b)   Type in your ID and PASSWORD (supplied in your CD-ROM packet).

c)   Type in

```
put filename.php3 <return>
quit
```

If you are running Linux or any other UNIX-like system, at the shell prompt follow exactly the same steps as above.

Running It

Open your web browser and type in the URL to get to your PHP3 script. For example, if your script is located in your local web server at */home/ httpd/html/test.php3* then the URL would be:

```
http://localhost/test.php3
```

Or, if your script is located at *http://www.php123.com* in your personal directory (**mydir**) in the file test.php3, then the URL would be:

```
http://www.php123.com/mydir/test.php3
```

A Note on Web Page Creation

Very often, you will find with a complicated PHP program, it is hard to generate valid HTML—for instance, it is very easy to forget to end a tag. There are some things you can do to find and fix these types of problems. A few of them are:

1. Validate your HTML using a syntax checker, like Weblint (*http://www.weblint.org/*), Doctor HTML (*http://www2.imagiware.com/RxHTML/*), or the W3C HTML Validation Service (*http://validator.w3.org/*).

2. View your HTML with a text-only browser, like Lynx.

3. Use both the newer and older versions of several browsers.

4. Try multiple graphical browsers with:

    *   graphics enabled,

    *   graphics disabled,

    *   no mouse (use the keyboard), or

    *   frames, style sheets, and applets not loaded.

5. Use your browser at several different resolutions.

6. Use a spell checker. This improves readability for most people. Also, someone reading the page with a speech synthesizer may not be able to understand the synthesizer's guess for a word with a spelling error.

If you do the above, your PHP programs will have the widest potential audience, and the world will see your message as you intend it to be seen. After all, isn't that what most web pages are about? You can also feel good about the fact that you won't be excluding someone with a physical disability from using your site.

Troubleshooting

So what can go wrong? About a million things. We have tried to isolate a few of the most common errors we've seen. Perhaps you have found something unique—if so, let us know.

If things aren't working on your local computer, we suggest you try your application directly on the Readers Only PHP3 Web Site, *http://www.php123.com/*. If it works there, then you have not installed PHP3 correctly on your machine. If it doesn't work there, then you have made an error in typing in the code.

Pay very close attention to how the code is written. Remember that the semicolon at the end of each logical phrase is very important.

12.2 Application 2—File-Based Counter

We will build a page that records each access by a visitor to the page by incrementing a *file-based* counter. The counter will display on the web page.

Here's what we're going to do:

1) Build a simple web page.

2) Write a PHP3 script that

   a) updates a number in a file every time someone pulls the page into a browser and

   b) displays the number on the web page.

Writing It

The Complete Code

```
<html>
<head>
  <title>PHP3 Application #2</title>
</head>
<body>
  <?PHP

  $counter_file = "/tmp/counter.txt";

  // IF the file doesn't exist THEN we start the count at 1
  if(!file_exists($counter_file)) {
    exec("/bin/echo 1 > $counter_file");
  }

  // Open the counter file and read the count
  $fp = fopen($counter_file, "r+");
  $count = fgets($fp, 10);
  $count += 1;

  // Overwrite the old count
  fseek($fp, 0);
  fwrite($fp, $count, 10);
  fclose($fp);

  //display the counter
  echo ˇYou are visitor $count to this page";

  ?>
</body>
</head>
```

Step By Step

1) We start with our simple web page:

```
<html>
<head>
   stuff here …
</head>
<body>
   stuff here …
</body>
</html>
```

2) We write our PHP3 script. First we make certain there is a file in which we can store the number reflecting the number of visitors.

```
$counter_file = "/tmp/counter.txt";
// IF the file doesn't exist THEN we start the count at 1
if(!file_exists($counter_file)) {
   exec("/bin/echo 1 > $counter_file");
}
```

Now, what's going on here?

```
$counter_file = "/tmp/counter.txt";
```

We are creating a string variable and filling it with the value contained in the text file "/tmp/coutner.txt". So what's "/tmp/counter.txt"? That's simply the name of the file we are going to use to put our counter number into. Of course, the "/tmp" at the beginning is the subdirectory in which we want to put it. On most UNIX systems, the "/tmp" directory is one where anybody can create files. You will probably want to use a different directory for a production counter.

The name of the file could just as easily be "mysubdirectory/counter.file.doc". (You may ask how we can create a file with a name like "counter.file.doc". Because we are operating in the UNIX operating system, file names are not limited to a single extension as in Microsoft Windows. Go ahead and be creative.) (Notice, also, that UNIX uses the forward slash /, not the backward slash \ used in Windows, to separate the parts of a pathname.)

```
// IF the file doesn't exist THEN we start the count at 1
```

This is how you put comments into your program. The PHP3 interpreter will ignore anything following the // on the *same* line. If your comment is going to span *more than one* line, you can put // in front of each line, or you can surround your comments with /* and */ symbols like this:

```
/*
IF the file doesn't exist THEN we start
the count at 1
*/
```

Next we perform a little logic. This little snippet of code can be broken apart as follows:

File_exists() is a function. Its purpose it to tell us whether a particular file exists. The syntax for the function is file_exists (name_of_file).

We have created a string variable $counter_file (which is holding the name of our counter file—"/tmp/counter.txt"). So, we plug in the string variable into the function like this: file_exists($counter_file). This is a valid expression all by itself. If the file exists, the function returns a TRUE; if it doesn't, then it returns a FALSE.

Now we want to put this function into a logical expression. In other words, we want to evaluate it. So,

```
if(!file_exists($counter_file))
{

}
```

tells the parser the following:

a) Evaluate file_exists($counter_file).

b) The **if** expression has the format if (something) { do this }. The curly braces { } demarcate what will happen if the expression between the parentheses ( ) is evaluated as TRUE. (**if** has many other formats, including **if..elseif..else**, which are included in the Language and Function Reference.)

c) We are interested in knowing whether the file does *not* exist, so we put the *not* operator ! in front of the expression we are evaluating. This then changes the logic of the expression to: **if** the file contained in $counter_file does **not** exist, then do whatever is between the curly braces.

So, let's say the file name contained in **$counter_file** does not exist. Then we perform the **exec** function: exec("/bin/echo 1 > $counter_file");. The exec function performs whatever operation is contained in its expression list (i.e., "/bin/echo 1 >

$counter_file"). So, what does that do? It basically creates what-ever file we've named in $counter_file and places the character 1 into it.

Notice that this statement terminates in a semicolon. All statements must be terminated with a semicolon. Don't forget to do this, otherwise the PHP3 interpreter won't know when you want to end your statement (and you'll get a nasty error message). (You may have noticed that expressions are not terminated with ; —they are terminated in other ways).

There is another way we could have written this same expression. Some of us prefer logically demarcating blocks in our programs with words, instead of curly braces. For us, there is a word syntax. The expression above can also be written like this:

```
if(!file_exists($counter_file)):
   exec("/bin/echo 1 > $counter_file");
endif;
```

You pick which method you prefer. The logical block begins with the colon and ends with the endif— terminated with a semicolon. We will use both type of expression blocks in these examples.

3) Next, we open the counter file and read the current count. Remember, if the file didn't exist a moment ago, we've just created it and filled it with the number 1.

```
// Open the counter file and read the count
$fp = fopen($counter_file, "r+");
$count = fgets($fp, 10);
$count += 1;

// Overwrite the old count
fseek($fp, 0);
fwrite($fp, $count, 10);
fclose($fp);
```

By now, you know what a comment is, so we'll avoid going over it again. **Fopen( )** is a function. It opens a file in one of several modes, including "read-only," "write-only," "both read and write," and so on. In our case we want to open $counter_file in "both read and write" mode: fopen($counter_file, "r+");. After opening the file, we are given a "file handle" that identifies the file to the operating system. We store this file handle in the variable $fp —thus $fp = fopen($counter_file, "r+w");.

Fgets( ) is a function. It reads something from a file referenced by the file handle. (Remember, we get the file handle from the function fopen(). You may ask, why not just use the file name? It's faster for the operating system to store the particular file in a special table and access it with a number—hence we use file handles.)

```
$count = fgets($fp, 10);
```

In this case, Fgets() takes the first 10 characters of data in the file and places it into a variable $count. (Isn't it great that we didn't have to declare the variable $count before we just began using it! It is automatically initialized as a float variable!)

Next, we increment the counter by 1 to show we just visited the page.

```
$count += 1;
```

We can just as easily increment the variable like this:

```
$count = $count + 1;
```

Notice that we end each logical statement with a semicolon. This is very important to remember!

Then we write back out the incremented number to our file. The function fwrite() allows us to write only a certain number of characters to the file, so we'll limit our number to 10 digits.

```
fwrite($fp, "$tcounter", 10);
```

Finally, we close the file to free up system resources. The function releases the file handle and forces the system to write all updated data to disk.

```
fclose($fp);
```

If we do not close (using fclose()) the file, then it is automatically closed at the end of the script's execution.

Then, to verify that everything is really working, we display the number on the monitor:

```
echo "You are visitor $tcounter to this page";
```

The function echo() takes any value contained between the quotation marks and sends it to the web browser. Among the many great features of echo() is that any variable contained between the quotation marks is automatically placed in the output. The output looks like:

```
You are visitor 2 to this page".
```

We could easily fancy up the output by embedding HTML directly into the **echo** statement, like this:

```
echo "You are <I>visitor</I> <b>$tcounter</b> to <font
    color=RED>this</font> page".
```

Our output would look like this:

```
You are visitor 2 to this page.
```

Now that wasn't so bad. Let's upload it and try it out.

Running It

Open your web browser and type in the URL to get to your PHP3 script. For example, if your script is located in your local web server at */home/httpd/ html/test.php3*, then the URL would be *http://localhost/test.php3*.

Or, if your script is located at *http://www.php123.com* in your personal directory (mydir) in the file test.php3, then the URL would be *http://www. php123.com/mydir/test.php3*.

Troubleshooting

So what can go wrong? About a million things. We have tried to isolate a few of the most common errors we've seen. Perhaps you have found something unique—if so, let us know.

If things aren't working on your local computer, we suggest you try your application directly on the Readers Only PHP3 Web Site, *http://http://www. php123.com/*. If it works there, then you have not installed either PHP3 or PostgreSQL (or both) correctly on your machine. If it doesn't work there, then you have made an error in typing in the code.

Pay very close attention to how the code is written. Remember that the semicolon at the end of each statement is very important.

12.3 Application 3—Database-Based Counter

We will build a page that records each access by a visitor to the page by incrementing a counter contained in a PostgreSQL database. The counter will display on the page.

Writing It

The Complete Code

```
<html>
<head>
  <title>PHP3 Application #4</title>
</head>
<body>
  <?PHP

  //open the database
  $conn = pg_connect("dbname=MyDatabase port=5432");
  if (!$conn) {echo "An error occurred in connection.\n";
    exit;}

  //update the counter
  $result = pg_Exec($conn, "SELECT id FROM counter");
  if (!$result) {echo "An error occured in query.\n";exit;}
  $tcounter = pg_Result($result, 0, "cal");
  $tcounter = $tcounter+1;
  $result = pg_Exec($conn, "UPDATE counter SET id =
    $tcounter");
  if (!$result) {echo "An error occurred in update.\n";exit;}

  //display the counter
  echo "You are visitor ".$tcounter." to this page";

  //perform housekeeping
  pg_FreeResult($result);
  pg_Close($conn);

  ?>
</body>
</head>
```

Tables to Build

```
CREATE TABLE counter(
  Idint
);
```

Step By Step

Building the Database. This is also done at a shell prompt on your local machine or over a Telnet connection (or, if you're using *www.php123.com,* just type in these commands from your shell prompt on the screen).

From your shell prompt you type in the following:

```
createdb MyDatabase
```

The database will be created. You will automatically become the owner and administrator of any database you create. In order for others to access your database you will need to grant them access to it.

Building the Table. Next, we add the Table **counter** to the database **MyDatabase** just created. Before you can build your table you must "Open" the database you have just created. It's as easy as typing in

```
psql MyDatabase
```

From here you can easily access any table that belongs to the Database.
Building the table involves using the SQL syntax for **CREATE TABLE**. Type in the following:

```
CREATE TABLE counter(
   Id     int
);
```

You can type it in like that, or like this:

```
CREATE TABLE counter(Id  int);
```

Do whichever is easiest for you. Just don't forget the semicolon at the end of the line. If you forget it, the command line parser will not accept your SQL command.

1) We start with the simple web page we built in Application 1 (see section 12.1).

2) Next, we open the database.

```
//open the database
$conn = pg_connect("dbname=MyDatabase port=5432");
if (!$conn) {echo "An error occurred in connection.\n";
  exit;}
```

pg_connect() is a function that opens a database. A database must be opened before it can be used. Pg_connect() requires the name of the database we wish to open, as well as the port on which the database server is listening.

The default port is always 5432. The port is specified when the Postmaster process is initiated.

When a database is opened by way of pg_connect(), a database handle is returned. This is a number that uniquely identifies the database. (It is similar in nature to the file handle that we dealt with in the previous example.) We place the database handle result into the variable $conn. (We could just as easily have put it in a variable called $XYZ.) So, $conn = pg_connect("dbname=MyDatabase port=5432"); opens a database and assigns the handle to a variable.

We need to make certain that the function opened the database. That's what the next line does.

```
if (!$conn) {echo "An error occured in connection.\n";
  exit;}
```

This says that if the variable $conn contains 0—i.e., **pg_connect()** was not able to open the database—then we are to perform whatever is contained within the if expression. We simply call the **echo()** function and pass it "An error has occurred in connection," plus we add "\n", which indicates "new line." This outputs the text to the monitor and moves to the next line. Then the last part of the expression statement will be executed—exit;.

Exit is a command that causes the PHP3 script to cease. If we've made it past this line, then the database has been opened correctly.

The next batch of code deals with reading the counter value from the database.

```
$result = pg_Exec($conn, "SELECT id FROM counter");
if (!$result) {echo "An error occurred in query.\n";
  exit;}
$tcounter = pg_Result($result, 0, "cal");
```

The function **pg_Exec()** takes a SQL command passed to the database server $conn.

The SQL query needs to return the data we want from the database. SQL follows a clearly defined syntax. The SQL statement "SELECT id FROM counter" tells PostgreSQL that we want to **SELECT ALL** rows of data from the field id contained in the table counter (in the database **MyDatabase**).

Again, if the $result variable receives the value 0, this tells us that the query didn't work. A query that results in no return items (a null return set) still has a $result= 0. $result=NULL (or nothing there) means there has been a processing error. Query failures can result from many facets of the operation, including improper SQL syntax, a database that has failed, connection errors, and so forth.

Next, we want to put the value of the database field "id" into the variable **$tcounter**. Because PHP3 dynamically allocates variables, you don't have to worry about predefining **$tcounter** as matching the data type of type of the field "id". (Of course, you can predefine a variable, if you wish.)

```
$tcounter = pg_Result($result, 0, "id");
```

The function **pg_Result()** takes the result set from our query (`"SELECT id FROM counter"`) and jumps to the first record in the result set (records are often numbered starting at zero), and takes the value from the field "cal" and places it in the variable `$tcounter`.

If we wanted the results from the second record, the script would read:

```
$tcounter = pg_Result($result, 1, "id");
```

If we wanted the results from the second record and the field "item_2" (if there was such a field in the database), the script would read:

```
$tcounter = pg_Result($result, 1, "item_2");
```

(There are many ways of extracting data from a PostgreSQL table, or any other database table using PHP3. We are showing you just one.)

To count our visit to this page, we increment the counter by 1. This is done by

```
$tcounter = $tcounter+1;
```

Next, we need to put the updated value back into the database. This is done by:

```
$result = pg_Exec($conn, "update counter set id =
    $tcounter");
if (!$result) {echo "An error occurred in update.\n";
    exit;}
```

You'll notice our `pg_Exec()` function again. This time it is performing a SQL "update." In this case, we simply set the field id of the table **counter** to the updated value now contained in the variable `$tcounter`. The function works exactly as previously noted. If the **pg_Exec()** function fails to perform its required mission, it returns a `$result=NULL`. This is interpreted by the following line, which prints `"An error occurred..."`, and the script exits.

If the program moves on to the next line, then the function pg_Exec() succeeded. To prove this to us we display the counter by the following:

```
echo "You are visitor ".$tcounter." to this page";
```

This uses the **echo()** function to perform the following sequence of events:

a) The message "You are visitor" is combined with the variable $tcounter that contains the updated counter, which in turn is combined with "to this page".

b) The entire string variable, which now says "You are visitor 2 to this page", is now passed to **echo()**, where it is displayed at the current cursor position on the monitor.

Lastly, we need to perform a little housekeeping on the databases. pg_FreeResult($result); frees up the memory associated with the results set from our query. The pg_Close() function closes the database connection created by pg_connect(). This releases the database handle. You will need to reissue the pg_connect() if you wish to use this database again. pg_Close($conn); closes the database associated with the handle $conn.

Running It

Open your web browser and type in the URL to get to your PHP3 script. For example, if your script is located in your local web server at */home/httpd/html/test.php3,* then the URL would be:

```
http://localhost/test.php3
```

Or, if your script is located at *http://www.php123.com* in your personal directory (mydir) in the file test.php3, then the URL would be:

```
http://www.php123.com/mydir/test.php3
```

Troubleshooting

So what can go wrong? About a million things. We have tried to isolate a few of the most common errors we've seen. Perhaps you have found something unique—if so, let us know.

If things aren't working on your local computer, we suggest you try your application directly on the Readers Only PHP3 Web Site, *http://http://www.*

php123.com/. If it works there, then you have not installed either PHP3 or PostgreSQL (or both) correctly on your machine. If it doesn't work there, then you have made an error in typing in the code.

Pay very close attention to how the code is written. Remember that the semicolon at the end of each logical phrase is very important.

12.4 Application 4—Real-Time Graphics

We will write an application that builds a series of run-time graphic "buttons" to be labeled based on the user's input. These buttons are then placed on a form.

Writing It

The Complete Code

```
<?PHP
//Example 4

Header("Content-type: image/gif");
$im = ImageCreateFromGif("images/logo1.gif");
$orange = ImageColorAllocate($im, 255, 128, 0);
$px = (imagesx($im) - 7.5 * strlen($string)) / 2;
ImageString($im, 3, $px, 9, $string, $orange);
ImageGif($im);

ImageDestroy($im);

?>
```

Step By Step. This application is included for those of you who enjoy graphics. PHP3 has a powerful built-in capability of creating GIF (as well as JPEG and PNG) graphics on the fly. How many other systems do you know that can build a custom series of graphic buttons based on user input in real time? Not many. (You PDF graphic aficionados, be sure to check out the PDF function library in the Reference Section.)

Our example uses the GIF graphic file format, developed by Compuserve in 1989 and trademarked and copyrighted by them. It is widely used on the web because GIF graphic files are compressible and can be made transparent to objects that lie beneath them (e.g., another graphic). PHP3 also creates JPEG and PNG graphic file formats.

Those of you who would like to build database applications may ask why this application is included in a book on database applications. We give it here because by using the techniques in this example, you will be able to modify GIF images stored in a database field.

We set the HTML document header to accommodate a GIF graphic image.

```
Header("Content-type: image/gif");
```

We then look to see if we will be putting any text on this graphic image. How do we know what the text will be? We check to see if a string has been passed to our little PHP3 script in the form. See, for example, *http://www. php123.com/example4.php3?string=TEST*.

Now we create an image based on a GIF that is read from our computer. In other words, an image containing the existing graphic is created for us on which to overlay text.

```
$im = ImageCreateFromGif("images/logo1.gif");
```

$im is a "handle" that represents the image created as a result of the function **ImageCreateFromGif()**. This identifier is used in other functions to manipulate the image.

A GIF contains a table of up to 255 colors. In order to use a color in a GIF, the color must be placed into the table as follows:

```
$orange = ImageColorAllocate($im, 255, 128, 0);
```

This places the color orange into our GIF's color table.

Now we are going to determine which coordinate in our graphic to start at in order to center the text contained in **$string**.

```
$px = (imagesx($im) - 7.5 * strlen($string)) / 2;
```

(We just happen to know that each character is 7.5 pixels wide in the default font. How do we know that? Trial and error.)

The next line is just like an **echo()** function, except we are placing the text into an image.

```
ImageString($im, 3, $px, 9, $string, $orange);
```

The next line simply outputs the created image. Output is directed by default to the screen, but can be directed to a file by specifying a filename as the second parameter:

```
ImageGif($im);
```

And we finish our program by deallocating the memory that was used in performing this little feat:

```
ImageDestroy($im);
```

Running It

Open your web browser and type in the URL to get to your PHP3 script. For example, if your script is located in your local web server at */home/httpd/ html/test.php3*, then the URL would be:

```
http://localhost/example4.php3?string=TEST
```

Or if your script is located at *http://www.php123.com* in your personal directory (mydir) in the file test.php3, then the URL would be:

```
http://www.php123.com/mydir/test.php3?string=TEST
```

Troubleshooting

So what can go wrong? If you see a strange-looking image, then you need to check that you have no output before the content header.

To debug further, you need change the content header from "image/gif" to "text/plain." This tells the web browser that you are sending text—not an image—and only text will be displayed. Then you can see any error messages resulting from the execution of your script.

12.5 Application 5—Jeff's Super-Form

This small application can take the output from any form and generate an e-mail message containing the form's contents. Because it is completely generic, you do not have to modify the program if you change the form that feeds it data. This can be a great time-saver. For example, here is a form:

```
<HTML>
<HEAD><TITLE>Example #5</TITLE></HEAD>
<BODY>
  <FORM METHOD=POST ACTION="example_5.php3">
    EMail Address:<INPUT TYPE=TEXT NAME="email_address"><BR>
    Phone Number:<INPUT TYPE=TEXT NAME="phone_number"><BR>
    <INPUT TYPE=SUBMIT NAME=SUBMIT>
  </FORM>
</BODY>
</HTML>
```

Note that the **action** is example_5.php3. Here is the source to that program:

```
<?PHP

  $message = sprintf("Form data --------------\n");
  while(list($key,$value) = each($HTTP_POST_VARS)) {
```

```
        $message .= sprintf(\#34>[%s]: %s\n", $key, $value);
    }
    $message .= "\n";

    $message .= "More Information ---------\n";
    $message .= "The user's IP address is ";
    $message .= getenv("remote_addr").".".\n";
    $message .= "The user is running the web browser ";
    $message .= getenv("http_user_agent").".".\n";

    mail("joeuser@php123.com, "Feedback Form",
      $message,
      "From: Feedback webmaster@php123.com");

?>
```

And here is an example of an e-mail message it generates:

```
To: joeuser@php123.com
Subject: Feedback Form
From: Feedback <webmaster@php123.com>

Form data --------------
[email_address]: joeuser@php123.com
[phone_number]: 555-1212
[SUBMIT]: Submit Query

More Information ----------
The user's IP address is 127.0.0.1.
The user is running the web browser Mozilla/4.0
  (compatible; MSIE 5.0; Windows 98; DigExt).
```

Step By Step

First, we make a string that will be the e-mail message body, to be used by the **mail()** function. The form elements are placed in an associative array named **$HTTP_POST_VARS** by the PHP interpreter before your script begins executing.

With the **for** loop, we append each form name/value pair to the message body string. Finally, we append the user's IP address and the web client he or she is using to the message body. Note, these two values are stored in environment variables.

Refer to Application 6 in section 12.6 for additional details.

12.6 Application 6—Application-Specific Form Processor

This nifty little application lets you create a form of any complexity on any web page and have the output e-mailed directly to you. Put anything in it that you want on your form. Whatever the user completes will be e-mailed to whatever e-mail address you indicate. Even better, it stores the data input into the form into a database table.

Of course, this can easily be expanded into all kinds of other applications, including a nifty shopping cart system.

Writing It

The Complete Code

```php
<?PHP
//step #2
// handle the output from the form

if ( strlen($NAME)>0 ):
  if (strlen($EMAIL)<1):
    echo "<center><b>Please enter an E-Mail address</b>
    <br>Use your browser's BACK key to return</center>";
    exit;
  endif;

  $NAME = addslashes($NAME);
  $EMAIL = addslashes($EMAIL);
  $PHONE = addslashes($PHONE);
  $MESSAGE = addslashes($MESSAGE);

  $subject_field = "My Form";
  $SENDTO = "webmaster@php123.com";

  $BODY = "From: $NAME
    \nPhone: $PHONE
    \nE-Mail: $EMAIL
    \nMessage: $COMMENTS";

  mail($SENDTO,
    $subject_field,
    $BODY,
    "From:$EMAIL" );

  //save the results in our table
```

```php
//open the database
$conn = pg_connect("dbname=MyDatabase port=5432");
if (!$conn) {echo "An error occurred in connection.\n";exit;}

//insert a new record to store the data
$result = pg_Exec($conn, "insert into MyForm (name, phone,
  email, message)
  VALUES ('$NAME', '$PHONE', '$EMAIL', '$MESSAGE' " );
if (!$result) {echo "An error occurred in update.\n";exit;}

//return to the form
$CP = "contactus.html";
Header("REFRESH: 2; URL=$CP");

echo "<html><bodybgcolor=WHITE><center>
  <p> <p> <p> ";
echo "<font face=\"helvetica,arial\" color=\"#000080\">";
echo "Your message has been <b>successfully</b> sent to
  <b>$SENDTO</b>";
echo "<br>Moving now to the <b>$CP</b> section ...";
echo "</center></body></html>";

exit;

endif;
?>

<html>
<head>
  <title>PHP3 Application #5 -- contactus.html </title>
</head>
<body>
//step #1
//create the form
<form method='PUT' action='contactus.html'>
<table>
  <tr><td>
    Type in your Name:
    <INPUT TYPE="text" NAME="NAME" VALUE="" SIZE=20
      MAXLENGTH=40 >
    <br>
    Type in your E-Mail:
    <INPUT TYPE="text" NAME="EMAIL" VALUE="" SIZE=20
      MAXLENGTH=40 >
```

```
<br>
Type in your Phone:
<INPUT TYPE="text" NAME="PHONE" VALUE="" SIZE=8
   MAXLENGTH=20 >
<br>
Type in your Message:
<TEXTAREA NAME="MESSAGE" ROWS=3 COLS=40 WRAP=VIRTUAL>
   </TEXTAREA>
<p>
<input type=SUBMIT name=SUBMIT value="Press to Submit">
</td></tr>
</table>
</body>
</head>
```

Tables to Build

```
CREATE TABLE MyForm(
  Name    varchar(50),
  Email   varchar(60),
  Phone   char(15),
  Message       varchar(100)
);
```

Step By Step

1) Build the table. Add the Table **MyForm** to your database **MyDatabase**.

2) Build a simple web page. This web page is preceded by some PHP3 code before the `<html>` beginning tag. What's going on here? We can construct any number of separate HTML documents in a single PHP3 script. That's what we're going to do here.

The portion of script that begins with the `<html>` and ends with `</html>`, let's call Part 1. The other portion, beginning at the top of the page and continuing down to just above the `<html>`, let's call Part 2. Why does Part 2 precede Part 1? It has to do with how the script works. Read on.

Let's deal with Part 1 first. We are going to create a simple form.

```
//create the form
<form method='PUT' action='contactus.html'>
```

Notice that we are pointing to the same HTML document we're in as our FORM action tag. This forces any results from this form back to this HTML document. These results will be (you guessed it) handled in Part 2 (that's why it's the top—so it can get to the return data before the `<html>` script kicks in).

To PHP, there is no difference between a GET and a PUT form method. This is because the PHP3 interpreter transparently handles these differences. When do you use the GET instead of the PUT method? The GET method is used when you want a link to be the results of the FORM. You should always use the PUT method when you have a lot of data to return because of length limitations in the browser return address. We are using the PUT form method because it accommodates more data.

Next, we're going to put our form into a *table*. A table simply creates rows and columns on a web page. `<table>` begins it, and `</table>` ends it. `<tr>` tells the browser to move to the next line; `<td>` tells the browser to move to the next column. The number of lines and columns your table contains is limited only by considerations of readability.

```
<table>
<tr><td>
```

Now we'll build the form:

```
Type in your Name:
<INPUT TYPE="text" NAME="NAME" VALUE="" SIZE=20 MAXLENGTH=40 >
```

The input command does just what it says—takes "input" from the user. There are several kinds of input, including "text," "radio," "checkbox," even "hidden." Refer to one of the reference books for more details. ▬▬▬

And so on, until the form is completed.

```
<br>
Type in your E-Mail:
<INPUT TYPE="text" NAME="EMAIL" VALUE="" SIZE=20
  MAXLENGTH=40 >
<br>
Type in your Phone:
<INPUT TYPE="text" NAME="PHONE" VALUE="" SIZE=8
  MAXLENGTH=20 >
<br>
Type in your Message:
<TEXTAREA NAME="MESSAGE" ROWS=3 COLS=40 WRAP=VIRTUAL>
  </TEXTAREA>
<p>
<input type=SUBMIT name=SUBMIT value="Press to Submit">
</td></tr>
</table>
```

Of course, you can place any type of user input into this form, including `<textarea>`s. What's important is that you give each input a different name. We strongly suggest using names that reflect the data being collected. We have specifically focused on standard text input, but checkboxes, radio buttons, and so forth all work in the same way. When a user clicks on the `<input type=SUBMIT name=SUBMIT value="Press to Submit">` button, the form is parsed by the browser and the data is sent back via the HTTP request to the web server.

So what happens? When you first called this web page, you created a URL that looked something like this:

```
http://php123.com/123456/contactus.html
```

However, after submitting the form, you will see your URL now looks something like this:

```
http://php123.com/123456/contactus.html?NAME=Craig+Williams
&EMAIL=craig@williams.nu&PHONE=555-1234&MESSAGE=This+is+my+
message
```

A bit more complex, eh! Well, our contacus.html page is again served up by the web server, only this time a bunch of additional information is appended to the URL. This is where Part 2 comes in.

The very first thing the page does is to start up the PHP3 interpreter

```
<?PHP
```

and evaluate the following expression:

```
if ( strlen($NAME)>0 ):
```

What does this tell us? If we've entered a name in the form and submitted it, the **name** string is contained in the variable $NAME. PHP3 automatically interprets any form elements contained in the submitted form (in our example, these include NAME, EMAIL, PHONE, and MESSAGE) and places them in variable with the same name: $NAME, $EMAIL, $PHONE, $MESSAGE. So, we simply check to see if the variable $NAME has anything in it.

Obviously, the first time we enter this page, there is no data in the URL, the expression evaluates to **FALSE**, and we jump straight to the `<html>` tag that creates the form. However, once we've submitted a form with something in the NAME field, our expression evaluates to **TRUE**, and so we enter the PHP3 script.

First, we want to make certain that an **EMAIL** address was entered by the person submitting the form.

```
if (strlen($EMAIL)<1):
  echo "<center><b>Please enter an E-Mail address</b>
  <br>Use your browser's BACK key to return</center>";
```

```
      exit;
   endif;
```

If we've made it this far, then this form has been submitted by someone who has at least taken the effort to fill in his or her name. To make certain the user has also entered something in the **EMAIL** field, we simply check to see if something is in the $EMAIL variable (as measured by the strlen() function). If there is nothing there, then it was never filled in. Our expression

```
   if (strlen($EMAIL)<1):
```

evaluates to **TRUE** and we jump to the **echo()** and exit. This terminates the script while displaying a nice sign at the top of the screen that reads

```
   "Please enter an E-Mail address - use your Browser's BACK
      key to return",
```

allowing the user to jump BACK to fix the error.

Assuming the user has entered something in the **EMAIL** field (see the web site for ways to verify a correct e-mail address), we move on to processing the data. The next section takes each string variable and escapes any occurrence of a single quote, a backslash, or a NULL character—a disaster for SQL syntax. Because we are going to be entering this data into a table using an SQL statement with PostgreSQL, we don't want any of these characters in our statement. We use the convenient function addslashes() to place a backslash (the SQL escape character) before every instance of a single quote, a backslash, or a NULL character.

```
   $NAME = addslashes($NAME);
   $EMAIL = addslashes($EMAIL);
   $PHONE = addslashes($PHONE);
   $MESSAGE = addslashes($MESSAGE);
```

Now we store information needed by the e-mail program. We'll want to put a "**Subject**" field in the email, so we store the subject in the variable **$subject_field**:

```
   $subject_field = "My Form";
```

We'll want to send the email to someone who is interested in the results of the form, so we store that recipient in **$SENDTO**. In this case, I'm going to send it to myself. You can send it to anyone you like (but remember our spamming rules!).

```
   $SENDTO = webmaster@php123.com;
```

And we put together the contents of the email and store it in the variable **$BODY**:

```
$BODY = "From: $NAME
        \nPhone: $PHONE
        \nE-Mail: $EMAIL
        \nMessage: $COMMENTS";
```

The variable $BODY concatenates each of the fields submitted by the form. The "\n" inserts a line-feed before each field. Remember, this is e-mail, so you can't use regular HTML tags here, such as <br> or <strong>.

Now that we have all the little pieces assembled, we create the mail message using the (what else?) **mail()** function:

```
mail($SENDTO,
     $subject_field,
     $BODY,
     "From:$EMAIL" );
```

And off the e-mail message goes.

Now that the e-mail message has been sent to us and we have an e-mail copy of the data on the form, we want to place the data into a table for storage (and later retrieval—see Application 7 in section 12.7). As in the previous example, we must open our database and assign it to the handle $conn.

```
$conn = pg_connect("dbname=MyDatabase port=5432");
if (!$conn) {echo "An error occurred in connection.\n";
  exit;}
```

Next, we want to insert a new record into the table, **MyForm**, that we have just built to store the data. The SQL insert command allows us to specify which fields we want to update and which values we want to place in each of them. Remember to keep the fields and values properly matched up!

```
$result = pg_Exec($conn, "insert into MyForm (name, phone,
  email, message)
  VALUES ('>$NAME', '$PHONE', '$EMAIL', '$MESSAGE' " );
```

Because SQL is not sensitive to spaces between words, we have found it is often easier to match up fields and values like this:

```
$result = pg_Exec($conn, "insert into MyForm
  (name,
  phone,
  email,
```

```
message)
VALUES
('$NAME',
'$PHONE',
'$EMAIL',
'$MESSAGE' " ·);
```

Notice that you do have to pay attention to the data type of the field when working in SQL. A character-based field (**char, varchar**) requires the value to be preceded and terminated by a single quote. A numeric field (**int, float**) requires nothing but a numeric value. A date field (**date**) requires single quotes to surround the date.

If the SQL insert fails, then this expression will execute:

```
if (!$result) {echo "An error occured in update.\n";exit;}
```

Now that we have performed both the e-mail and database operations, we need to decide what we want to do with the user. In this example, we want to send them right back to a blank form.

```
$CP = "contactus.html";
Header("REFRESH: 2; URL=$CP");
```

Calling the Header() function with **REFRESH** sends the user to whatever page you have specified in $CP. Of course, you could just as easily type in the name of the URL like this: Header("REFRESH: 2; URL=contactus.html");.

This operation takes a couple of seconds to perform in the browser, so we want to leave the user with something to look at. Let's create a little mini-page that shows what we've just done:

```
echo "<html><bodybgcolor=WHITE><center><p>
   <p> <p> ";
echo "<font face=\"helvetica,arial\" color=\"#000080\">";
echo "Your message has been <b>successfully</b> sent to
  <b>$SENDTO</b>";
echo "<br>Moving now to the <b>$CP</b> section ...";
echo "</center></body></html>";
```

And we want to call **exit()** to make certain we don't keep right on going down into Part 1.

```
exit;
```

The final two lines close the logical expression we opened on the second line, and the ?> closes the PHP3 interpreter:

```
endif;
?>
```

Try it out a dozen times. We'll be using the data you've typed in with our next application.

Running It. Open your web browser and type in the URL to get to your PHP3 script. For example, if your script is located in your local web server at */home/httpd/html/test.php3*, then the URL would be:

```
http://localhost/test.php3
```

Or, if your script is located at *http://www.php123.com* in your personal directory (mydir) in the file test.php3, then the URL would be:

```
http://www.php123.com/mydir/test.php3
```

Troubleshooting. So what can go wrong? About a million things. We have tried to isolate a few of the most common errors we've seen. Perhaps you have found something unique—if so, let us know.

If things aren't working on your local computer, we suggest you try your application directly on the Readers Only PHP3 Web Site, *http://www. php123.com/*. If it works there, then you have not installed either PHP3 or PostgreSQL (or both) correctly on your machine. If it doesn't work there, then you have made an error in typing in the code.

Pay very close attention to how the code is written. Remember that the semicolon at the end of each logical phrase is very important.

12.7 Application 7—Querying Application 6

We now write a short application to let us query the data we are gathering from our on-line form in Application 6 (section 12.6).

Writing It

The Complete Code

```php
<?PHP
//step #2
// perform the query
if ( strlen($NAME)>0 ):
  $NAME = addslashes($NAME);

  //open the database
```

```php
$conn = pg_connect("dbname=MyDatabase port=5432");
if (!$conn) {echo "An error occurred in
  connection.\n";exit;}

//query the database
if ($HOW=="A"):
   $result = pg_Exec($conn, "SELECT * FROM MyForm
     where  name = '$NAME' ." );
else:
   $result = pg_Exec($conn, "SELECT * FROM MyForm
     where  name *~ '$NAME' " );
endif;
if (!$result) {echo "An error occurred in update.\n";exit;}

//show the results
$num = pg_NumRows($result);
$i=0;
while ($i < $num) {
   $cname = pg_Result($result, $i, "name");
   $cemail = trim(pg_Result($result, $i, "email"));
   $cphone = trim(pg_Result($result, $i, "phone"));
   $cmessage = trim(pg_Result($result, $i, "message"));

   echo $cname." ".$cemail."<br>";
   echo "cphone    <br> <b>$cmessage</b> <p>";

   $i++;
   }

   //provide for a return
   echo "<p> <a href='queryform.html'> Return to the Main
     Page </a>";

   exit;

endif;
?>

<html>
<head>
  <title>PHP3 Application #6 -- queryform.html </title>
</head>
<body>

<?PHP
```

```
//step #1
//create the form
<form method='PUT' action='queryform.html'>
<table>
  <tr><td>
    Indicate a value to be searched.
    Then indicate how you want the data searched.
    <p>
    Find by What Name:
    <INPUT TYPE="text" NAME="NAME" VALUE="" SIZE=10
      MAXLENGTH=10 >
    <br>
    Search by which method?
    <INPUT TYPE="checkbox" NAME="HOW" VALUE="A" CHECKED><b>
      Anywhere</b> in the field
    <INPUT TYPE="checkbox" NAME="HOW" VALUE="B">At the
      <b>Beginning</b> only
    <p>
    <input type=SUBMIT name=SUBMIT value="Press to Submit">
  </td></tr>
</table>
?>
</body>
</head>
```

Step By Step. In this application we build a form to let us indicate values that we will use to query our database. As in Application 6, we divide the code into two parts. Part 1 begins at `<html>` and ends at `</html>`, and creates the form where we will enter our query information. Part 2 begins at the top of the code and ends on the line above `<html>`, and performs the actual query and results display.

We'll focus first on Part 1. We create a form. We point the FORM results back to the calling HTML page:

```
<form method='PUT' action='queryform.html'>
```

We build a table:

```
<table>
<tr><td>
```

And we add sufficient instructions to allow a visitor to figure out what is to be done on the form.

```
Indicate a value to be searched.
Then indicate how you want the data searched.
<p>
```

Next we build the input fields. We need to give this a little thought. How do we want to search our data? The first question perhaps should be, What data do we have to search? Well, we're storing the **NAME, EMAIL, PHONE,** and **MESSAGE** of every person who has filled in our form. How do we want to search it?

We can search the data by any combination of fields or expressions, but this would accomplish little other than frustrating a user who just wants to get at the data. So, let's decide we want to locate the data by the NAME of the person who's completed the form.

```
Find by What Name:
<INPUT TYPE="text" NAME="NAME" VALUE="" SIZE=10 MAXLENGTH=10 >
<br>
```

The next issue is how to search the name field. Will we require an "exact" match before displaying the data? Or will we require the search criterion to be at the beginning of the name field? Or may a search criterion be found anywhere in the **NAME** field? Decisions, decisions.

It's always a good idea to let the user make these kinds of decisions. So, we give the user two choices and preselect one of them as a default (that's the CHECKED in the INPUT tag):

```
Search by which method?
<INPUT TYPE="checkbox" NAME="HOW" VALUE="A" CHECKED>
  <b>Anywhere</b> in the field
<INPUT TYPE="checkbox" NAME="HOW" VALUE="B">At the
  <b>Beginning</b> only
<p>
```

Lastly, we add a **SUBMIT** button that sends our form to the action address specified in the FORM (in our case, it's coming right back to this document):

```
<input type=SUBMIT name=SUBMIT value="Press to Submit">
```

and we terminate our table

```
</td></tr>
</table>
```

and PHP3

```
?>
```

and the rest of the document

```
</body>
</head>
```

Now, let's assume a user has completed the form we've just written, has entered the name "Craig" and selected the "anywhere in the field" check-box, and has just pressed the Submit button.

The form is sent to itself and runs Part 2. We move into the PHP3 inter-preter.

```
<?PHP
```

Next, we see if the URL arguments contain a **NAME** field. If they do, then we can safely assume that someone has completed our form and has entered a search criterion. If nothing is there, then we bypass the expression of Part 2 and rebuild Part 1.

```
if ( strlen($NAME)>0 ):
```

We escape any single quotes, backslashes, or NULL characters in $NAME:

```
$NAME = addslashes($LNAME);
```

We open up our database and store the database handle to **$conn**. If the con-nection fails, we exit our program.

```
$conn = pg_connect("dbname=MyDatabase port=5432");
if (!$conn) {echo "An error occurred in connection.\n";
  exit;}
```

Now we set up our query. Because the SQL syntax is different depending on whether we will be matching from the front of the field or anywhere in the field, we need to know how the user wants us to proceed. We evaluate the results of the checkbox input. If the user selected the checkbox "Any-where in the field", the value associated with the variable $HOW is **A**—so

```
if ($HOW=="A"):
```

evaluates TRUE and we create a SQL SELECT statement and run it using **pg_Exec()**.

```
$result = pg_Exec($conn, "SELECT * FROM MyForm
   WHERE  name = '$NAME' " );
```

If $HOW does not evaluate to A, let's assume it's the other choice:

```
else:
```

and we create another SQL statement:

```
$result = pg_Exec($conn, "SELECT * FROM MyForm
   WHERE  name *~ '$NAME' " );
```

You will want to review a good book on SQL syntax, but notice how easy it is to locate data based on such different requirements.

To find data that begins with a particular search criterion, you just set the condition to

```
WHERE name = '$NAME'
```

Here the SQL server evaluates all data contained in the field, beginning at the first letter as an exact match until it runs out of comparison letters. So, $NAME = "Craig" would create a result set of names like "Craig", "CraigA", "CraigABCD", but not "craig" (notice that we need to match the field type of name (character) with the type of $NAME (also character), which we do with the single quotes).

Similarly, to locate all data that contains the search criterion anywhere in the data, you can use the very nifty syntax

```
WHERE  name *~ '$NAME'
```

This tells the SQL server to find all records with the value contained in $NAME located anywhere in the field. The asterisk also tells the engine to ignore case. So, if $NAME = "Craig", then we would return such name field data as "CRAIG", "craig", "CraigABC", "ABCcraigDEF", and "ABC-CraigDEF".

Don't forget to terminate the logical expression we just evaluated:

```
endif;
```

If something goes wrong with the query, then handle it next:

```
if (!$result) {echo "An error occured in update.\n";exit;}
```

Now, let's display the results of our query. First, it will be nice to know how many different records we have returned. (Remember, the first record is record number 0.)

```
$num = pg_NumRows($result);
```

Next, we'll create a counting variable (of course, there are many ways of doing this, including using the FOR..NEXT expression):

```
$i=0;
```

Now let's create a loop that begins at the first record (0) and loop around as many times as there are records in the result set (as indicated by $num):

```
while ($i < $num) {
```

Everything we do now is done once for each record in the result set. If we find 10 matches, then this is repeated 10 times. 10,000 matches will result in this being repeated 10,000 times. (So it often a good idea to check how large the result set is before starting your loop—it's easy to reduce the size of the displayed results. That is, if ($num>100: $num=100; endif; limits any size result set to only showing the first 100 records.)

We use the function **pg_Result()** to place the values from each of the various fields in the result set into variables. For example, at the very beginning, $i = 0, so we could interpret the following expression as: Go to record number 0 (first one) of the result set (contained in $result) and place the value found in the "name" field into the variable $cname.

```
$cname = pg_Result($result, $i, "name");
```

and so on for the other fields we're interested in.

```
$cemail = trim(pg_Result($result, $i, "email"));
$cphone = trim(pg_Result($result, $i, "phone"));
$cmessage = trim(pg_Result($result, $i, "message"));
```

Notice that we have combined another function **trim()** surrounding the **pg_Result()** function. We use parentheses to separate the individual functions. How does the PHP3 interpreter know which function to handle first? Easy: It works from the inside to the outside (**pg_Result()** first, followed by the **trim()**). This is just a shortcut for writing

```
$cmessage = pg_Result($result, $i, "message");
$cmessage = trim($cmessage);
```

Now we place the data on the screen. This is where your originality and creativity come in. Build as fancy a layout as you like. Here is something as simple as it can get:

```
echo $cname." ".$cemail."<br>";
echo "cphone    <br>
    <b>$cmessage</b> <p>";
```

This echoes the data contained in $cname followed by a space, followed by $cemail, followed by a carriage return, and so on. We could jazz it up a little by simply adding a couple of tags:

```
echo "<b>$cname</b>   <font
color=RED><b>$cemail</b></font><br>";
    echo "cphone    <br>
    <font color=BLUE><I><b>$cmessage</b></I><p>";
```

Of course, we need to increment our counter variable, otherwise we would stay on the same record forever!

```
$i++;
```

and we end our logical statement

```
}
```

Because we don't know how long the user will want to study the result set, we can't issue a Header() REFRESH. So, let's just place a nice tag at the bottom of the form to give the user somewhere to go when done:

```
echo "<p> <a href='queryform.html'> Return to the Main Page
    </a>";
```

Then we exit the page,

```
exit;
```

and we close our logical expression evaluating whether the form of Part 2 was completed:

```
endif;
```

and we terminate the PHP3 interpreter to allow the HTML of Part 1 to begin:

```
?>
```

You may ask: Suppose I don't want to terminate my PHP3 script? Suppose I want the entire HTML document to be contained in a single PHP3 script?

You can do that. It's just a little more coding work. `<html>` is in PHP3. So, here's how you would code the following:

```
<input type=TEXT name=NAME value=""> Here is what I want
<a href='ABC.COM'> Here is where I want to go </a>
```

Or, in straight PHP3 using **echo()**:

```
echo "<input type=TEXT name=NAME value="> Here is what I
  want ";
echo "<a href='ABC.COM'> Here is where I want to go </a>";
```

Notice that PHP3 does not allow double quotes—just replace them with single quotes, or replace them with the in-line \" double quote substitution.

Running It. Open your web browser and type in the URL to get to your PHP3 script. For example, if your script is located in your local web server at */home/httpd/html/test.php3*, then the URL would be:

```
http://localhost/test.php3
```

Or, if your script is located at *http://www.php123.com* in your personal directory (mydir) in the file test.php3, then the URL would be:

```
http://www.php123.com/mydir/test.php3
```

Troubleshooting. So what can go wrong? About a million things. We have tried to isolate a few of the most common errors we've seen. Perhaps you have found something unique—if so, let us know.

If things aren't working on your local computer, we suggest you try your application directly on the Readers Only PHP3 Web Site, *http://www.php123.com/*. If it works there, then you have not installed either PHP3 or PostgreSQL (or both) correctly on your machine. If it doesn't work there, then you have made an error in typing in the code.

Pay very close attention to how the code is written. Remember that the semicolon at the end of each logical phrase is very important.

12.8 Application 8—Login Authentication

This nifty little piece of code requires all visitors to a web page to pass a login verification before being able to access the page. Users permitted into the page are maintained in a database.

Writing It

The Complete Code

```php
<>?PHP
   if(!($PHP_AUTH_USER)):
      Header( "WWW-authenticate: basic realm=Restricted Area");
      Header(  "HTTP/1.0 401 Unauthorized");
      echo "<meta http-equiv=\"refresh\" content=\"0;url=failed.
        php3\">";
      exit;
   else:
      $conn = pg_connect("dbname=generic port=5432");
      if (!$conn) {echo "An error occurred in connection.\n";
        exit;}

      $user_id=strtoupper($PHP_AUTH_USER);
      $password=$PHP_AUTH_PW;
      $result = pg_Exec($conn, "SELECT id,password,name FROM
        user
        WHERE id = '$user_id'
        and password~*'$password'");
      if (!$result): echo "An error occurred.\n"; exit; endif;
      $num = pg_NumRows($result);
      if (pg_NumRows($result)>0):
         SetCookie("BuyID1",$user_id );
         SetCookie( "BuyID1", $user_id, 0,  "/",  ".betaclub.
           org");
         //always update profile
         echo "<meta http-equiv=\"refresh\" content=\"0;
           url=secretpage.html\">";
         exit;
      else:
         Header(  "WWW-authenticate: basic realm=Restricted
           Area");
         Header(  "HTTP/1.0 401 Unauthorized");
         echo "<center><p> 
           <p><table width='350' border=1>
           <tr><td bgcolor=#D8E9D6 align='center'>
           <font face='helvetica' color=#000080 size=2>
           <b>Please check your ID and PASSWORD
           <br>Your login has FAILED</b>
           <br><font size=1>Use your Browser's BACK key to
             return</font>
```

```
            </td></tr>
            </table></center>";
        exit;
    endif;
endif;
?>
```

Tables to Build

```
CREATE TABLE user(
    IDchar(10),
    Name varchar(60),
    Password      char(15),
);
```

Step By Step

1) Build a simple form.

2) First, we determine whether the user has already been authenticated. An authenticated user is allowed to continue, whereas an unauthenticated user is stopped. We determine that a user is not authenticated by examining the global PHP3 variable $PHP_AUTH_USER. If the variable does *not* exist (the !), then the present user has not been authenicated:

   ```
   if(!($PHP_AUTH_USER)):
   ```

   We "push" into the return header several tags that pop up an authentication window, which will vary in form from one browser to another. The "realm" is what you want to call your authentication window, and it will appear to the user:

   ```
   Header( "WWW-authenticate: basic realm=Restricted
     Area");
   ```

   Authentication windows contain a "Login ID" and a "Password" field, and usually contain wording such as "Enter your ID and PASS-WORD to continue" followed by the realm. See Figure 12.1.

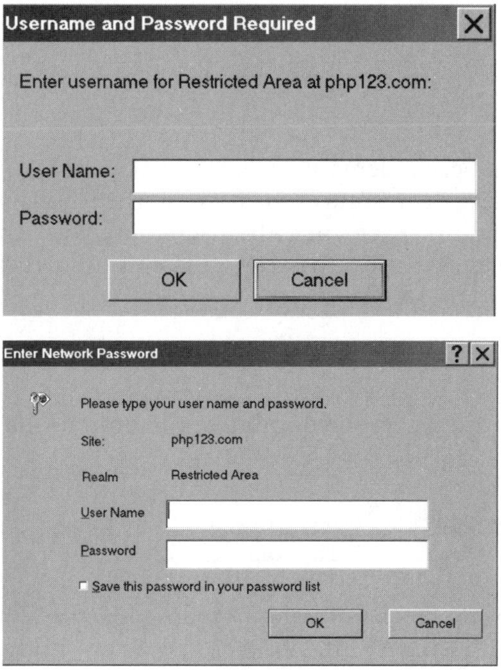

Figure 12.1 The login windows generated by
Netscape Navigator (top) and Microsoft
Internet Explorer (bottom).

The second header tag creates a minimal version requirement and assumes the present user is "Unauthorized" (not yet authenticated).

```
Header(  "HTTP/1.0 401 Unauthorized");
```

At this point, the user must complete the information requested in the authentication window or no further activity within the browser can be accomplished.

If the user fails a set number of times to authenticate (usually three), the next line of the script is executed:

```
echo "<meta http-equiv=\"refresh\" content=\"0;url=
  failed.php3\">";
```

This line moves the user to whatever URL is indicated. In this case, the script "failed.php3" is called. Failed.php3 may contain a page requesting the user to check on their **ID** and **PASSWORD**. The script could just as easily return the user to the main page (i.e., index.html).

Because the authentication has failed, we exit the user from the rest of the script:

```
exit;
```

Part 2: The second section of the script, demarcated by the keyword `else`, actually contains the code to validate the results of the user's authentication attempt in the authentication window. Each time the user completes the window and presses the Submit key, the script passes to the part following the expression

```
else:
```

In this section, we first open the database containing our login information

```
$conn = pg_connect("dbname=generic port=5432");
if (!$conn) {echo "An error occurred in connection.\n";exit;}
```

Next we convert the results of the authentication window, specifically the user ID and the user PASSWORD. These are stored, respectively, in the global variables `$PHP_AUTH_USER` and `$PHP_AUTH_PW`. In this case, we convert `$PHP_AUTH_USER` to uppercase and store the value to the variable `$user_id`, because we are storing all IDs in uppercase in our database. (Of course, this is not necessary.)

```
$user_id=strtoupper($PHP_AUTH_USER);
```

and we convert the password to the string variable `$password`:

```
$password=$PHP_AUTH_PW;
```

Next, we check to see if the values entered by the user match the values in the database. First, we issue a query to look for all **IDs** that match the variable `$user_id` and **PASSWORDs** that "wild-card match" the variable `$password`. A "wild-card match" returns any instances where the search value is contained anywhere in the data field, without respect to case.

```
$result = pg_Exec($conn, "SELECT id,password,name,firsttime
  FROM user
  WHERE id = '$user_id'
  and password~*'$password'");
```

As before, we verify that the query executed correctly. If not, we jump out of the program after displaying an error message:

```
if (!$result): echo "An error occurred.\n"; exit; endif;
```

Now we need to see how many result rows were returned from our query. The function `pg_NumRows()` gives us that information.

```
$num = pg_NumRows($result);
```

And, if the number of result rows is greater than zero, we know that we have at least one match to our **ID** and **PASSWORD**:

```
if (pg_NumRows($result)>0):
```

We proceed into the next section of script, reserved for users who used a correct **ID** and **PASSWORD** combination. First, we set a standard cookie on the user's computer to identify him or her in subsequent sessions.

```
SetCookie("BuyID1",$user_id );
```

We also go ahead and set a cookie for pre-version 4.0 Microsoft Explorer browsers, which require a directory location:

```
SetCookie( "BuyID1", $user_id, 0,  "/",  ".php123.com");
```

Then we move the user to the next step using the refresh meta-tag. Here, we will pass them to "secretpage.html".

```
echo "<meta http-equiv=\"refresh\"
  content=\"0;url=secretpage.html\">";
```

and finally, we exit the script:

```
exit;
```

Otherwise, the user failed to enter a correct ID or PASSWORD (or both) and we proceed down the other logical partition. Here, we begin by resetting the header on the client page.

```
Header(  "WWW-authenticate: basic realm=Restricted Area");
Header(  "HTTP/1.0 401 Unauthorized");
```

Then we generate a nice little message to say that something was not right with the login attempt:

```
echo "<center><p> 
<p><table width='350' border=1>
```

```
<tr><td bgcolor=#D8E9D6 align='center'>
  <font face='helvetica' color=#000080 size=2>
  <b>Please check your ID and PASSWORD<br>Your login has
    FAILED</b>
  <br><font size=1>Use your Browser's BACK key to return
    </font>
</td></tr>
</table></center>";
```

This echo statement calls the **echo()** function and passes the argument of everything contained between the quotation marks. In this case, we want to create a box that displays a message.

We begin by centering the script output on the monitor <center>, skipping two lines (<p>) (creating a "paragraph") and a space ( ), and then skipping another couple of lines (<p>).

We then create a <table> with a width of 350 pixels with a border. We create a row in our table (<tr>), then a single column (<td>) with a background color represented by the hexidecimal number Red=D8 Green=E9 Blue=D6 (bgcolor=#D8E9D6), where anything contained in the column is horizontally aligned to the center (**align='center'**) and vertically aligned to the top (**valign='top'**).

We then set the <font> we want to use in the column we've just created with a font face of helvetica, a hexidemical color of Red=00 Green=00 Blue=80 and a size of 2. We then print our message in <b>old. We skip a line (**
) and set the font size down to the smallest size possible (size=1**) and print another line of text. We finally end our </table> and end our </center>ing.

Instead of the echo statement above, we could just as easily have issued a meta-tag refresh pointing the user to a script named "failed.php3" to do whatever we want:

```
echo "<meta http-equiv=\"refresh\" content=\"0;url=failed.
  php3\">";
```

And lastly, we exit out of the script

```
exit;
```

Restricted Page Access: What's to prevent anyone from going directly to *secretpage.html* and bypassing the authentication step? How do we restrict access to a page by requiring authentication?

Simply insert the following code into at the top of any page that you want to require authentication (we assume that the name of the script that contains this example's authentication code is called *login.html*):

```
if(!($PHP_AUTH_USER)):
  echo "<meta http-equiv=\"refresh\"
    content=\"0;url=login.html\">";
endif;
```

If this code snippet is located at the top of your page, it is the first thing a client encounters. Clients who have not been authenticated will be forced to your login.html script.

Running It. Open your web browser and type in the URL to get to your PHP3 script. For example, if your script is located in your local web server at */home/httpd/html/test.php3*, then the URL would be:

```
http://localhost/test.php3
```

Or, if your script is located at *http://www.php123.com* in your personal directory (mydir) in the file test.php3, then the URL would be:

```
http://www.php123.com/mydir/test.php3
```

Troubleshooting. So what can go wrong? About a million things. We have tried to isolate a few of the most common errors we've seen. Perhaps you have found something unique—if so, let us know.

Because you are working with the header of a client page, a programming error may require you to terminate your entire session. Once you have perfected your own authentication system, however, it will be well worth the effort.

Pay very close attention to how the code is written. Remember that the semicolon at the end of each logical phrase is very important.

12.9 Where Next?

Now that you have finished these eight basic applications, it's time to take yourself to the next level.

This level relies on your own creativity and imagination. There is no better way to learn a new language than to build a test application of your own design. Now that you have been through these applications, you are ready to come up with something that you would like to build. What is it? It doesn't matter. Start off with a simple web page and start adding PHP3 statements that apply from your study of the Reference section.

If you develop a particularly interesting application, or examples that we can use in the Language and Function Reference Section, please send them on to us so that we can share them with others.

Chapter 13

Technical Notes

"State" and Interactive Web Design

Remember, HTTP is *stateless*. It is impossible to identify a unique client without using forms or cookies.

Authentication

The HTTP authentication hooks in PHP3 are available *only* when it is running as an Apache module. In an Apache module PHP3 script, it is possible to use the **Header()** function to send an "Authentication Required" message to the client browser causing it to pop up a Username/Password input window. Once the user has filled in a username and a password, the URL containing the PHP3 script is called again with the variables $PHP_AUTH_USER, $PHP_AUTH_PW, and $PHP_AUTH_TYPE, set to the user name, password, and authentication type respectively.

A sample script is found in Chapter 12, Application 8.

To prevent someone from writing a script revealing the password for a page that was authenticated through a traditional external mechanism, the PHP_AUTH variables will not be set if external authentication is enabled for that particular page.

Note, however, that the above does not prevent someone who controls a non-authenticated URL from stealing passwords from authenticated URLs on the same server.

XML Parser

PHP3 includes XML (eXtensible Markup Language) functions. XML is a markup language for highly structured documents. It is a standard defined by the World Wide Web consortium (W3C). Information about XML can be found at *http://www.w3.org/XML/*. The XML functions use the expat library available at *http://www.jclark.com/xml/*.

Because the standard is still in the formative stage, we have chosen not to develop sample applications using XML in this book. Look for examples at *www.php123.com*. ▬▬

Lightweight Directory Access Protocol (LDAP)

LDAP is the lightweight directory access protocol. See *http://www.openldap.com/* for an OpenSource™ LDAP server.

LDAP is a TCP/IP-based protocol that is used to access directory servers. LDAP uses a hierarchal data model that lends itself to multiple-user directories organized by logical business units, similar to (but in some ways more adaptable than) either Microsoft Active Directory (MAD) or Novell Directory Services (NDS).

The LDAP directories are special-purpose databases that hold information in a tree structure. At the root of this structure is "the world." The first level below the root are "countries." Below this level can be entries for companies, organizations, places, and so on. At the bottom level of this structure can be people, passwords, text, equipment, URLs, and so forth. ▬▬

Want to test it out? We have it running at *www.php123.com*.

SNMP Functions

The Simple Network Management Protocol (SNMP) provides a method of monitoring and managing systems over a network. Various things can be monitored and managed by SNMP in a PHP3 program, including routers, hubs, air conditioning systems, well, almost anything with an interface. The SNMP functions use the ucd-snmp library available from *http://www.ece.ucdavis.edu/ucd-snmp/*. ▬▬

IMAP Functions

PHP3 provides functions to retrieve mail from an Internet Message Access Protocol (IMAP) server. IMAP provides a method of accessing e-mail stored on a server.

Post Office Protocol Version 3 (POP3) is a more commonly used protocol to retrieve e-mail from mail servers. However, IMAP has several important features that POP3 lacks.

POP3 simply downloads messages from a server. In addition, IMAP:

- Allows the same mailbox to be accessed from multiple computers (e.g., laptop and desktop)

- Supports concurrent access to shared mailboxes

- Provides server-based MIME parsing

- Supports disconnected operation

- Provides for searching of messages before download

- Provides an offline synchronization client with server

For more information on IMAP, see RFC 2060. PHP3 uses the IMAP library available from *ftp://ftp.cac.washington.edu/imap/imap-4.4.tar.Z*.

Why use IMAP? First, IMAP is an open standard. The specifications are publicly available to anyone and several implementations are available in source-code form. Second, IMAP is well suited for accessing mailboxes on servers rather than merely fetching mail to a local machine. With IMAP you can list mailboxes, copy or move mail between them, and request parts of multipart e-mail messages. The advantage of IMAP is that users can access their e-mail using any mail client, even from different machines.

So, how is this done? First, the prerequisites. You will need PHP3 compiled with the IMAP libraries. Or, just access the Readers Only site at *http://www.php123.com*, where we have it running for you.

The authors are not, however, wild about IMAP. It seems to us to be overly complicated and to shift too much processing requirement from the client to the server.

Image Functions

PHP3 can generate JPEG, GIF, and PNG (Portable Network Graphics) images. PNG is a replacement for the GIF standard (which is owned by Unisys).

PHP3 can also determine the size of these images on disk, for example, to automatically generate HEIGHT= and WIDTH= attributes in <IMG> tags.

In order to use these functions, the GD library must be compiled in. It is available from *http://www.boutell.com/gd/#buildgd*. The GD library also provides a collection of functions to draw images (points, lines, arcs), manipulate colors, and generate text.

In addition to the basic text functions built into the GD library, PHP3 also supports the FreeType library. This gives PHP3 the ability to render type using True Type fonts, which can greatly improve the appearance of text in images generated by PHP3.

This library is available from *http://www.freetype.org/*.

Hyperwave Functions

Hyperwave is an information management system similar to a database. It is predominantly used in the storage and management of large documents. For more information, see *http://www.hyperwave.com/*.

Gz-File Functions

PHP3 can transparently read and write gzip (.gz) compressed files.

 To do this, PHP3 uses the zlib library written by Jean-Loup Gailly and Mark Adler, available from *http://www.cdrom.com/pub/infozip/zlib/*.

HTTP-Related Functions

Using these functions, PHP3 can directly manipulate HTTP headers.

 For example, the `Content-Type` header can be changed to specify output other than text/html, and the `Location` header can be used to perform a redirect. PHP3 can also set and manipulate cookies by using either the **header()** function or the **SetCookie()** function.

Data Conversion Functions

The calendar functions in PHP3 simplify converting between different date formats.

 The intermediary step in the conversion is based on the Julian Day Count. The Julian Day Count is a count of days since November 25, 4714 BC. To convert between date formats, you must first convert to Julian Day Count, then to the appropriate date format.

The Julian Day Count is different from the Julian Calendar.

 For more information on date formats, see *http://genealogy.org/~scottlee/cal-overview.html*.

To enable these functions, the calendar extension must have been enabled at compile time. This is enabled on the Readers Only web site.

Spelling Functions

Using the aspell library, PHP3 can check the spelling of a word and suggest possible corrections. To use this feature, the aspell library must be compiled into PHP. This is available from *http://metalab.unc.edu/kevina/aspell/*. These features have been enabled on the Readers Only web site.

Arbitrary-Precision Functions

 PHP3 includes a set of arbitrary-precision math functions based upon the Unix program bc, a POSIX standard.

This precision is both in the integer part and the fractional part. The numbers are represented internally in decimal, and all calculations are done in decimal.

Numbers have two attributes, the length and the scale. The length is the total number of significant decimal digits in the number, and the scale is the total number of decimal digits after the decimal point.

To enable the BC functions, PHP3 should be compiled with the enable-bcmath configure option. These functions have been enabled on the Readers Only web site.

FilePro Functions

These functions provide read-only access from data stored in FilePro databases. For more information on filePro, see *http://www.fileproplus.com/*.

Oracle 7–8 Functions

These functions allow access to Oracle8 and Oracle7 databases. The driver requires the Oracle8 client libraries and uses the Oracle8 Call-Interface (OCI8).

PDF Functions

With the PDF library (available from *http://www.ifconnection.de/~tm/*) by Thomas Merz, PHP3 can create PDF files. PDF files are a convenient way to distribute documents for viewing and printing while preserving their original appearance. However, anyone accessing PDF documents needs a special program to view or print them. The two most popular are *xpdf* (on the attached CD-ROM) and *Adobe Acrobat*.

Be certain to review the examples of PDF output online at *http://www.php123.com/pdf/*.

InterBase Functions

PHP3 provides functions to interface with the InterBase RDBMS, which is a multi-platform RDBMS with a small footprint.

For more information on InterBase, see *http://www.interbase.com/*.

VmailMgr Functions

PHP3 supports the VMailMgr package by Bruce Guenter.

VMailMgr (short for Virtual Mail ManaGeR) is a package of programs designed to manage multiple groups of mail addresses and mailboxes on a single host. It cooperates with *qmail (http://www.qmail.org/)* for mail delivery.

These functions require qmail and the VMailMgr package from *http://www.qcc.sk.ca/~bguenter/distrib/vmailmgr/*.

Shared Memory and Semaphore Functions

PHP3 provides semaphore functions using System V semaphores.

Semaphores may be used to provide exclusive access to resources on the current machine, or to limit the number of processes that may simultaneously use a particular resource. They also provide shared-memory functions using System V shared memory. Shared memory may be used to provide access to global variables. Different web servers and even other programs are able to access this data to provide a global data exchange.

Note that shared memory is not safe against simultaneous access. Semaphores should be used for process synchronization.

Using the PHP3 Debugger

PHP3 includes an internal debugger. Please refer to the on-line documention for more information on topics such as setting breakpoints or examining variables.

The debugger works by connecting to a TCP port on the local machine or a remote machine every time PHP3 starts up. All error messages from PHP3 are sent to this TCP connection.

To set up the PHP3 debugger:

1) Set up a TCP port for the debugger in php3.ini (debugger.port) and enable it (debugger.enabled).

2) Set up a program to listen on the specified port. The netcat utility program can be used for this purpose, *http://www.10pht.com/~weld/netcat/*.

3) In the PHP3 program, include "debugger_on(host)", where host is the IP address or host name of the host listening on the specified port.

Now, all warnings, notices, and so forth will show up on the listener socket, even if they have been turned off with **error_reporting()**.

Linking User-Defined Functions into the Built-In PHP3 Library

We have left the topic of adding user-developed built-in functions into your PHP3 core library for the reference section of the Readers Only web site. This can be quite complex. Please refer to *www.php123.com/userfunctions/* for more information.

What's Coming for PHP?

Zend *http://www.zend.com/* is a complete rewrite of the PHP3 engine and is expected to be the scripting engine for PHP4. Zend also adds several important new features:

- More efficient on long and complex PHP3 scripts
- Generation of obfuscated PHP3 code allowing distribution of PHP3 programs without providing source-code access
- A new boolean data type
- Runtime binding of functions
- A full-featured debugger with breakpoints, expression evaluation, step-in/over, function call backtrace, and more.

We expect future releases of PHP3 to continue the tradition of adding many new additional features, to support many more additional libraries and to support many more database systems. From reading the TODO list included with PHP4, we expect the following features to be added soon:

- Support for PGP encryption
- Support for the Informix OORDBS
- Support for the DB2 database
- Support for FastCGI *http://fastcgi.idle.com/*
- File locking

PHP4 was released for Beta testing in the last half of 1999. Expect to see the production version in early 2000.

Work is progressing by several groups on support for NSAPI (on Windows), ISAPI, and WSAPI, which will all allow PHP3 to be used as a plug-in on multithreaded servers like Netscape FastTrack, Microsoft's Internet Information Server (IIS), and O'Reilly's WebSite Pro.

Reference Section

Language and Function Reference

Language Reference Layout

— *Function Name*

— *Function Library*

aspell_new (spell) — *Function Short Description*
load a dictionary — *Function Syntax*

```
int aspell_new(string master, string personal);
```

— *Function Description*

This function opens a new dictionary and returns an identifier for use with other aspell functions.

— *Function Example*

Example

```
<?PHP
$spell = aspell_new("english");
?>
```

Index by Functional Category

(See Function Index for alphabetical listing.)

EXPRESSIONS

IF (expressions)
provide for conditional execution of code fragments

```
IF (expr)
  statement
```

> expr is evaluated to its truth value. If expr evaluates to TRUE, PHP executes the statement; if it evaluates to FALSE, the statement is ignored.
>
> The PHP IF sentence is similar to that of C.

Example 1

```
if ($a > $b)
  print "a is bigger than b";
```

> There is no limit to the number of individual statements that can be conditionally executed by a single evalution.

Example 2

This example executes two statements, one following the other. This is often referred to as sequential processing.

```
if ($a>$b) {
  print "a is bigger than b";
  $b = $a;
}
```

> IF statements can be nested indefinitely within other IF statements, providing comprehensive flexibility for conditional execution of the program.

Example 3

```
 if ($a>$b) {
  print "a is bigger than b";
  if ($a==2) {
   print "a is equal to 2";
```

```
    }
}
```

ELSE (expressions)
provide for a default condition to the IF expression

```
IF (expr)
   Statement
ELSEIF (expr2)
   Statement
ELSE
   Statement
```

> It is often necessary to execute a statement if a certain condition is met, and execute a different statement if the condition is not met. This is what ELSE does. ELSE extends an IF statement to execute a separate statement in case the expression in the IF statement evaluates to FALSE.
>
> The ELSE statement is executed only *after* the IF expression has been evaluated to FALSE.

Example 1
```
if ($a>$b) {
   print "a is bigger than b";
} else {
   print "a is NOT bigger than b";
}
```

Example 2

This example is the same as the previous example, except it uses the alternative syntax.

```
if ($a>$b) :
   print "a is bigger than b";
else:
   print "a is NOT bigger than b";
endif;
```

ELSEIF

> The ELSEIF statement is executed after the initial IF expression has been evaluated to FALSE. There is no limit to the number of ELSEIF conditions that can be evaluated within an IF expression.
>
> After every ELSEIF statement has been evaluated to FALSE, the ELSE statement is expressed.

Example 1

```
$a = 5
$b = 6

if ($a>$b) {
  print "a is bigger than b";
} elseif ($b>$a) {
  print "a is NOT bigger than b";
} else {
  print "a and b are the same";
}
```

Output

```
A is NOT bigger than b
```

Example 2

This example is the same as the previous example, except it uses the alternative syntax.

```
if ($a>$b) :
  print "a is bigger than b";
elseif ($b>$a):
  print "a is NOT bigger than b";
else:
  print "a and b are the same";
endif;
```

WHILE (expressions)
provide for looping with the truth evaluation occurring at the top of the loop.

```
WHILE(expr) statement
```

> WHILE loops are the simplest type of loop. They behave like their C counterparts.

A WHILE statement executes the nested statement(s) repeatedly, as long as the WHILE expression evaluates to TRUE.

The value of the expression is checked at the *beginning* of each loop. So, even if the evaluation value changes during the execution of the nested statement(s), execution will not stop until the top of the succeeding iteration.

If the WHILE expression evaluates to FALSE at the beginning of the loop, the nested statement(s) will not be executed.

As with the IF statement, multiple statements can be grouped within the same WHILE loop by surrounding a group of statements with curly braces, OR by using the alternate syntax:

```
WHILE(expr): statement ... ENDWHILE;
```

Examples 1 and 2:

The following examples are identical, and both print numbers from 1 to 10.

Example 1

```
$i=1;
while ($i<=10) {
  print $i++;
}
```

Example 2

```
$i=1;
while ($i<=10):
  print $i;
  $i++;
endwhile;
```

DO..WHILE (expressions)
provide for looping with the truth evaluation occurring at the bottom of the loop, insuring that all statements contained within the expression are evaluated at least once.

```
DO
  Statement
WHILE
```

> DO..WHILE loops are similar to WHILE loops, except the truth expression is checked at the *end* of each iteration instead of at the beginning.
>
> Because the truth expression is checked at the end of the loop, the DO..WHILE loop is guaranteed to run *at least once*.
>
> There is just one syntax for DO..WHILE loops:

Example 1

The above loop will run only once, until the truth expression is checked at the bottom of the expression.

```
$i = 0;
do {
  print $i;
} while ($i>0);
```

> The DO..WHILE loop can also be used to stop execution in the middle of a code block, by encapsulating the block with DO..WHILE(0), and using the BREAK statement.

Example 2

The following code fragment demonstrates encapsulating.

```
do {
   if ($i < 5) {
     print "i is not big enough";
     break;
   }
   $i *= $factor;
   if ($i < $minimum_limit) {
     break;
   }
   print "i is ok now ";
} while(0);
```

FOR (expressions)
provide for the most complex execution loops.

```
FOR (expr1; expr2; expr3) statement
```

FOR loops are the most comprehensive loops in PHP. They behave
like their C counterparts.

The first expression (expr1) is evaluated (executed) unconditionally at
the beginning of the loop.

In the beginning of each iteration, expr2 is evaluated. If it evaluates to
TRUE, the loop continues and the nested statement(s) are executed. If
it evaluates to FALSE, the execution of the loop ends. At the end of
each iteration, expr3 is evaluated (executed).

Each of the expressions can be empty. If expr2 is empty, the loop
should be run indefinitely (PHP implicitly considers it as TRUE, like
C). (Why? Often program logic wants to end the loop using a conditional BREAK statement instead of using the FOR truth expression.)

FOR(expr): ... ENDFOR; is NOT supported.

Example 1

```
for ($i=1; $i<=10; $i++) {
   print $i;
}
```

Output

```
1 2 3 4 5 6 7 8 9 10
```

Example 2

```
for ($i = 1;;$i++) {
   if ($i > 10) {
      break;
   }
   print $i;
}
```

Output

```
1 2 3 4 5 6 7 8 9 10
```

Example 3

```
$i = 1;
for (;;) {
   if ($i > 10) {
      break;
   }
```

```
    print $i;
    $i++;
}
```

Output

```
1 2 3 4 5 6 7 8 9 10
```

SWITCH (expressions)
execute one statement at a time

```
SWITCH (var)
   case expr:
   statement(s);
   break;
   default:
    print "i equals 1";
```

> The SWITCH statement is similar to a series of IF statements based on the same expression.
>
> SWITCH is useful when it is necessary to compare the same variable (or expression) with many different values, and execute a different piece of code depending on which value it is equal to.

Example

Compares using the IF expression and SWITCH expression to accomplish the same logic.

IF Logic Example

```
$1=2
if ($i == 0) {
  print "i equals 0";
}
if ($i == 1) {
  print "i equals 1";
}
if ($i == 2) {
  print "i equals 2";
}
```

Output

```
I equals 2
```

SWITCH Logic Example

```
switch ($i) {
  case 0:
    print "i equals 0";
    break;
  case 1:
    print "i equals 1";
    break;
  case 2:
    print "i equals 2";
    break;
}
```

Output

```
I equals 2
```

> The SWITCH statement executes one statement at a time.
>
> There is no default execution logic (as in ELSE). Only when a CASE statement is found with a value that matches the value of the SWITCH expression does PHP execute the code block.
>
> PHP continues to execute the statements until the end of the SWITCH block, or until the BREAK statement is encountered. If a BREAK statement is not contained at the end of each CASE statement list, PHP continues executing all subsequent CASE statements.

Example 1

This snippet does not contain BREAK statements. If $i equals to 0, PHP will execute all of the print statements! If $i equals to 1, PHP will execute the last two print statements. Only if $i equals to 2 will PHP execute the anticipated results. So, unless the logic requires succeeding CASE comparisons, inserting a BREAK is important to terminate a sequential SWITCH evaluation.

```
switch ($i) {
  case 0:
    print "i equals 0";
  case 1:
    print "i equals 1";
  case 2:
    print "i equals 2";
}
```

Example 2

A special case is the default case. This case matches anything that wasn't matched by the other cases. For example:

```
/* example 4 */
switch ($i) {
  case 0:
    print "i equals 0";
    break;
  case 1:
    print "i equals 1";
    break;
  case 2:
    print "i equals 2";
    break;
  default:
    print "i is not equal to 0, 1 or 2";
}
```

> The CASE expression may be any expression that evaluates to a scalar type (integer or real numbers and strings).
>
> Arrays and objects are meaningless in CASE comparisons.

REQUIRE (expressions)
replace itself with the specified file.

`Require`(file)

> The REQUIRE statement replaces itself with the file specified by *expressions*. The expression works much like the C preprocessor #include.
>
> The REQUIRE() expressions cannot be placed inside a loop structure to iteratively include the contents of a different file with each loop. For this purpose use the INCLUDE expression.

Example 1

Include the contents of a file called "header.inc".

```
require('header.inc');
```

INCLUDE (expressions)
include the file specified by *expressions*

```
Include(file)
```

The replacement occurs each time the INCLUDE statement is encountered.
The INCLUDE expression can be used within a looping structure to include
a number of different files.

Example 1

Include a number of different files.

```
$files = array('first.inc', 'second.inc', 'third.inc');
for ($i = 0; $i < count($files); $i++) {
   include($files[$i]);
}
```

FUNCTION (expressions)
define a function

```
function foo( $arg_1, $arg_2, ..., $arg_n ) {
   echo "PHP 123...\n";
   return $retval;
}
```

Any valid PHP3 code may appear inside a function, even other functions and
class definitions. Refer to Section 2.4.2.2 for more detail.

FUNCTIONS

DATA-RELATED

abs (math)
absolute value

```
mixed abs(mixed number);
```

This function calculates and returns the absolute value of *number*.
If *number* is a float, then the return type is also a float. Otherwise, it is
an int.

Example

```
<?PHP
echo abs(10)."\n";
echo abs(-10)."\n";
echo abs(0)."\n";
?>
```

Output

```
10
10
0
```

---

acos (math)
arc cosine

```
float acos(float number);
```

> This function calculates and returns the arc cosine of *number* in radians.

Example

```
<?PHP
echo acos(1)."\n";
echo acos(0)."\n";
?>
```

Output

```
0
1.5707963267949
```

See also asin() and atan().

---

addSlashes (string)
quote string with slashes

```
string addslashes(string str);
```

> This function returns a string with backslashes before the single quote
> ('), double quote ("), and backslash (\) characters.
>
> These characters must be escaped in certain database queries.

Example

```
<?PHP
$word="F:\NETWORK";
echo "String: ".$word."\n";
echo "Escaped string: ".addslashes($word)."\n";

$word="'a'";
echo "String: ".$word."\n";
echo "Escaped string: ".addslashes($word)."\n";
?>
```

Output

```
String: F:\NETWORK
Escaped string: F:\\NETWORK
String: 'a'
Escaped string: \'a\'
```

See also stripslashes() and quotemeta().

----

array (array)
create an array

```
array array(...);
```

> This function returns an array of the parameters. The parameters can
> be given an index with the => operator. Note that array() really is a lan-
> guage construct used to represent literal arrays, and is not a regular
> function.

Example 1

The code below will create an array with four elements.

```
<?PHP
$student = array("Joe", "Bob", "Jill", "Janice");
?>
```

Example 2

The code below creates an associative array.
```
<?PHP
$id  = array("Joe" => 123, "Bob" => 345, "Jill" => 678,
  "Janice" => 901);
echo $id[Joe]."\n";
```

```
echo $id[Janice]."\n";
?>
```

Output

```
123
901
```

See also list().

----

array_walk (array)
apply a user function to each member of an array

```
int array_walk(array a, string function);
```

This function calls the user-defined *function* on each element of *a*.

Example 1

The code below will call the user-defined function lower() on each element of an array.

```
<?PHP
function lower($str) {
  $str = strtolower($str);
}

$a = array("Joe", "Bob", "Jill", "Janice");
array_walk($a, 'lower');
do {
  echo current($a)."<br>";
} while (next($a));
?>
```

Output

```
Joe
bob
jill
janice
```

----

arsort (array)
sort an array in reverse order and maintain index association

```
void arsort(array array);
```

This function sorts *array* in reverse order such that the array indices maintain their correlation with the array elements they are associated with. This is useful when sorting associative arrays.

Example

```php
<?PHP
$id  = array("Joe" => 333, "Bob" => 222, "Jill" => 111,
"Janice" => 999);
arsort($id);
do {
   echo key($id)." ID # ".current($id)."\n";
} while (next($id));
?>
```

Output

```
Janice ID # 999
Joe ID # 333
Bob ID # 222
Jill ID # 111
```

See also asort(), rsort(), ksort(), and sort().

---

asin (math)
arc sine

```php
float asin(float number);
```

This function calculates and returns the arc sine of *number* in radians.

Example

```php
<?PHP
echo asin(1)."\n";
echo asin(0)."\n";
?>
```

Output

```
1.5707963267949
```

See also acos() and atan().

---

asort (array)
sort an array and maintain index association

```
void asort(array array);
```

> This function sorts *array* such that the array indices maintain their
> correlation with the array elements they are associated with. This is
> useful when sorting associative arrays.

Example

```php
<?PHP
$id  = array("Joe" => 333, "Bob" => 222, "Jill" => 111,
"Janice" => 999);
asort($id);
do {
  echo key($id)." ID # ".current($id)."\n";
} while (next($id));
?>
```

Output

```
Jill ID # 111
Bob ID # 222
Joe ID # 333
Janice ID # 999
```

See also arsort(), rsort(), ksort(), and sort().

----

aspell_new (spell)
load a dictionary

```
int aspell_new(string master, string personal);
```

> This function opens a new dictionary, and returns an identifier for use
> with other aspell functions.

Example

```php
<?PHP
$spell = aspell_new("english");

$word = "test";
if(aspell_check($spell, $word))
```

```
  echo $word." is spelled correctly.\n";
else
  echo $word." is not spelled correctly.\n";
?>
```

Output

```
test is spelled correctly.
```

---

aspell_check (spell)
check spelling

```
boolean aspell_check(int dictionary_link, string word);
```

> This function checks spelling of *word*. It returns TRUE if *word* is
> spelled correctly and FALSE if it is not.

Example

```
<?PHP
$spell = aspell_new("english");

$word = "test";
if(aspell_check($spell, $word))
  echo $word." is spelled correctly.\n";
else
  echo $word." is not spelled correctly.\n";

$word = "testf";
if(aspell_check($spell, $word))
  echo $word." is spelled correctly.\n";
else
  echo $word." is not spelled correctly.\n";
?>
```

Output

```
test is spelled correctly.
testf is not spelled correctly.
```

See also aspell_new().

---

aspell_check_raw (spell)
check a word's spelling without changing its case or removing white space

```
boolean aspell_check_raw(int dictionary_link, string word);
```

> This function is similar to aspell_check(). The difference is that with aspell_check(), *word* is made lower-case and trimmed.

Example

```
<?PHP
$spell = aspell_new("english");

$word = "test";
if(aspell_check_raw($spell, $word))
  echo $word." is spelled correctly.\n";
else
  echo $word." is not spelled correctly.\n";

$word = "TEST";
if(aspell_check_raw($spell, $word))
  echo $word." is spelled correctly.\n";
else
  echo $word." is not spelled correctly.\n";
?>
```

Output

```
test is spelled correctly.
TEST is not spelled correctly.
```

---

aspell_suggest (spell)
suggest possible correct spellings of a word

```
array aspell_suggest(int dictionary_link, string word);
```

> This function returns an array of possible correct spellings of *word*.

Example

```
<?PHP
$spell = aspell_new("english");

$word = "testf";
if(aspell_check($spell, $word))
  echo $word." is spelled correctly.\n";
else {
  echo $word." is not spelled correctly.\n";
```

```
    echo "Suggested correct spellings:\n";
    $suggest = aspell_suggest($spell, $word);
    for ($x = 0; $x < count($suggest); $x++)
    echo $suggest[$x]."\n";
}
?>
```

Output

```
testf is not spelled correctly.
Suggested correct spellings:
testify
test
tests
testy
test's
tester
```

----

atan (math)
arc tangent

```
float atan(float number);
```

> This function calculates and returns the arc tangent of *number* in radians.

Example

```
<?PHP
echo atan(1)."\n";
echo atan(0)."\n";
?>
```

Output

```
0.78539816339745
0
```

See also acos() and atan().

----

base64_encode (url)
encode data with MIME base64

```
string base64_encode(string data);
```

This function returns *data* encoded with base64. This encoding was designed to convert binary data to a form that will survive being sent through systems or protocols that are not 8-bit clean, such as the body of e-mail messages. Base64-encoded data takes about one-third more space than the original binary data. For more information on Base64, see RFC 2045, "Multipurpose Internet Mail Extensions (MIME) Part One: Format of Internet Message Bodies."

Example

```
<?PHP
$str = base64_encode("example@php123.com");
echo $str;
?>
```

Output

```
ZXhhbXBsZUBwaHAxMjMuY29t
```

See also base64_decode(), section 6.8.

---

base64_decode> (url)
decode data encoded with MIME base64

```
string base64_decode(string encoded_data);
```

This function decodes the Base64-encoded *encoded_data*, and returns the original binary data. Typically, decoding Base64 data is done when extracting files from e-mail messages. For more information on Base64, see RFC 2045, "Multipurpose Internet Mail Extensions (MIME) Part One: Format of Internet Message Bodies."

Example

```
<?PHP
$str = base64_decode("ZXhhbXBsZUBwaHAxMjMuY29t");
echo $str;
?>
```

Output

```
example@php123.com
```

See also base64_encode()

---

bcadd (AP)
add two arbitrary-precision numbers

```
string bcadd(string left operand, string right operand,
[int scale]);
```

This function adds the *left operand* to the *right operand,* and returns the sum as a string. The optional *scale* parameter is used to set the number of digits after the decimal point in the result.

Example

```
<?PHP
$str = bcadd(1000000, 2000000);
echo "one million + two million = ".$str."\n";
?>
```

Output

```
one million + two million = 3000000
```

See also bcsub().

----

bccomp (AP)(x)
compare two arbitrary-precision numbers

```
int bccomp(string left operand, string right operand,
[int scale]);
```

This function compares the *left operand* to the *right operand,* and returns the result as an integer. The optional *scale* parameter is used to set the number of digits after the decimal point, which will be used in the comparison. The return value is 0 if the two operands are equal. If the *left operand* is larger than the *right operand,* then the return value is +1. If the *left operand* is less than the *right operand,* then the return value is −1.

Example

```
<?PHP
// bccomp()
$int = bccomp(5, 6);
if($int == 0)
```

```
    echo "Values are equal\n";
else if ($int > 0)
    echo "The first value is greater\n";
else if ($int < 0)
    echo "The second value is greater\n";
?>
```

Output

```
The second value is greater
```

----

bcdiv (AP)
divide two arbitrary-precision numbers

```
string bcdiv(string left operand, string right operand,
[int scale]);
```

> This function divides the *left operand* to the *right operand,* and
> returns the result as a string. The optional *scale* parameter is used
> to set the number of digits after the decimal point in the result.

Example

```
<?PHP
$str = bcdiv(22, 7, 10);
echo "pi is approximately ".$str."\n";
?>
```

Output

```
pi is approximately 3.1428571428
```

See also bcmul().

----

bcmod (AP)
get the modulus of an arbitrary-precision number

```
string bcmod(string left operand, string modulus);
```

> This function computes modulus of the *left operand* using *modulus,*
> and returns the result as a string.

Example

```
<?PHP
$str = bcmod(15, 6);
echo "15 % 6 = ".$str."\n";
?>
```

Output

```
15 % 6 = 3
```

See also bcdiv().

---

bcmul (AP)
multiply two arbitrary-precision numbers

```
string bcadd(string left operand, string right operand, [int
scale]);
```

> This function multiplies the *left operand* by the *right operand*, and
> returns the result as a string. The optional *scale* parameter is used to
> set the number of digits after the decimal point in the result.

Example

```
<?PHP
$str = bcmul(5, 10, 5);
echo "5 * 10 = ".$str."\n";
?>
```

Output

```
5 * 10 = 50
```

See also bcdiv().

---

bcpow (AP)
raise an arbitrary-precision number to the power of another

```
string bcpow(string left operand, string right operand,
[int scale]);
```

> This function raises the *left operand* to the power of *right operand*,
> and returns the sum as a string. The optional *scale* parameter is used
> to set the number of digits after the decimal point in the result.

Example

```
<?PHP
$str = bcpow(2, 20);
echo "2 to the 20th is ".$str;
?>
```

Output

```
2 to the 20th is 1048576
```

See also bcsqrt().

----

bcscale (AP)
set default scale

```
string bcscale(int scale);
```

> This function sets the default scale parameter for all arbitrary preci-
> sion math functions that do not explicitly specify a scale parameter.

----

bcsqrt (AP)
find the square root of an arbitrary-precision number

```
string bcsqrt(string operand, [int scale]);
```

> This function finds the square root of the *operand*, and returns it as a
> string. The optional *scale* parameter is used to set the number of digits
> after the decimal point in the result.

Example

```
<?PHP
$str = bcsqrt(10,5);
echo $str;
?>
```

Output

```
3.16227
```

See also bcscale() and bcpow().

----

bcsub (AP)
subtract one arbitrary precision number from another

```
string bcsub(string left operand, string right operand,
[int scale]);
```

> This function subtracts the *right operand* to the *left operand*, and
> returns the difference as a string. The optional *scale* parameter is used
> to set the number of digits after the decimal point in the result.

Example

```
<?PHP
$str = bcsub(1, 10);
echo $str;
?>
```

Output

```
-9
```

See also bcadd().

----

binDec (math)
binary to decimal

```
int bindec(string binary_string);
```

> This function converts *binary_string* to the decimal equivalent. This
> function converts a binary number in a string to a decimal number.
> The largest number that can be converted is 31 bits of 1's, which is
> equivalent to 2147483647 in decimal.

Example

```
<?PHP
echo bindec("1")."\n";
echo bindec("0")."\n";
echo bindec("1111111111111111111111111111111")."\n";
?>
```

Output

```
1
2147483647
```

See also decbin().

----

ceil (math)
round fractions up

```
int ceil(float number);
```

> This function returns the smallest integer value not less than *number*.
> Using ceil() on an integer simply returns that integer.

Example

```php
<?PHP
echo ceil(1)."\n";
echo ceil(1.1)."\n";
echo ceil(1.9)."\n";
echo ceil(2)."\n";
?>
```

Output

```
1
2
```

See also floor() and round().

----

chunk_split (string)
split a string into smaller chunks

```
string chunk_split(string str, int [chunklen] , string
[end] );
```

> This function is used to insert string *end* into string *str* every *chunklen* characters. By default, the optional parameter *chunklen* is 76 characters, which is appropriate for e-mail. By default, the optional parameter *end* is "\r\n".

Example

```php
<?PHP
$text =
"ABCDEFGHIJKLMNOPQRSTUVWXYZABCDEFGHIJKLMNOPQRSTUVWXYZ";
echo chunk_split($text, 20);
?>
```

Output

```
ABCDEFGHIJKLMNOPQRST
UVWXYZABCDEFGHIJKLMN
OPQRSTUVWXYZ
```

See also base64_encode().

----

checkdate (date-time)
validate a date/time

```
int checkdate(int month, int day, int year);
```

> This function returns TRUE if the date given is valid, otherwise it returns FALSE. It checks the validity of the date formed by the arguments. A date is considered valid if:
>
> - year is between 1900 and 32767 inclusive;
>
> - month is between 1 and 12 inclusive; and
>
> - day is within the allowed number of days for the given month with leap years taken into account.

Example

```php
<?PHP
// Is the date January 99, 1999 valid?
if (checkdate(1, 99, 1999))
  echo "Date is valid\n";
else
  echo "Date is invalid\n";

// Is the data January 2, 1999 valid?
if (checkdate(1, 2, 1999))
  echo "Date is valid\n";
else
  echo "Date is invalid\n";
?>
```

Output

```
Date is invalid
Date is valid
```

----

chop (string)
remove trailing whitespace

```
string chop(string str);
```

> This function returns the string *str* with any trailing white space removed.

Example

```
<?PHP
$word="ABCabc                    ";
echo "String: '".$word."'\n";
echo "String after chop(): '".chop($word)."'\n";
?>
```

Output

```
String: 'ABCabc
String after chop(): 'ABCabc'
```

See also trim().

----

chr (string)
return a specific character

```
string chr(int ascii);
```

> This function returns a single character string containing the character specified by *ascii*. This function is the opposite of ord().

Example

```
<?PHP
for($x = 32;$x < 65; $x++) {
   echo chr($x);
?>
```

Output

```
!"#$%&'()*+,-./0123456789:;<=>?@
```

See also ord().

----

cos (math)
cosine

```
float cos(float number);
```

> This function calculates and returns the cosine of *number* in radians.

Example

```
<?PHP
echo cos(pi()/4)."\n";
echo cos(pi()/2)."\n";
?>
```

Output

Note: The second value displayed should be zero (0), but due to floating-point rounding errors, it is a number very close to zero.

```
0.70710678118655
6.1230317691119E-17
```

See also sin() and tan().

----

count (array)
count elements in a variable

```
int count(mixed var);
```

> This function returns the number of elements in var, which is typically an array (since anything else will have one element). It returns 0 if the variable is not set, and it returns 1 if the variable is not an array.

Example

```
<?PHP
$student = array("Joe", "Bob", "Jill", "Janice");
echo "The number of elements: ".count($student)."\n";
?>
```

Output

```
The number of elements: 4
```

See also sizeof(), isset(), and is_array().

----

crypt (string)
DES-encrypt a string

```
string crypt(string str, string salt);
```

This function will encrypt string *str* using the standard Unix DES encryption method. *salt* is an optional two-character string to base the encryption on. This function is most often used to create or verify Unix passwords in /etc/passwd. Note: No decrypt function exists because crypt() uses a one-way algorithm.

Example

```php
<?PHP
$username = "jsmith";
$password = "test";
echo crypt($password, $username);
?>
```

Output

```
jsOrmWx9.tReo
```

---

current (array)
return the current element in an array

```
mixed current(array array);
```

Each array variable has an internal pointer that points to one of its elements. In addition, all of the elements in the array are linked by a bi-directional linked list for traversing purposes. The internal pointer points to the first element that was inserted to the array until you run one of the functions that modify that pointer on that array.

The current() function simply returns the array element that is currently being pointed to by the internal pointer. It does not move the pointer in any way. If the internal pointer points beyond the end of the elements list, current() returns FALSE.

Example

```php
<?PHP

$student = array("Joe", "Bob", "Jill", "Janice");
```

```
do {
  echo current($student)."<br>";
} while (each($student));

?>
```

Output

```
Joe
Bob
Jill
Janice
```

See also end(), next(), prev(), and reset().

----

date (date-time)
date-format a local time/date

```
string date(string format, int timestamp);
```

> This function returns a string formatted according to the specified format string using the given timestamp; if no timestamp is specified, then the current local time is used.

The following characters are recognized in the format string:

U   seconds since the epoch
Y   year, numeric, 4 digits
y   year, numeric, 2 digits
F   month, textual, long; e.g., "January"
M   month, textual, 3 letters; e.g., "Jan"
m   month, numeric
z   day of the year, numeric; e.g., "299"
d   day of the month, numeric
l   day of the week, textual, long; e.g., "Friday"
D   day of the week, textual, 3 letters; e.g., "Fri"
w   day of the week, numeric, 1 digit
H   hour, numeric, 24 hour format
h   hour, numeric, 12 hour format
i   minutes, numeric
s   seconds, numeric
A   "AM" or "PM"
a   "am" or "pm"
S   English ordinal suffix, textual, 2 characters; e.g., "th", "nd"

> Unrecognized characters in the format string are printed as is.

Example 1

Prints today's date in the format Friday, 1st of January 1999 00:00:00 AM

```
echo date( "l dS of F Y h:i:s A" );
```

Example 2

Prints the day of the week on which January 1, 2000 falls

```
echo "January 1, 2000 is on a " . date("l", mktime(0,0,0,1,1,
    2000));
```

See also gmdate() and mktime().

---

decBin (math)
decimal to binary

```
string decbin(int number);
```

> This function converts *number* to a string containing its binary representation. The largest number that can be converted is 2147483647 in decimal. This value is a string of 31 1s.

Example

```
<?PHP
echo decbin(0)."\n";
echo decbin(1)."\n";
echo decbin(32)."\n";
echo decbin(2147483647)."\n";
?>
```

Output

```
0
1
100000
1111111111111111111111111111111
```

See also bindec().

---

decHex (math)
decimal to hexadecimal

```
string dechex(int number);
```

> This function converts *number* to a string containing its hexadecimal representation. The largest number that can be converted is 2147483647 in decimal. This value returns "7fffffff".

Example

```
<?PHP
echo dechex(0)."\n";
echo dechex(1)."\n";
echo dechex(32)."\n";
echo dechex(2147483647)."\n";
?>
```

Output

```
0
1
20
7fffffff
```

See also hexdec().

----

decOct (math)
decimal to octal

```
string decoct(int number);
```

> This function converts *number* to a string containing its octal representation. The largest number that can be converted is 2147483647 in decimal. This value returns "17777777777".

Example

```
<?PHP
echo decoct(0)."\n";
echo decoct(1)."\n";
echo decoct(32)."\n";
echo decoct(2147483647)."\n";
?>
```

Output

```
0
1
40
17777777777
```

See also octdec().

----

doubleVal (variable)
get double value of a variable

```
double doubleval(mixed var);
```

> This function returns the double (floating-point) value of *var*. *var* may
> be any scalar type. This function cannot be used on arrays or objects.

Example

```php
<?PHP
echo doubleval(10)."\n";
echo doubleval("20 boxes of crayons")."\n";
?>
```

Output

```
10
20
```

See also intval(), strval(), and settype().

----

each (array)
return next key/value pair from an array

```
array each(array array);
```

> This function returns the current key/value pair from the array *array*,
> and it advances the array cursor. This pair is returned in a four-element
> array, with the keys 0, 1, key, and value. Elements 0 and key each
> contain the key name of the array element, and 1 and value contain
> the data.

Example 1

Display each element of an array using the each() function to advance
through the array:

```
<?PHP

$student = array("Joe", "Bob", "Jill", "Janice");

do {
  echo current($student)."<br>";
} while (each($student));

?>
```

Output

```
Joe
Bob
Jill
Janice
```

Example 2

Each() is typically used in conjunction with list() to traverse an array; for instance, $HTTP_POST_VARS:

```
<?PHP
echo "Values submitted via POST method:<br>";
while ( list( $key, $val ) = each( $HTTP_POST_VARS ) ) {
  echo "$key => $val<br>";
}
?>
```

See also key(), current(), reset(), next(), and prev().

----

empty (variable)
determine whether a variable is set

```
int empty(mixed var);
```

> This function returns FALSE if *var* exists and has a value. It returns TRUE otherwise.

Example

```
<?PHP
$a = 1;
if(empty($a))
  echo "\$a does not exist.";
if(empty($b))
  echo "\$b does not exist.";
?>
```

Output

```
$b does not exist.
```

See also isset().

----

echo (string)
output one or more strings

```
string echo(string arg1, string argn...);
```

> This function outputs all of its parameters. echo() is actually a part of
> the PHP language, therefore placing the arguments inside parentheses
> is not required.

Example

```php
<?PHP
echo date("F d, Y, H:i:s", time())."\n";
echo "ABCabc\n";
?>
```

Output

```
January 1, 2000, 00:00:00
ABCabc
```

See also print(), printf(), and flush()

----

end (array)

```
array end(array array);
```

> end() advances array's internal pointer to the last element.

Example

```php
<?PHP
$student = array("Joe", "Bob", "Jill", "Janice");
end($student);
echo current($student)."<br>";
?>
```

Output

```
Janice
```

See also current(), end(), next(), and reset().

----

ereg (string)
regular expression match

```
int ereg(string pattern, string string, array regs);
```

> This function searches *string* for matches to the regular expression
> given in *pattern*. Searching is case-sensitive. This function returns
> TRUE if a match for pattern was found or FALSE if no matches were
> found or if an error occurred.

Example

The first call to ereg() looks for a simple pattern in the string. The second
looks for a pattern that is at the end of a line. The third call to ereg() looks for
a pattern at the start of a line. The last looks for a string that looks like a
Social Security Number (SSN, ###-##-####).

```
<?PHP
$word = "Testing 123";
$pat = "123";
if(ereg($pat, $word))
   echo "$pat was found in $word.\n";
else
   echo "$pat was not found in $word.\n";
$word = "Testing 123";
$pat = "123$";
if(ereg($pat, $word))
   echo "$pat was found in $word.\n";
else
   echo "$pat was not found in $word.\n";
$word = "Testing 123";
$pat = "^Testing";
if(ereg($pat, $word))
   echo "$pat was found in $word.\n";
else
   echo "$pat was not found in $word.\n";
$word = "123-45-6789";
```

```
$pat = "[0-9][0-9][0-9]-[0-9][0-9]-[0-9][0-9][0-9][0-9]";
if(ereg($pat, $word))
   echo "$pat was found in $word.\n";
else
   echo "$pat was not found in $word.\n";
?>
```

Output

```
123 was found in Testing 123.
123$ was found in Testing 123.
^Testing was found in Testing 123.
[0-9][0-9][0-9]-[0-9][0-9]-[0-9][0-9][0-9][0-9] was found in
123-45-6789.
```

---

ereg_replace (string)
replace regular expression

```
string ereg_replace(string pattern, string replacement,
string string);
```

> This function searches *string* for matches to *pattern*, then it replaces
> the matched text with *replacement*.

Example

The first call to ereg_replace() is used to delete all occurrences of a string.
Next, it is used to replace the contents of one string with another.

```
<?PHP
$text = "Testing 123";
echo ereg_replace("123", "", $text)."\n";
$text = "Testing 123";
echo ereg_replace("123", "456", $text)."\n";
?>
```

Output

```
Testing
Testing 456
```

See also ereg(), eregi(), and eregi_replace().

---

eregi (string)
case-insensitive regular expression match

```
int eregi(string pattern, string string, array regs);
```

> This function is identical to ereg(), except that case is ignored when matching alphabetic characters.

Example: see ereg()

See also ereg(), ereg_replace(), and eregi_replace().

---

eregi_replace (string)
replace regular expression case-insensitive

```
string eregi_replace(string pattern, string replacement,
string string);
```

> This function is identical to ereg_replace(), except that case is ignored when matching alphabetic characters.

Example: see ereg_replace()

See also ereg(), eregi(), and ereg_replace().

---

explode (string)
split a string by string

```
array explode(string separator, string string);
```

> This function returns an array of strings containing the elements separated by *separator*.

Example

The first use of explode() shows how to divide a line of text into individual words. The second shows how to use explode() to divide /etc/passwd up into separate elements.

```
<?PHP
$text = "A quick brown fox";
$words = explode(" ", $text);
```

```
echo $words[0].$words[1].$words[2]."\n";

$line = "joeuser:*:1100:100:Joe User:/home/joeuser:/bin/sh";
$element = explode(":", $line);
echo "UID: ".$element[2]."\n";
echo "Home directory: ".$element[5]."\n";
?>
```

Output

```
Aquickbrown
UID: 1100
Home directory: /home/joeuser
```

See also split() and implode().

----

exp (math)
e to the power of...

```
float exp(float number);
```

> This function calculates and returns e (approximately
> 2.718281828459) raised to the power of *number*.

Example

```
<?PHP
echo exp(0)."\n";
echo exp(1)."\n";
?>
```

Output

```
1
2.718281828459
```

See also pow() and log().

----

floor (math)
round fractions down

```
int floor(float number);
```

This function returns the largest integer value not greater than *number*. Using ceil() on an integer simply returns that integer.

Example

```php
<?PHP
echo floor(1)."\n";
echo floor(1.1)."\n";
echo floor(1.9)."\n";
echo floor(2)."\n";
?>
```

Output

```
1
1
1
2
```

See also ceil() and round().

---

flush (string)
flush the output buffer

```
void flush(void);
```

This function flushes PHP's output buffers. The effect of this function is to push all output so far to the user's browser. This function is typically used before executing a time-consuming action.

Example

```php
<?PHP
echo "Updating database.\n";
flush();
// Now, do time-consuming work
?>
```

---

getdate (date-time)
get date/time information

```
array getdate(int timestamp);
```

This function returns an associative array containing the timestamp in the form of the following array elements:

"seconds"	seconds
"minutes"	minutes
"hours"	hours
"mday"	day of the month
"wday"	day of the week, numeric
"mon"	month, numeric
"year"	year, numeric
"yday"	day of the year, numeric; e.g., "299"
"weekday"	day of the week, textual, full; e.g., "Friday"
"month"	month, textual, full; e.g., "January"

Example

```
<?PHP
$date_array = getdate(mktime());
echo "Today is ".$date_array[weekday];
?>
```

----

get_meta_tags (string)
extract all meta tag content attributes from a file and return an array

```
array get_meta_tags(string filename, int [use_include_path]);
```

This function opens *filename* and parses it line by line for <META> tags of the form:

<META NAME="*index*" CONTENT="*content*">

The value of the name property becomes the key, and the value of the content property becomes the value of the returned array.

Example

Assuming /home/httpd/html/index.html contains the following:

```
<META NAME="author" CONTENT="Joe User">
<META NAME="keywords" CONTENT="PHP programming">
```

Then get_meta_tags() can be used to extract the information below.

```
<?PHP
$tags = get_meta_tags("/home/httpd/html/index.html");
echo $tags[author]."\n";
echo $tags[keywords]."\n";
?>
```

Output

```
Joe User
PHP programming
```

---

getRandMax (math)
show largest possible random value

```
int getrandmax(void );
```

> This function returns the maximum value that can be returned by a call to rand().

Example

```
<?PHP
echo getrandmax()."\n";
?>
```

Output

```
2147483647
```

See also rand() and srand().

---

getType (variable)
get the type of a variable.

```
string gettype(mixed var);
```

This function returns the variable type of *var*. Possible values for the returned string are:

integer

double

string

array

class

object

unknown type

Example

```php
<?PHP
$i = 1;
echo gettype($i)."\n";
$a = "Test";
echo gettype($a)."\n";
$x = 1.1;
echo gettype($x)."\n";
?>
```

Output

```
Integer
String
double
```

See also settype().

----

getTimeofDay (date-time)
get the time of day

```
array gettimeofday(void);
```

This function is an interface to the system function gettimeofday().
It returns an associative array containing the elements sec, usec,
minuteswest, and dsttime. These elements correspond to the
timeval.tv_sec, timeval.tv_usec, timezone.tz_minuteswest, and
timezone.tz_dsttime system data structures, respectively. Note that if

this function returns 0, then your system does not have a gettimeofday()
function. Typically, using the value in timezone is not recommended,
because representing world-wide time zones (with all of their political
peculiarities) cannot be done so simply. For more information, refer to
your system's documentation on the gettimeofday() C function.

Example

```php
<?PHP
$today = gettimeofday();
echo "Current time in seconds: ".$today[sec]."\n";
echo "Current time in microseconds: ".$today[usec]."\n";
echo "Minutes west of Greenwich time:
  ".$today[minuteswest]."\n";
echo "Type of Daylight Savings Time correction:
  ".$today[dsttime]."\n";
?>
```

Output

```
Current time in seconds: 932349559
Current time in microseconds: 255050
Minutes west of Greenwich time: 240
Type of Daylight Savings Time correction: 0
```

See also date().

---

gmDate (date-time)
format a GMT/CUT date/time

```
string gmdate(string format, int timestamp);
```

This function is identical to the date() function, except that the time
returned is Greenwich Mean Time (GMT).

Example

For example, when run in the EST (GMT -0500) time zone, the first line
below prints *"Dec 31 1998 23:00:00"*, while the second line prints *"Jan 01
1999 04:00:00"*.

```php
<?PHP
echo date( "M d Y H:i:s",mktime(23,0,0,12,31,1998) );
echo gmdate( "M d Y H:i:s",mktime(23,0,0,12,31,1998) );
?>
```

Output

```
Dec 31 1998 23:00:00
Jan 01 1999 04:00:00
```

See also date(), mktime(), and gmmktime().

---

gmmkTime (date-time)
get UNIX timestamp for a GMT date

```
int gmmktime(int hour, int minute, int second, int month, int
day, int year);
```

> This function is identical to mktime() except the passed parameters
> represent a GMT date.

See also mktime().

---

hexDec (math)
hexadecimal to decimal

```
int hexdec(string hex_string);
```

> This function calculates and returns the decimal equivalent of the
> hexadecimal number represented by the hex_string argument. HexDec
> converts a hexadecimal string to a decimal number. The largest num-
> ber that can be converted is 7fffffff or 2147483647 in decimal.

Example

```
<?PHP
echo hexdec("0")."\n";
echo hexdec("1")."\n";
echo hexdec("20")."\n";
echo hexdec("7fffffff")."\n";
?>
```

Output

```
0
32
2147483647
```

See also dechex().

---

htmlEntities (string)
convert all applicable characters to HTML entities

```
string htmlentities(string string);
```

> This function is similar to htmlspecialchars(), except that it performs a more complete conversion to HTML special characters. The ISO-8859-1 character set is used, and because you cannot depend on browsers always to send out data in this format, avoiding the use of this function is best if you expect to support users with alternative character sets (international).

Example

```
<?PHP
for($x = 200; $x <= 220; $x++)
   echo htmlentities(chr($x));
?>
```

Output

```
&Egrave;
&Eacute;
&Ecirc;
&Euml;
&Igrave;
&Iacute;
&Icirc;
&Iuml;
&ETH;
&Ntilde;
&Ograve;
&Oacute;
&Ocirc;
&Otilde;
&Ouml;
&times;
&Oslash;
&Ugrave;
&Uacute;
&Ucirc;
&Uuml;
```

See also htmlspecialchars() and nl2br().

----

htmlSpecialChars (string)
convert special characters to HTML entities

```
string htmlspecialchars(string string);
```

> This function returns a string with HTML special characters converted
> to its equivalent HTML representation. This function returns a string
> with these conversions made. The conversions applied are:
>
> '&' (ampersand)   → '&'
>
> '"' (double quote) → '"'
>
> '<' (less than)   → '<'
>
> '>' (greater than) → '>'

Note that htmlentities() should be used if a more complete conversion is
required.

Example

```
<?PHP
$text = "<http://www.php123.com/test.php3?ID=1&NAME=>";
echo htmlspecialchars($text)."\n";
?>
```

Output

```
&lt;http://www.php123.com/test.php3?ID=1&amp;NAME=&gt;
```

See also htmlentities() and nl2br().

----

implode (string)
join array elements with a string

```
string implode(array pieces, string glue);
```

> This function returns a string containing a string representation of all
> the array elements in the same order, with the glue string between
> each element. It is the opposite of explode().

Example

The following code takes the words in the array and places them into a
single string with a space between them.

```
<?PHP
$words = array("The", "quick", "brown", "fox");
$text = implode($words, " ");
echo $text."\n";
?>
```

Output

```
The quick brown fox
```

See also explode(), join(), and split().

---

intVal (variable)
get integer value of a variable

```
int intval(mixed var, int base);
```

> This function returns the integer value of *var*, using the specified *base*
> for the conversion. The default base is 10. The system function strtol()
> is used to handle the conversion. *var* may be any scalar type. This
> function cannot be used on arrays or objects.

Example

```
<?PHP
echo intval("10", 16)."\n";
echo intval("10", 8)."\n";
echo intval("10", 2)."\n";
?>
```

Output

```
16
2
```

See also doubleval(), strval(), settype(), and Type juggling.

---

is_array (variable)
find whether a variable is an array

```
int is_array(mixed var);
```

> This function returns TRUE if *var* is an array. Otherwise, it returns
> FALSE.

Example

```
<?PHP
$a = array(1, 2, 3);
$b = 1;
if(is_array($a))
  echo "\$a is an array.";
else
  echo "\$a is not an array.";
if(is_array($b))
  echo "\$b is an array.";
else
  echo "\$b is not an array.";
?>
```

Output

```
$a is an array.
$b is not an array.
```

See also is_double(), is_float(), is_int(), is_integer(), is_real(), is_string(), is_long(), and is_object().

----

is_double (variable)
find whether a variable is a double

```
int is_double(mixed var);
```

This function returns TRUE if *var* is a double. Otherwise, it returns FALSE.

Example

```
<?PHP
$a = 1.1;
$b = 1;
if(is_double($a))
  echo "\$a is a double.";
else
  echo "\$a is not a double.";
if(is_double($b))
  echo "\$b is a double.";
else
  echo "\$b is not a double.";
?>
```

Output

```
$a is a double.
$b is not a double.
```

See also is_array(), is_float(), is_int(), is_integer(), is_real(), is_string(), is_long(), and is_object().

----

is_float (variable)
find whether a variable is a float

```
int is_float(mixed var);
```

This function is an alias for is_double().

Example: see is_double()

See also is_double(), is_real(), is_int(), is_integer(), is_string(), is_object(), is_array(), and is_long().

----

is_int (variable)
find whether a variable is an integer

```
int is_int(mixed var);
```

This function is an alias for is_long().

Example: see is_long()

See also is_double(), is_float(), is_integer(), is_string(), is_real(), is_object(), is_array(), and is_long().

----

is_integer (variable)
find whether a variable is an integer

```
int is_integer(mixed var);
```

This function is an alias for is_long().

Example: see is_long()

See also is_double(), is_float(), is_int(), is_string(), is_real(), is_object(), is_array(), and is_long().

----

is_long (variable)
find whether a variable is an integer

```
int is_long(mixed var);
```

> This function returns TRUE if *var* is an integer. Otherwise, it returns FALSE.

Example

```php
<?PHP
$a = 1.1;
$b = 1;
if(is_long($a))
  echo "\$a is a long.";
else
  echo "\$a is not a long.";
if(is_long($b))
  echo "\$b is a long.";
else
  echo "\$b is not a long.";
?>
```

Output

```
$a is not a long.
$b is a long.
```

See also is_double(), is_float(), is_int(), is_real(), is_string(), is_object(), is_array(), and is_integer().

----

is_object (variable)
find whether a variable is an object

```
int is_object(mixed var);
```

> This function returns TRUE if *var* is an object. Otherwise it returns FALSE.

Example

```php
<?PHP
class abc {}
$a = new abc;
```

```
$b = 1;
if(is_object($a))
  echo "\$a is an object.";
else
  echo "\$a is not an object.";
if(is_object($b))
  echo "\$b is an object.";
else
  echo "\$b is not an object.";
?>
```

Output

```
$a is an object.
$b is not an object.
```

See also is_long(), is_int(), is_integer(), is_float(), is_double(), is_real(), is_string(), and is_array().

----

is_real (variable)
find whether a variable is a real

```
int is_real(mixed var);
```

> This function is an alias for is_double().

Example: See is_double().

See also is_long(), is_int(), is_integer(), is_float(), is_double(), is_object(), is_string(), and is_array().

----

is_string (variable)
find whether a variable is a string

```
int is_string(mixed var);
```

> This function returns TRUE if *var* is a string. Otherwise, it returns FALSE.

Example

```
<?PHP
$a = 1.1;
$b = "abc";
```

```
if(is_string($a))
   echo "\$a is a string.";
else
   echo "\$a is not a string.";
if(is_string($b))
   echo "\$b is a string.";
else
   echo "\$b is not a string.";
?>
```

Output

```
$a is not a string.
$b is a string.
```

See also is_long(), is_int(), is_integer(), is_float(), is_double(), is_real(), is_object(), and is_array().

----

isSet (variable)
determine whether a variable is set

```
int isset(mixed var);
```

> This function returns TRUE if *var* exists and has a value. Otherwise, it returns FALSE.

Example

```
<?PHP
$a = 1;
if(isset($a))
   echo "\$a exists.";
if(isset($b))
   echo "\$b exists.";
?>
```

Output

```
$a exists.
```

See also empty().

----

jDToJulian (calendar)
convert a Julian Day Count to a Julian calendar date

```
string jdtojulian(int julianday);
```

> Converts Julian Day Count to a string containing the Julian Calendar
> Date in the format month/day/year.

---

join (string)
join array elements with a string

```
string join(array pieces, string glue);
```

This function is identical to implode().

Example: See implode().

See also implode().

JulianToJD (calendar)
convert a Julian calendar date to Julian Day Count

```
int juliantojd(int month, int day, int year);
```

> This function converts the given Julian calendar date to a Julian Day
> Count. The Julian Day Count is used as an intermediary in converting
> between different calendar formats. The valid range for Julian calendar
> dates are from 4713 B.C. to 9999 A.D. Note that the Julian calendar
> was created in 46 B.C., therefore the use of this function on dates
> before this date is not meaningful.

See also JDToJulian().

---

key (array)
fetch a key from an associative array

```
mixed key(array array);
```

> key() returns the index element of the current array position.

See also current() next().

---

ksort (array)
sort an array by key

```
int ksort(array array);
```

> This function sorts an associative array by key, while maintaining key-to-data correlations. This is useful mainly for associative arrays.

Example

```
<?PHP
$id  = array("Joe" => 333, "Bob" => 222, "Jill" => 111,
  "Janice" => 999);
ksort($id);
do {
  echo key($id)." ID # ".current($id)."\n";
} while (next($id));
?>
```

Output

```
Bob ID # 222
Janice ID # 999
Jill ID # 111
Joe ID # 333
```

See also asort(), arsort(), sort(), and rsort().

----

list (array)
assign variables as if they were an array

```
void list(...);
```

> This function is used to assign an array to a list of variables.

Example

```
<?PHP
$ar = array(1, 2, 3);
list($a, $b, $c) = $ar;
echo $a."\n";
echo $b."\n";
echo $c."\n";
?>
```

Output

```
1
2
3
```

See also array().

---

log (math)(x)
natural logarithm

```
float log(float number);
```

> This function calculates and returns the natural logarithm of *number*.

Example

```
<?PHP
echo log(1)."\n";
echo log(exp(1))."\n";
echo log(exp(1) * exp(1))."\n";
?>
```

Output

```
0
1
2
```

See also exp().

---

log10 (math)(x)
base-10 logarithm

```
float log10(float number);
```

> This function calculates and returns the base-10 logarithm of *number*.

Example

```
<?PHP
echo log10(1)."\n";
echo log10(10)."\n";
echo log10(10 * 10)."\n";
?>
```

Output

```
0
1
2
```

See also pow().

----

ltrim (string)
strip white space from the beginning of a string

```
string ltrim(string str);
```

> This function strips white space from the start of a string, and returns
> the stripped string.

Example

```
<?PHP
$word="     ABCabc        ";
echo "String: '".$word."'\n";
echo "String after ltrim(): '".ltrim($word)."'\n";
?>
```

Output

```
String: '     ABCabc        '
String after ltrim(): 'ABCabc        '
```

See also chop() and trim().

----

max (math)
find largest value

```
mixed max(mixed number1, mixed number2, mixed numberN);
```

> This function returns the numerically largest value of the given values.
> If the first parameter is an array, max() returns the highest value in that
> array. If the first parameter is an integer, string or double, then you need
> at least two parameters and max() returns the largest of these values.
> With this function, you can compare an unlimited number of values. If
> one or more of the values is a double, then all the values will be treated
> as doubles, and a double is returned. If none of the values is a double,
> then all of them will be treated as integers, and an integer is returned.

Example

```
<?PHP
echo max(0, 1)."\n";
echo max(1, 2, 3, 4, 5)."\n";
$a = array(0, 1, 2, 3, 4, 5, 6);
echo min($a)."\n";
?>
```

Output

```
1
5
6
```

See also min().

----

md5 (string)
calculate the md5 hash of a string

```
string md5(string str);
```

> This function calculates the MD5 hash of *str* using the MD5 Message-Digest Algorithm from RSA Data Security, Inc. The MD5 hash is a 128-bit fingerprint of *str*. It is believed to be computationally impossible to find two strings that have the same MD5 hash or to generate an arbitrary string given its MD5 hash. See RFC 1321 for more information on MD5.

Example

The code below shows how to calculate the MD5 hash of a file.

```
<?PHP
$file_name = "/home/httpd/html/index.html";
$index = file($file_name);
echo md5($index);
?>
```

Output

```
4410ec34d9e6c1a68100ca0ce033fb17
```

----

microtime (date-time)
return current UNIX timestamp with microseconds

```
string microtime(void);
```

> This function returns a string containing "msec sec" where sec is the current time measured in the number of seconds since the Unix Epoch (0:00:00 January 1, 1970 GMT), and msec is the microseconds part. This function is available only on operating systems that support the gettimeofday() system call.

Example 1.

The code below shows the number of microseconds and seconds since the Epoch. The microsecond time is displayed before the second time.

```
<?PHP
echo "The number of seconds and microseconds since the
Epoch: ";
echo microtime() . "\n";
?>
```

Output

```
The number of seconds and microseconds since the Epoch:
0.36525700 921112347
```

Example 2

The code below shows a more useful application of microtime() using a user-defined function to parse out the time in microseconds to calculate time intervals.

```
<?PHP
function getmicrotime(){
   $t = microtime();
   $t = explode(" ", $t);
   $total = $t[1] + $t[0];
   return ($total);
}

$start = getmicrotime();
sleep(1);
$finish = getmicrotime();
```

```
echo "Elapsed: ".($finish - $start);
?>
```

Output

```
Elapsed: 1.0070600509644
```

See also time().

---

min (math)
find smallest value

```
mixed min(mixed number1, mixed number2, mixed numberN);
```

> This function returns the numerically smallest of the given values. If
> the first parameter is an array, min() returns the smallest value in that
> array. If the first parameter is an integer, string or double, then you
> need at least two parameters and min() returns the smallest of these
> values. With this function, you can compare an unlimited number of
> values. If one or more of the values is a double, then all the values will
> be treated as doubles, and a double is returned. If none of the values is
> a double, then all of them will be treated as integers, and an integer is
> returned.

Example

```
<?PHP
echo max(0, 1)."\n";
echo max(1, 2, 3, 4, 5)."\n";
$a = array(0, 1, 2, 3, 4, 5, 6);
echo min($a)."\n";
?>
```

Output

```
0
1
0
```

See also max().

---

mktime (date-time)
get UNIX timestamp for a date

```
int mktime(int hour, int minute, int second, int month,
int day, int year);
```

> This function returns the Unix timestamp corresponding to the given arguments. This timestamp is a long integer containing the number of seconds that have elapsed between the Unix Epoch (00:00:00 on January 1, 1970) and the specified time. Arguments may be omitted in order from right to left. Any arguments that are omitted will be set to the current value according to the local date and time. MkTime is generally useful for doing date arithmetic.

Example

The following code will display the number of seconds in a year using arithmetic on UNIX timestamps.

```
<?PHP
echo "There are ";
echo mktime(0,0,0,1,1,1999) - mktime(0,0,0,1,1,1998);
echo " seconds in a year.\n";
?>
```

Output:

```
There are 31536000 seconds in a year.
```

See also date(), time(), and gmmktime().

----

next (array)
advance the internal array pointer

```
mixed next(array array);
```

> This function returns the array element in the next place that is pointed by the internal array pointer, or FALSE If there are no more elements. Warning: If the array contains empty elements then this function will return FALSE for these elements as well. To properly traverse an array that may contain empty elements, see the each() function.

next() behaves like current(), with one difference: It advances the internal array pointer one place forward before returning the element. That means it returns the next array element and advances the internal array pointer by one. If advancing the internal array pointer results in going beyond the end of the element list, next() returns FALSE.

Example:

```
<?PHP
$student = array("Joe", "Bob", "Jill", "Janice");

do {
  echo current($student)."<br>";
} while (next($student));
?>
```

Output

```
Joe
Bob
Jill
Janice
```

See also current(), end(), prev() and reset().

----

nl2br (string)
convert newlines to HTML line breaks

```
string nl2br(string string);
```

This function returns a string with "<BR>" (HTML line break) inserted before all newlines ('\n').

Example

```
<?PHP
$hosts = file("/etc/hosts");
$x = 0;
while($hosts[$x])
  echo nl2br($hosts[$x++]);
?>
```

Output

(output will vary depending on the contents of /etc/hosts)

```
127.0.0.1  localhost localhost.localdomain<br>
192.168.0.1  example.com<br>
```

See also htmlspecialchars() and htmlentities().

---

number_format (math)

format a number with grouped thousands

```
string number_format (float number, int decimals, string
dec_point, string thousands_sep);
```

> This function returns a formatted version of *number*. This function
> can accept one, two, or four parameters, but not three. If only one
> parameter is given, *number* will be formatted without decimals, but
> with a comma (,) between every group of thousands. If two parameters
> are given, *number* will be formatted with *decimals* decimals with a
> dot (.) in front and a comma (,) between every group of thousands. If all
> four parameters are given, *number* will be formatted with *decimals*
> decimals, *dec_point* instead of a dot (.) before the decimals and *thou-
> sands_sep* instead of a comma (,) between every group of thousands.

Example

```
<?PHP
echo number_format(0)."\n";
echo number_format(1000)."\n";
echo number_format(1000000, 2)."\n";
echo number_format(1000000, 2, ",", ".")."\n";
?>
```

Output

```
0
1,000
1,000,000.00
1.000.000,00
```

---

octDec (math)
octal to decimal

```
int octdec(string octal_string);
```

> This function calculates and returns the decimal equivalent of the
> octal number represented by *octal_string*. The largest number that can
> be converted is 17777777777 in octal or 2147483647 in decimal.

Example

```php
<?PHP
echo octdec("0")."\n";
echo octdec("1")."\n";
echo octdec("20")."\n";
echo octdec("17777777777")."\n";
?>
```

Output

```
0
1
16
2147483647
```

See also decoct().

---

ord (string)
return ASCII value of character

```
int ord(string string);
```

> This function returns the ASCII value of the first character of string.
> This function is the opposite of chr().

Example

```php
<?PHP
$str = "ABCDEF";
for($x = 0; $x < strlen($str); $x++)
  echo ord($str[$x])." ";
?>
```

Output

```
65 66 67 68 69 70
```

----

parse_str (string)
parse the string into variables

```
void parse_str(string str);
```

> This function parses *str* as if it were the query string passed via an URL, and it sets the appropriate variables.

Example

```php
<?PHP
$url = "http://www.php123.com/test.php3?id=123&name=Joe+User";
$url = strtok($url, "?");
$url = strtok("?");
parse_str($url);
echo "ID #: ".$id."\n";
echo "Name: ".$name."\n";
?>
```

Output

```
ID #: 123
Name: Joe User
```

----

parse_url (url)
parse a URL and return its components

```
array parse_url(string url);
```

> This function returns an associative array containing the broken-down components of the specified URL. The elements in the associative array returned are:
>
> | Array | Description |
> | --- | --- |
> | *$a[scheme]* | This specifies the protocol used. Some of the more common schemes are ftp, http, gopher, mailto, and news. |

Array	Description
$a[host]	The domain name or IP address of a network host.
$a[port]	The port to connect to. Most schemes have a default port number, such as port 80 for http.
$a[user]	An optional user name. Some schemes, such as ftp, allow the specification of a user name.
$a[pass]	An optional password. Some schemes, such as ftp, allow the specification of a password.
$a[path]	Some schemes, such as ftp and httpd, allow for the specification of a hierarchical path. It is separated from the host name with a slash (/).
$a[query]	HTTP allows for the specification of a query string. It is separated from the path with a question mark (?).
$a[fragment]	The HTTP scheme defines a fragment, also called an anchor, separated from the path with a pound sign (#).

For more information on how URLs are constructed, see RFC1738, "Uniform Resource Locators (URL)."

Example

```
<?PHP
$url =
parse_url("http://www.php123.com:8080/test/abc.php3?ID=1");
echo "scheme: ".$url[scheme]."\n";
echo "host: ".$url[host]."\n";
echo "port: ".$url[port]."\n";
echo "user: ".$url[user]."\n";
echo "password: ".$url[pass]."\n";
echo "path: ".$url[path]."\n";
echo "query: ".$url[query]."\n";
echo "fragment: ".$url[fragment]."\n\n";

$url =
parse_url("ftp://user_name:password@www.php123.com/pub/php.
  zip");
echo "scheme: ".$url[scheme]."\n";
echo "host: ".$url[host]."\n";
echo "port: ".$url[port]."\n";
echo "user: ".$url[user]."\n";
echo "password: ".$url[pass]."\n";
echo "path: ".$url[path]."\n";
```

```
echo "query: ".$url[query]."\n";
echo "fragment: ".$url[fragment]."\n";
?>
```

Output

```
scheme: http
host: www.php123.com
port: 8080
user:
password:
path: /test/abc.php3
query: ID=1
fragment:

scheme: ftp
host: www.php123.com
port:
user: user_name
password: password
path: /put/php.zip
query:
fragment:
```

---

pi (math)
get value of pi

```
double pi(void );
```

> This function returns an approximation of pi.

Example

```
<?PHP
echo pi()."\n";
?>
```

Output

```
3.1415926535898
```

---

pos (array)
return the current element in an array

```
mixed pos(array array);
```

> This is an alias for current().

Example

```PHP
<?PHP

$student = array("Joe", "Bob", "Jill", "Janice");

do {
  echo pos($student)."<br>";
} while (each($student));

?>
```

Output

```
Joe
Bob
Jill
Janice
```

See also end(), next(), prev(), and reset().

----

pow (math)
exponential expression

```
float pow(float base, float exp);
```

> This function calculates and returns *base* raised to the power of *exp*.

Example

```PHP
<?PHP
echo pow(1, 0)."\n";
echo pow(1, 1)."\n";
echo pow(2, 20)."\n";
echo pow(2, 31)."\n";
?>
```

Output

```
1
1
1048576
2147483648
```

See also exp().

----

prev (array)
rewind internal array pointer

```
mixed prev(array array);
```

> This function returns the array element from *array* in the previous place that is pointed by the internal array pointer, or it returns FALSE if there are no more elements. Note: If the array contains empty elements, then this function will return FALSE for these elements as well. To properly traverse an array that may contain empty elements, see the each() function. This function is like next(), except it rewinds the internal array pointer one place instead of advancing it.

Example

```
<?PHP
$student = array("Joe", "Bob", "Jill", "Janice");
end($student);
echo current($student)."<br>";
prev($student);
echo current($student)."<br>";
?>
```

Output

```
Janice
Jill
```

See also current(), end(), next(), and reset().

---

print (string)
print — output a string

```
print(string arg);
```

> This function outputs whatever string is contained in *arg*.

Example

```
<?PHP
print date("F d, Y, H:i:s", time())."\n";
print "ABCabc\n";
?>
```

Output

```
January 1, 2000, 00:00:00
ABCabc
```

See also echo(), printf(), and flush().

----

printf (string)
output a formatted string

```
int printf(string format, mixed args...);
```

> This function produces formatted output. It is a way to exert finer
> control over the output than either *echo*() or *print*() provides. Its out-
> put is specified according to *format*. The format string is described in
> the documentation for sprintf(). This function is similar to the Unix C
> function printf().

Example

The first call to printf simply outputs the specified string. The second call
formats the output so that it has leading #s, for example, an amount printed
on a check. The next uses the default padding character, a space. The next
two calls show how positive and negative padding values can be used
to either left- or right-justify the output. The next-to-last call shows how
floating-point number output can be controlled. The last call shows how to
display values in hexadecimal.

```
<?PHP
$str = '$101.95';
$amount = 0.12;
printf("%s\n", $str);
printf("%'#10s##\n", $str);
printf("%10s\n", $str);
printf("%-10s\n", $str);
printf("%2.1f\n", $amount);
printf("%X\n", 255);
?>
```

Output

```
$101.95
###$101.95##
   $101.95
$101.95
```

```
0.1
FF
```

See also print(), sprintf(), and flush().

---

quoted_printable_decode (string)
convert a quoted-printable string to an 8-bit string

```
string quoted_printable_decode(string str);
```

> This function takes a quoted-printable string *str* and returns an 8-bit
> binary decoded version of it. Quoted-printable encoding is intended to
> be used on data that consists mainly of human-readable ASCII text
> with a few 8-bit binary characters. If the text encoded is largely ASCII
> text, then the encoded version of it is mostly human-readable, and it
> will survive being sent via e-mail through most character-translating
> and line-wrapping systems. The most common use for this function is
> to decode e-mail. For more information on quoted_printable_decode(),
> see RFC 1521, "MIME (Multipurpose Internet Mail Extensions) Part
> One: Mechanisms for Specifying and Describing the Format of Inter-
> net Message Bodies."

Example

```
<?PHP
$str = "Aim=E9e\nJean-Ren=E9\n";
echo quoted_printable_decode($str);
?>
```

Output

```
Aimée
Jean-René
```

---

quoteMeta (string)
quote meta characters

```
int quotemeta(string str);
```

> This function accepts a string *str* and returns a version with a back-
> slash character (\) before every character that is one of the following:
> . \ + * ? [^] ($)

Example

```
<?PHP
$str = "C:\WINDOWS\*.*";
echo quotemeta($str);
?>
```

Output

```
C:\\WINDOWS\\\*\.\*
```

See also addslashes(), htmlentities(), htmlspecialchars(), and nl2br().

----

rand (math)
generate a random value

```
int rand(void );
```

> This function returns a pseudo-random value between 0 and
> RAND_MAX. For example, if you want a random number between
> 100 and 1000, use "rand() % 1000 + 100." Typically, you should seed
> the random number generator before use with srand(). The sequence of
> numbers is repeatable if srand() is called with the same number.

Example

The first three calls to rand() are used to generate a random number between
0 and RAND_MAX. The next line generates a random number between 0
and 9. The next line generates a random number between 0 and 100. The
last line generates a random number between 100 and 1199.

```
<?PHP
echo rand()."\n";
echo rand()."\n";
echo rand()."\n";
echo (rand() % 10)."\n";
echo (rand() % 100)."\n";
echo ((rand() % 1000) + 100)."\n";
?>
```

Output

(output will vary depending upon the return value of rand())

```
716248711
843591640
```

```
379949409
7
56
349
```

See also srand() and getrandmax().

----

rawURLdecode (string)
decode URL encoded strings

```
string rawurldecode(string str);
```

> This function accepts string *str* and returns a string in which URL-encoded characters (percent (%) sign followed by two hex digits) have been replaced with the characters that they represent. For more information on URL encoding, see RFC 1738, "Uniform Resource Locators (URL)."

Example

```
<?PHP
$str = "http://www.php123.com/%7Ejoeuser";
echo rawurldecode($str)."\n";
$str = "joeuser%40php123.com";
echo rawurldecode($str)."\n";
?>
```

Output

```
http://www.php123.com/~joeuser
joeuser@php123.com
```

See also rawurlencode().

----

rawURLencode (string)
URL-encode a string

```
string rawurlencode(string str);
```

> This function accepts a string *str*, and returns a string that is URL-encoded. Certain characters are replaced by a percent (%) sign followed by two hexadecimal digits that represent the ASCII value of the character. All non-alphanumeric characters except - (dash), _ (underscore), and . (period) are replaced in this manner. For more information on URL encoding, see RFC 1738, "Uniform Resource Locators (URL)."

Example

```
<?PHP
$str = "http://www.php123.com/~joeuser";
echo rawurlencode($str)."\n";
$str = "joeuser@php123.com";
echo rawurlencode($str)."\n";
?>
```

Output

```
http%3A%2F%2Fwww.php123.com%2F%7Ejoeuser
joeuser%40php123.com
```

See also rawurldecode().

----

reset (array)
set internal pointer of array to first element

```
reset(array array);
```

reset() rewinds the array's internal pointer to the first element.

Example

```
<?PHP
$student = array("Joe", "Bob", "Jill", "Janice");
end($student);
echo current($student)."<br>";
reset($student);
echo current($student)."<br>";
?>
```

Output

```
Janice
Joe
```

See also current(), next(), prev(), and reset().

----

round (math)
round a float

```
double round(double number);
```

This function calculates and returns the rounded value of *number*.

Example

```php
<?PHP
echo round(1)."\n";
echo round(1.1)."\n";
echo round(1.49)."\n";
echo round(1.5)."\n";
?>
```

Output

```
1
1
2
2
```

See also ceil() and floor().

----

rsort (array)
sort an array in reverse order

```
void rsort(array array);
```

This function sorts an array in reverse order (highest to lowest).

Example

```php
<?PHP

$student = array("Joe", "Bob", "Jill", "Janice");

rsort($student);

do {
  echo current($student)."<br>";
} while (each($student));

?>
```

Output

```
Joe
Jill
Janice
Bob
```

See also arsort(), asort(), ksort(), sort(), and usort().

----

setLocale (string)
set locale information

```
string setlocale(string category, string locale);
```

category is a string specifying the category of the functions affected by the locale setting:

- LC_ALL for all of the below
- LC_CTYPE for character classification and conversion, for example, strtolower()
- LC_MONETARY for localeconv() (not currently implemented in PHP)
- LC_NUMERIC for decimal separator
- LC_TIME for date and time formatting with strftime()

If locale is the empty string "", the locale names will be set from the values of environment variables with the same names as the above categories, or from "LANG".

If locale is zero or "0", the locale setting is not affected and only the current setting is returned.

Setlocale returns the new current locale, or FALSE if the locale functionality is not implemented in the platform, the specified locale does not exist or the category name is invalid. Attempting to use an invalid category name will cause a warning message to be printed.

---

setType (variable)
set the type of a variable

```
int settype(string var, string type);
```

This function sets the type of variable *var* to *type*. Possible values of *type* are:

```
integer
double
string
array
object
```

This function returns TRUE if successful. Otherwise, it returns FALSE.

Example

```
<?PHP
$a = 123;
echo "\$a is now an ".gettype($a)."\n";
settype($a, "array");
echo "\$a is now an ".gettype($a)."\n";
echo $a[0]."\n";

$a = 123;
settype($a, "string");
echo "\$a is now a ".gettype($a)."\n";
echo $a."\n";
?>
```

Output

```
$a is now an integer
$a is now an array
123
$a is now a string
123
```

See also gettype().

----

sin (math)
sine

```
float sin(float number);
```

> This function calculates and returns the sine of *number* in radians.

Example

```
<?PHP
echo sin(pi()/4)."\n";
echo sin(pi()/2)."\n";
?>
```

Output

```
0.70710678118655
1
```

See also cos() and tan().

----

sizeof (array)
get size of array

```
int sizeof(array array);
```

This function returns the number of elements in the array. It is identical to the *count()* function.

Example

```
<?PHP
$student = array("Joe", "Bob", "Jill", "Janice");
echo "The number of elements: ".sizeof($student)."\n";
?>
```

Output

```
The number of elements: 4
```

See also count().

----

similar_text (string)
calculate the similarity between two strings

```
int similar_text(string first, string second, double
[percent]);
```

This function calculates the similarity between the two given strings. The number of matching characters in the two strings is returned. If the third parameter is passed by reference, then this function will calculate the percentage.

Example

```
<?PHP
$str1 = "The quick brown fox";
$str2 = "The quick red fox";
echo similar_text($str1, $str2, &$a)."\n";
echo $a."\n";

$str1 = "ABCDEFFFFFFGHIJKLMN";
$str2 = "ABCDEFGHIJKLMN";
echo similar_text($str1, $str2, &$a)."\n";
```

```
echo $a."\n";
?>
```

Output

```
15
83.333333333333
14
84.848484848485
```

---

sort (array)
sort an array

```
void sort(array array);
```

> This function sorts an array. Elements are arranged from lowest to highest when this function completes.

Example

```php
<?PHP

$student = array("Joe", "Bob", "Jill", "Janice");

sort($student);

do {
  echo current($student)."<br>";
} while (each($student));

?>
```

Output

```
Bob
Janice
Jill
Joe
```

See also arsort(), asort(), ksort(), rsort(), and usort().

---

soundex (string)
calculate the soundex key of a string

```
string soundex(string str);
```

This function returns the Soundex key for the given string *str*. Soundex maps similar-sounding words to the same codes. It was originally designed to discover similar-sounding names for telephone directory assistance, but it can also be used on arbitrary words. This function can be used to simplify searches in databases where you know the pronunciation but are not sure of spelling. This soundex function returns a string four characters long, starting with a letter. The soundex function used in PHP is the one described by Donald Knuth in *The Art of Computer Programming, Vol. 3: Sorting and Searching*, Addison-Wesley (1973), pp. 391–392.

Example

```
<?PHP
$str1 = "Smith";
$str2 = "Smyth";
echo soundex($str1)." ".soundex($str2)."\n";

$str1 = "Frye";
$str2 = "Fry";
echo soundex($str1)." ".soundex($str2)."\n";

$str1 = "Boan";
$str2 = "Bone";
echo soundex($str1)." ".soundex($str2)."\n";
?>
```

Output

```
S530 S530
F600 F600
B500 B500
```

split (string)
split string into array by regular expression

```
array split(string pattern, string string, int limit);
```

This function uses the regular expression *pattern* to split *string* into parts. It returns an array of strings, where each is a substring of *string* divided by occurrences of *pattern*. If an error occurs, it returns FALSE.

Example

Below, the first call to split() is used to separate a /etc/passwd entry into its components. The second call is used to extract a query string from a URL.

```
<?PHP
$line = "joeuser:*:1100:100:Joe User:/home/joeuser:/bin/sh";
$passwd = split(":", $line);
echo "UID: ".$passwd[2]."\n";
echo "Home directory: ".$passwd[5]."\n";

$url = "http://www.php123.com/test.php3?id=1&name=Joe+User";
$query_string = split("\?", $url, 5);
echo $query_string[1]."\n";
?>
```

Output

```
UID: 1100
Home directory: /home/joeuser
id=1&name=Joe+User
```

----

sprintf (string)
return a formatted string

```
sprintf(string format, mixed args...);
```

> This function returns a string generated according to a set of rules
> defined by the *format* string applied to the subsequent arguments.

The format string is composed by zero or more directives. They are ordinary
characters (other than %) that are copied directly to the output string, and
conversion specifications, each of which is applied to the next parameter,
in sequence.

Each conversion specification consists of these elements, in order:

1. An optional number that specifies the character to use to pad the
   results of the string. The default pad character is a space. A common
   pad character is 0. An alternate padding character can be specified by
   prefixing it with a single quote ('). See the examples below.

2. An optional alignment specifier that says if the result should be left-
   justified or right-justified. The default is right-justified. A - character
   placed here will make it left-justified.

3. An optional width specifier that says the minimum number of characters this conversion should produce.

4. An optional precision specifier that says how many decimal digits
   should be displayed for floating-point numbers. This option has no
   effect for other types than double.

5. A type specifier that says what type the argument data should be
    treated as. Possible types:

    %   a literal percent character. No argument is required.
    b   the argument is treated as an integer, and presented as a binary
        number.
    c   the argument is treated as an integer, and presented as the char-
        acter with that ASCII value.
    d   the argument is treated as an integer, and presented as a decimal
        number.
    f   the argument is treated as a double, and presented as a floating-
        point number.
    o   the argument is treated as an integer, and presented as an octal
        number.
    s   the argument is treated as and presented as a string.
    x   the argument is treated as an integer and presented as a hexadec-
        imal number (with lowercase letters).
    X   the argument is treated as an integer and presented as a hexadec-
        imal number (with uppercase letters).

Note: The above description of format specifiers applies to both sprintf() and
printf().

Example

The first call to sprintf simply places the specified string in the output
string. The second call formats the output string so that it has leading #'s,
for example, an amount printed on a check. The next uses the default
padding character, a space. The next two calls show how positive and negative padding values can be used to either left- or right-justify the string. The
next-to-last call shows how floating-point number output can be controlled.
The last call shows how to display values in hexadecimal.

```php
<?PHP
$str = '$101.95';
$amount = 0.12;
echo sprintf("%s", $str)."\n";
echo sprintf("%'#10s##", $str)."\n";
echo sprintf("%10s", $str)."\n";
echo sprintf("%-10s", $str)."\n";
echo sprintf("%2.1f", $amount)."\n";
echo sprintf("%X", 255)."\n";
?>
```

Output

```
$101.95
###$101.95##
  $101.95
$101.95
 0.1
FF
```

See also printf().

----

sql_regcase (string)
make regular expression for case-insensitive match

```
string sql_regcase(string string);
```

This function returns a regular expression that will make a case-insensitive match to *string*. This expression is *string* with each character converted to a bracket expression. This bracket expression contains the character's uppercase and lowercase form, or the original character twice, if it does not have an appropriate upper- and lowercase form. This function can be used to add case-insensitive pattern matching to functions and databases that support only case-sensitive regular expressions.

Example

```
<?PHP
$str = "Joe User";
echo sql_regcase($str);
?>
```

Output

```
[Jj][Oo][Ee][ ][Uu][Ss][Ee][Rr]
```

----

strchr (string)
find first occurrence of a character

```
string strchr(string haystack, string needle);
```

This function is identical to strstr().

Example: See strstr().

----

strcmp (string)
binary-safe string comparison

```
int strcmp(string str1, string str2);
```

> This function compares two strings. It returns less than zero (0) if *str1*
> is less than *str2*, greater than zero (0) if str1 is greater than str2, and
> zero (0) if they are equal. It is similar to the Unix C function strcmp().
> Note: The comparison is case-sensitive.

Example

```
<?PHP
$str1 = "Carter";
$str2 = "Johnson";
echo strcmp($str1, $str2)."\n";

$str1 = "Johnson";
$str2 = "Carter";
echo strcmp($str1, $str2)."\n";

$str1 = "Johnson";
$str2 = "Johnson";
echo strcmp($str1, $str2)."\n";
?>
```

Output

```
-7
7
0
```

See also ereg(), substr(), and strstr().

----

strcspn (string)
find length of initial segment not matching mask

```
int strcspn(string str, string reject);
```

> This function ("string complement span") returns the number of ini-
> tial characters in *str* that do not contain any of the characters of *reject*.
> In other words, the return value is the offset of the first character of *str*
> that is a member of the set *reject*.

Example

```
<?PHP
$url = "http://www.php123.com/test.php3?id=123";
echo "The query string is at location: ".strcspn($url,
"?")."\n";
?>
```

Output

```
The query string is at location: 31
```

See also strspn().

----

stripSlashes (string)
unquote string quoted with addslashes

```
string stripslashes(string str);
```

This function accepts string *str*, and returns a string with backslashes stripped off.

Example

```
<?PHP
$str = "2\' 10 \" in length";
echo stripslashes($str);
?>
```

Output

```
2' 10 " in length
```

See also addslashes().

----

strlen (string)
get string length

```
int strlen(string str);
```

This function returns the length of string.

Example

```
<?PHP
$str = "The quick brown fox";
echo strlen($str);
?>
```

Output

19

---

strrpos (string)
find position of last occurrence of a char in a string

```
string strrpos(string haystack, char needle);
```

> This function looks for the string *needle* in the string *haystack*. It
> returns the numeric position of the last occurrence of *needle* in
> *haystack*. *needle* can be only a single character. If *needle* contains
> more than one character, then only the first one is used. If *needle* is
> not found, then it returns FALSE.

Example

```
<?PHP
$str = "The quick brown fox";
echo strrpos($str, "o");
?>
```

Output

17

See also strpos(), strrchr(), substr(), and strstr().

---

strpos (string)
find position of first occurrence of a string

```
string strpos(string haystack, string needle);
```

> This function looks for the string *needle* in the string *haystack*. It
> returns the numeric position of the first occurrence of *needle* in the
> *haystack*. If needle is not found, then it returns FALSE.

Example

```php
<?PHP
$str = "The quick brown fox";
echo strpos($str, "o");
?>
```

Output

12

See also strrpos(), strrchr(), substr(), and strstr().

---

strrchr (string)
find the last occurrence of a character in a string

```
string strrchr(string haystack, string needle);
```

> This function looks for the string *needle* in the string *haystack* starting at the end of *haystack*. It returns a string containing the last occurrence of *needle* in the string *haystack*. If *needle* is not found, then it returns FALSE. If *needle* contains more than one character, then the only first one is used.

Example

```php
<?PHP
$str = "The quick brown fox";
echo strrchr($str, "o");
?>
```

Output

ox

See also substr() and strstr().

---

strrev (string)
reverse a string

```
string strrev(string string);
```

> This function returns any string in the reverse order.

Example

```
<?PHP
$str = "The quick brown fox";
echo strrev($str);
?>
```

Output

```
xof nworb kciuq ehT
```

---

strspn (string)
find length of initial segment matching mask

```
int strspn(string str, string accept);
```

> This function ("string span") returns the initial number of characters in *str* that consist entirely of characters of the set *accept*. The order of the characters in *accept* is not important. In other words, the return value is the offset of the first character of *str* that is not a member of *accept*.

Example

```
<?PHP
$str = "the quick brown fox...";
echo "The first character that is not either a lower case
  letter or a space is at: ".strspn($str,
"abcdefghijklmnopqrstuvwxyz ")."\n";
?>
```

Output

```
The first character that is not either a lower case letter or a
space is at: 19
```

See also strcspn().

---

strstr (string)
find first occurrence of a string

```
string strstr(string haystack, string needle);
```

> This function looks for the string *needle* in the string *haystack*. It returns a string containing the first occurrence of *needle* to the end on the string *haystack*. If *needle* is not found, then it returns FALSE.

Example

```
<?PHP
$str = "The quick brown fox";
echo strstr($str, "brown");
?>
```

Output

```
Brownfox
```

See also strrchr(), substr(), and ereg().

----

strtok (string)
tokenize string

```
string strtok(string arg1, string arg2);
```

> This function is called multiple times to split a string into a series of tokens. For example, the string "The quick brown fox" could tokenize into its individual words by using the space character as the token. The first call to strtok() has two parameters. The first is the string to tokenize, and the second is the token. Subsequent calls to strtok() need only the token as a parameter.

Example 1

```
<?PHP
$str = "The quick brown fox";
$word = strtok($str, " ");
while($word) {
   echo $word;
   $word = strtok(" ");
?>
```

Output 1

```
Thequickbrownfox
```

Example 2

The example below shows how to use strtok() to convert a date in one format (YYYY-MM-DD) read from a database into the format that most people are used to seeing (MM-DD-YYYY);

```
<?PHP
$date_str = "2000-01-01";
$y = strtok($date_str, "-");
$m = strtok("-");
$d = strtok("-");
printf("%02d-%02d-%04d", $m, $d, $y);
?>
```

Output 2

```
01-01-2000
```

See also split() and explode().

----

strtolower (string)
make a string lower-case

```
string strtolower(string str);
```

> This function accepts a string *str*, and returns a string with all alphabetic characters converted to lowercase. Note that 'alphabetic' is determined by the current locale. For instance, in the default "C" locale, characters such as umlaut-A (Ä) will not be converted.

Example

```
<?PHP
$str = "The quick brown fox";
echo strtolower($str);
?>
```

Output

```
the quick brown fox
```

See also strtoupper() and ucfirst().

----

strtoupper (string)
make a string uppercase

```
string strtoupper(string string);
```

> This function accepts a string *str*, and returns a string with all alphabetic characters converted to uppercase. Note that 'alphabetic' is determined by the current locale. For instance, in the default "C" locale, characters such as umlaut-A (Ä) will not be converted.

Example

```
<?PHP
$str = "The quick brown fox";
echo strtoupper($str);
?>
```

Output

```
THE QUICK BROWN FOX
```

See also strtolower() and ucfirst().

---

strtr (string)
translate certain characters

```
string strtr(string str, string from, string to);
```

> This function accepts a string *str* and translates all occurrences of each character in *from* to the corresponding character in *to*. The result is returned. Note: If *from* and *to* are different lengths, then the extra characters in the longer one are ignored.

Example

```
<?PHP
$str = "The quick brown fox";
echo strtr($str, " ", "-")."\n";
$str = "The quick brown fox";
echo strtr($str, "q", "Q")."\n";
?>
```

Output

```
The-quick-brown-fox
The Quick brown fox
```

See also ereg_replace().

----

strval (variable)
get string value of a variable

```
string strval(mixed var);
```

> This function returns the string value of *var. var* may be any scalar
> type. This function cannot be used on arrays or objects.

Example
```
<?PHP
$a = 123456;
$str = strval($a);
echo "The third character of $a is $str[2]\n";
?>
```

Output
```
The third character of 123456 is 3
```

See also doubleval(), intval(), settype(), and Type juggling.

----

substr (string)
return part of a string

```
string substr(string string, int start, int length);
```

> This function accepts a string *str,* and returns a portion of the string
> specified by *start* and *length.* If start is positive, the returned string
> will begin at the *start* characters into the string. If *start* is negative,
> the returned string will begin at the *start* characters from the end of
> string. If *length* is given and it is positive, the string returned will end
> *length* characters from start. If this would result in a string with nega-
> tive length, then the returned string will contain the single character
> at *start.* If *length* is given and it is negative, the string returned will
> end *length* characters from the end of string. If this would result in a
> string with negative length, then the returned string will contain the
> single character at *start.*

Example 1

```
<?PHP
$str = "The quick brown fox";
echo substr($str, 4, 5);
echo substr($str, 3, -3)."\n";
?>
```

Output 1

```
quick
quick brown
```

Example 2

The example below demonstrates how to use substr() to shorten an expanded ZIP-code (also called ZIP+4) to just the first 5 digits.

```
<?PHP
$zip = "29301-1234";
echo substr($zip, 0, 5)."\n";
?>
```

Output 2

```
29301
```

See also strrchr() and ereg().

---

sqrt (math)
square root

```
float sqrt(float arg);
```

This function calculates and returns the square root of *number*.

Example

```
<?PHP
echo sqrt(0)."\n";
echo sqrt(1)."\n";
echo (sqrt(2) / 2)."\n";
?>
```

Output

```
0
1
0.70710678118655
```

----

srand (math)
seed the random number generator

```
void srand(int seed);
```

> This function seeds the random number generator with *seed*. Typically, the seed is a number based upon the time of day. For debugging, it may be useful to seed the generator with a constant value. This will cause rand() to generate the same sequence of random numbers each time the PHP script is executed.

Example 1

Seed the random number generator with a random value based upon the current time in microseconds.

```
<?PHP
srand((double)microtime() * 1000000);
?>
```

Example 2

Seed the random number generator with a constant value so that rand() generates a repeatable set of numbers.

```
<?PHP
srand(1);
?>
```

See also rand() and getrandmax().

----

strftime (date-time)
format a local time/date according to locale settings

```
string strftime(string format, int timestamp);
```

> This function returns a string formatted according to the specified format string; if no timestamp is specified, then the current local time is used. Month and day names and other language-dependent strings respect the current locale set with setlocale().

Month and weekday names and other language-dependent strings respect the current language and cultural rules as set by setlocale().

The following conversion specifiers are recognized in the format string:

%a   abbreviated day name according to the current locale
%A   full day name according to the current locale
%b   abbreviated month name according to the current locale
%B   full month name according to the current locale
%c   preferred date and time representation for the current locale
%d   day of the month as a decimal number (range 0 to 31)
%H   hour as a decimal number using a 24-hour clock (range 00 to 23)
%I   hour as a decimal number using a 12-hour clock (range 01 to 12)
%j   day of the year as a decimal number (range 001 to 366)
%m   month as a decimal number (range 10 to 12)
%M   minute as a decimal number
%p   either 'am' or 'pm' according to the given time value, or the corresponding strings for the current locale
%S   second as a decimal number
%U   week number of the current year as a decimal number, starting with the first Sunday as the first day of the first week
%W   week number of the current year as a decimal number, starting with the first Monday as the first day of the first week
%w   day of the week as a decimal, Sunday being 0
%x   preferred date representation for the current locale without the time
%X   preferred time representation for the current locale without the date
%y   year as a decimal number without a century (range 00 to 99)
%Y   year as a decimal number including the century
%Z   time zone or name or abbreviation
%%   a literal '%' character

Example

This shows the week day in the local language and works only if you have the respective locales installed in your system.

```
setlocale ("LC_TIME", "C");
print(strftime("%A in Finnish is "));
```

```
setlocale ("LC_TIME", "fi");
print(strftime("%A, in French "));
setlocale ("LC_TIME", "fr");
print(strftime("%A and in German "));
setlocale ("LC_TIME", "de");
print(strftime("%A.\n"));
```

See also setlocale() and mktime().

---

tan (math)
tangent

```
float tan(float number);
```

> This function calculates and returns the tangent of *number* in radians.

Example

```
<?PHP
echo tan(pi()/4)."\n";
echo tan(pi()/2)."\n";
?>
```

Output

Note that the second value displayed should be zero (0), but due to floating-point rounding errors, it is a number very close to zero.

```
1
1.6331778728384E+16
```

See also sin() and cos().

---

time (date-time)
return current UNIX timestamp

```
int time(void);
```

> This function returns the current time measured in the number of seconds elapsed the Unix Epoch (00:00:00 on January 1, 1970).

Example

The following code displays the current seconds since January 1, 1970.

```
<?PHP
echo "The number of seconds since the Epoch: ";
echo time() . "\n";
?>
```

Output:

```
The number of seconds since the Epoch: 921112347
```

See also date().

----

trim (string)
Strip white space from the beginning and end of a string.

```
string trim(string str);
```

> This function removes white space from the start and the end of the
> given string. The resulting string is returned.

Example

```
<?PHP
$word="      ABCabc      ";
echo "String: '".$word."'\n";
echo "String after trim(): '".trim($word)."'\n";
?>
```

Output

```
String: '      ABCabc      '
String after trim(): 'ABCabc'
```

See also chop() and ltrim().

----

uasort (array)
sort an associative array by values using a user-defined comparison function

```
void usort(array array, function cmp_function);
```

> This function sorts the values of *array* using a user-supplied compari-
> son function. This function should be used when the array needs to be
> sorted on non-trivial criteria.

Example

The example below uses a comparison function to sort the items in reverse order.

```php
<?PHP
function cmp($a, $b) {
  if ($a > $b)
    return 1;
  else if ($a < $b)
    return -1;
  else
    return 0;
}

$id  = array("Joe" => 333, "Bob" => 222, "Jill" => 111,
"Janice" => 999);
uasort($id, cmp);
do {
  echo key($id)." ID # ".current($id)."\n";
} while (next($id));
?>
```

Output

```
Jill ID # 111
Bob ID # 222
Joe ID # 333
Janice ID # 999
```

See also uasort(), arsort(), asort(), ksort(), rsort(), and sort().

----

ucfirst (string)
make a string's first character uppercase

```
string ucfirst(string str);
```

> This function will capitalize the first character of *str* if it is alphabetic. Note that 'alphabetic' is determined by the current locale. For instance, in the default "C" locale characters such as umlaut-A (Ä) will not be converted.

Example

```php
<?PHP
$str = "user";
```

```
echo ucfirst($str);
?>
```

Output

```
User
```

See also strtoupper() and strtolower().

---

ucwords (string)
uppercase the first character of each word in a string

```
string ucwords(string str);
```

> This function capitalizes the first character of each word in *str* if that
> character is alphabetic.

Example

```
<?PHP
$str = "The quick brown fox";
echo ucwords($str);
?>
```

Output

```
The Quick Brown Fox
```

See also strtoupper(), strtolower(), and ucfirst().

---

uksort (array)
sort an array by keys using a user-defined comparison function

```
void usort(array array, function cmp_function);
```

> This function sorts the keys of *array* using a user-supplied comparison
> function. This function should be used when the array needs to be
> sorted on nontrivial criteria.

Example

The following example uses a comparison function to sort the items in
reverse order.

```PHP
<?PHP
function cmp($a, $b) {
  if ($a > $b)
    return 1;
  else if ($a < $b)
    return -1;
  else
    return 0;
}

$id  = array("Joe" => 333, "Bob" => 222, "Jill" => 111,
"Janice" => 999);
uksort($id, cmp);
do {
  echo key($id)." ID # ".current($id)."\n";
} while (next($id));
?>
```

Output

```
Joe ID # 333
Jill ID # 111
Janice ID # 999
Bob ID # 222
```

See also arsort(), asort(), ksort(), rsort(), and sort().

----

urldecode (url)
decode URL-encoded string

```
string urldecode(string str);
```

> This function decodes any URL encoding in the given string. It undoes
> what urlencode() does. The decoded string is returned.

Example

The code below uses urldecode() to decode an e-mail address that could have
been given as a query string in a URL.

```PHP
<?PHP
$str = urldecode("example%40php123.com");
echo $str;
?>
```

Output

```
example@php123.com
```

See also urlencode().

----

urlencode (url)
URL-encode string

```
string urlencode(string str);
```

> This function returns a string in which all non-alphanumeric characters, except dash(-), underscore (_), and period (.), in *str* have been replaced with a percent sign (%) followed by two hex digits. Spaces are encoded as plus signs (+). Data posted from a WWW form is encoded in this way. The MIME type for this media type is "application/x-www-form-urlencoded". Typically, this function is used to convert arbitrary strings into a safe form that can be used in the query part of an URL.

Example 1

The code below demonstrates how to use urlencode() to convert an arbitrary string into a form that can be used in a query string in an URL (the part after the question mark).

```
<?PHP
$str = urlencode("/www/~user/test.html");
echo $str;
?>
```

Output 1

```
%2Fwww%2F%7Euser%2Ftest.html
```

Example 2

The code below demonstrates how to use urlencode() to convert arbitrary strings passed in the URL to another PHP3 program.

```
<?PHP
$name = "Joe User";
$password = "123!!";
echo "http://www.php123.com/contact.php3?name=";
echo urlencode($name);
echo '&password=';
```

```
echo urlencode($password);
?>
```

Output 2

```
http://www.php123.com/contact.php3?name=Joe+User&password=
123%21%21
```

See also urldecode().

----

unset (variable)
unset a given variable

```
int unset(mixed var);
```

> This function destroys the specified variable, and it returns TRUE.

Example

```
<?PHP
if(isset($a))
   echo "1. \$a exists.";
$a = 123456;
if(isset($a))
   echo "2. \$a exists.";
unset($a);
if(isset($a))
   echo "3. \$a exists.";
?>
```

Output

```
2. $a exists.
```

See also isset() and empty().

----

usort (array)
sort an array using a user-defined comparison function

```
void usort(array array, function cmp_function);
```

> This function sorts *array* using a user-supplied comparison function.
> This function should be used when the array needs to be sorted on
> nontrivial criteria.

Example

The example below uses a comparison function to sort the items in reverse order.

```
<?PHP
function cmp($a, $b) {
   if ($a > $b)
      return -1;
   else if ($a < $b)
      return 1;
   else
      return 0;
}

$ar = array(1, 2, 3);
usort($ar, cmp);
echo $ar[0]."\n";
echo $ar[1]."\n";
echo $ar[2]."\n";
?>
```

Output

3
2
1

See also arsort(), asort(), ksort(), rsort(), and sort().

PROCESS-RELATED

escapeShellCmd (execution)
escape shell metacharacters

```
string escapeshellcmd(string command);
```

EscapeShellCmd() escapes any characters in a string that might be used to trick a shell command into executing arbitrary commands. This function should be used to make sure that any data coming from user input is escaped before this data is passed to the exec() or system() functions. The use of this function is required if you want to execute external programs safely with command lines created with data from untrusted sources. The characters:

& ; ' ' " | * ? ~ < > ^ ( ) [ ] { } $ [0x0A] [0xFF]

are removed, because they have a special meaning to most shells.

Example 1

Below is a demonstration of how escaping shell characters can make your system more secure.

```
<?PHP
$binary = "/bin/arbitrary_program";
$evil_string = " ;cat /etc/passwd";
system($binary . $evil_string);
$evil_string = escapeshellcmd($evil_string);
system($evil_string);
?>
```

Explanation

In the above PHP program, if the string $evil_string was controlled by an untrusted user, say, input from a web form, then that user could construct command lines that could be potentially harmful. In $evil_string above, the shell command separator, the semicolon (;), is used to turn the single string into two shell commands. What was a command with an argument becomes an exploitable tool that will allow anyone to execute any arbitrary command on the server. After using escapeshellcmd() on $evil_string, however, it becomes "/bin/arbitrary_program \; cat /etc/passwd". The semicolon is escaped-out, so the shell is never at risk of running an unintended program.

----

error_log (info)
send an error message somewhere

```
int error_log(string message, int message_type, string
destination, string extra_headers);
```

This function sends an error message to the web server's error log, a TCP port, or to a file. *message* is the error message that will be logged. *message_type* specifies where the message should go. Valid message types are:

0   Message is sent to PHP's system logger, using the operating system's system logging mechanism or a file, depending on how the error_log configuration directive is set.

> 1   Message is sent by e-mail to the address in the destination para-
>   meter. This is the only message type in which the fourth para-
>   meter, extra_headers, is used. This message type uses the same
>   internal function as Mail().
>
> 2   Message is sent through the PHP debugging connection. This
>   option is available only if remote debugging has been enabled. In
>   this case, the destination parameter specifies the host name or
>   IP address and, optionally, port number of the socket receiving
>   the debug information.
>
> 3   Message is appended to the file destination.

Example 1

The example below will append the specified message to the web server's
error_log.

```php
<?PHP
error_log((date("F d, Y, H:i:s", time())))." student add
  failed", 0);
?>
```

Output

(the line appended to the web server's error_log)

```
[Sat Jan 01 00:00:00 2000] [error] January 01, 2000, 00:00:00
  student add failed
```

Example 2

The code below will send an e-mail message to *alarm@php123.com* containing the specified text.

```php
<?PHP
error_log((date("F d, Y, H:i:s", time())))." Could not write to
  student ID database.", 1, "alarm@php123.com");
?>
```

Output

```
(the e-mail message)
To: alarm@php123.com
Subject: PHP3 error_log message

January 01, 2000, 00:00:00 Could not write to student ID
database.
```
----

error_reporting (info)
set which PHP errors are reported

```
int error_reporting(int level);
```

This function sets PHP's error-reporting level, and returns the old level. The error-reporting level is a bitmask of the following values:

Value	Internal Name	Description
1	E_ERROR	Notices are not printed by default, and indicate that the script encountered something that could indicate an error, but could also happen in the normal course of running the script: for example, trying to access the value of a variable that has not been set, or calling *stat()* on a nonexistent file.
2	E_WARNING	Warnings are printed by default, but do not interrupt script execution. These indicate a problem that should have been trapped by the script before the call was made: for example, calling *ereg()* with an invalid regular expression.
4	E_PARSE	Errors are also printed by default, and execution of the script is halted after the function returns. These indicate errors that cannot be recovered from, such as a memory-allocation problem.
8	E_NOTICE	Parse errors should be generated only by the parser. The code is listed here only for the sake of completeness.
16	E_CORE_ERROR	This is like an E_ERROR, except it is generated by the core of PHP. Functions should not generate this type of error.
32	E_CORE_WARNING	This is like an E_WARNING, except it is generated by the core of PHP. Functions should not generate this type of error.

Example 1

```
<?PHP
echo "The current reporting level: ".error_reporting();
?>
```

Output

```
55 means display every type of error message except for
   E_NOTICE.
The current reporting level: 55
```

Example 2

The code below demonstrates how to use error_reporting to suppress an error message. The first attempt to open the file displays an error message. After calling error_report(), the second attempt does not generate an error message.

```
<?PHP
echo "Try to open a file that does not exist.\n";
file("/etc/does_not_exist");
error_reporting(0);
echo "Try to open file again\n");
file("/etc/does_not_exist");
?>
```

Output

```
Try to open a file that does not exist.
```

Warning: File("/etc/does_not_exist") - No such file or
   directory in **/www/tmp/tmp.php3** on line **4**
Try to open file again

----

exec (execution)
execute an external program

```
string exec(string command, string array, int return_var);
```

Exec executes the given command; however, it does not output anything. It simply returns the last line from the result of the command. If you need to execute a command and have all the data from the command passed directly back without any interference, use the PassThru() function.

If the array argument is present, then the specified array will be filled with every line of output from the command. Note that if the array already contains some elements, exec() will append to the end of the array. If you do not want the function to append elements, call unset() on the array before passing it to exec().

If the return_var argument is present along with the array argument, then the return status of the executed command will be written to this variable.

Note that if you are going to allow data coming from user input to be passed to this function, then you should be using EscapeShellCmd() to make sure that users cannot trick the system into executing arbitrary commands.

Note that you will not see any output that is sent to stderr. As with any other CGI program, Apache captures this output and places it in a log file, typically named /var/log/httpd/error_log.

Example

The code below will display the last line of the output from the command /bin/ls.

```
<?PHP
$str = exec("/bin/ls");
echo $str;
?>
```

See also system(), PassThru(), popen(), and EscapeShellCmd().

----

getEnv (info)
get the value of an environment variable

```
string getenv(string varname);
```

This function returns the value of the environment variable *varname*, or FALSE in case of an error. The most common error is that the environment variable does not exist. This function is useful in reading environment variables set by the web server before the PHP script is called. For more information on CGI and the environment variables that the web server provides for PHP, see *http://www.w3.org/CGI/*.

Example

```php
<?PHP
echo getenv("GATEWAY_INTERFACE")."\n";
echo getenv("SERVER_PROTOCOL")."\n";
echo getenv("REMOTE_ADDR")."\n";
?>
```

Output

```
CGI/1.1
HTTP/1.1
192.168.0.100
```

See also putenv().

---

get_cfg_var (info)
get the value of a PHP configuration option

```
string get_cfg_var(string name);
```

> This function returns the current value of the PHP configuration variable specified by *name*, or FALSE if an error occurs.

Example

```php
<?PHP
echo "Maximum allowed script execution time:"
  .get_cfg_var("max_execution_time")."\n";
?>
```

Output

```
Maximum allowed script execution time: 30
```

---

get_current_user (info)
get the name of the owner of the current PHP script

```
string get_current_user(void);
```

> This function returns the name of the owner of the current PHP script. It uses the Unix C function getpwuid(getuid()).

Example

```
<?PHP
echo get_current_user()."\n";
?>
```

Output

```
nobody
```

See also getmyuid(), getmypid(), getmyinode(), and getlastmod().

----

getLastMod (info)
get time of last page modification

```
int getlastmod(void);
```

> This function returns the time of the last modification of the current
> page. The value returned is a Unix timestamp (number of seconds
> since Epoch). This function returns FALSE on error.

Example

```
<?PHP
echo date("F d, Y, H:i:s", getlastmod())."\n";
?>
```

Output

```
January 01, 2000, 00:00:00
```

See also date(), getmyuid(), get_current_user(), and getmyinode().

----

get_magic_quotes_gpc (info)
get the current magic quotes Get/Post/Cookie setting

```
long get_magic_quotes_gpc(void);
```

> This function returns TRUE when magic quotes are enabled for all
> Get/Post/Cookie operations. Otherwise, it returns FALSE. When
> magic quotes are on, all single quote ('), double quote ("), backslash (\),
> and NULL characters are escaped automatically. This can save time
> by eliminating extra calls to addslashes() and stripslashes().

See also set_magic_quotes_gpc().

---

set_magic_quotes_gpc (info)
set the current magic quotes Get/Post/Cookie setting

```
long get_magic_quotes_gpc(int new_setting);
```

> This function sets the magic quote setting for all Get/Post/Cookie oper-
> ations. When magic quotes are on, all single quote ('), double quote ("),
> backslash (\), and NULL characters are escaped automatically. This can
> save time by eliminating extra calls to addslashes() and stripslashes().

See also get_magic_quotes_gpc().

---

get_magic_quotes_runtime (info)
get the current magic quotes setting

```
long get_magic_quotes_runtime(void);
```

> This function returns TRUE when magic quotes are enabled for most
> operations that return data from an external source. Otherwise, it
> returns FALSE. When magic quotes are on, all single quote ('), double
> quote ("), backslash (\), and NULL characters are escaped automati-
> cally. This can save time by eliminating extra calls to addslashes() and
> stripslashes().

Refer to *www.php123.com* for on-line example.

See also set_magic_quotes_runtime().

---

getMyinode (info)
get the inode of the current script

```
int getmyinode(void);
```

> This function returns the current script's inode, or FALSE on error.

Example

```
<?PHP
echo getmyinode()."\n";
?>
```

Output

```
45910
```

See also getmyuid(), get_current_user(), getmypid(), and getlastmod().

----

getMypid (info)
get PHP's process ID

```
int getmypid(void);
```

> This function returns the current PHP process ID, or FALSE on error.
> Note that when PHP is running as a server module, separate script
> executions are not guaranteed to have different pids.

Example

```
<?PHP
echo getmypid()."\n";
?>
```

Output

```
4212
```

See also getmyuid(), get_current_user(), getmyinode(), and getlastmod().

----

getMyuid (info)
get PHP script owner's UID

```
int getmyuid(void);
```

> This function returns the UNIX user ID of the current script, or
> FALSE on error.

Example

```
<?PHP
echo getmyuid()."\n";
?>
```

Output

```
(will vary depending upon your setup)
100
```

See also getmypid(), get_current_user(), getmyinode(), and getlastmod().

----

getrusage (info)
get a PHP script's resource limits and usage

```
array getrusage([int userid]);
```

> This function returns an associative array of the data returned from
> the getrusage() system function. For more information on this func-
> tion, see the man page for getrusage(2) on your system.

Example

```
<?PHP
$a = getrusage();
echo "Number of page faults: ".$a["ru_majflt"]."\n";
echo "CPU usage in seconds: ".$a["ru_utime.tv_sec"]."\n";
echo "CPU usage in microseconds:
".$a["ru_utime.tv_usec"]."\n";
?>
```

Output

```
Number of page faults: 176
CPU usage in seconds: 0
CPU usage in microseconds: 180000
```

----

leak (special)
Leak memory

```
void leak(int bytes);
```

> This function leaks *bytes* bytes of memory. This function is really
> useful only in debugging PHP itself or in testing process limits.

Example

```
<?PHP
leak(1000000);
?>
```

----

phpInfo (info)
output PHP information

```
int phpinfo(void);
```

> This function prints-out a large amount of information about the copy
> of PHP running. This includes information about PHP compilation
> options and extensions, the PHP version, server information and envi-
> ronment (if compiled as a module), the PHP environment, OS version
> information, paths, master and local values of configuration options,
> HTTP headers, and the PHP License.

Example

```
<?PHP
echo phpinfo();
?>
```

Output

PHP Version 3.0.9 by Rasmus Lerdorf, Andi Gutmans, Zeev Suraski, Stig Bakken, Shane Caraveo, Jim Winstead, and countless others.

System: Linux www.php123.com 2.2.10 #1 Mon Jun 28 09:40:25 EDT 1999
i686 unknown
Build Date: Jun 28 1999

Extensions

Extensions	Additional Information
PHP core	CFLAGS=-fPIC HSREGEX=no
Basic Functions	No additional information.
PHP_DL	Dynamic Library support enabled.
PHP_dir	No additional information.
PHP_filestat	No additional information.
PHP_file	No additional information.
PHP_head	No additional information.
Sendmail	Path to sendmail: /usr/sbin/sendmail -t
Debugger	No additional information.
Syslog	No additional information.

MySQL	Allow persistent links: Yes
	Persistent links: 0/Unlimited
	Total links: 0/Unlimited
	Client API version: 3.22.23b
	Compilation definitions: MYSQL_INCLUDE=-I/usr/include/mysql MYSQL_LFLAGS=-Wl,'-rpath /usr/lib/mysql' -L/usr/ lib/mysql MYSQL_LIBS=-lmysqlclient
DBase	No additional information.
Socket functions	No additional information.

(Note: Table has been truncated for space purposes.)

PHP License

This program is free software; you can redistribute it and/or modify
it under the terms of:

A) the GNU General Public License as published by the Free Software
   Foundation; either version 2 of the License, or (at your option) any
   later version.

B) the PHP License as published by the PHP Development Team and
   included in the distribution in the file: LICENSE

This program is distributed in the hope that it will be useful, but WITHOUT
ANY WARRANTY; without even the implied warranty of MERCHANT-
ABILITY or FITNESS FOR A PARTICULAR PURPOSE. See the GNU Gen-
eral Public License for more details.

You should have received a copy of both licenses referred to here.

If you did not, or have any questions about PHP licensing, please contact
core@php.net.

See also phpversion().

----

phpVersion (info)
get the current PHP version

```
string phpversion(void);
```

> This function returns a string containing the version of PHP that is running.

Example

```
<?PHP
echo "PHP Version ".phpversion();
?>
```

Output

```
PHP Version 3.0.10
```

See also phpinfo().

----

putEnv (info)
set the value of an environment variable

```
void putenv(string setting);
```

> This function sets an environment variable. This function is typically used when an external program is executed that uses values in the environment.

Example

```
<?PHP
putenv("PATH=/bin");
?>
```

See also getenv().

----

set_magic_quotes_runtime (info)
set the current magic quotes setting

```
long set_magic_quotes_runtime(int new_setting);
```

> This function sets the magic quotes setting for most operations that return data from an external source. When magic quotes are on, all single quote ('), double quote ("), backslash (\), and NULL characters are escaped automatically. This can save time by eliminating extra calls to addslashes() and stripslashes().

Example

```php
<?PHP
$FILE_NAME = "/tmp/quote_test";
echo "Magic quotes are ".display_magic_quotes_setting()."\n";
$a = file($FILE_NAME);
echo $a[0]."\n";
set_magic_quotes_runtime(1);
echo "Magic quotes are ".display_magic_quotes_setting()."\n";
$a = file($FILE_NAME);
echo $a[0]."\n";
?>
```

Output

```
Magic quotes are OFF
John's jacket  ... C:\WINDOWS ... "The Quick Brown Fox"
Magic quotes are ON
John\'s jacket  ... C:\\WINDOWS ... \"The Quick Brown Fox\"
```

See also get_magic_quotes_runtime().

----

set_time_limit (info)
limit the maximum execution time

```
void set_time_limit(int seconds);
```

> This function sets the number of *seconds* a script is allowed to run. When this time is reached, the script returns a fatal error. The default time limit is 30 seconds or, if it exists, the max_execution_time value defined in php3.ini. If seconds is set to zero (0), then no time limit is set. When called, set_time_limit() restarts the timeout counter. In other words, if the timeout is the default of 30 seconds, and 15 seconds into script, set_time_limit(50) is called, then the script will run for a total of 65 seconds before timing out.

----

sleep (special)(x)
delay execution N seconds

```
void sleep(int seconds);
```

> This function delays execution of the program until at least *seconds* seconds have elapsed.

Example

```
<?PHP
echo gmdate("M d Y H:i:s", time());
sleep(10);
echo gmdate("M d Y H:i:s", time());
?>
```

Output

```
Jan 01 2000 00:00:00
Jan 01 2000 00:00:10
```

See also usleep().

----

system (execution)
execute an external program and display output

```
string system(string command, int return_var);
```

> System() is just like the C version of the function in that it executes the given command and outputs the result. If a variable is provided as the second argument, then the return status code of the executed command will be written to this variable.
>
> Note that if you are going to allow data coming from user input to be passed to this function, then you should be using the EscapeShell-Cmd() function to make sure that users cannot trick the system into executing arbitrary commands.
>
> The System() call also tries to flush the web server's output buffer automatically after each line of output if PHP is running as a server module.

> If you need to execute a command and have all the data from the command passed directly back without any interference, use the PassThru() function.
>
> Note that you will not see any output that is sent to **stderr**. As with any other CGI program, Apache captures this output and places it in a log file, typically named/var/log/httpd/error_log.

Example

The code below will list the files in the /tmp directory.

```
<?PHP
$str = system("/bin/ls /tmp");
?>
```

See also exec(), popen().

---

passthru (execution)
execute an external program and display raw output

```
string passthru(string command, int return_var);
```

> The passthru() function is similar to the Exec() function in that it executes a command. If the return_var argument is present, the return status of the Unix command will be placed in return_var. This function should be used in place of Exec() or System() when the output from the Unix command is binary data that needs to be passed directly back to the browser. A common use for this function is to execute the pbmplus utilities so that you can output an image stream directly. By setting the content-type to image/gif and then calling a pbmplus program to output a gif, you can create PHP scripts that output images directly.

Example

The code below will send out a .GIF image.

```
<?PHP
header("Content-type: image/gif");
passthru("cat /tmp/test.gif");
?>
```

See also exec() and fpassthru().

---

usleep (special)
delay execution N microseconds

```
void usleep(int micro_seconds);
```

> This function delays execution of the program until at least
> *micro_seconds* microseconds have passed.

Example

```
<?PHP
echo gmdate("M d Y H:i:s", time());
usleep(10);
echo gmdate("M d Y H:i:s", time());
usleep(1000000);
echo gmdate("M d Y H:i:s", time());
?>
```

Output

```
Jan 01 2000 00:00:00
Jan 01 2000 00:00:00
Jan 01 2000 00:00:01
```

See also sleep().

----

uniqid (special)
generate a unique id

```
int uniqid(string prefix);
```

> This function returns a unique identifier prefixed with *prefix* based on
> current time in microseconds taken from the system call gettimeof-
> day(). The prefix can be necessary when a different host may happen
> to generate the identifier at the same micorsecond. *prefix* can be up to
> 114 characters long. The generated id contains 14 characters after the
> prefix.

Example

```
<?PHP
echo uniqid("")."\n";
echo uniqid("sql")."\n";
?>
```

Output

```
371eef73262b8
sql371eef732b0cb
```

See also tempnam().

NETWORK-RELATED

virtual (Apache)
perform an Apache sub-request

```
int virtual(string filename);
```

> virtual() is an Apache-specific function equivalent to <!--#include
> virtual...--> in mod_include. It performs an Apache sub-request. It is
> useful for including CGI scripts or .shtml files, or anything else that
> you would parse through Apache. Note that a CGI script must gener-
> ate valid CGI headers. At the minimum, that means it must generate
> a Content-type header. For PHP files, you should use include() or
> require().

Example

```
<?PHP
  echo "You are visitor ";
  virtual("/cgi-bin/counter.cgi");
  echo "<br>\n";
?>
```

Output

```
You are visitor 101
```

----

getallHeaders (Apache)
retrieve all HTTP request headers

```
array getallheaders(void);
```

> This function returns an associative array of all the HTTP headers in
> the current request. GetAllHeaders() is supported only when PHP runs
> as an Apache module.

Example

This code displays all the request headers for the current request.

```php
<?PHP
$headers = getallheaders();
while (list($header, $value) = each($headers)) {
  echo "$header: $value<br>\n";
?>
```

Output

```
Accept: */*
Accept-Encoding: gzip, compress
Accept-Language: en
Host: 127.0.0.1
Referer: http://127.0.0.1/index.html
User-Agent: Lynx/2.8rel.3 libwww-FM/2.14
```

----

checkdnsrr (network)
check DNS records of different types given an IP address or host name

```
int checkdnsrr(string host, string [type]);
```

This function searches DNS for resource records of *type* for *host*. It returns TRUE if any records are found. It returns FALSE if no records were found or in case of error. The resource record can be any one of the types below:

Type	Description
A	a host address (dotted-quad IP address)
NS	an authoritative name server (domain)
MX	a mail exchanger (domain), preceded by a preference value (0..32767), with lower numeric values representing higher logical preferences
CNAME	the canonical name for an alias (domain)
SOA	marks the start of a zone of authority (domain of originating host, domain address of maintainer, a serial number and the following parameters in seconds: refresh, retry, expire, and minimum TTL (see RFC 883)

Type	Description
NULL	a null resource record (no format or data)
RP	a responsible person for some domain name (mailbox, TXT-referral)
PTR	a domain name pointer (domain)
HINFO	host information (cpu_type OS_type)

The default type is MX; host can be either a domain name or an IP address.

Example

The example below shows how to check to see if a hostname has an associated IP address and to see if it has a mail server (MX, mail exchange).

```
<?PHP
echo "Has IP address".checkdnsrr("www.php123.com", "A")."\n";
echo "Has mail server".checkdnsrr("www.php123.com", "MX").
  "\n";
echo "Has IP address: ".checkdnsrr("www.non-existant-domain.
  com", "A")."\n";
?>
```

Output

```
Has IP address: 1
Has mail server: 1
Valid address:
```

See also gethostbyaddr() and gethostbyname().

----

debugger_on (network)
enable internal PHP debugger

```
void debugger_on(string address);
```

This function enables the internal PHP debugger, connecting it to address.

The debugger is still under development.

Refer to *www.php123.com* for on-line example.

----

debugger_off (network)
disable internal PHP debugger

```
void debugger_off(void);
```

> This function disables the internal PHP debugger.
>
> The debugger is still under development. The authors do not recommend using the version current as of the printing of this book.

---

closelog (network)
close connection to system logger

```
int closelog(void);
```

> This function closes the connection to the system logger. Its use is optional.

Example

```
<?PHP
openlog("PHP", LOG_PID | LOG_PERROR, LOG_USER);
syslog(LOG_INFO, "Doing daily updates");
closelog();
?>
```

Output

```
The above message will be appended to the appropriate log file.
```

See also openlog().

---

fsockopen (network)
open Internet or Unix domain socket connection

```
int fsockopen(string hostname, int port, int [errno], string
[errstr]);
```

> This function opens an Internet domain socket connection to *hostname* on *port*.
>
> A file pointer that may be used with fgets(), fgetss(), fputs(), and fclose() is returned.

If the call fails, then it will return FALSE and the optional *errno* and *errstr* parameters will contain the actual system-level error that occurred on the system connect() call.

If *errno* is 0 but the function returned FALSE, then the error occurred before the connect() call. Note that the *errno* and *errstr* parameters should be passed by reference.

To connect using Unix sockets, set the *port* to zero and specify the filename of the Unix domain socket in *hostname*.

Example

In the example below, fsockopen() is used to connect to a web server and display the generated HTTP headers.

```
<?PHP
$web = fsockopen("www.php123.com", 80);
fputs($web, "GET / HTTP/1.0\n\n");
while(!feof($web)) {
  $str =  fgets($web, 1024);
  if(!strcmp($str, "\n"))
    break;
  echo $str;
}
fclose($web);
?>
```

Output

```
HTTP/1.1 200 OK
Date: Sat, 01 Jan 2000 00:00:00 GMT
Server: Apache/1.3.3 (Unix)
Connection: close
Content-Type: text/html
```

See also fclose().

----

getallheaders (apache)
get all HTTP request headers

```
array getallheaders(void);
```

This function returns an associative array of all the HTTP headers from the current request. Note that this function works only when PHP runs as an Apache module.

Example

```
<?PHP
$headers = getallheaders();
while (list($header, $value) = each($headers)) {
  printf("$header: $value\n");
}
?>
```

Output

```
Accept: */*
Accept-Encoding: gzip, deflate
Accept-Language: en-us
Host: www.php123.com
Pragma: no-cache
Referer: http://www.php123.com/
User-Agent: Mozilla/4.0 (compatible; MSIE 5.0; Windows 98)
```

See also gethostbyname().

----

gethostbyaddr (network)
get a host's name given an IP address

```
string gethostbyaddr(string ip_address);
```

> This function returns the host name given the IP address *ip_address*.
> In case of error, the IP address is returned.

Example

```
<?PHP
echo gethostbyaddr("127.0.0.1");
echo gethostbyaddr("2.0.0.0");
?>
```

Output

```
localhost
2.0.0.0
```

See also gethostbyname().

----

gethostbyname (network)
get a host's IP address given its host name

```
string gethostbyname(string hostname);
```

> This function returns the IP address given the *hostname*. In case of error, the hostname is returned.

Example

```
<?PHP
echo gethostbyname("www.php123.com");
echo gethostbyname("www.non-existant-domain.com");
?>
```

Output

```
209.11.12.44
www.non-existant-domain.com
```

See also gethostbyaddr() and gethostbynamel().

---

gethostbynamel (network)
get a list of host IP addresses given its host name

```
array gethostbynamel(string hostname);
```

> This function returns a list of IP addresses given the *hostname*.

Example

```
<?PHP
$addr = gethostbynamel("www.aol.com");
do {
  echo current($addr)." ";
} while(next($addr));
?>
```

Output

```
152.163.210.23 152.163.210.25 152.163.210.24 152.163.210.27
```

See also gethostbyaddr() and gethostbyname().

---

getmxrr (network)
get a host's MX server

```
int getmxrr(string hostname, array mxhosts, array [weight]);
```

This function searches DNS for MX (mail exchange) resource records
for hostname. It returns TRUE if any records are found. It returns
FALSE if no records were found or in case of error. A list of MX records
is placed in the array mxhosts.

If the weight parameter is given, then it will be filled with the weight
(preference values) information obtained from DNS. In other words,
this function can be used to find the mail server(s) for a given host
name, and their order of preference.

Example

```
<?PHP
getmxrr("php123.com", &$mxhosts, &$weight);
for($x = 0; $x < count($mxhosts); $x++)
   echo $mxhosts[$x]." ".$weight[$x]."\n";
?>
```

Output

```
smtp.php123.com 10
smtp2.php123.com 20
```

See also checkdnsrr().

----

header (http)
send a raw HTTP header

```
int header(string string);
```

This function is used at the top of an HTML file to send a raw HTTP
header string. See the HTTP specification (RFC 2068) for more information on raw HTTP headers. Note: header() must be called before
any actual output is sent either by normal HTML tags or from PHP.
In other words, it must be at the very top of the web page. A common
mistake is to have a blank line before the start of the PHP code. For
example, this function will let you specify the "Location:" header
to redirect the client to a different web page. Also, you can set the

Content-Type HTTP header. By default, PHP sends "text/html", but you can set it to other values. By setting the content-type to "image/gif", you can use PHP to generate GIF images dynamically. An example of the images you can create on the fly are buttons, graphs, and charts generated with perhaps data from either a database or user input. Other examples of different content you can create are plain text files (text/plain), .ZIP compressed files (application/zip), JPEG images (application/jpeg), PDF documents, and even sound files.

Example 1

When placed on a web page by itself, the following redirects the client to *http://www.example.com/.*

```
<?PHP
Header("Location: http://www.example.com");
?>
```

Example 2

When placed at the top of a web page, the following lets the web client know that the content it is about to receive is a .gif image.

```
<?PHP
header("Content-type: image/gif");
passthru("cat /tmp/test.gif");
?>
```

Example 3

When placed at the top of a web page, the following lets the web client know that the content it is about to receive is a jpeg image.

```
<?PHP
header("Content-type: image/jpeg");
passthru("cat /tmp/test.jpeg");
?>
```

Example 4

When placed at the top of a web page, the following lets the web client know that the content it is about to receive is a plain text file. This will keep the web browser from attempting to interpret the text.

```
<?PHP
header("Content-type: text/plain");
echo "Annual Report";
```

```
...
?>
```

----

imap_Append (IMAP)

append a string to a specified mailbox

```
int imap_append(int imap_stream, string mbox, string message,
stringflags);
```

> This function appends the string *message* to the specified mailbox
> *mbox*. The string *message* should be a properly formatted mail mes-
> sage. If the optional parameter *flags* is specified, then the *flags* are
> written to the mailbox. The mailbox must already exist, because the
> server will not automatically create it.

Example

```
<?PHP
$server = "{php123.com:143}";
$mailbox = "INBOX";
$mbox = imap_open("$server$mailbox", "joeuser", "secret");
if(!$mbox)
  echo "Connect to IMAP server failed\n";
if(!imap_append($mbox, $server.$mailbox, "Subject:
test\n\nTesting...))
  echo "append failed.\n";
imap_close($mbox);
?>
```

Output

(none)

See also IMAP_createmailbox().

----

imap_base64 (IMAP)

decode base64-encoded text

```
string imap_base64(string text);
```

> This function returns a string containing the base-64 decoded version
> of *text*.

Example

```php
<?PHP
// A binary string
$str = "ÿû1234á";
echo imap_binary($str);
echo imap_base64(imap_binary($str));
?>
```

Output

```
//sxMjM04Q==
ÿû1234á
```

See also imap_binary().

----

imap_body (IMAP)
read the message body

```
string imap_body(int imap_stream, int msg_number, int flags);
```

> This function returns the body of the message specified by *msg_number* in the current mailbox. The *flags* are a bit mask with the meaning:
>
> | | |
> |---|---|
> | FT_UID | the *msg_number* is a UID |
> | FT_PEEK | do not set the \Seen flag if not already seen |
> | FT_INTERNAL | CRLF ### |

Example

The code below displays the body of the first message, if it exists.

```php
<?PHP
$server = "{php123.com:143}";
$mailbox = "INBOX";
$mbox = imap_open("$server$mailbox","joeuser", "secret");
if(!$mbox)
   echo "Connect to IMAP server failed\n";
$info = imap_mailboxmsginfo($mbox);
if ($info->Nmsgs >= 1)
   echo imap_body($mbox, 1);
imap_close($mbox);
?>
```

Output

```
(the body of the first message)
```

See also imap_fetchbody().

----

imap_check (IMAP)
check current mailbox

```
array imap_check(int imap_stream);
```

> This function checks the current mailbox status on the server, and
> returns with the information in an object with the properties below:
>
> | | |
> |---|---|
> | Date: | date of message |
> | Driver: | type of connection |
> | Mailbox: | name of mailbox |
> | Nmsgs: | total number of messages |
> | Recent: | total number of recent messages |

Example

```php
<?PHP
$server = "{php123.com:143}";
$mailbox = "INBOX";
$mbox = imap_open("$server$mailbox","joeuser", "secret");
if(!$mbox)
   echo "Connect to IMAP server failed\n";
$check=imap_check($mbox);
echo $check->Date."<br>\n";
echo "Connection Type: ",$check->Driver,"<br>\n";
echo "Mbox: ",$check->Mailbox,"<br>\n";
echo "Number Messages: ",$check->Nmsgs."\n";
echo "Recent: ",$check->Recent,"<br>\n";
imap_close($mbox);
?>
```

Output

```
Sat, 01 May 2000 00:00:00 -0400 (EDT)
Connection Type: imap
Mbox: {imap.php123.com:143/imap/user=joeuser}INBOX
Number Messages: 3 Recent: 0
```

See also imap_ping().

----

imap_close (IMAP)
close an IMAP stream

```
int imap_close(int imap_stream, int flags);
```

> This function closes an IMAP stream. It returns TRUE on success and
> FALSE on error.

Example

```php
<?PHP
$server = "{php123.com:143}";
$mailbox = "INBOX";
$mbox = imap_open("$server$mailbox","joeuser", "secret");
if(!$mbox)
  echo "Connect to IMAP server failed\n";
echo "This mail box has ".imap_num_msg($mbox)." message(s)\n";
imap_close($mbox);
?>
```

Output

```
This mail box has 2 message(s)
```

See also imap_open().

----

imap_createmailbox(IMAP)
create a new mailbox

```
int imap_createmailbox(int imap_stream, string mbox);
```

> This function creates a new mailbox *mbox*. It returns TRUE on suc-
> cess and FALSE on error.

Example

```php
<?PHP
$server = "{php123.com:143}";
$mailbox = "INBOX";
$mbox = imap_open("$server$mailbox","joeuser", "secret");
```

```
if(!$mbox)
    echo "Connect to IMAP server failed\n";
if(!imap_createmailbox($mbox, $server."sent-mail"))
    echo "Error creating mailbox.";
imap_close($mbox);
?>
```

Output

```
(no output unless error)
```

See also imap_deletemailbox() and imap_listmailbox().

----

imap_delete (IMAP)
mark a message for deletion from the current mailbox

```
int imap_delete(int imap_stream, int msg_number);
```

> This function marks the message *msg_number* for deletion. The
> actual deletion is handled by the function imap_expunge(). This func-
> tion always returns TRUE.

Example

The following code deletes the first message in the mailbox, if it exists.

```
<?PHP
$server = "{php123.com:143}";
$mailbox = "INBOX";
$mbox = imap_open("$server$mailbox","joeuser", "secret");
if(!$mbox)
    echo "Connect to IMAP server failed\n";
if(imap_num_msg($mbox) >= 1) {
    imap_delete($mbox, 1);
    imap_expunge($mbox, 1);
}
imap_close($mbox);
?>
```

Output

```
(no output, unless error)
```

See also imap_expunge() and imap_undelete().

----

imap_deletemailbox (IMAP)
delete a mailbox

```
int imap_deletemailbox(int imap_stream, string mbox);
```

> This function deletes the specified mailbox, *mbox*. It returns TRUE on success and FALSE on error.

Example

```
<?PHP
$server = "{php123.com:143}";
$mailbox = "INBOX";
$mbox = imap_open("$server$mailbox","joeuser", "secret");
if(!$mbox)
   echo "Connect to IMAP server failed\n";
if(!imap_deletemailbox($mbox, $server.$mailbox))
   echo "Error deleting mailbox.";
imap_close($mbox);
?>
```

Output

```
(no output, unless error)
```

See also imap_createmailbox().

----

imap_expunge (IMAP)
delete all messages marked for deletion

```
int imap_expunge(int imap_stream);
```

> This function deletes all messages marked for deletion by imap_delete(). It always returns TRUE.

Example

```
<?PHP
$server = "{php123.com:143}";
$mailbox = "INBOX";
$mbox = imap_open("$server$mailbox","joeuser", "secret");
if(!$mbox)
```

```
      echo "Connect to IMAP server failed\n";
if(imap_num_msg($mbox) >= 1) {
   imap_delete($mbox, 1);
   imap_expunge($mbox, 1);
}
imap_close($mbox);
?>
```

Output

```
Integer
```

See also imap_delete() and imap_undelete().

----

imap_fetchbody (IMAP)
fetch a particular section of the body of the message

```
string imap_fetchbody(int imap_stream, int msg_number, int
part_number, flags flags);
```

> This function returns contents of the part *part_number* of the body of
> message *msg_number* in a string.

Example

```
<?PHP
$server = "{php123.com:143}";
$mailbox = "INBOX";
$mbox = imap_open("$server$mailbox","joeuser", "secret");
if(!$mbox)
   echo "Connect to IMAP server failed\n";
echo "<p>The contents of message #1:\n";
$header_struct = imap_fetchstructure($mbox, 1);
$num_parts = count($header_struct->parts);
echo "The message has ".$num_parts." parts.\n";
for($part_no = 0; $part_no <= $num_parts; $part_no++) {
   echo "<B>$part_no</B><br>".imap_fetchbody($mbox, 1,
      $part_no);
   echo "————-\n";
}
imap_close($mbox);
?>
```

Output

```
(varies depending upon contents of mailbox)
```

See also imap_fetchstructure() and imap_body().

----

imap_fetchstructure (IMAP)
read the structure of a particular message

```
array imap_fetchstructure(int imap_stream, int msg_number);
```

> This function returns an array of objects with the following elements:
> type, encoding, ifsubtype, subtype, ifdescription, description, ifid, id,
> lines, bytes, and ifparameters. If the message is multipart, then it also
> returns an array of parts.

Example

```php
<?PHP
$server = "{php123.com:143}";
$mailbox = "INBOX";
$mbox = imap_open("$server$mailbox","joeuser", "secret");
if(!$mbox)
   echo "Connect to IMAP server failed\n";
$header_struct = imap_fetchstructure($mbox, 1);
$num_parts = count($header_struct->parts);
echo "The message has ".$num_parts." parts.\n";
imap_close($mbox);
?>
```

Output

```
(varies depending upon contents of mailbox)
```

See also imap_fetch().

----

imap_header (IMAP)
read the header of the message

```
object imap_header(int imap_stream, int msg_number, int
fromlength, int subjectlength, int defaulthost);
```

> This function returns an object containing several different header
> elements.

Example

```php
<?PHP
$server = "{php123.com:143}";
$mailbox = "INBOX";
$mbox = imap_open("$server$mailbox","joeuser", "secret");
if(!$mbox)
   echo "Connect to IMAP server failed\n";
$headers = imap_header($mbox, 1);
echo "\n".$headers->Subject;
echo "\n".$headers->message_id;
imap_close($mbox);
?>
```

Output

```
Re: your message
<200001010000.AAA00000@smtp.php123.com>
```

See also imap_headers().

----

imap_headers (IMAP)
return headers for all messages in a mailbox

```
array imap_headers(int imap_stream);
```

> This function returns with an array of strings with formatted header information.

Example

```php
<?PHP
$server = "{php123.com:143}";
$mailbox = "INBOX";
$mbox = imap_open("$server$mailbox","joeuser", "secret");
if(!$mbox)
   echo "Connect to IMAP server failed\n";
$headers = imap_headers($mbox);
echo "This mail box has ".count($headers)." message(s)\n";
echo "of which ".imap_num_recent($mbox)." are recent
   message(s)\n";
echo "The messages (Status # Date from Subject Size):\n";
echo $headers[0]."\n";
echo $headers[1]."\n";
echo $headers[2]."\n";
```

```
imap_close($mbox);
?>
```

Output

```
This mail box has 3 message(s)
of which 0 are recent message(s)

The messages (Status # Date from Subject Size):

   1) 16-Jan joe                Re: your message (1388 chars)
   2) 16-Jan james              Information Request (991 chars)
```

See also imap_header().

----

imap_listmailbox (IMAP)
read the list of mailboxes

```
array imap_listmailbox(int imap_stream, string ref, string
pat);
```

> This function returns an array containing the names of all of the mail-
> boxes.

Example

```
<?PHP
$server = "{php123.com:143}";
$mailbox = "INBOX";
$mbox = imap_open("$server$mailbox","joeuser", "secret");
if(!$mbox)
   echo "Connect to IMAP server failed\n";
$list = imap_listmailbox($mbox, "{php123.com:143}", "*");
echo "There are ".count($list)." mailbox(es). They are:\n";
echo "-- START --\n";
for($x = 0; $x < count($list); $x++)
   echo $list[$x]."\n";
echo "-- END --\n";
imap_close($mbox);
?>
```

Output

```
There are 8 mailbox(es). They are:
-- START --
```

```
{php123.com:143}INBOX
{php123.com:143}sent-mail
{php123.com:143}personal
{php123.com:143}risks-digest
{php123.com:143}php
{php123.com:143}php-dev
{php123.com:143}old
{php123.com:143}drafts
-- END --
```

See also PHP_createmailbox().

---

imap_listsubscribed (IMAP)
list all the subscribed mailboxes

```
array imap_listsubscribed(int imap_stream, string ref, string
pattern);
```

> This function returns with an array of all of the mailboxes currently
> subscribed to.

Example

```php
<?PHP
$server = "{php123.com:143}";
$mailbox = "INBOX";
$mbox = imap_open("$server$mailbox","joeuser", "secret");
if(!$mbox)
  echo "Connect to IMAP server failed\n";
if(!imap_subscribe($mbox, $server."sent-mail"))
  echo "Could not subscribe.\n";
$list = imap_listsubscribed($mbox, $server.$mailbox, "*");
for($x = 0; $x < count($list); $x++)
  echo "list[$x]:".$list[$x]."\n";
imap_close($mbox);
?>
```

Output

```
list[0]:{php123.com:143}INBOX
list[1]:{php123.com:143}sent-mail
```

See also imap_subscribe() and imap_unsubscribe().

---

imap_mail_copy (IMAP)
copy specified messages to a mailbox

```
int imap_mail_copy(int imap_stream, string msglist, string
mbox, int flags);
```

This function copies the messages specified by *msglist* to the mailbox
mbox. It returns TRUE on success, and FALSE on error.

Example

```
<?PHP
$server = "{php123.com:143}";
$mailbox = "INBOX";
$mbox = imap_open("$server$mailbox","joeuser", "secret");
if(!$mbox)
  echo "Connect to IMAP server failed\n";
if(!imap_mail_copy($mbox, "1", "sent-mail"))
  echo "imap_mail_copy() failed.\n";
imap_close($mbox);
?>
```

Output

```
(no output, unless error)
```

See also imap_mail_move().

----

imap_mail_move (IMAP)
move specified messages to a mailbox

```
int imap_mail_move(int imap_stream, string msglist, string
mbox);
```

This function moves the messages specified by *msglist* to the mailbox,
mbox. It returns TRUE on success, and FALSE on error.

Example

```
<?PHP
$server = "{php123.com:143}";
$mailbox = "INBOX";
$mbox = imap_open("$server$mailbox","joeuser", "secret");
```

```
if(!$mbox)
   echo "Connect to IMAP server failed\n";
if(!imap_mail_move($mbox, "1", "sent-mail"))
   echo "imap_mail_move() failed.\n";
imap_close($mbox);
?>
```

Output

```
(no output, unless error)
```

See also imap_mail_copy().

----

imap_num_msg (IMAP)
return the number of messages in the current mailbox

```
int imap_num_msg(int imap_stream);
```

> This function returns the number of messages in the current mailbox.

Example

```
<?PHP
$server = "{php123.com:143}";
$mailbox = "INBOX";
$mbox = imap_open("$server$mailbox","joeuser", "secret");
if(!$mbox)
   echo "Connect to IMAP server failed\n";
echo "This mail box has ".imap_num_msg($mbox)." message(s)\n";
echo "This mail box has ".imap_num_recent($mbox)." recent
message(s)\n";
imap_close($mbox);
?>
```

Output

```
This mail box has 3 message(s)
This mail box has 0 recent message(s)
```

See also imap_num_recent().

----

imap_num_recent (IMAP)
return the number of recent messages in current mailbox

```
int imap_num_recent(int imap_stream);
```

> This function returns the number of recently received messages in the current mailbox.

Example

```
<?PHP
$server = "{php123.com:143}";
$mailbox = "INBOX";
$mbox = imap_open("$server$mailbox","joeuser", "secret");
if(!$mbox)
   echo "Connect to IMAP server failed\n";
echo "This mail box has ".imap_num_msg($mbox)." message(s)\n";
echo "This mail box has ".imap_num_recent($mbox)." recent
message(s)\n";
imap_close($mbox);
?>
```

Output

```
This mail box has 3 message(s)
This mail box has 0 recent message(s)
```

See also imap_num_msg().

----

imap_open (IMAP)
open an IMAP stream to a mailbox

```
int imap_open(string mailbox, string username, string
password, int flags);
```

> This function returns an IMAP stream on success, and FALSE on error. This function can be used to connect to both IMAP and POP3 servers.

Example 1

The following example demonstrates how to connect to an IMAP server as username joeuser with the password secret.

```
<?PHP
$server = "{php123.com:143}";
$mailbox = "INBOX";
$mbox = imap_open("$server$mailbox","joeuser", "secret");
if(!$mbox)
   echo "Connect to IMAP server failed\n";
echo "This mail box has ".imap_num_msg($mbox)." message(s)\n";
imap_close($mbox);
?>
```

Output 1

```
This mail box has 3 messsage(s).
```

Example 2

The example below demonstrates how to connect to a POP3 server as user-name joeuser with the password secret.

```
<?PHP
$mbox =
imap_open("{php123.com/pop3:110}INBOX","joeuser","secret");
if(!$mbox)
   echo "Connect to POP server failed\n";
echo "This mail box has ".imap_num_msg($mbox)." message(s)\n";
imap_close($mbox);
?>
```

Output 2

```
This mail box has 3 message(s).
```

See also imap_close().

----

imap_ping (IMAP)
check if the IMAP stream is still active

```
int imap_ping(int imap_stream);
```

> This function returns TRUE if the connection is still active. It can be used a keep-alive to reset server inactivity counters, or as a way to check for new mail.

Example

```
<?PHP
$server = "{php123.com:143}";
$mailbox = "INBOX";
$mbox = imap_open("$server$mailbox","joeuser", "secret");
if(!$mbox)
   echo "Connect to IMAP server failed\n";
$ret = imap_ping($mbox);
if(!$ret)
   echo "ping failed\n";
imap_close($mbox);
?>
```

Output

```
(no output, unless error)
```

See also imap_open().

---

imap_rename (IMAP)
rename an old mailbox to new mailbox

```
int imap_renamemailbox(int imap_stream, string old_mbox,
string new_mbox);
```

> This function renames the mailbox *mbox* to *new_mbox*. It returns
> TRUE on success, and FALSE on error.

Example

```
<?PHP
$server = "{php123.com:143}";
$mailbox = "INBOX";
$mbox = imap_open("$server$mailbox","joeuser", "secret");
if(!$mbox)
   echo "Connect to IMAP server failed\n";
if(!imap_renamemailbox($mbox, $server."sent-mail",
   $server."sent-mail.old"))
   echo "mailbox rename failed.\n";
imap_close($mbox);
?>
```

Output

```
(no output, unless error)
```

See also imap_createmailbox() and imap_deletemailbox().

---

imap_reopen (IMAP)
reopen IMAP stream to new mailbox

```
int imap_reopen(string imap_stream, string mailbox, string
[flags]);
```

> This function reopens the specified IMAP stream.

Example

```php
<?PHP
$server = "{php123.com:143}";
$mailbox = "INBOX";
$mbox = imap_open("$server$mailbox","joeuser", "secret");
if(!$mbox)
   echo "Connect to IMAP server failed\n";
echo "This mail box has ".imap_num_msg($mbox)." message(s)\n";
if(!($mbox = imap_reopen($mbox, $server.$mailbox,
   OP_READONLY)))
   echo "mailbox reopen failed.\n";
imap_close($mbox);
?>
```

Output

```
(no output, unless error)
```

---

imap_subscribe (IMAP)
subscribe to a mailbox

```
int imap_subscribe(int imap_stream, string mbox);
```

> This function subscribes to the specified mailbox *mbox*. It returns
> TRUE on success, and FALSE on error.

Example

```php
<?PHP
$server = "{php123.com:143}";
$mailbox = "INBOX";
```

```
$mbox = imap_open("$server$mailbox","joeuser", "secret");
if(!$mbox)
   echo "Connect to IMAP server failed\n";
if(!imap_subscribe($mbox, $server."sent-mail"))
   echo "Could not subscribe.\n";
$list = imap_listsubscribed($mbox, $server.$mailbox, "*");
for($x = 0; $x < count($list); $x++)
   echo "list[$x]:".$list[$x]."\n";
imap_close($mbox);
?>
```

Output

```
list[0]:{php123.com:143}INBOX
list[1]:{php123.com:143}sent-mail
```

See also imap_listsubscribed() and imap_unsubscribe().

---

imap_undelete (IMAP)
unmark the message that is marked deleted

```
int imap_undelete(int imap_stream, int msg_number);
```

> This function removes the deletion flag for message *msg_number*.
> Note that messages are not permanently deleted until IMAP_expunge()
> is called. It returns TRUE on success, and FALSE on error.

Example

The code below deletes the first message in the mailbox, if it exists.

```
<?PHP
$server = "{php123.com:143}";
$mailbox = "INBOX";
$mbox = imap_open("$server$mailbox","joeuser", "secret");
if(!$mbox)
   echo "Connect to IMAP server failed\n";
if(imap_num_msg($mbox) >= 1) {
   imap_delete($mbox, 1);
   imap_undelete($mbox, 1);
}
imap_close($mbox);
?>
```

Output

```
(no output, unless error)
```

See also imap_delete() and imap_expunge().

----

imap_unsubscribe (IMAP)
unsubscribe from a mailbox

```
int imap_unsubscribe(int imap_stream, string mbox);
```

> This function unsubscribes from the specified mailbox *mbox*. It returns TRUE on success, and FALSE on error.

Example

```php
<?PHP
$server = "{php123.com:143}";
$mailbox = "INBOX";
$mbox = imap_open("$server$mailbox","joeuser", "secret");
if(!$mbox)
   echo "Connect to IMAP server failed\n";
if(!imap_unsubscribe($mbox, $server."INBOX"))
   echo "Could not subscribe.\n";
imap_close($mbox);
?>
```

Output

```
(no output, unless error)
```

See also imap_listsubscribed() and imap_subscribe().

----

imap_qprint (IMAP)
convert a quoted-printable string to an 8-bit string

```
string imap_qprint(string string);
```

> This function returns a converted 8-bit string giving a quoted-printable string.

See also imap_8bit().

----

imap_8bit (IMAP)
convert an 8-bit string to a quoted-printable string

```
string imap_8bit(string string);
```

> This function returns a converted quoted-printable string given an 8-bit string.

See also imap_qprint().

----

imap_binary (IMAP)
convert an 8-bit string to a base-64 string

```
string imap_binary(string string);
```

> This function returns a converted base-64 string given an 8-bit string.

Refer to *www.php123.com* for on-line example.
See also imap_base64().

----

imap_mailboxmsginfo (IMAP)
get information about the current mailbox

```
array imap_mailboxmsginfo(int imap_stream);
```

> This function returns an object containing information about the current mailbox status. It has the following properties:
>
> | Property | Description |
> | --- | --- |
> | date | date of message |
> | driver | name of driver |
> | mailbox | name of mailbox |
> | nmsg | total number of messages |
> | recent | total number of recent messages |
> | unread | total number of unread messages |
> | size | size of mailbox |

Example

```
<?PHP
$server = "{php123.com:143}";
$mailbox = "INBOX";
$mbox = imap_open("$server$mailbox","joeuser", "secret");
if(!$mbox)
   echo "Connect to IMAP server failed\n";
$info = imap_mailboxmsginfo($mbox);
echo "This box has ".$info->Nmsgs." message(s).\n";
imap_close($mbox);
?>
```

Output

```
This box has 3 message(s).
```

----

imap_rfc822_write_address (IMAP)

return a properly formatted email address given the mailbox, host, and personal info

```
string imap_rfc822_write_address(string mailbox, string
host, string personal);
```

Example

```
<?PHP
echo imap_rfc822_write_address("joeuser", "php123.com", "Joe
  User");
?>
```

Output

```
Joe User <joeuser@php123.com>
```

See also imap_rfc822_parse_adrlist().

----

imap_rfc822_parse_adrlist (IMAP)

parse an address string

```
string imap_rfc822_parse_adrlist(string address, string
default_host);
```

This function parses the given address string and returns an array of objects containing:

mailbox	the mailbox name (username)
host	hostname
personal	personal name
adl	domain source route

Example

```php
<?PHP
$list = imap_rfc822_parse_adrlist("joeuser@php123.com, joe,
  \"Joe  User\" <joeuser@php123.com>", "php123.com");
for($x = 0; $x < count($list); $x++) {
  echo "mailbox: ".$list[$x]->mailbox."\n";
  echo "host: ".$list[$x]->host."\n";
  echo "personal: ".$list[$x]->personal."\n";
  echo "adl: ".$list[$x]->adl."\n";
}
?>
```

Output

```
mailbox: joeuser
host: php123.com
personal:
adl:
mailbox: joe
host: php123.com
personal:
adl:
mailbox: joeuser
host: php123.com
personal: Joe User
adl:
```

See also imap_rfc822_write_address().

---

imap_setflag_full (IMAP)
set flags on messages

```
string imap_setflag_full(int stream, string sequence, string
flag, string options);
```

This function sets the specified flags for the messages specified in *sequence*. Valid flag values are:

Flag	Description
\Seen	message has been read
\Answered	message has been answered
\Flagged	message has been marked urgent
\Deleted	message has been marked as deleted
\Draft	message is stored to be finished later
\Recent	message has recently arrived

See also imap_clearflag_full().

----

imap_clearflag_full (IMAP)
clear flags on messages

```
string imap_clearflag_full(int stream, string sequence, string
flag, string options);
```

This function clears the specified flags for the messages specified in *sequence*. Valid flag values are:

Flag	Description
\Seen	message has been read
\Answered	message has been answered
\Flagged	message has been marked urgent
\Deleted	message has been marked as deleted
\Draft	message is stored to be finished later
\Recent	message has recently arrived

See also imap_setflag_full().

----

imap_fetchheader (IMAP)
return the header of a message

```
stringimap_fetchheader(int imap_stream, int msgno, int flags);
```

> This function returns a string containing the complete format header from the specified message.

Example

```php
<?PHP
$server = "{php123.com:143}";
$mailbox = "INBOX";
$mbox = imap_open("$server$mailbox","joeuser", "secret");
if(!$mbox)
   echo "Connect to IMAP server failed\n";
echo imap_fetchheader($mbox, 1);
imap_close($mbox);
?>
```

Output

```
Message-Id: <200001010000.AAA00000@smtp.php123.com>
To: joeuser@php123.com
From: admin@php123.com
Subject: Re: your message
Content-Type: text
```

See also imap_fetchbody().

----

mail (mail)
send mail

```
void mail(string receiver, string subject, string message,
string additional_headers);
```

> This function automatically mails *message* to the *receiver* with sub-ject *subject*. Multiple recipients may be specified by putting a space between each address in the *receiver* string. This function is simply a wrapper for an external program, typically sendmail. The program is specified when PHP is configured, before it is compiled and installed.

Example 1

Send a message to *info@php123.com*.

```php
mail("info@php123.com",
   "Message Subject",
   "Message body line 1\nline 2\nline 3");
```

Example 2

Send a message to *webmaster@php123.com* with the additional header "X-Priority: 1". Some mail user agents take a special action (list it first, place an exclamation pioint beside the message, etc.) on a message when that header is present.

```
mail("webmaster@php123.com", "Sub", "Testing 123",
  "X-Priority: 1");
```

Example 3

Send a message to *info@php123.com* and make it appear to be from test@php123.com.

```
mail("info@php123.com",
  "Sub",
  "Testing 123",
  " From: Test <test@php123.com>\nX-Priority: 1");
```

---

openlog (network)
open connection to system logger

```
int openlog(string ident, int option, int facility);
```

This function opens a connection to the system logger. The string ident is added to each message. The facility is one of the below values:

Facility	Description
LOG_AUTH	security/authorization messages (DEPRECATED. Use LOG_AUTHPRIV instead)
LOG_AUTHPRIV	security/authorization messages (private)
LOG_CRON	clock daemon (cron and at)
LOG_DAEMON	other system daemons
LOG_KERN	kernel messages
LOG_LOCAL0 through LOG_LOCAL7	reserved for local use
LOG_LPR	line printer subsystem
LOG_MAIL	mail subsystem

LOG_NEWS	USENET news subsystem
LOG_SYSLOG	messages generated internally by syslogd
LOG_USER(default)	generic user-level messages
LOG_UUCP	UUCP subsystem

option is one of the following values:

Option	Description
LOG_CONS	write directly to system console if there is an error while sending to system logger
LOG_NDELAY	open the connection immediately (normally, the connection is opened when the first message is logged)
LOG_PERROR	print to stderr as well
LOG_PID	Include PID with each message

Example

```PHP
<?PHP
openlog("PHP", LOG_PID | LOG_PERROR, LOG_USER);
syslog(LOG_INFO, "Doing daily updates");
closelog();
?>
```

Output

The above message will be appended to the appropriate log file. It will look something like:

```
Jan 01 00:00:00 www PHP[28935]: Doing daily updates
```

See also closelog().

----

pfsockopen (network)
.... Not yet in PHP. Look for the updated function at *www.php123.com*.

----

setcookie (http)
send a cookie

```
int setcookie(string name, string value, int expire, string
path, string domain, int secure);
```

SetCookie() defines a cookie to be sent along with the rest of the header information. The *name* argument is required; the other arguments are optional. If only the *name* argument is present, the cookie by that name will be deleted from the remote client. If the *value, path,* or *domain* arguments are skipped, they should be replaced with an empty string (" "). The *expire* and *secure* arguments are integers, and should have a 0 (zero) in their places if they are skipped. The *expire* argument is a regular Unix time integer (seconds since the Epoch) as returned by the time() function. The *secure* argument indicates that the cookie should be transmitted only over a secure HTTPS connection. Note that the value portion of the cookie will automatically be urlencoded when you send the cookie; when it is received, it is automatically decoded. It is assigned to a variable by the same name as the cookie name. For more information on cookies, see Netscape's cookie specification at *http://www.netscape.com/newsref/std/cookie_spec.html.*

Example 1

Set a cookie that expires when the client's web client is closed.

```
<?PHP
SetCookie("Student_ID","12345");
?>
```

Example 2

The code below shows how to read the value of the cookie that was set above.

```
<?PHP
echo $Student_ID;
?>
```

Example 3

The code below shows how to set a cookie that expires in 2 hours.

```
<?PHP
SetCookie("Student_ID", $id, time() + 7200);
?>
```

set_socket_blocking (network)
set blocking/non-blocking mode on a socket

```
int set_socket_blocking(int socket_descriptor, int mode);
```

> This function is used to set a socket descriptor to blocking or non-blocking mode.
>
> If *mode* is FALSE, it will be set to non-blocking mode. If *mode* is TRUE, it will be set to blocking mode (the default). This affects calls that read from a socket, like fgets() and fputs().
>
> In non-blocking mode, these calls will return immediately, before the data is read or written.

Example

In the example below, set_socket_blocking() is used to make the fgets() function return immediately without waiting for input.

```PHP
<?PHP
$web = fsockopen("www.php123.com", 80);
set_socket_blocking($web, 0);
$str = fgets($web, 1024);
echo $str;
fclose($web);
?>
```

Output

(none)

See also fsockopen().

---

snmpget (SNMP)
fetch an SNMP object

```
int snmpget(string hostname, string community, string object_id);
```

> This function returns the SNMP object value on success, and returns FALSE on error. Simple Network Management Protocol (SNMP) provides a method of monitoring and managing systems over a network. The various things that can be monitored and managed by SNMP,

collectively called the Management Information Base (MIB), are defined in several different RFCs. For more information on SNMP (Version 2), refer to the documents that define it, RFCs 1441, 1445, 1446, 1447, and 1901 through 1909.

Example

The code below uses the snmpwalk() function to return information about the specified system.

```
<?PHP
$info = snmpget("pm3.php123.com", "public",
"system.sysDescr.0");
echo $info;
?>
```

Output

(The output below is from a Livingston dial-up server. The information available via SNMP will vary depending upon the type of system.)

```
Livingston PortMaster PM-3 ComOS 3.8.2
```

See also snmpwalk().

----

snmpwalk (SNMP)
fetch an SNMP object

```
int snmpget(string hostname, string community, string
object_id);
```

This function returns the SNMP object value on success, and returns FALSE on error. Simple Network Management Protocol (SNMP) provides a method of monitoring and managing systems over a network. The various things that can be monitored and managed by SNMP, collectively called the Management Information Base (MIB), are defined in several different RFCs. For more information on SNMP (Version 2), refer to the documents that define it, RFCs 1441, 1445, 1446, 1447, and 1901 through 1909.

Example

The following code uses snmpwalk() function to return a large amount of information about the host.

```
<?PHP
$info = snmpwalk("router.php123.com", "public", "");

for($x = 0; $x < count($info); $x++)
  echo $info[$x]."\n";
?>
```

Output

(The output below is from a Cisco router. The information available via SNMP will vary depending upon the type of system.)

```
system.sysDescr.0 = OCTET STRING: "Cisco Internetwork
  Operating System Software (IGS-I-L), Version 11.0(21),
  RELEASE SOFTWARE (fc1)..Copyright (c) 1986-1998 by cisco
  Systems, Inc...Compiled Mon 31-Aug-98 16:55 by jaturner"
system.sysObjectID.0 = OBJECT IDENTIFIER: enterprises.9.1.17
system.sysUpTime.0 = Timeticks: (285623660) 33 days, 1:23:56
system.sysContact.0 = OCTET STRING: ""
system.sysName.0 = OCTET STRING: "router.php123.com"
[... and so on ...]
```

See also snmpget().

----

syslog (network)
make a system log entry

```
int syslog(int priority, string message);
```

This function makes a system log entry that is sent to syslog. The priority is one of the below values:

Priority	Description
LOG_EMERG	system is unusable
LOG_ALERT	action must be taken immediately
LOG_CRIT	critical conditions
LOG_ERR	error conditions
LOG_WARNING	warning conditions
LOG_NOTICE	normal, but significant, condition
LOG_INFO	informational message
LOG_DEBUG	debug-level message

Example

```
<?PHP
syslog(LOG_INFO, "Doing daily updates");
?>
```

Output

The above message is appended to the appropriate log file.)

See also openlog().

DATABASE-RELATED

DATABASE FUNCTIONS

NON-SQL DATABASE FUNCTIONS

dBase™ Functions (dbase)

> PHP provides tools that access data stored in dBase-format (.dbf) databases. There is no support for indexes or memo fields, nor is there support for file locking. dBase databases are not a good choice for production databases. You should use one of the many SQL databases that PHP supports. Instead, it can be used as an excellent solution for importing and exporting of your data.

General Example

The program below creates a .dbf database. It adds records to it, and then it reads them back.

```
<?PHP
// Create a database and write to it
$dbf_file_name = "/tmp/test.dbf";
// Define the fields
$def =
  array(
    array("name", "C", 50),
    array("id", "C", 8)
  );

// Create the new database
if(!($test_dbf = dbase_create($dbf_file_name, $def)))
  print "Error:  Could not create database.\n";
```

```
// Append three records to the db
$rec = array("Joe User", "1");
if(!dbase_add_record($test_dbf, $rec))
  print "Error:  Could not add record.\n";
$rec = array("John Smith", "2");
if(!dbase_add_record($test_dbf, $rec))
  print "Error:  Could not add record.\n";
$rec = array("Mary Jones", "3");
if(!dbase_add_record($test_dbf, $rec))
  print "Error:  Could not add record.\n";

// Close the database
dbase_close($test_dbf);

// Display the contents of the database
// Open the database for reading
if(!($test_dbf = dbase_open($dbf_file_name, 0)))
  print "Could not open database.\n";

// Display each record from the database
for($i = 0; $i <= dbase_numrecords($test_dbf); $i++) {
  $field = dbase_get_record($test_dbf, $i);
  echo $field[0].$field[1]."\n";
}

// Close the database
dbase_close($test_dbf);
?>
```

----

dbase_create (dbase)
create a dBase database

```
int dbase_create(string filename, array fields);
```

The fields parameter is an array of arrays. Each array describes the format of one field in the database. Each field consists of a name, a character indicating the field type, a length, and a precision.

The types of fields available are:

L	Boolean. These do not have a length or precision.
M	Memo. (Note that these are not supported by PHP.) These do not have a length or precision.
D	Date (stored as YYYYMMDD). These do not have a length or a precision.

> N   Number. These have both a length and a precision
>   (the number of digits after the decimal point).
>
> C   String.
>
> If the database is successfully created, a dbase_identifier is returned,
> otherwise FALSE is returned.
>
> A quick note about the dbase libraries: Although PHP provides tools
> to access data stored in dBase-format (.dbf) databases, there is no sup-
> port for indexes or memo fields, nor is there support for file locking.
> dBase databases are not a good choice for production databases. You
> should use one of the many SQL databases that PHP supports. Instead,
> it can be used as an excellent solution for importing and exporting
> data from legacy systems.

Example

```
<?PHP
$dbf_file_name = "/tmp/test.dbf";
// Define the fields
$def =
  array(
    array("name", "C", 50),
    array("id", "C", 8)
  );

// Create the new database
if(!($test_dbf = dbase_create($dbf_file_name, $def)))
  print "Error:  Could not create database.\n";
?>
```

Output

(none)

See also dbase_open().

----

dbase_open (dbase)
open a dBase database

```
int dbase_open(string filename, int flags);
```

> The flags correspond to those for the open() system call. Typically 0
> means read-only, 1 means write-only, and 2 means read and write. It
> returns a dbase_identifier for the opened database, or FALSE if the
> database could not be opened.

Example

```
<?PHP
$dbf_file_name = "/tmp/test.dbf";

// Open the database for reading
if(!($test_dbf = dbase_open($dbf_file_name, 0)))
  print "Could not open database.\n";

// Close the database
dbase_close($test_dbf);
?>
```

Output

(none)

See also dbase_close() and dbase_create().

----

dbase_close (dbase)
close a dBase database

```
bool dbase_close(int dbase_identifier);
```

> This function closes the database associated with dbase_identifier.

Example

```
<?PHP
$dbf_file_name = "/tmp/test.dbf";

// Open the database for reading
if(!($test_dbf = dbase_open($dbf_file_name, 0)))
  print "Could not open database.\n";

// Close the database
dbase_close($test_dbf);
?>
```

Output

(none)

See also dbase_open() and dbase_create().

----

dbase_pack (dbase)
pack a dBase database

```
bool dbase_pack(int dbase_identifier);
```

> Use this function to pack the specified database. It permanently deletes all records that have been previously marked for deletion (dbase_delete_record).

See also dbase_delete_record().

---

dbase_add_record (dbase)
add a record to a dBase database

```
bool dbase_add_record(int dbase_identifier, array record);
```

> This function adds the data in the record to the database. If the number of items in the supplied record is not equal to the number of fields in the database, the operation will fail and FALSE will be returned.

Example

```php
<?PHP
$dbf_file_name = "/tmp/test.dbf";

// Define the fields
$def =
  array(
    array("name", "C", 50),
    array("id", "C", 8)
  );

// Create the new database
if(!($test_dbf = dbase_create($dbf_file_name, $def)))
  print "Error:  Could not create database.\n";

// Append three records to the db
$rec = array("Joe User", "1");
if(!dbase_add_record($test_dbf, $rec))
  print "Error:  Could not add record.\n";
$rec = array("John Smith", "2");
if(!dbase_add_record($test_dbf, $rec))
  print "Error:  Could not add record.\n";
$rec = array("Mary Jones", "3");
if(!dbase_add_record($test_dbf, $rec))
  print "Error:  Could not add record.\n";
```

```
// Close the database
dbase_close($test_dbf);
?>
```

Output

(none)

See also dbase_delete_record().

---

dbase_delete_record (dbase)
delete a record from a dBase database

```
bool dbase_delete_record(int dbase_identifier, int record);
```

> This function marks the record to be deleted from the database. To actually remove the record from the database, you must also call dbase_pack().

Example

```
<?PHP
$dbf_file_name = "/tmp/test.dbf";

// Open the database for writing
if(!($test_dbf = dbase_open($dbf_file_name, 1)))
  print "Could not open database.\n";

// Delete each record from the database
for($i = 0; $i <= dbase_numrecords($test_dbf); $i++) {
  dbase_delete_record($test_dbf, $i);
}

// Close the database
dbase_close($test_dbf);
?>
```

Output

(none)

See also dbase_pack().

---

dbase_get_record (dbase)
get a record from a dBase database

```
array dbase_get_record(int dbase_identifier, int record);
```

This function returns the data from a record and places it into an array. The array is indexed starting at 0, and includes an associative member named 'deleted' that is set to 1 if the record has been marked for deletion (see dbase_delete_record()).

Each field is converted to the appropriate PHP type. (Dates are left as strings.)

Example

```
<?PHP
// Display the contents of the database

// Open the database for reading
if(!($test_dbf = dbase_open($dbf_file_name, 0)))
  print "Could not open database.\n";

// Display each record from the database
for($i = 0; $i <= dbase_numrecords($test_dbf); $i++) {
  $field = dbase_get_record($test_dbf, $i);
  echo $field[0].":".$field[1]."\n";
}

// Close the database
dbase_close($test_dbf);
?>
```

Output

```
Joe User:1
John Smith:2
Mary Jones:3
```

See also dbase_open().

----

dbase_numfields (dbase)
find out how many fields are in a dBase database

```
int dbase_numfields(int dbase_identifier);
```

This function returns the number of fields (columns) in the specified database.

----

dbase_numrecords (dbase)
find out how many records are in a dBase database

```
int dbase_numrecords(int dbase_identifier);
```

> This function returns the number of records (rows) in the specified
> database.

Example

```php
<?PHP
// Display the contents of the database
$dbf_file_name = "/tmp/test.dbf";

// Open the database for reading
if(!($test_dbf = dbase_open($dbf_file_name, 0)))
  print "Could not open database.\n";

// Display each record from the database
for($i = 0; $i <= dbase_numrecords($test_dbf); $i++) {
  $field = dbase_get_record($test_dbf, $i);
  echo $field[0].":".$field[1]."\n";
}

// Close the database
dbase_close($test_dbf);
?>
```

Output

```
Joe User:1
John Smith:2
Mary Jones:3
```

----

dbm Functions (dbm)

> These functions allow you to store records stored in a dbm-style data-
> base. This type of database (supported by the Berkeley db, gdbm, and
> some system libraries, as well as a built-in flatfile library) stores
> key/value pairs (as opposed to the full-blown records supported by
> relational databases).

Example

```
$dbm = dbmopen("lastseen", "w");
if (dbmexists($dbm, $userid)) {
$last_seen = dbmfetch($dbm, $userid);
} else {
dbminsert($dbm, $userid, time());
}
do_stuff();
dbmreplace($dbm, $userid, time());
dbmclose($dbm);
```
----

dbmopen (dbm)
open a dbm database

```
int dbmopen(string filename, string flags);
```

The first argument is the full-path filename of the dbm file to be opened and the second is the file open mode, which is one of "r", "n", or "w" for read-only, new (implies read-write, and may truncate an already existing database of the same name) and read-write, respectively. This function returns an identifier to be passed to the other dbm functions on success, or FALSE on failure. If ndbm support is used, ndbm will actually create filename.dir and filename.pag files. gdbm uses only one file, as does the internal flat-file support, and Berkeley db creates a filename.db file. Note that PHP does its own file locking in addition to any file locking that may be done by the dbm library itself. PHP does not delete the .lck files it creates. It uses these files simply as fixed inodes on which to do the file locking. For more information on dbm files, see your Unix man pages, or obtain GNU's gdbm from *ftp://prep.ai.mit.edu/pub/gnu*.

----

dbmclose (dbm)
close a dbm database

```
bool dbmclose(int dbm_identifier);
```

This function unlocks and closes the specified database.

----

dbmexists (dbm)

tell if a value exists for a key in a dbm database

```
bool dbmexists(int dbm_identifier, string key);
```

This function returns TRUE if there is a value associated with the key.

Refer to *www.php123.com* for on-line example.

----

dbmfetch (dbm)

fetch a value for a key from a dbm database

```
string dbmfetch(int dbm_identifier, string key);
```

This function returns the value associated with key.

Refer to *www.php123.com* for on-line example.

----

dbminsert (dbm)

insert a value for a key in a dbm database

```
int dbminsert(int dbm_identifier, string key, string value);
```

This function adds the value to the database with the specified key. It returns −1 if the database was opened read-only, 0 if the insert was successful, and 1 if the specified key already exists. (To replace the value, use dbmreplace().)

Refer to *www.php123.com* for on-line example.

----

dbmreplace (dbm)

replace the value for a key in a dbm database

```
bool dbmreplace(int dbm_identifier, string key, string value);
```

This function replaces the value for the specified key in the database. This will also add the key to the database if it didn't already exist.

Refer to *www.php123.com* for on-line example.

----

dmdelete (dbm)
delete the value for a key from a dbm database

```
bool dbmdelete(int dbm_identifier, string key);
```

> This function deletes the value for key in the database. It returns FALSE if the key didn't exist in the database.

Refer to *www.php123.com* for on-line example.

----

dbmfirstkey (dbm)
retrieve the first key from a dbm database

```
string dbmfirstkey(int dbm_identifier);
```

> This function returns the first key in the database. Note that no particular order is guaranteed, since the database may be built using a hash table, which doesn't guarantee any ordering.

Refer to *www.php123.com* for on-line example.

----

dbmnextkey (dbm)
retrieve the next key from a dbm database

```
string dbmnextkey(int dbm_identifier, string key);
```

> This function returns the next key after key. By calling dbmfirstkey(), followed by successive calls to dbmnextkey(), it is possible to visit every key/value pair in the dbm database.

Example

```
$key = dbmfirstkey($dbm_id);
while ($key) {
  echo "$key = " . dbmfetch($dbm_id, $key) . "\n";
  $key = dbmnextkey($dbm_id, $key);
}
```

----

dblist (dbm)
describe the dbm-compatible library being used

```
string dblist(void);
```

Refer to *www.php123.com* for on-line example.

----

filePro Functions (fp)

> These functions allow read-only access to data stored in filePro databases.
>
> filePro is a registered trademark by Fiserv, Inc. You can find more information about filePro at http://www.fileproplus.com/.

filepro (fp)
read and verify the map file

```
bool filepro(string directory);
```

> This function reads and verifies the map file, storing the field count and info. No locking is done, so you should avoid modifying your filePro database while it may be opened in PHP.

Refer to *www.php123.com* for on-line example.

---

filepro_fieldname (fp)
get the name of a field

```
string filepro_fieldname(int field_number);
```

> This function returns the name of the field corresponding to field_number filepro_fieldtype (fp)().
>
> It gets the type of a field: string filepro_fieldtype(int field_number); and it returns the edit type of the field corresponding to field_number.

Refer to *www.php123.com* for on-line example.

---

filepro_fieldwidth (fp)
get the width of a field

```
int filepro_fieldwidth(int field_number);
```

> This function returns the width of the field corresponding to field_number.

---

filepro_retrieve (fp)
retrieve data from a filePro database

```
string filepro_retrieve(int row_number, int field_number);
```

> This function returns the data from the specified location in the database.

Refer to *www.php123.com* for on-line example.

----

filepro_fieldcount (fp)
find out how many fields are in a filePro database

```
int filepro_fieldcount(void);
```

> This function returns the number of fields (columns) in the opened filePro database. See also filepro().

Refer to *www.php123.com* for on-line example.

----

filepro_rowcount (fp)
find out how many rows are in a filePro database

```
int filepro_rowcount(void);
```

> This function returns the number of rows in the opened filePro database. See also filepro().

Refer to *www.php123.com* for on-line example.

SQL DATABASE FUNCTIONS

mSQL Database Functions (msql)

msql (msql)
send an mSQL query to the mSQL engine

```
int msql(string database, string query, int link_identifier);
```

This function returns a positive mSQL result identifier to the query result, or FALSE on error.

msql() selects a database specified by database and executes a query on it. If the optional link identifier isn't specified, the function will try to find an open link to the mSQL server. If no open link is found, the function will attempt to create a data link as if msql_connect() had been called with no arguments.

Refer to *www.php123.com* for on-line example.

See also msql_connect().

----

msql_close (msql)
close an mSQL database connection

```
int msql_close(int link_identifier);
```

This function returns TRUE on success, FALSE on error.

msql_close() closes the data link to a mSQL database that's associated with the specified link identifier. If the link identifier is not specified, the last opened link will be closed.

It is not generally necessary to call this function, as non-persistent open links are automatically closed at the end of the a script execution. msql_close() will not close persistent links generated by msql_pconnect().

Refer to *www.php123.com* for on-line example.

See also msql_connect() and msql_pconnect().

----

msql_connect (msql)
open mSQL connection

```
int msql_connect(string hostname);
```

This function returns a positive mSQL link identifier on success, or FALSE on error. msql_connect() establishes a connection to a mSQL database server. The hostname argument is optional. If it is missing, localhost is assumed.

> If a second call is made to msql_connect() with the same arguments, no new link is established; instead, the link identifier of the already opened link is returned.
>
> Any open links are closed when execution of the script ends, unless closed earlier by explicitly calling msql_close().

Refer to *www.php123.com* for on-line example.

See also msql_pconnect(), msql_close().

----

msql_create_db (msql)
create mSQL database

```
int msql_create_db(void);
```

> msql_create_db() creates a new database on the server associated with the specified link identifier.

Refer to *www.php123.com* for on-line example.

See also msql_drop_db().

----

msql_createdb (msql)
create mSQL database

```
int msql_createdb(void);
```

> This function is identical to msql_create_db().

Refer to *www.php123.com* for on-line example.

----

msql_data_seek (msql)
move internal row pointer

```
int msql_data_seek(int result_identifier, int row_number);
```

> This function returns TRUE on success, FALSE on failure.
>
> msql_data_seek() moves the internal row pointer of the mSQL result associated with result_identifier to the row number specified by row_number. The next call to msql_fetch_row() will return the specified row.

Refer to *www.php123.com* for on-line example.

See also msql_fetch_row().

---

msql_dbname (msql)
get current mSQL database name

```
string msql_dbname(string result, int i);
```

> msql_dbname() returns the database name stored in position i of the
> result pointer returned from the msql_listdbs() function. This function
> can be used to determine how many database names are available.

Refer to *www.php123.com* for on-line example.

---

msql_drop_db (msql)
drop (delete) mSQL database

```
int msql_drop_db(string database_name, int link_identifier);
```

> This function returns TRUE on success, FALSE on failure.
>
> msql_drop_db() attempts to drop (or remove) an entire database from
> the server associated with the specified link identifier.
>
> Use this function with caution, as an entire database and all underly-
> ing tables and indexes can be destroyed in a single command.

Refer to *www.php123.com* for on-line example.

See also msql_create_db().

---

msql_dropdb (msql)
drop (or remove) an mSQL database

```
int msql_dropdb(string database_name, int link_identifier);
```

> This function is identical to msql_drop_db().

Refer to *www.php123.com* for on-line example.

---

msql_error (msql)
return error message of last msql call

```
string msql_error( );
```

Errors coming back from the mSQL database backend retrieve the error-message string. Warnings are no longer issued.

Refer to *www.php123.com* for on-line example.

----

msql_fetch_array (msql)
fetch row as array

```
int msql_fetch_array(int result);
```

This function returns an array that corresponds to the fetched row, or FALSE if there are no more rows.

msql_fetch_array() is an expanded version of msql_fetch_row(). In addition to storing the data in the numeric indices of the result array, it also stores the data in associative indices, using the field names as keys. msql_fetch_array() is not significantly slower than msql_fetch_row().

Refer to *www.php123.com* for on-line example.

See also msql_fetch_row().

----

msql_fetch_field (msql)
get field information

```
object msql_fetch_field(int result, int field_offset);
```

This function returns an object containing field information.

msql_fetch_field() can be used to obtain information about fields in a certain query result. If the field offset is not specified, the next unretrieved field is fetched.

The properties of the object are:

name   column name

table	name of the table the column belongs to
not_null	1 if the column cannot be null
primary_key	1 if the column is a primary key
unique	1 if the column is a unique key
type	the type of the column

Refer to *www.php123.com* for on-line example.

See also msql_field_seek().

----

msql_fetch_object (msql)
fetch row as object

```
int msql_fetch_object(int result);
```

This function returns an object with properties that correspond to the fetched row, or FALSE if there are no more rows.

msql_fetch_object() is similar to msql_fetch_array(), with one difference: an object is returned, instead of an array. Indirectly, that means that you can access the data only by the field names, and not by their offsets (numbers are illegal property names).

The function is as fast as msql_fetch_array(), and almost as fast as msql_fetch_row() (the difference is insignificant).

Refer to *www.php123.com* for on-line example.

See also msql_fetch_array() and msql_fetch_row().

----

msql_fetch_row (msql)
get row as enumerated array

```
array msql_fetch_row(int result);
```

This function returns an array that corresponds to the fetched row, or FALSE if there are no more rows.

msql_fetch_row() fetches one row of data from the result associated with the specified result identifier. The row is returned as an array. Each result column is stored in an array offset, starting at offset 0. Subsequent call to msql_fetch_row() returns the next row in the result set, or FALSE if there are no more rows.

Refer to *www.php123.com* for on-line example.

See also msql_fetch_array(), msql_fetch_object(), msql_data_seek(), and msql_result().

---

msql_fieldname (msql)
get field name

```
string msql_fieldname(int result, int field);
```

> msql_fieldname() returns the name of the specified field. result is the result identifier, and field is the field index. msql_fieldname($result, 2); will return the name of the second field in the result associated with the result identifier.

Refer to *www.php123.com* for on-line example.

---

msql_field_seek (msql)
set field offset

```
int msql_field_seek(int result, int field_offset);
```

> This function seeks for the specified field offset. If the next call to msql_fetch_field() won't include a field offset, this field would be returned.

Refer to *www.php123.com* for on-line example.

See also msql_fetch_field().

---

msql_fieldtable (msql)
get table name for field

```
int msql_fieldtable(int result, int field);
```

> This function returns the name of the table from which that field was fetched.

Refer to *www.php123.com* for on-line example.

---

msql_fieldtype (msql)
get field type

```
string msql_fieldtype(string result, int i);
```

> msql_fieldtype() is similar to the msql_fieldname() function. The arguments are identical, but the field type is returned. This will be one of "int", "string", or "real".

Refer to *www.php123.com* for on-line example.

----

msql_fieldflags (msql)
get field flags

```
string msql_fieldflags(string result, int i);
```

> msql_fieldflags() returns the field flags of the specified field. Currently this is "not null", "primary key", a combination of the two, or "" (an empty string).

Refer to *www.php123.com* for on-line example.

----

msql_fieldlen (msql)
get field length

```
int msql_fieldlen(string result, int i);
```

> msql_fieldlen() returns the length of the specified field.

Refer to *www.php123.com* for on-line example.

----

msql_free_result (msql)
free result memory

```
int msql_free_result(int result);
```

> msql_free_result() frees the memory associated with result. When PHP completes a request, this memory is freed automatically, so you need to call this function only when you want to make sure you don't use too much memory while the script is running.

Refer to *www.php123.com* for on-line example.

----

msql_freeresult (msql)
free result memory

```
int msql_freeresult(int result);
```

> This function is identical to msql_free_result().

Refer to *www.php123.com* for on-line example.

----

msql_list_fields (msql)
list result fields

```
int msql_list_fields(string database, string tablename);
```

> msql_list_fields() retrieves information about the given tablename.
> Arguments are the database name and the table name. A result pointer
> is returned that can be used with msql_fieldflags(), msql_fieldlen(),
> msql_fieldname(), and msql_fieldtype(). A result identifier is a positive
> integer. The function returns −1 if an error occurs. A string describing
> the error will be placed in $phperrmsg, and unless the function was
> called as @msql_list_fields(), this error string will also be printed out.

Refer to *www.php123.com* for on-line example.

See also msql_error().

----

msql_listfields (msql)
list result fields

```
int msql_listfields(string database, string tablename);
```

> This function is identical to msql_list_fields().

Refer to *www.php123.com* for on-line example.

----

msql_list_dbs (msql)
list mSQL databases on server

```
int msql_list_dbs(void);
```

> msql_list_dbs() returns a result pointer containing the databases available from the current msql daemon. Use the msql_dbname() function to traverse this result pointer.

Refer to *www.php123.com* for on-line example.

----

msql_listdbs (msql)
list mSQL databases on server

```
int msql_listdbs(void);
```

> This function is identical to msql_list_dbs().

Refer to *www.php123.com* for on-line example.

----

msql_list_tables (msql)
list tables in an mSQL database

```
int msql_list_tables(string database);
```

> msql_list_tables() takes a database name and result pointer, much like the msql() function. The msql_tablename() function should be used to extract the actual table names from the result pointer.

Refer to *www.php123.com* for on-line example.

----

msql_listtables (msql)
list tables in an mSQL database

```
int msql_listtables('string database);
```

> This function is identical to msql_list_tables().

Refer to *www.php123.com* for on-line example.

----

msql_num_fields (msql)
get number of fields in result

```
int msql_num_fields(int result);
```

> msql_num_fields() returns the number of fields in a result set.

Refer to *www.php123.com* for on-line example.

See also msql(), msql_query(), msql_fetch_field(), and msql_num_rows().

----

msql_num_rows (msql)
get number of rows in result

```
int msql_num_rows(string result);
```

> msql_num_rows() returns the number of rows in a result set.

Refer to *www.php123.com* for on-line example.

See also msql(), msql_query(), and msql_fetch_row().

----

msql_numfields (msql)
get number of fields in result

```
int msql_numfields(int result);
```

> This function is identical to msql_num_fields().

Refer to *www.php123.com* for on-line example.

----

msql_numrows (msql)
get number of rows in result

```
int msql_numrows(void);
```

> This function is identical to msql_num_rows().

Refer to *www.php123.com* for on-line example.

----

msql_pconnect (msql)
open persistent mSQL connection

```
int msql_pconnect(string hostname);
```

> This function returns a positive mSQL persistent link identifier on success, or FALSE on error. msql_pconnect() acts very much like msql_connect(), with two major differences:
>
> First, when connecting, the function first tries to find a (persistent) link that's already open with the same host. If one is found, an identifier for it will be returned instead of opening a new connection.
>
> Second, the connection to the SQL server is not closed when the execution of the script ends. Instead, the link will remain open for future use (msql_close() will not close links established by msql_pconnect()).
>
> This type of link is therefore called 'persistent'. See Section 2.2.3.

Refer to *www.php123.com* for on-line example.

----

msql_query (msql)
send mSQL query

```
int msql_query(string query, int link_identifier);
```

> msql_query() sends a query to the currently active database on the server that's associated with the specified link identifier. If the link identifier isn't specified, the last opened link is assumed. If no link is open, the function tries to establish a link as if msql_connect() was called, and use it.
>
> This function returns a positive mSQL result identifier on success, or FALSE on error.

Refer to *www.php123.com* for on-line example.

See also msql(), msql_select_db(), and msql_connect().

----

msql_regcase (msql)
make regular expression for case-insensitive match

Refer to *www.php123.com* for on-line example.

See also sql_regcase().

----

msql_result (msql)
get result data

```
int msql_result(int result, int i, mixed field);
```

This function returns the contents of the cell at the row and offset in the specified mSQL result set.

msql_result() returns the contents of one cell from a mSQL result set. The field argument can be the field's offset, or the field's name, or the field's table dot field's name (fieldname.tablename). If the column name has been aliased ('select foo as bar from...'), use the alias instead of the column name.

When working on large result sets, you should consider using one of the functions that fetch an entire row (specified below). As these functions return the contents of multiple cells in one function call, they're MUCH quicker than msql_result(). Also, note that specifying a numeric offset for the field argument is much quicker than specifying a fieldname or tablename.fieldname argument.

Recommended high-performance alternatives: msql_fetch_row(), msql_fetch_array(), and msql_fetch_object().

Refer to *www.php123.com* for on-line example.

msql_select_db (msql)
select mSQL database

```
int msql_select_db(string database_name, int link_identifier);
```

This function returns TRUE on success, FALSE on error.

msql_select_db() sets the current active database on the server that's associated with the specified link identifier. If no link identifier is specified, the last opened link is assumed. If no link is open, the function will try to establish a link as if msql_connect() was called, and use it.

Every subsequent call to msql_query() is made on the active database.

Refer to *www.php123.com* for on-line example.

See also msql_connect(), msql_pconnect(), and msql_query().

msql_selectdb (msql)
select mSQL database

```
int msql_selectdb(string database_name, int link_identifier);
```

This function is identical to msql_select_db().

Refer to *www.php123.com* for on-line example.

----

msql_tablename (msql)
get table name of field

```
string msql_tablename(int result, int field);
```

> msql_tablename() takes a result pointer returned by the
> msql_list_tables() function as well as an integer index and returns
> the name of a table. The msql_numrows() function may be used to
> determine the number of tables in the result pointer.

Example
```php
<?php
msql_connect ("localhost");
$result = msql_list_tables("wisconsin");
$i = 0;
while ($i < msql_numrows($result)) {
  $tb_names[$i] = msql_tablename($result, $i);
  echo $tb_names[$i] . "<BR>";
  $i++;
}
?>
```

ODBC Database Functions (odbc)

odbc_autocommit (obdb)
toggle autocommit behavior

```
int odbc_autocommit(int connection_id, int OnOff);
```

> This function returns TRUE on success, FALSE on failure. By default,
> autocommit is on for a connection.

Refer to *www.php123.com* for on-line example.

See also odbc_commit() and odbc_rollback().

----

odbc_binmode (obdb)
handle binary column data

```
int odbc_binmode(int result_id, int mode);
```

(ODBC SQL types affected: BINARY, VARBINARY, LONGVARBINARY)

  0: Passthrough BINARY data

  1: Return as is

  2: Return and convert to char

When binary SQL data is converted to character C data, each byte (8 bits) of source data is represented as two ASCII characters. These characters are the ASCII character representation of the number in its hexadecimal form. For example, a binary 00000001 is converted to "01" and a binary 11111111 is converted to "FF".

Refer to *www.php123.com* for on-line example.

----

odbc_close (obdb)
close an ODBC connection

```
void odbc_close(int connection_id);
```

odbc_close() closes down the connection to the database server associated with the given connection identifier.

This function fails if there are open transactions on this connection. The connection remains open in this case.

Refer to *www.php123.com* for on-line example.

----

odbc_close_all (obdb)
close all ODBC connections

```
void odbc_close_all(void);
```

odbc_close_all() will close down all connections to database server(s).

This function fails if there are open transactions on a connection. This connection remains open in this case.

Refer to *www.php123.com* for on-line example.

----

odbc_commit (obdb)
commit an ODBC transaction

```
int odbc_commit(int connection_id);
```

This function returns TRUE on success, FALSE on failure. All pending transactions on connection_id are committed.

Refer to *www.php123.com* for on-line example.

---

odbc_connect (obdb)
connect to a datasource

```
int odbc_connect(string dsn, string user, string password);
```

This function returns an ODBC connection id or 0 (FALSE) on error.

The connection id returned by this function is needed by other ODBC functions. You can have multiple connections open at once. For persistent connections see odbc_pconnect().

Refer to *www.php123.com* for on-line example.

---

odbc_cursor (obdb)
get cursorname

```
string odbc_cursor(int result_id);
```

odbc_cursor will return a cursorname for the given result_id.

Refer to *www.php123.com* for on-line example.

---

odbc_do (obdb)
get cursorname

```
string odbc_cursor(int result_id);
```

odbc_cursor will return a cursorname for the given result_id.

Refer to *www.php123.com* for on-line example.

---

odbc_exec (obdb)
prepare and execute a SQL statement

```
int odbc_exec(int connection_id, string query_string);
```

> This function returns FALSE on error, and returns an ODBC result identifier if the SQL command was executed successfully.
>
> odbc_exec() will send an SQL statement to the database server specified by connection_id. This parameter must be a valid identifier returned by odbc_connect() or odbc_pconnect().

Refer to *www.php123.com* for on-line example.

See also odbc_prepare() and odbc_execute() for multiple execution of SQL statements.

---

odbc_execute (obdb)
execute a prepated statement

```
int odbc_execute(int result_id, array parameters_array);
```

> This function executes a statement prepared with odbc_prepare(). It returns TRUE on successful execution, FALSE otherwise. The array parameters_array must be given only if you really have parameters in your statement.

Refer to *www.php123.com* for on-line example.

---

odbc_fetch_into (obdb)
fetch one result row into array

```
int odbc_fetch_into(int result_id, int rownumber, array
result_array);
```

> This function returns the number of columns in the result, FALSE on error. result_array must be passed by reference, but it can be of any type since it will be converted to type array. The array will contain the column values starting at array index 0.

Refer to *www.php123.com* for on-line example.

---

odbc_fetch_row (obdb)
fetch a row

```
int odbc_fetch_row(int result_id, int row_number);
```

> If odbc_fetch_row() was succesful (there was a row), TRUE is returned. If there are no more rows, FALSE is returned.
>
> odbc_fetch_row() fetches a row of the data that was returned by odbc_do() / odbc_exec(). After odbc_fetch_row() is called, the fields of that row can be accessed with odbc_result().
>
> If row_number is not specified, odbc_fetch_row() will try to fetch the next row in the result set. Calls to odbc_fetch_row() with and without row_number can be mixed.
>
> To step through the result more than once, you can call odbc_fetch_row() with row_number 1, and then continue doing odbc_fetch_row() without row_number to review the result. If a driver doesn't support fetching rows by number, the row_number parameter is ignored.

Refer to *www.php123.com* for on-line example.

----

odbc_field_name (obdb)
get the column name

```
string odbc_fieldname(int result_id, int field_number);
```

> odbc_field_name() will return the name of the field occupying the given column number in the given ODBC result identifier. Field numbering starts at 1. FALSE is returned on error.

Refer to *www.php123.com* for on-line example.

----

odbc_field_num (obdb)
return column number

```
int odbc_fieldnum(int result_id, string field_name);
```

> odbc_field_num() will return the number of the column slot that corresponds to the named field in the given ODBC result identifier. Field numbering starts at 1. FALSE is returned on error.

Refer to *www.php123.com* for on-line example.

----

odbc_field_type (obdb)
get datatype of a field

```
string odbc_field_type(int result_id, mixed field);
```

> odbc_field_type() will return the SQL type of the field referenced by
> name or number in the given ODBC result identifier. Field numbering
> runs from 1.

Refer to *www.php123.com* for on-line example.

----

odbc_free_result (obdb)
free resources associated with a result

```
int odbc_free_result(int result_id);
```

> This function always returns TRUE.
>
> odbc_free_result() must be called only if you are worried about using
> too much memory while your script is running. All result memory
> will automatically be freed when the script is finished. But if you are
> sure you are not going to need the result data any more in a script, you
> may call odbc_free_result(), and the memory associated with result_id
> will be freed.
>
> If auto-commit is disabled (see odbc_autocommit()) and you call
> odbc_free_result() before commiting, all pending transactions are
> rolled back.

Refer to *www.php123.com* for on-line example.

----

odbc_longreadlen (obdb)
handle LONG columns

```
int odbc_longreadlen(int result_id, int length);
```

> (ODBC SQL types affected: LONG, LONGVARBINARY)
>
> The number of bytes returned to PHP is controlled by the parameter
> length. If it is set to 0, Long column data is passed through to the client.
>
> Handling of LONGVARBINARY columns is also affected by
> odbc_binmode().

Refer to *www.php123.com* for on-line example.

----

odbc_num_fields (obdb)
return number of columns in a result

```
int odbc_num_fields(int result_id);
```

odbc_num_fields() returns the number of fields (columns) in an ODBC result. This function will return −1 on error. The argument is a valid result identifier returned by odbc_exec().

Refer to *www.php123.com* for on-line example.

----

odbc_pconnect (obdb)
open a persistent database connection

```
int odbc_pconnect(string dsn, string user, string password);
```

Returns an ODBC connection id or 0 (FALSE) on error. This function is much like odbc_connect(), except that the connection is not really closed when the script has finished. Future requests for a connection with the same dsn, user, password combination (via odbc_connect() and odbc_pconnect()) can reuse the persistent connection.

Refer to *www.php123.com* for on-line example.

----

odbc_prepare (obdb)
prepare a statement for execution

```
int odbc_prepare(int connection_id, string query_string);
```

This function returns FALSE on error, and returns an ODBC result identifier if the SQL command was prepared successfully. The result identifier can be used later to execute the statement with odbc_execute().

Refer to *www.php123.com* for on-line example.

----

odbc_num_rows (obdb)
return number of rows in a result

```
int odbc_num_rows(int result_id);
```

odbc_num_rows() will return the number of rows in an ODBC result. This function will return −1 on error. For INSERT, UPDATE, and DELETE statements, odbc_num_rows() returns the number of rows affected. For a SELECT clause this can be the number of rows available.

Using odbc_num_rows() to determine the number of rows available after a SELECT will return −1 with many drivers.

Refer to *www.php123.com* for on-line example.

----

odbc_result (obdb)
get result data

```
string odbc_result(int result_id, mixed field);
```

This function returns the contents of the field.

Field indices start from 1. For the way binary or long column data is returned, refer to odbc_binmode () and odbc_longreadlen().

Refer to *www.php123.com* for on-line example.

----

odbc_result_all (obdb)
print result as HTML table

```
int odbc_result_all(int result_id, string format);
```

This function returns the number of rows in the result or FALSE on error.

odbc_result_all() prints all rows from a result identifier produced by odbc_exec(). The result is printed in HTML table format. With the optional string argument format, additional overall table formatting can be done.

Refer to *www.php123.com* for on-line example.

----

odbc_rollback (obdb)
roll back a transaction

```
int odbc_rollback(int connection_id);
```

> This function rolls back all pending statements on connection_id; it returns TRUE on success, FALSE on failure.

Refer to *www.php123.com* for on-line example.

Oracle™ Database Functions *(oracle)*

ora_Bind *(oracle)*
bind a PHP variable to an Oracle parameter

```
int ora_bind(int cursor, string PHP variable name, string SQL
parameter name, int length, int type);
```

> This function returns TRUE if the bind succeeds, otherwise FALSE. Details about the error can be retrieved using the ora_error() and ora_errorcode() functions.
>
> This function binds the named PHP variable with a SQL parameter. The SQL parameter must be in the form ":name". With the optional type parameter, you can define whether the SQL parameter is an in/out (0, default), in (1) or out (2) parameter. As of PHP 3.0.1, you can use the constants ORA_BIND_INOUT, ORA_BIND_IN, and ORA_BIND_OUT instead of the numbers.
>
> ora_bind must be called after ora_parse() and before ora_exec(). Input values can be given by assignment to the bound PHP variables; after calling ora_exec() the bound PHP variables contain the output values if available.

Example

```php
<?php
ora_parse($curs, "declare tmp INTEGER; begin tmp := :in; :out
  := tmp; :x := 7.77; end;");
ora_bind($curs, "result", ":x", $len, 2);
ora_bind($curs, "input", ":in", 5, 1);
ora_bind($curs, "output", ":out", 5, 2);
$input = 765;
ora_exec($curs);
echo "Result: $result<BR>Out: $output<BR>In: $input";
?>
```

---

ora_Close (oracle)
close an Oracle cursor

```
int ora_close(int cursor);
```

> This function returns TRUE if the close succeeds, otherwise FALSE. Details about the error can be retrieved using the ora_error() and ora_errorcode() functions.
>
> This function closes a data cursor opened with ora_open().

Refer to *www.php123.com* for on-line example.

----

ora_ColumnName (oracle)
get name of Oracle result column

```
string Ora_ColumnName(int cursor, int column);
```

> This function returns the name of the field/column column on the cursor cursor. The returned name is in all-uppercase letters.

Refer to *www.php123.com* for on-line example.

----

ora_ColumnType (oracle)
get type of Oracle result column

```
string Ora_ColumnType(int cursor, int column);
```

> This function returns the Oracle data type name of the field/column column on the cursor cursor. The returned type will be one of the following:
>
> VARCHAR2, VARCHAR, CHAR, NUMBER, LONG, LONG RAW, ROWID, DATE, CURSOR

Refer to *www.php123.com* for on-line example.

----

ora_Commit (oracle)
commit an Oracle transaction

```
int ora_commit(int conn);
```

This function returns TRUE on success, FALSE on error. Details about the error can be retrieved using the ora_error() and ora_errorcode() functions. This function commits an Oracle transaction. A transaction is defined as all the changes on a given connection since the last commit/rollback, since autocommit was turned off, or since the connection was established.

Refer to *www.php123.com* for on-line example.

----

ora_CommitOff (oracle)
disable automatic commit

```
int ora_commitoff(int conn);
```

This function returns TRUE on success, FALSE on error. Details about the error can be retrieved using the ora_error() and ora_errorcode() functions.

This function turns off automatic commit after each ora_exec().

Refer to *www.php123.com* for on-line example.

----

ora_CommitOn (oracle)
enable automatic commit

```
int ora_CommitOn(int conn);
```

Refer to *www.php123.com* for on-line example.

----

ora_Error (oracle)
get Oracle error message

```
string Ora_Error(int cursor);
```

This function returns an error message of the form XXX-NNNNN, where XXX is where the error comes from and NNNNN identifies the error message.

Refer to *www.php123.com* for on-line example.

----

ora_ErrorCode (oracle)
get Oracle error code

```
int Ora_ErrorCode(int cursor);
```

> This function returns the numeric error code of the last executed statement on the specified cursor.

Refer to *www.php123.com* for on-line example.

----

ora_Exec (oracle)
execute parsed statement on an Oracle cursor

```
int ora_exec(int cursor);
```

> This function returns TRUE on success, FALSE on error. Details about the error can be retrieved using the ora_error() and ora_errorcode() functions.

Refer to *www.php123.com* for on-line example.

----

ora_Fetch (oracle)
fetch a row of data from a cursor

```
int ora_fetch(int cursor);
```

> This function returns TRUE (a row was fetched) or FALSE (no more rows, or an error occurred). If an error occured, details can be retrieved using the ora_error() and ora_errorcode() functions. If there was no error, ora_errorcode() will return 0. Retrieves a row of data from the specified cursor.

Refer to *www.php123.com* for on-line example.

----

ora_GetColumn (oracle)
get data from a fetched row

```
mixed ora_getcolumn(int cursor, mixed column);
```

> This function returns the column data. If an error occurs, FALSE is returned and ora_errorcode() will return a non-zero value. Note, however, that a test for FALSE on the results from this function may be TRUE in cases where there is no error as well (NULL result, empty string, the number 0, the string "0"). Fetches the data for a column or function result.

Refer to *www.php123.com* for on-line example.

----

ora_Logoff (oracle)
close an Oracle connection

```
int ora_logoff(int connection);
```

> This function returns TRUE on success, FALSE on error. Details about the error can be retrieved using the ora_error() and ora_errorcode() functions. Logs out the user and disconnects from the server.

Refer to *www.php123.com* for on-line example.

----

ora_Logon (oracle)
open an Oracle connection

```
int ora_logon(string user, string password);
```

> This function establishes a connection between PHP and an Oracle database with the given username and password.
>
> This function returns a connection index on success, or FALSE on failure. Details about the error can be retrieved using the ora_error() and ora_errorcode() functions.

Refer to *www.php123.com* for on-line example.

----

ora_Open (oracle)
open an Oracle cursor

```
int ora_open(int connection);
```

> This function opens an Oracle cursor associated with connection. It
> returns a cursor index or False on failure. Details about the error can
> be retrieved using the ora_error() and ora_errorcode() functions.

Refer to *www.php123.com* for on-line example.

----

ora_Parse (oracle)
parse an SQL statement

```
int ora_parse(int cursor_ind, string sql_statement, int
defer);
```

> This function parses an SQL statement or a PL/SQL block and associ-
> ates it with the given cursor. It returns 0 on success or −1 on error.

Refer to *www.php123.com* for on-line example.

----

ora_Rollback (oracle)
roll back transaction

```
int ora_rollback(int connection);
```

> This function undoes an Oracle transaction. (See ora_commit() for the
> definition of a transaction.) It returns TRUE on success, FALSE on
> error. Details about the error can be retrieved using the ora_error() and
> ora_errorcode() functions.

Refer to *www.php123.com* for on-line example.

Oracle 8 Functions (or8)

ocIDefineByName (or8)
use a PHP variable for the define-step during a SELECT

```
int OCIDefineByName(int stmt, string Column-Name, mixed
&variable, int [type]);
```

> OCIDefineByName() uses fetches SQL-Columns into user-defined
> PHP-Variables. Be careful that Oracle uses ALL-UPPERCASE column-
> names, whereby in your select statement you can also write lowercase.

OCIDefineByName() expects the Column-Name to be in uppercase. If you define a variable that doesn't exist in your select statement, no error will be given! If you need to define an abstract Datatype (LOB/ROWID/BFILE), you need to allocate it first using OCINewDescriptor() function. See also the OCIBindByName() function.

Example

```php
<?php
/* OCIDefineByPos example thies@digicol.de (980219) */

$conn = OCILogon("scott","tiger");

$stmt = OCIParse($conn,"select empno, ename from emp");

/* the define MUST be done BEFORE ociexecute! */

OCIDefineByName($stmt,"EMPNO",&$empno);
OCIDefineByName($stmt,"ENAME",&$ename);

OCIExecute($stmt);

while (OCIFetch($stmt)) {
   echo "empno:".$empno."\n";
   echo "ename:".$ename."\n";
}
OCIFreeStatement($stmt);
OCILogoff($conn);
?>
```

---

ociBindByName (or8)
bind a PHP variable to an Oracle Placeholder

```
int OCIBindByName(int stmt, string ph_name, mixed &variable,
intlength, int [type]);
```

OCIBindByName()binds the PHP variable variable to the Oracle placeholder ph_name. Whether it will be used for input or output will be determined at run time, and the necessary storage space will be allocated. The length parameter sets the maximum length for the bind. If you set length to −1, OCIBindByName() will use the current length of variable to set the maximum length.

Refer to *www.php123.com* for on-line example.

---

ocILogon (or8)
establish a connection to Oracle

```
int OCILogon(string username, string password, string
[OCACLE_SID]);
```

> OCILogon() returns an connection identified as needed for most other OCI calls.

Refer to *www.php123.com* for on-line example.

---

ocILogOff (or8)
disconnect from Oracle

```
int OCILogOff(int connection);
```

> OCILogOff() closes an Oracle connection.

Refer to *www.php123.com* for on-line example.

---

ocIExecute (or8)
execute a statement

```
int OCIExecute(int statement, int [mode]);
```

> OCIExecute() executes a previously parsed statement (see OCIParse()). The optional mode allows you to specify the execution mode (default is OCI_COMMIT_ON_SUCCESS). If you don't want statements to be commited automatically, specify OCI_DEFAULT as your mode.

Refer to *www.php123.com* for on-line example.

---

ocICommit (or8)
commit outstanding transactions

```
int OCICommit(int connection);
```

> OCICommit() commits all outstanding statements for Oracle connection connection.

Refer to *www.php123.com* for on-line example.

----

ociRollback (or8)

rolls back outstanding transactions

```
int OCIRollback(int connection);
```

> OCIRollback() rolls back all outstanding statements for Oracle con-
> nection connection.

Refer to *www.php123.com* for on-line example.

----

ociNumRows (or8)

get the number of affected rows

```
int OCINumRows(int statement);
```

> OCINumRows() returns the number of rows affected for (e.g.) update-
> statements. This function will not tell you the number of rows that a
> select will return.

Refer to *www.php123.com* for on-line example.

----

ociResult (or8)

returns column value for fetched row

```
int OCIResult(int statement, mixed column);
```

> OCIResult() returns the data for column column in the current row
> (see OCIFetch()). OCIResult() will return everything as strings except
> for abstract types (ROWIDs, LOBs and FILEs).

Refer to *www.php123.com* for on-line example.

----

ociFetch (or8)

fetch the next row into result buffer

```
int OCIFetch(int statement);
```

> OCIFetch() fetches the next row (for SELECT statements) into the internal result buffer.

Refer to *www.php123.com* for on-line example.

----

ociFetchInto (or8)
fetch the next row into resul array

```
int OCIFetchInto(array &result, int [mode]);
```

> OCIFetchInto() fetches the next row (for SELECT statements) into the result array. OCIFetchInto() will overwrite the previous content of result. By default result will contain a one-based array of all columns that are not NULL.

Refer to *www.php123.com* for on-line example.

----

ociColumnIsNULL (or8)
test whether a result column is NULL

```
int OCIColumnIsNULL(int stmt, mixed column);
```

> OCIColumnIsNULL() returns TRUE if the returned column col in the result from the statement *stmt* is NULL. You can use either the column-number (1-based) or the column-name for the col parameter.

Refer to *www.php123.com* for on-line example.

----

ociColumnSize (or8)
return result column size

```
int OCIColumnSize(int stmt, mixed column);
```

> OCIColumnSize() returns the size of the column as given by Oracle. You can use either the column-number (1-based) or the column-name for the col parameter.

Refer to *www.php123.com* for on-line example.

PostgreSQL Database Functions (postgresql)

pg_Close (postgresql)
close a PostgreSQL connection

```
bool pg_close(int connection);
```

> The function closes the specified connection. It returns FALSE if connection is not a valid connection index.

Example

```php
<?PHP
$conn = pg_pConnect("dbname=test port=5432");
if(!$conn) {
  print "Error: Could not connect to database.<br>\n";
  exit;
}
pg_close($conn);
?>
```

Output

```
(none, unless error)
```

See also pg_Connect() and pg_pConnect().

----

pg_cmdTuples (postgresql)
return number of affected tuples

```
int pg_cmdtuples(int result_id);
```

> This function returns the number of rows affected by INSERT, UPDATE, and DELETE queries. If no rows are affected, the function returns 0.

Example

```php
<?PHP
$conn = pg_pConnect("dbname=test port=5432");
if(!$conn) {
  print "Error: Could not connect to database.<br>\n";
  exit;
}
```

```
$result = pg_Exec("UPDATE student SET password='abc' WHERE
  id='1'");
echo pg_cmdTuples($result);

pg_close($conn);
?>
```

Output

```
1
```

See also pg_Exec() and pg_Result().

----

pg_Connect (postgresql)
open a connection

```
int pg_connect(string host, string port, string options,
string tty, string dbname);
```

> This function opens a connection to a PostgreSQL database and
> returns a connection index on success, or FALSE in case of error. The
> return value is used by other PostgreSQL functions.

Example

```
<?PHP
$conn = pg_Connect("dbname=test port=5432");
if(!$conn) {
  print "Error: Could not connect to database.<br>\n";
  exit;
}

$result = pg_Exec("SELECT * FROM student");
for($x = 0; $x < pg_NumRows($result); $x++) {
  $id = trim(pg_Result($result, $x, "id"));
  $password = trim(pg_Result($result, $x, "password"));
  echo "ID #:".$id."/".$password."\n";
}

pg_close($conn);
?>
```

Output

```
ID #:1/abc
ID #:2/def
```

See also pg_pConnect() and pg_close().

----

pg_Dbname (postgresql)
return database name

```
string pg_dbname(int connection);
```

This function returns the name of the database the given PostgreSQL connection index is connected to. In case of error, it returns FALSE.

Example

```php
<?PHP
$conn = pg_Connect("dbname=test port=5432");
if(!$conn) {
  print "Error: Could not connect to database.<br>\n";
  exit;
}

echo pg_DBname($conn);

pg_close($conn);
?>
```

Output

```
test
```

See also pg_Connect().

----

pg_ErrorMessage (postgresql)
return error message

```
string pg_errormessage(int connection);
```

This function returns a string containing an error message returned from the PostgreSQL server. If no error was returned, then this function returns FALSE. To use this function effectively, you may want to put an @ sign before each pg_ function call. This will turn off PHP's usual error reporting. Often with web pages, more control over the format of error messages is needed.

Example

In the code shown below, the SQL SELECT statement contains a typo. pg_ErrorMessage() is used to display the error message returned from the server. Also, note that the call to pg_Exec has an @ sign in front of it.

```
<?PHP
$conn = pg_pConnect("dbname=test port=5432");
if(!$conn) {
  echo "Error: Could not connect to database.<br>\n";
  exit;
}

$result = @pg_Exec("SELECT * FROM studentttt");
if(!$result) {
  echo "[".__FILE__."]/[".__LINE__."]->
".pg_errormessage($conn)."\n";
}

pg_close($conn);
?>
```

Output

```
[/www/example.php3]/[14]-> ERROR: studentttt: Table does not
exist.
```

See also pg_connect() and pg_result().

----

pg_Exec (postgresql)
execute a query

```
int pg_exec(int connection, string query);
```

> This function sends the SQL statement *query* to the PostgreSQL database specified by the *connection* parameter. A result index is returned if the query can be executed. FALSE is returned on failure or if connection index is not valid. Details about the error can be found using the pg_ErrorMessage() function. The return value of this function is an index that is used to access the returned results.

Example

```
<?PHP
$conn = pg_Connect("dbname=test port=5432");
if(!$conn) {
  print "Error: Could not connect to database.<br>\n";
  exit;
}

$result = pg_Exec("SELECT * FROM student");
for($x = 0; $x < pg_NumRows($result); $x++) {
  $id = trim(pg_Result($result, $x, "id"));
```

```
    $password = trim(pg_Result($result, $x, "password"));
@Normal:   echo "ID #:".$id."/".$password."\n";
}

pg_close($conn);
?>
```

Output

```
ID #:1/abc
ID #:2/def
```

See also pg_Connect() and pg_Result().

----

pg_Fetch_Array (postgresql)
fetch row as an associative array

```
array pg_fetch_array(int result, int row);
```

> This function returns an associative array containing the row speci-
> fied by the result set/row pair. It returns FALSE if there are no more
> rows. Sequential calls to pg_fetch_row() will return the next row in
> the result set, or FALSE if there are no more rows.

Example

```
<?PHP
$conn = pg_Connect("dbname=test port=5432");
if(!$conn) {
  print "Error: Could not connect to database.<br>\n";
  exit;
}

$result = pg_Exec("SELECT * FROM student WHERE id='1'");

$row = pg_fetch_array($result, 0);
echo $row["id"].":".$row["password"]."\n";

pg_close($conn);
?>
```

Output

```
1:abc
```

See also pg_fetch_object() and pg_fetch_row().

----

pg_Fetch_Object (postgresql)

fetch row as object

```
object pg_fetch_object(int result, int row);
```

> This function returns an object with properties that correspond to the fetched row. It returns FALSE if there are no more rows. Sequential calls to pg_fetch_row() will return the next row in the result set, or FALSE if there are no more rows.

Example

```
<?PHP
$conn = pg_Connect("dbname=test port=5432");
if(!$conn) {
  print "Error: Could not connect to database.<br>\n";
  exit;
}

$result = pg_Exec("SELECT * FROM student WHERE id='1'");

$row = pg_fetch_object($result, 0);
echo $row->id.":".$row->password."\n";

pg_close($conn);
?>
```

Output

```
1:abc
```

See also pg_fetch_array() and pg_fetch_row().

----

pg_Fetch_Row (postgresql)

get row as an array

```
array pg_fetch_row(int result, int row);
```

> This function returns an array containing the row specified by the result set/row pair. It returns FALSE if there are no more rows. Sequential calls to pg_fetch_row() will return the next row in the result set, or FALSE if there are no more rows.

Example

```
<?PHP
$conn = pg_Connect("dbname=test port=5432");
```

```
if(!$conn) {
  print "Error: Could not connect to database.<br>\n";
  exit;
}

$result = pg_Exec("SELECT * FROM student WHERE id='1'");

$row = pg_fetch_row ($result, 0);
echo $row[0].":".$row[1]."\n";

pg_close($conn);
?>
```

Output

```
1:abc
```

See also pg_fetch_array(), pg_fetch_object(), and pg_result().

----

pg_FieldIsNull (postgresql)
test if a field is NULL

```
int pg_fieldisnull(int result_id, int row, mixed field);
```

This function returns TRUE if the specified field is NULL. It returns FALSE if the row is not NULL. The field can be specified as number or fieldname. Row numbering starts at 0.

Example

```
<?PHP
$conn = pg_Connect("dbname=test port=5432");
if(!$conn) {
  print "Error: Could not connect to database.<br>\n";
  exit;
}

$result = pg_Exec("SELECT * FROM student WHERE id='1'");

if (!pg_fieldisnull($result, 0, "id"))
  echo "Field is not NULL.\n";
else
  echo "Field is NULL.\n";

pg_close($conn);
?>
```

Output

```
Field is not NULL.
```

See also pg_fieldnum() and pg_Exec().

----

pg_FieldName (postgresql)
return the name of a field

```
string pg_fieldname(int result_id, int field_number);
```

> This function returns the name of the field specified by the field number. Field numbering starts from 0.

Example

```
<?PHP
$conn = pg_Connect("dbname=test port=5432");
if(!$conn) {
  print "Error: Could not connect to database.<br>\n";
  exit;
}

$result = pg_Exec("SELECT * FROM student WHERE id='1'");
echo pg_fieldname($result, 2);
pg_close($conn);
?>
```

Output

```
grade
```

See also pg_fieldnum() and pg_Exec().

----

pg_FieldNum (postgresql)
return a column number given its name

```
string pg_fieldnum(int result_id, int field_name);
```

> This functions returns the column number for the field of the specified *name*. Field numbering starts at 0. This function returns -1 on error.

Example

```
<?PHP
$conn = pg_Connect("dbname=test port=5432");
if(!$conn) {
  print "Error: Could not connect to database.<br>\n";
  exit;
}
```

```
$result = pg_Exec("SELECT * FROM student WHERE id='1'");
echo pg_fieldnum($result, "grade");

pg_close($conn);
?>
```

Output

2

See also pg_fieldname() and pg_Exec().

----

pg_FieldPrtLen (postgresql)
return the printed length

```
int pg_fieldprtlen(int result_id, int row_number, string
field_name);
```

> This function returns the actual printed length (number of characters)
> of a specific value in a PostgreSQL result. Row numbering starts at 0.
> This function returns −1 on an error.

Example

```
<?PHP
$conn = pg_Connect("dbname=test port=5432");
if(!$conn) {
  print "Error: Could not connect to database.<br>\n";
  exit;
}

$result = pg_Exec("SELECT * FROM student WHERE id='1'");
echo pg_fieldprtlen($result, 0, 0);

pg_close($conn);
?>
```

Output

10

See also pg_fieldtype() and pg_Exec().

----

pg_FieldSize (postgresql)
return the internal storage size of the named field

```
int pg_fieldsize(int result_id, string field_name);
```

> This function returns the internal storage size (in bytes) of the named field in the given PostgreSQL result. A field size of 0 indicates a variable length field. This function will return −1 on error.

Example

```PHP
<?PHP
$conn = pg_Connect("dbname=test port=5432");
if(!$conn) {
  print "Error: Could not connect to database.<br>\n";
  exit;
}

$result = pg_Exec("SELECT * FROM student WHERE id='1'");
echo pg_fieldsize($result, 2);

pg_close($conn);
?>
```

Output

4

See also pg_fieldtype() and pg_Exec().

----

pg_FieldType (postgresql)
return the type of the given field

```
int pg_fieldtype(int result_id, int field_number);
```

> This function returns a string containing the type of the given field specified by the PostgreSQL result identifier. Field numbering starts at 0.

Example

```PHP
<?PHP
$conn = pg_Connect("dbname=test port=5432");
if(!$conn) {
  print "Error: Could not connect to database.<br>\n";
  exit;
}

$result = pg_Exec("SELECT * FROM student WHERE id='1'");
echo pg_fieldtype($result, 2);

pg_close($conn);
?>
```

Output

```
int4
```

See also pg_fieldname() and pg_Exec().

----

pg_FreeResult (postgresql)
free up memory

```
int pg_freeresult(int result_id);
```

> This function frees memory that was previously allocated to store a
> result. It accepts the result ID as a the single parameter. Calling this
> function is usually not necessary, because all result memory will
> automatically be freed when the script is finished.

----

pg_GetLastOid (postgresql)
return the last object identifier

```
int pg_getlastoid(int result_id);
```

> This function returns the oid assigned to an inserted row given the
> result_id returned from pg_Exec. oids are unique identifiers assigned
> by PostgreSQL to each row. This function returns a positive integer if
> there was a valid oid, or -1 if an error occurred.

Example

```
<?PHP
$conn = pg_Connect("dbname=test port=5432");
if(!$conn) {
  print "Error: Could not connect to database.<br>\n";
  exit;
}

$result = pg_Exec("INSERT INTO student VALUES ('ghi', 3)");
echo pg_getlastoid($result);

pg_close($conn);
?>
```

Output

```
779616
```

See also pg_Exec().

----

pg_Host (postgresql)
return the host name

```
string pg_host(int connection_id);
```

> pg_Host() will return the host name that the given PostgreSQL connection identifier is connected to.

---

pg_loclose (postgresql)
close a large object

```
void pg_loclose(int fd);
```

> pg_loclose() closes an Inversion Large Object. fd is a file descriptor for the large object from pg_loopen().

Refer to *www.php123.com* for on-line example.

---

pg_locreate (postgresql)
create a large object

```
int pg_locreate(int conn);
```

> pg_locreate() creates an Inversion Large Object and returns the oid of the large object. conn specifies a valid database connection. PostgreSQL access modes INV_READ, INV_WRITE, and INV_ARCHIVE are not supported. The object is always created with both read and write access. INV_ARCHIVE has been removed from PostgreSQL itself (version 6.3 and above).

Refer to *www.php123.com* for on-line example.

---

pg_loopen (postgresql)
open a large object

```
int pg_loopen(int conn, int objoid, string mode);
```

pg_loopen() open an Inversion Large Object and returns file descriptor of the large object. The file descriptor encapsulates information about the connection. Do not close the connection before closing the large object file descriptor. objoid specifies a valid large object oid and mode can be "r", "w", or "rw".

Refer to *www.php123.com* for on-line example.

---

pg_loread (postgresql)
read a large object

```
string pg_loread(int fd, int len);
```

pg_loread() reads at most *len* bytes from a large object and returns it as a string. fd specifies a valid large object file descriptor and *len* specifies the maximum allowable size of the large object segment.

Refer to *www.php123.com* for on-line example.

---

pg_loreadall (postgresql)
read a entire large object

```
void pg_loreadall(int fd);
```

pg_loreadall() reads a large object and passes it straight through to the browser after sending all pending headers. It is primarily intended for sending binary data such as images or sound.

Refer to *www.php123.com* for on-line example.

---

pg_lounlink (postgresql)
delete a large object

```
void pg_lounlink(int conn, int lobjid);
```

pg_lounlink() deletes a large object with the *lobjid* identifier for that large object.

Refer to *www.php123.com* for on-line example.

---

pg_lowrite (postgresql)
write a large object

```
int pg_lowrite(int fd, string buf);
```

> pg_lowrite() writes at most to a large object from a variable buf and returns the number of bytes actually written, or FALSE in the case of an error. *fd* is a file descriptor for the large object from pg_loopen().

Refer to *www.php123.com* for on-line example.

---

pg_NumFields (postgresql)()
return the number of fields

```
int pg_numfields(int result_id);
```

> This function returns the number of fields (columns) in a PostgreSQL result. The argument is a valid result identifier returned by pg_Exec(). This function returns –1 in case of error.

Example

```
<?PHP
$conn = pg_Connect("dbname=test port=5432");
if(!$conn) {
  print "Error: Could not connect to database.<br>\n";
  exit;
}

$result = pg_Exec("SELECT id FROM student");
echo pg_NumFields($result)."\n";
$result = pg_Exec("SELECT id, password FROM student");
echo pg_NumFields($result)."\n";

pg_close($conn);
?>
```

Output

```
1
2
```

See also pg_Exec() and pg_NumRows().

---

pg_NumRows (postgresql)
return the number of rows

```
int pg_numrows(int result_id);
```

> This function returns the number of rows in a PostgreSQL result. The argument is a valid result identifier returned by pg_Exec(). This function returns –1 in case of error.

Example

The code below uses the pg_NumRows() function as a control variable in a FOR loop to process the entire set of results.

```
<?PHP
$conn = pg_Connect("dbname=test port=5432");
if(!$conn) {
  print "Error: Could not connect to database.<br>\n";
  exit;
}

$result = pg_Exec("SELECT * FROM student");
for($x = 0; $x < pg_NumRows($result); $x++) {
  $id = trim(pg_Result($result, $x, "id"));
  $password = trim(pg_Result($result, $x, "password"));
  echo "ID #:".$id."/".$password."\n";
}

pg_close($conn);
?>
```

Output

```
ID #:1/abc
ID #:2/def
```

See also pg_Exec() and pg_NumFields().

----

pg_Options (postgresql)
return options

```
string pg_options(int connection_id);
```

> This function returns a string containing the options specified on the given PostgreSQL connection identifier.

See also pg_Connect().

----

pg_pConnect (postgresql)
make a persistent database connection

```
int pg_pconnect(string host, string port, string options,
string tty, string dbname);
```

> This function opens a persistent connection to a PostgreSQL database.
> It returns a connection index on success, or FALSE if the connection
> cannot be made. The return value is used by other PostgreSQL func-
> tions. You can have multiple persistent connections open at once.

Example

```
<?PHP
$conn = pg_pConnect("dbname=test port=5432");
if(!$conn) {
  print "Error: Could not connect to database.<br>\n";
  exit;
}

$result = pg_Exec("SELECT * FROM student");
for($x = 0; $x < pg_NumRows($result); $x++) {
  $id = trim(pg_Result($result, $x, "id"));
  $password = trim(pg_Result($result, $x, "password"));
  echo "ID #:".$id."/".$password."\n";
}

pg_close($conn);
?>
```

Output

```
ID #:1/abc
ID #:2/def
```

See also pg_Connect() and pg_Exec().

----

pg_Port (postgresql)
return the port number

```
int pg_port(int connection_id);
```

> This function returns the port number to which the given connection
> id is connected.

Example

```php
<?PHP
$conn = pg_pConnect("dbname=test port=5432");
if(!$conn) {
  print "Error: Could not connect to database.<br>\n";
  exit;
}

echo pg_Port($conn);

pg_close($conn);
?>
```

Output

```
5432
```

----

pg_Result (postgresql)
return values from a result identifier

```
mixed pg_result(int result_id, int row_number, mixed
fieldname);
```

> This function returns individual values from the specified *result_id*
> returned from pg_Exec(). Result ID's point to data in multiple rows
> and fields. The *row_number* parameter specifies which group of
> results to examine, and *fieldname* specifies which individual field.
> The field name can be specified as either a number or a string. Both
> row numbers and field names start at 0. The types of the returned data
> are integer, double, and strings.

Example

```php
<?PHP
$conn = pg_Connect("dbname=test port=5432");
if(!$conn) {
  print "Error: Could not connect to database.<br>\n";
  exit;
}

$result = pg_Exec("SELECT * FROM student");
for($x = 0; $x < pg_NumRows($result); $x++) {
  $id = trim(pg_Result($result, $x, "id"));
  $password = trim(pg_Result($result, $x, "password"));
  echo "ID #:".$id."/".$password."\n";
}

pg_close($conn);
?>
```

Output

```
ID #:1/abc
ID #:2/def
```

See also pg_Exec().

----

pg_tty (postgresql)
return the tty name

```
string pg_tty(int connection_id);
```

> This function returns the tty name that server-side debugging output
> is sent to on the given PostgreSQL connection identifier.

Refer to *www.php123.com* for on-line example.

MySQL Functions *(mysql)*
These functions allow you to access MySQL database servers. More information about MySQL can be found at http://www.mysql.com/.

mysql_affected_rows *(mysql)*
get number of affected rows in last query

```
int mysql_affected_rows([int link_identifier]);
```

> This function returns the number of affected rows by the last INSERT,
> UPDATE, or DELETE query. If optional parameter *link_identifier*
> identifier isn't specified, then the last opened link is assumed. Note
> that this command does not work with SELECT statements, only on
> those that modify records. To find the number of rows returned from a
> SELECT, use the function mysql_num_rows().

Example

```php
<?PHP
$conn = mysql_connect("localhost", "username", "password");

mysql_select_db("test_db");
if(mysql_errno()) {
  echo mysql_errno().": ".mysql_error()."\n";
  exit;
}
```

```
mysql_query("CREATE TABLE test (id char(10), last_name
  char(50))");
mysql_query("INSERT INTO test (id, last_name) VALUES
  ('123','Smith')");

echo "Number of rows affected by the last query:".
  mysql_affected_rows()."\n";

mysql_close($conn);
?>
```

Output

```
Number of rows affected by the last query:1
```

----

mysql_close (mysql)
close MySQL connection

```
int mysql_close([int link_identifier]);
```

This function closes a previously opened connection. If the optional parameter *link_identifier* is not specified, then the last opened link is used. It returns TRUE on success, and FALSE on error. Calling this function is not required, because open connections are automatically closed at the end of the script.

Example

```
<?PHP
$conn = mysql_connect("localhost", "username", "password");

...

mysql_close($conn);
?>
```

Output

```
(none)
```

See also mysql_connect() and mysql_pconnect().

----

mysql_connect (mysql)
open MySQL server connection

```
int mysql_connect([string hostname], [string username],
[string password]);
```

This function creates a connection to a MySQL server. On success, it returns a link identifier to be used as a parameter to other MySQL library functions; it returns FALSE on error. This function must be called successfully before any other MySQL functions can be used. All of the parameters are optional. If they are omitted, then the default values are localhost for *hostname*, the owner of the process for *username*, and an empty password. The *hostname* parameter can also specify a port number as "hostname:port". If mysql_connect() is called twice with the same arguments, the link identifier of the already opened link will be returned. The link will be closed automatically at the end of the execution of the script or when mysql_close() is called.

Example

```
<?PHP
$conn = mysql_connect("localhost", "username", "password");

mysql_select_db("test_db");
if(mysql_errno()) {
  echo mysql_errno().": ".mysql_error()."\n";
  exit;
}

mysql_close($conn);
?>
```

Output

```
(no output)
```

See also mysql_pconnect() and mysql_close().

---

mysql_create_db (mysql)
create MySQL database

```
int mysql_create_db(string database name, int link_identifier );
```

This function creates a new database. It returns TRUE if the database was created successfully, or FALSE otherwise. Note that this function has been deprecated in the MySQL C API. It is suggested that the SQL CREATE DATABASE command be used instead.

Example 1

```PHP
<?PHP
$conn = mysql_connect("localhost", "username", "password");

mysql_create_db("test_db", $conn);
if(mysql_errno()) {
   echo mysql_errno().": ".mysql_error()."\n";
   exit;
}

$result = mysql_list_dbs();
$x = 0;
while ($x < mysql_num_rows($result)) {
   $db_names[$x] = mysql_tablename($result, $x);
   echo $db_names[$x]."\n";
   $x++;
}

mysql_close($conn);
?>
```

Output 1

```
test_db
mysql
```

Example 2

The example below shows how the mysql_create_db() function can be replaced with a SQL CREATE DATABASE command.

```PHP
<?PHP
$conn = mysql_connect("localhost", "username", "password");

$result = mysql_query("CREATE DATABASE test_db");
if(mysql_errno()) {
   echo mysql_errno().": ".mysql_error()."\n";
   exit;
}

$result = mysql_list_dbs();
$x = 0;
while ($x < mysql_num_rows($result)) {
   $db_names[$x] = mysql_tablename($result, $x);
   echo $db_names[$x]."\n";
   $x++;
}

mysql_close($conn);
?>
```

Output 2

```
test_db
mysql
```

See also mysql_drop_db().

----

mysql_data_seek (mysql)
move internal row pointer

```
int mysql_data_seek(int result_identifier, int row_number);
```

> The function moves the internal row pointer and returns TRUE on success, FALSE on failure.
>
> mysql_data_seek() moves the internal row pointer of the MySQL result associated with the specified result identifier to pointer to the specified row number. The next call to mysql_fetch_row() would return that row.

Example

```
<?PHP
$conn = mysql_connect("localhost", "username", "password");

mysql_select_db("invalid_db_name");
if(mysql_errno()) {
  echo mysql_errno().": ".mysql_error()."\n";
  exit;
}

mysql_close($conn);
?>
```

Output

```
1049: Unknown database 'invalid_db_name'
```

See also mysql_data_seek().

----

mysql_dbname (mysql)
get current MySQL database name

```
string mysql_dbname(string result, int i);
```

This function returns the database name stored in position i of the result pointer returned from the mysql_list_dbs() function. The mysql_num_rows() function can be used to determine how many database names are available.

Example

```
<?PHP
$conn = mysql_connect("localhost", "username", "password");

mysql_select_db("invalid_db_name");
if(mysql_errno()) {
   echo mysql_errno().": ".mysql_error()."\n";
   exit;
}

mysql_close($conn);
?>
```

Output

```
1049: Unknown database 'invalid_db_name'
```

---

mysql_db_query (mysql)
send MySQL query

```
int mysql_db_query(string database, string query, int
link_identifier);
```

This function returns a positive MySQL result identifier to the query result, or FALSE on error.

mysql_db_query() selects a database and executes a query on it. If the optional link identifier isn't specified, the function will try to find an open link to the MySQL server and if no such link is found, it will try to create one, as if mysql_connect() had been called with no arguments.

Example

```
<?PHP
$conn = mysql_connect("localhost", "username", "password");

mysql_select_db("invalid_db_name");
if(mysql_errno()) {
   echo mysql_errno().": ".mysql_error()."\n";
```

```
   exit;
}

mysql_close($conn);
?>
```

Output

```
1049: Unknown database 'invalid_db_name'
```

See also mysql_connect().

----

mysql_drop_db (mysql)
drop (delete) MySQL database

```
int mysql_drop_db(string database_name, int link_identifier );
```

> This function deletes a database. It returns TRUE if the database was
> deleted, or FALSE otherwise. Note that this function has been depre-
> cated in the MySQL C API. It is suggested that the SQL DROP DATA-
> BASE command be used instead.

Example 1

```
<?PHP
$conn = mysql_connect("localhost", "username", "password");

mysql_drop_db("test_db", $conn);
if(mysql_errno()) {
   echo mysql_errno().": ".mysql_error()."\n";
   exit;
}

$result = mysql_list_dbs();
$x = 0;
while ($x < mysql_num_rows($result)) {
   $db_names[$x] = mysql_tablename($result, $x);
   echo $db_names[$x]."\n";
   $x++;
}

mysql_close($conn);
?>
```

Output 1

```
mysql
```

Example 2

The example below shows how the mysql_drop_db() function can be replaced with a SQL DROP DATABASE command.

```php
<?PHP
$conn = mysql_connect("localhost", "username", "password");
$result = mysql_query("CREATE DATABASE test_db");
if(mysql_errno()) {
   echo mysql_errno().": ".mysql_error()."\n";
   exit;
}

$result = mysql_list_dbs();
$x = 0;
while ($x < mysql_num_rows($result)) {
   $db_names[$x] = mysql_tablename($result, $x);
   echo $db_names[$x]."\n";
   $x++;
}

mysql_close($conn);
?>
```

Output 2

```
mysql
```

See also mysql_create_db().

----

mysql_errno (mysql)
return error number of last mysql call

```
int mysql_errno();
```

> This function returns the error number returned from the most recent MySQL request. A return value of zero means that no error occurred.

Example

```php
<?PHP
$conn = mysql_connect("localhost", "username", "password");

mysql_select_db("invalid_db_name");
if(mysql_errno()) {
   echo mysql_errno().": ".mysql_error()."\n";
   exit;
}
```

```
mysql_close($conn);
?>
```

Output

```
1049: Unknown database 'invalid_db_name'
```

See also mysql_error().

----

mysql_error (mysql)
return error message of last mysql call

```
string mysql_error();
```

> This function returns a string containing the error returned from the
> most recent MySQL request. An empty result string indicates no error.

Example

```
<?PHP
$conn = mysql_connect("localhost", "username", "password");

mysql_select_db("invalid_db_name");
if(mysql_errno()) {
  echo mysql_errno().": ".mysql_error()."\n";
  exit;
}

mysql_close($conn);
?>
```

Output

```
1049: Unknown database 'invalid_db_name'
```

See also mysql_errno().

----

mysql_fetch_array (mysql)
fetch row as array

```
array mysql_fetch_array(int result);
```

> This function takes a result set and returns an associative array contain-
> ing the next fetched row, or FALSE if there are no more rows in the set.

Example

```
<?PHP
$conn = mysql_connect("localhost", "username", "password");

mysql_select_db("test_db");
if(mysql_errno()) {
  echo mysql_errno().": ".mysql_error()."\n";
  exit;
}

$result = mysql_query("SELECT * FROM test WHERE last_name =
  'Smith' LIMIT 3");
while($student = mysql_fetch_array($result))
  echo $student["id"].": ".$student["last_name"]."\n";

mysql_close($conn);
?>
```

Output

```
1: Smith
24: Smith
29: Smith
```

See also mysql_fetch_row().

----

mysql_fetch_field (mysql)
get field information

```
object mysql_fetch_field(int result, [int field_offset]);
```

This function returns an object containing information about the field specified by the result set. If the field offset parameter is not specified, then the next field is retreived.

The properties of the returned object are:

name	name of column
table	name of the table the column belongs to
max_length	maximum length of the column
not_null	TRUE if the column cannot be NULL
primary_key	TRUE if the column is a primary key
unique_key	TRUE if the column is a unique key

multiple_key	TRUE if the column is a non-unique key
numeric	TRUE if the column is numeric
blob	TRUE if the column is a BLOB
type	column's type
unsigned	TRUE if the column is unsigned
zerofill	TRUE if the column is zero-filled

Example

```php
<?PHP
$conn = mysql_connect("localhost", "username", "password");
mysql_select_db("test_db");
if(mysql_errno()) {
  echo mysql_errno().": ".mysql_error()."\n";
  exit;
}
$result = mysql_query("SELECT * FROM test WHERE last_name =
     'Smith' LIMIT 1");

$info = mysql_fetch_field($result);
echo "Column name:".$info->name."\n";
echo "Table name:".$info->table."\n";
echo "Maximum length of column:".$info->max_length."\n";
if($info->not_null)
  echo "Column can not be NULL\n";
else
  echo "Column can be NULL\n";
echo "Column type:".$info->type."\n";

mysql_close($conn);
?>
```

Output

```
Column name:id
Table name:test
Maximum length of column:3
Column can be NULL
Column type:string
```

See also mysql_field_seek().

----

mysql_fetch_lengths (mysql)
get length of a result

```
array mysql_fetch_lengths(int result);
```

> This function returns an array containing the length of each field in the last row fetched by mysql_fetch_row(), mysql_fetch_array(), or mysql_fetch_object(). On error, it returns FALSE. This function can be used to avoid calling strlen(). Using this function can often be faster than calling strlen(), and it, unlike strlen(), is binary-safe.

Example

```
<?PHP
$conn = mysql_connect("localhost", "username", "password");

mysql_select_db("invalid_db_name");
if(mysql_errno()) {
  echo mysql_errno().": ".mysql_error()."\n";
  exit;
}

$result = mysql_query("SELECT * FROM test WHERE last_name =
    'Smith' LIMIT 1");
$column = mysql_fetch_object($result);
$lengths = mysql_fetch_lengths($result);
echo "The first column is ".$lengths[0]." bytes.\n";
echo "The second column is ".$lengths[1]." bytes.\n";

mysql_close($conn);
?>
```

Output

```
The first column is 3 bytes.
The second column is 5 bytes.
```

See also mysql_fetch_row().

---

mysql_fetch_object (mysql)
fetch row as object

```
int mysql_fetch_object(int result);
```

> This function returns an object with properties that correspond to the fetched row, or FALSE if there are no more rows. mysql_fetch_object() is similar to mysql_fetch_array(), with one difference—an object is returned, not an array. Indirectly, that means that you can access the data only by the field names, and not by their offsets (numbers are illegal property names).
>
> In terms of speed, the function is identical to mysql_fetch_array(), and almost as quick as mysql_fetch_row() (the difference is insignificant).

Example

```php
<?PHP
$conn = mysql_connect("localhost", "username", "password");

mysql_select_db("test_db");
if(mysql_errno()) {
  echo mysql_errno().": ".mysql_error()."\n";
  exit;
}

$result = mysql_query("SELECT * FROM test WHERE last_name =
    'Smith' LIMIT 3");

while($student = mysql_fetch_object($result))
  echo $student->id.":".$student->last_name."\n";

mysql_close($conn);
?>
```

Output

```
1: Smith
24: Smith
29: Smith
```

See also mysql_fetch_array() and mysql_fetch_row().

---

mysql_fetch_row (mysql)
get row as enumerated array

```
array mysql_fetch_row(int result);
```

> This function returns an array containing the next row in a result set, or FALSE if there are no more rows. Subsequent calls to the function will return the next row in the result set, or FALSE if there are no more rows.

Example

```
<?PHP
$conn = mysql_connect("localhost", "username", "password");

mysql_select_db("test_db");
if(mysql_errno()) {
  echo mysql_errno().": ".mysql_error()."\n";
  exit;
}

$result = mysql_query("SELECT * FROM test WHERE last_name =
    'Smith' LIMIT 3");

while($student = mysql_fetch_row($result))
  echo $student[0].":".$student[1]."\n";

mysql_close($conn);
?>
```

Output

```
1: Smith
24: Smith
29: Smith
```

See also mysql_fetch_array(), mysql_fetch_object(), mysql_data_seek(), mysql_fetch_lengths(), and mysql_result().

---

mysql_field_name (mysql)
get field name

```
string mysql_field_name(string result, int field_index);
```

> This function returns the name of the specified field. The arguments to the function are a result set and a field index.

Example

```
<?PHP
$conn = mysql_connect("localhost", "username", "password");

mysql_select_db("test_db");
if(mysql_errno()) {
  echo mysql_errno().": ".mysql_error()."\n";
  exit;
}
```

```
$result = mysql_query("SELECT * FROM test LIMIT 1");

$x = 0;
while($field_name = mysql_field_name($result, $x++)) {
  echo $field_name."\n";
}

mysql_close($conn);
?>
```

Output

```
id
last_name
first_name
```

See also mysql_query().

----

mysql_field_seek (mysql)
set field offset

```
int mysql_field_seek(int result, int field_offset);
```

> This function seeks to the specified field offset. If the next call to mysql_fetch_field() does not include the optional field offset parameter, then this specified field will examined.

Example

The example below uses the function mysql_field_seek() to "advance" to the next field in the result set so that each field can be examined.

```
<?PHP
$conn = mysql_connect("localhost", "username", "password");

mysql_select_db("test_db");
if(mysql_errno()) {
  echo mysql_errno().": ".mysql_error()."\n";
  exit;
}

$result = mysql_query("SELECT * FROM test LIMIT 1");

for($x = 0;$x < mysql_num_fields($result); $x++) {
  mysql_field_seek($result, $x);

  $info = mysql_fetch_field($result);
  echo "Column name:".$info->name."\n";
  echo "Table name:".$info->table."\n";
```

```
    echo "Maximum length of column:".$info->max_length."\n";
    if($info->not_null)
       echo "Column can not be NULL\n";
    else
       echo "Column can be NULL\n";
    echo "Column type:".$info->type."\n";
    }
}

mysql_close($conn);
?>
```

Output

```
Column name:id
Table name:test
Maximum length of column:3
Column can be NULL
Column type:string
Column name:last_name
Table name:test
Maximum length of column:5
Column can be NULL
Column type:string
```

See also mysql_fetch_field().

----

mysql_field_table (mysql)
get table name for a field in a result set

```
string mysql_field_table(int result, int field_offset);
```

> This function returns the table name for the specified field in a result set.

Example

```
<?PHP
$conn = mysql_connect("localhost", "username", "password");

mysql_select_db("test_db");
if(mysql_errno()) {
   echo mysql_errno().": ".mysql_error()."\n";
   exit;
}
```

```
$result = mysql_query("SELECT * FROM test LIMIT 1");
```

```
echo "The first field in the result set came from the table:
".mysql_field_table($result, 0);
```

```
mysql_close($conn);
?>
```

Output

```
The first field in the result set came from the table: test
```

---

mysql_field_type (mysql)
get field type

```
string mysql_field_type(string result, int field_offset);
```

> This function is similar to the mysql_field_name() function, except
> that the type of the field is returned rather than the table name. The
> types returned are int, real, string, blob, date, time, or any other valid
> MySQL type.

Example

```php
<?PHP
$conn = mysql_connect("localhost", "username", "password");
mysql_select_db("test_db");
if(mysql_errno()) {
  echo mysql_errno().": ".mysql_error()."\n";
  exit;
}
```

```
$result = mysql_query("SELECT * FROM test LIMIT 1");
```

```
echo "The first field in the result set is of the type:
".mysql_field_type ($result, 0);
```

```
mysql_close($conn);
?>
```

Output

```
The first field in the result set is of the type: string
```

---

mysql_field_flags (mysql)
get field flags

```
string mysql_field_flags(string result, int field_offset);
```

This function returns the field flags for the specified field. Valid values are:

Flag	Description
not_null	field can't be NULL
primary_key	field is part of a primary key
unique_key	field is part of a unique key
multiple_key	field is part of a key
unsigned	field is unsigned
zerofill	field has the zerofill attribute (are 0 padded to the left, for example 00004)
binary	field has the binary attribute

All the applicable flags are returned in the string and separated by a space. Note: Formerly, enum, blob, and timestamp were valid values for a field flag, but they have since been deprecated because they indicated the type of field rather than an attribute.

Example

```
<?PHP
$conn = mysql_connect("localhost", "username", "password");

mysql_select_db("test_db");
if(mysql_errno()) {
  echo mysql_errno().": ".mysql_error()."\n";
  exit;
}
$result = mysql_query("SELECT * FROM test LIMIT 1");

echo mysql_field_flags($result, 0);

mysql_close($conn);
?>
```

Output

```
not_null primary_key auto_increment
```

----

mysql_field_len (mysql)
get field length

```
int mysql_field_len(string result, int field_offset);
```

> This function returns the length of the specified field.

Example

```PHP
<?PHP
$conn = mysql_connect("localhost", "username", "password");

mysql_select_db("test_db");
if(mysql_errno()) {
   echo mysql_errno().": ".mysql_error()."\n";
   exit;
}
$result = mysql_query("SELECT * FROM test LIMIT 1");

echo "The first field is ".mysql_field_len($result, 0)." bytes
   long.";

mysql_close($conn);
?>
```

Output

```
The first field is 10 bytes long.
```

See also pg_query().

----

mysql_free_result (mysql)
free result memory

```
int mysql_free_result(int result);
```

> This function frees memory that was previously allocated to store a
> result. It accepts the result set as the single parameter. Calling this
> function is usually not necessary, because all result memory will
> automatically be freed when the script is finished.

Example

```PHP
<?PHP
$conn = mysql_connect("localhost", "username", "password");

mysql_select_db("test_db");
if(mysql_errno()) {
   echo mysql_errno().": ".mysql_error()."\n";
   exit;
}
```

```
$result = mysql_query("SELECT * FROM test WHERE last_name =
  'Smith'");

. . .

mysql_free_result($result);

mysql_close($conn);
?>
```

Output

```
(no output)
```

See also mysql_query.

----

mysql_insert_id (mysql)
get generated id from last INSERT

```
int mysql_insert_id(void);
```

> This function returns the automatically generated ID # for an
> AUTO_INCREMENTED field. This function has no arguments.
> It returns the ID # generated by the last INSERT.

Example

```
<?PHP
$conn = mysql_connect("localhost", "username", "password");

mysql_select_db("test_db");
if(mysql_errno()) {
  echo mysql_errno().": ".mysql_error()."\n";
  exit;
}

$result = mysql_query("INSERT INTO test (last_name) VALUES
  ('Smith')");

echo "The last ID #: ".mysql_insert_id()."\n";

mysql_close($conn);
?>
```

Output

```
The last ID #: 1248
```

See also mysql_query().

----

mysql_list_fields (mysql)
list result fields

```
int mysql_list_fields(string database, string tablename, [int
link_identifier]);
```

> This function retrieves information about the given tablename. It takes
> the database name and the table name as arguments. The result set
> returned can be examined with mysql_field_flags(), mysql_field_len(),
> mysql_field_name(), and mysql_field_type(). Note: This function has
> been deprecated. It is suggested that the SQL command SHOW
> COLUMNS FROM be used instead.

Example

```
<?PHP
$conn = mysql_connect("localhost", "username", "password");

mysql_select_db("test_db");
if(mysql_errno()) {
  echo mysql_errno().": ".mysql_error()."\n";
  exit;
}

$result = mysql_list_fields("test_db", "students");
echo mysql_field_flags($result, 0);

mysql_close($conn);
?>
```

Output

```
not_null primary_key auto_increment
```

----

mysql_list_dbs (mysql)
list MySQL databases on server

```
int mysql_list_dbs(void);
```

> This function returns a pointer containing the databases available
> from the current mysql installation. The mysql_tablename() function
> is used to traverse the returned data.

Example

```
<?PHP
$conn = mysql_connect("localhost", "username", "password");

$result = mysql_list_dbs();
$x = 0;
while ($x < mysql_num_rows($result)) {
  $db_names[$x] = mysql_tablename($result, $x);
  echo $db_names[$x]."\n";
  $x++;
}

mysql_close($conn);
?>
```

Output

```
test_db
mysql
```

See also mysql_tablename().

----

mysql_list_tables (mysql)
list tables in a MySQL database

```
int mysql_list_tables(string database);
```

> This function takes a database name as an argument, and returns a
> pointer to a list of tables. The mysql_tablename() function is used to
> traverse the returned data to discover the actual table names. The
> mysql_num_rows() function may be used to determine the number
> of tables given the result pointer.

Example

```
<?PHP
$conn = mysql_connect("localhost", "username", "password");

$result = mysql_list_tables("mysql");
$x = 0;
while ($x < mysql_num_rows($result)) {
  $table_names[$x] = mysql_tablename($result, $x);
  echo $table_names[$x]."\n";
  $x++;
}
```

```
mysql_close($conn);
?>
```

Output

```
columns_priv
db
func
host
tables_priv
user
```

See also mysql_tablename().

----

mysql_num_fields (mysql)
get number of fields in result

```
int mysql_num_fields(int result);
```

> This function returns the number of fields in a result set.

Example

```
<?PHP
$conn = mysql_connect("localhost", "username", "password");

mysql_select_db("test_db");
if(mysql_errno()) {
   echo mysql_errno().": ".mysql_error()."\n";
   exit;
}
$result = mysql_query("SELECT * FROM test WHERE last_name =
   'Smith'");
echo mysql_num_fields($result)." fields in the result set.\n";

$result = mysql_query("SELECT id FROM test WHERE last_name =
   'Smith'");
echo mysql_num_fields($result)." fields in the result set.\n";

mysql_close($conn);
?>
```

Output

```
42 fields in the result set.
1 fields in the result set.
```

See also mysql_db_query(), mysql_query(), mysql_fetch_field(), mysql_num_rows().

----

mysql_num_rows (mysql)
get number of rows in result

```
int mysql_num_rows(string result);
```

> This function returns the number of rows in a result set.

Example

```php
<?PHP
$conn = mysql_connect("localhost", "username", "password");

mysql_select_db("test_db");
if(mysql_errno()) {
  echo mysql_errno().": ".mysql_error()."\n";
  exit;
}

$result = mysql_query("SELECT * FROM test.WHERE last_name =
  'Smith'");
echo "The number of rows in the
  result:".mysql_num_rows($result)."\n";

mysql_close($conn);
?>
```

Output

```
The number of rows in the result: 140
```

See also mysql_db_query(), mysql_query(), and, mysql_fetch_row().

----

mysql_pconnect (mysql)
open persistent MySQL connection

```
int mysql_pconnect(string hostname , string username , string
password );
```

> This function creates a persistent connection to a MySQL server. It
> returns a positive MySQL persistent link identifier on success, or
> FALSE on error. This function is much like mysql_connect(), with one
> difference: When this function is called, it first tries to find a persistent

connection that is already open with the same host, username and password. If one is found, an identifier for this existing connection is returned instead of opening a new connection. The connection to the SQL server is not closed when the execution of the script ends. Instead, the link remains open for future use. The function mysql_close() does not close a persistent connection.

Example

```
<?PHP
$conn = mysql_pconnect("localhost", "username", "password");

mysql_select_db("test_db");
if(mysql_errno()) {
   echo mysql_errno().": ".mysql_error()."\n";
   exit;
}

mysql_close($conn);
?>
```

Output

```
1049: Unknown database 'invalid_db_name'
```

See also mysql_connect() and mysql_close().

---

mysql_query (mysql)
send MySQL query

```
int mysql_query(string query, int link_identifier );
```

This function sends a query to the active database. If the optional parameter *link_identifier* is not specified, then the last opened link is used. It returns a result identifier on success, or FALSE on error.

Example

```
<?PHP
$conn = mysql_connect("localhost", "username", "password");

mysql_select_db("test_db");
if(mysql_errno()) {
   echo mysql_errno().": ".mysql_error()."\n";
   exit;
```

```
}
$result = mysql_query("SELECT * FROM test WHERE last_name =
    'Smith'");
echo "The number of rows in the result:".mysql_num_rows
    ($result)."\n";

mysql_close($conn);
?>
```

Output

```
The number of rows in the result: 140
```

See also mysql_db_query(), mysql_select_db(), and mysql_connect().

----

mysql_result (mysql)
get result data

```
int mysql_result(int result, int row, mixed field);
```

> This function returns the contents of one field in a MySQL result set.
> The argument *field* can be the field's numerical offset, the name of the
> field, or the name of the field with the table. For example, the field
> could be 1, "last_name", or "students.last_name", respectively. Note:
> When working with large result sets, it is much faster to use functions
> that work on multiple columns of the table in one MySQL call, like
> mysql_fetch_row(), mysql_fetch_array(), and mysql_fetch_object().

Example

```
<?PHP
$conn = mysql_connect("localhost", "username", "password");

mysql_select_db("test_db");
if(mysql_errno()) {
  echo mysql_errno().": ".mysql_error()."\n";
  exit;
}

$result = mysql_query("SELECT * FROM test WHERE last_name =
    'Smith' LIMIT 5");

for($x = 0; $x < mysql_num_rows($result); $x++) {
  echo mysql_result($result, $x, "last_name")."\n";
}

mysql_close($conn);
?>
```

Output

```
Smith
Smith
Smith
Smith
Smith
```

See also mysql_fetch_row(), mysql_fetch_array(), and mysql_fetch_object().

----

mysql_select_db (mysql)
select MySQL database

```
int mysql_select_db(string database_name, [int
link_identifier]);
```

> This function sets the current active database. It returns TRUE on
> success and FALSE on error. If *link_identifier* is not specified, then the
> last opened link is assumed. The selected database is used in future
> calls to mysql_query().

Example

```php
<?PHP
$conn = mysql_connect("localhost", "username", "password");

mysql_select_db("invalid_db_name");
if(mysql_errno()) {
   echo mysql_errno().": ".mysql_error()."\n";
   exit;
}

mysql_close($conn);
?>
```

Output

```
1049: Unknown database 'invalid_db_name'
```

See also mysql_connect(), mysql_pconnect(), and mysql_query().

----

mysql_tablename (mysql)
get table name of field

```
string mysql_tablename(int result, int i);
```

> This function takes a result pointer returned by the mysql_list_tables()
> function and an integer index. It returns a string containing the name
> of a table.

Example

```
<?PHP
$conn = mysql_connect("localhost", "username", "password");
$result = mysql_list_tables("mysql");
$x = 0;
while ($x < mysql_num_rows($result)) {
   $table_names[$x] = mysql_tablename($result, $x);
   echo $table_names[$x]."\n";
   $x++;
}

mysql_close($conn);
?>
```

Output

```
columns_priv
db
func
host
tables_priv
user
```

Informix Functions *(ifx)*

The Informix driver for Online (ODS) 7.x, SE 7.x, and Universal Server (IUS)
9.x is implemented in "functions/ifx.ec" and "functions/php3_ifx.h". At the
time of writing, ODS 7.2 support is fairly complete, with full BLOB support.
IUS 9.1 support is partly finished: the new data types are there, but SLOBS
support is still under construction.

ifx_connect *(ifx)*
open Informix server connection

```
int ifx_connect(string [database] , string [userid] , string
[password] );
```

ifx_connect() establishes a connection to an Informix server. It returns an connection identifier on success, or FALSE on error. All the arguments are optional; if they're omitted, defaults are taken from values supplied in php3.ini (ifx.default_host for the host (Informix libraries will use $INFORMIXSERVER environment value if not defined), ifx.default_user for user, ifx.default_password for the password (none if not defined)).

In case a second call is made to ifx_connect() with the same arguments, no new link is established, but instead, the link identifier of the already opened link is returned.

The link to the server will be closed as soon as the execution of the script ends, unless it's closed earlier by explicitly calling ifx_close().

Example

```
$conn_id = ifx_pconnect (mydb@ol_srv1, "imyself",
   "mypassword");
```

See also ifx_pconnect() and ifx_close().

----

ifx_pconnect (ifx)
open persistent Informix connection

```
int ifx_pconnect(string [database] , string [userid] , string
[password] );
```

This function returns a positive Informix persistent link identifier on success, or FALSE on error.

Refer to *www.php123.com* for on-line example.

----

ifx_close (ifx)
close Informix connection

```
int ifx_close(int [link_identifier] );
```

This function always returns TRUE.

Refer to *www.php123.com* for on-line example.

----

ifx_query (ifx)
send Informix query

```
int ifx_query(string query, int [link_identifier], int
[cursor_type], mixed [blobidarray] );
```

> This function returns a positive Informix result identifier on success, or FALSE on error.

Refer to *www.php123.com* for on-line example.

----

ifx_prepare (ifx)
prepare an SQL-statement for execution

```
int ifx_prepare(string query, int conn_id, int [cursor_def],
mixed blobidarray);
```

> This function returns a integer result_id for use by ifx_do() and sets affected_rows for retrieval by the ifx_affected_rows() function.
>
> It prepares query on connection *conn_id.* For "select-type" queries a cursor is declared and opened. The optional cursor_type parameter allows you to make this a "scroll" and/or "hold" cursor. It's a mask and can be either IFX_SCROLL, IFX_HOLD, or both or'd together.

Refer to *www.php123.com* for on-line example.

----

ifx_do (ifx)
execute previously prepared query or open a cursor for it

```
int ifx_do(int result_id);
```

> This function returns TRUE on success, FALSE on error.

Refer to *www.php123.com* for on-line example.

----

ifx_error (ifx)
return error code of last Informix call

```
string ifx_error(void);
```

> The Informix error codes (SQLSTATE & SQLCODE) formatted as follows:
>
> x [SQLSTATE = aa bbb SQLCODE=cccc] where x = space : no error
>
> E : error
>
> N : no more data
>
> W : warning
>
> ? : undefined
>
> If the "x" character is anything other than space, SQLSTATE and SQL-CODE describe the error in more detail.

Refer to *www.php123.com* for on-line example.

----

ifx_errormsg (ifx)
return error message of last Informix call

```
string ifx_errormsg(int [errorcode]);
```

> This function returns the Informix error message associated with the most recent Informix error, or, when the optional "errorcode" parameter is present, the error message corresponding to "errorcode".

Refer to *www.php123.com* for on-line example.

----

ifx_affected_rows (ifx)
get number of rows affected by query

```
int ifx_affected_rows(int result_id);
```

> result_id is a valid result id returned by ifx_query() or ifx_prepare().
> This function returns the number of rows affected by a query associated with result_id.

Refer to *www.php123.com* for on-line example.

----

ifx_fetch_row (ifx)
get row as enumerated array

```
array ifx_fetch_row(int result_id, mixed [position] );
```

> This function returns an associative array that corresponds to the fetched row, or FALSE if there are no more rows.

Refer to *www.php123.com* for on-line example.

----

ifx_htmltbl_result (ifx)
format all rows of query into a HTML table

```
int ifx_htmltbl_result(int result_id, string
[html_table_options]);
```

> This function returns the number of rows fetched or FALSE on error. It formats all rows of the result_id query into a html table. The optional second argument is a string of <table> tag options.

Refer to *www.php123.com* for on-line example.

----

ifx_fieldtypes (ifx)
list Informix SQL fields

```
array ifx_fieldtypes(int result_id);
```

> This function returns an associative array with fieldnames as key and the SQL fieldtypes as data for query with result_id. It returns FALSE on error.

Refer to *www.php123.com* for on-line example.

----

ifx_fieldproperties (ifx)
list SQL fieldproperties

```
array ifx_fieldproperties(int result_id);
```

> This function returns an associative array with fieldnames as key and the SQL fieldproperties as data for a query with result_id. It returns FALSE on error, and returns the Informix SQL fieldproperies of every field in the query as an associative array. Properties are encoded as:
>
> "SQLTYPE;length;precision;scale;ISNULLABLE"
>
> where SQLTYPE = the Informix type like "SQLVCHAR", etc., and ISNULLABLE = "Y" or "N".

Refer to *www.php123.com* for on-line example.

----

ifx_num_fields (ifx)
return number of columns in query

```
int ifx_num_fields(int result_id);
```

> This function returns the number of columns in query for result_id or
> FALSE on error. After preparing or executing a query, this call gives
> you the number of columns in the query.

Refer to *www.php123.com* for on-line example.

----

ifx_num_rows (ifx)
count the rows already fetched in query

```
int ifx_num_rows(int result_id);
```

> This function returns the number of rows fetched so far for a query
> with result_id after a ifx_query() or ifx_do() query.

Refer to *www.php123.com* for on-line example.

----

ifx_free_result (ifx)
release resources for query

```
int ifx_free_result(int result_id);
```

> This function releases resources for the query associated with
> result_id, and returns FALSE on error.

Refer to *www.php123.com* for on-line example.

----

ifx_create_char (ifx)
create char object

```
int ifx_create_char(string param);
```

> This function creates a char object. param is the char content.

Refer to *www.php123.com* for on-line example.

----

ifx_free_char (ifx)
delete char object

```
int ifx_free_char(int bid);
```

> This function deletes the char object for the given char object-id bid, and returns FALSE on error, otherwise TRUE.

Refer to *www.php123.com* for on-line example.

----

ifx_update_char (ifx)
update content of char object

```
int ifx_update_char(int bid, string content);
```

> This function updates the content of the char object for the given char object bid, where content is a string with new data. It returns FALSE on error, otherwise TRUE.

Refer to *www.php123.com* for on-line example.

----

ifx_get_char (ifx)
return content of char object

```
int ifx_get_char(int bid);
```

> This function returns the content of the char object for the given char object-id bid.

Refer to *www.php123.com* for on-line example.

----

ifx_create_blob (ifx)
creates blob object

```
int ifx_create_blob(int type, int mode, string param);
```

> This function creates a blob object of type 1 = TEXT, 0 = BYTE, mode:
> 0 = blob-object holds the content in memory, 1 = blob-object holds the
> content in file. If mode = 0, then param will be a pointer to the con-
> tent; if mode = 1, then param will be a pointer to the filestring. It
> returns FALSE on error, otherwise the new blob object-id.

Refer to *www.php123.com* for on-line example.

----

ifx_copy_blob (ifx)
duplicate the given blob object

```
int ifx_copy_blob(int bid);
```

> This function duplicates the given blob object. bid is the ID of the blob
> object. It returns FALSE on error, otherwise the new blob object-id.

Refer to *www.php123.com* for on-line example.

----

ifx_free_blob (ifx)
delete blob object

```
int ifx_free_blob(int bid);
```

> This function deletes the blob object for the given blob object-id bid. It
> returns FALSE on error, otherwise TRUE.

Refer to *www.php123.com* for on-line example.

----

ifx_get_blob (ifx)
return content of blob object

```
int ifx_get_blob(int bid);
```

> This function returns the content of the blob object for the given blob
> object-id bid.

Refer to *www.php123.com* for on-line example.

----

ifx_update_blob (ifx)
update content of blob object

```
ifx_update_blob(int bid, string content);
```

> This function updates the content of the blob object for the given blob object bid. content is a string with new data. It returns FALSE on error, otherwise TRUE.

Refer to *www.php123.com* for on-line example.

----

ifx_blobinfile_mode (ifx)
set default blob mode for all select queries

```
void ifx_blobinfile_mode(int mode);
```

> This function sets the default blob mode for all select queries. Mode "0" means save Byte-Blobs in memory, and mode "1" means save Byte-Blobs in a file.

Refer to *www.php123.com* for on-line example.

----

ifx_textasvarchar (ifx)
set default text mode

```
void ifx_textasvarchar(int mode);
```

> This function sets the default text mode for all select-queries. Mode "0" returns a blob id, and mode "1" returns a varchar with text content.

Refer to *www.php123.com* for on-line example.

----

ifx_byteasvarchar (ifx)
set default byte mode

```
void ifx_byteasvarchar(int mode);
```

> This function sets the default byte mode for all select-queries. Mode "0" returns a blob id, and mode "1" returns a varchar with text content.

Refer to *www.php123.com* for on-line example.

----

ifx_nullformat (ifx)
set default return value on a fetch row

```
void ifx_nullformat(int mode);
```

> This function sets the default return value of a NULL-value on a fetch row. Mode "0" returns "", and mode "1" returns "NULL".

Refer to *www.php123.com* for on-line example.

----

ifxus_create_slob (ifx)
create slob object and open it

```
int ifxus_create_slob(int mode);
```

> This function creates an slob object and opens it. The modes are:
>
>   1 = LO_RDONLY,
>
>   2 = LO_WRONLY,
>
>   4 = LO_APPEND,
>
>   8 = LO_RDWR,
>
>   16 = LO_BUFFER,
>
>   32 = LO_NOBUFFER -> or-mask.
>
> You can also use constants named IFX_LO_RDONLY, IFX_LO_WRONLY, etc. This function returns FALSE on error, otherwise the new slob object-id.

Refer to *www.php123.com* for on-line example.

----

ifx_free_slob (ifx)
delete slob object

```
int ifxus_free_slob(int bid);
```

> This function deletes the slob object. bid is the id of the slob object. It returns FALSE on error, otherwise TRUE.

Refer to *www.php123.com* for on-line example.

----

ifxus_close_slob (ifx)
delete slob object

```
int ifxus_close_slob(int bid);
```

> This function deletes the slob object on the given slob object-id bid. It returns FALSE on error, otherwise TRUE.

Refer to *www.php123.com* for on-line example.

----

ifxus_open_slob (ifx)
open slob object

```
int ifxus_open_slob(long bid, int mode);
```

> This function opens a slob object. bid should be an existing slob id.
>
> The modes are:
>
> 1 = LO_RDONLY,
>
> 2 = LO_WRONLY,
>
> 4 = LO_APPEND,
>
> 8 = LO_RDWR,
>
> 16 = LO_BUFFER,
>
> 32 = LO_NOBUFFER -> or-mask.
>
> It returns FALSE on error, otherwise the new slob object-id.

Refer to *www.php123.com* for on-line example.

----

ifxus_tell_slob (ifx)
return current file or seek position of an open slob object

```
int ifxus_tell_slob(long bid);
```

> This function returns the current file or seek position of an open slob object. bid should be an existing slob id. It returns FALSE on error, otherwise the seek position.

Refer to *www.php123.com* for on-line example.

----

ifxus_seek_slob (ifx)
set current file or seek position of an open slob object

```
int ifxus_seek_blob(long bid, int mode, long offset);
```

> bid should be an existing slob id. The modes are:
>
>   0 = LO_SEEK_SET,
>
>   1 = LO_SEEK_CUR,
>
>   2 = LO_SEEK_END.
>
> offset is an byte offset. It returns FALSE on error, otherwise the seek position.

Refer to *www.php123.com* for on-line example.

----

ifxus_read_slob (ifx)
read n bytes of the slob object

```
int ifxus_read_slob(long bid, long nbytes);
```

> This function reads n bytes of the slob object. bid is an existing slob id and nbytes is the number of bytes to read. It returns FALSE on error, otherwise the string.

Refer to *www.php123.com* for on-line example.

----

ifxus_write_slob (ifx)
write a string into slob object

```
int ifxus_write_slob(long bid, string content);
```

> This function writes a string into the slob object. bid is a existing slob id and content is the content to write. It returns FALSE on error, otherwise bytes written.

Refer to *www.php123.com* for on-line example.

MS SQL Server Functions (msql)

mssql_affected_rows (msql)
get number of affected rows in last query

```
int mssql_affected_rows(int [link_identifier] );
```

> mssql_affected_rows() returns the number of rows affected by the last INSERT, UPDATE, or DELETE query on the server associated with the specified link identifier. If the link identifier isn't specified, the last opened link is assumed. This command is not effective for SELECT statements, only on statements that modify records. To retrieve the number of rows returned from a SELECT, use mssql_num_rows().

Refer to *www.php123.com* for on-line example.

----

mssql_close (msql)
close MS SQL server connection

```
int mssql_close(int link_identifier);
```

> This function returns TRUE on success, FALSE on error. It closes the link to a MS SQL Server database that's associated with the specified link identifier. If the link identifier isn't specified, the last opened link is assumed. Note that this isn't usually necessary, as non-persistent open links are automatically closed at the end of the script's execution. mssql_close() will not close persistent links generated by mssql_pconnect().

See also mssql_connect(), mssql_pconnect().

Refer to *www.php123.com* for on-line example.

----

mssql_connect (msql)
open MS SQL server connection

```
int mssql_connect(string servername, string username, string password);
```

> mssql_connect() establishes a connection to a MS SQL server. It returns a positive MS SQL link identifier on success, or FALSE on error. The servername argument must be a valid servername that

is defined in the 'interfaces' file. In case a second call is made to mssql_connect() with the same arguments, no new link will be established, but instead, the link identifier of the already opened link will be returned. The link to the server will be closed as soon as the execution of the script ends, unless it's closed earlier by explicitly calling mssql_close().

See also mssql_pconnect(), mssql_close().

Refer to *www.php123.com* for on-line example.

---

mssql_data_seek (msql)
move internal row pointer

```
int mssql_data_seek(int result_identifier, int row_number);
```

mssql_data_seek() moves the internal row pointer of the MS SQL result associated with the specified result identifier to pointer to the specified row number. It returns TRUE on success, or FALSE on failure. The next call to mssql_fetch_row() would return that row.

Refer to *www.php123.com* for on-line example.

---

mssql_fetch_array (msql)
fetch row as array

```
int mssql_fetch_array(int result);
```

mssql_fetch_array() is an extended version of mssql_fetch_row(). It returns an array that corresponds to the fetched row, or FALSE if there are no more rows. In addition to storing the data in the numeric indices of the result array, it also stores the data in associative indices, using the field names as keys. Note that using mssql_fetch_array() is NOT significantly slower than using mssql_fetch_row(), while it provides a significant added value.

See also mssql_fetch_row().

Refer to *www.php123.com* for on-line example.

---

mssql_fetch_field (msql)
get field information

```
object mssql_fetch_field(int result, int field_offset);
```

This function returns an object containing field information. mssql_fetch_field() can be used in order to obtain information about fields in a certain query result. If the field offset isn't specified, the next field not yet retrieved by mssql_fetch_field() is retrieved.

The properties of the object are:

name	column name. If the column is a result of a function, this property is set to computed #N, where #N is a serial number.
column_source	the table from which the column was taken
max_length	maximum length of the column
numeric	1 if the column is numeric

Refer to *www.php123.com* for on-line example.

See also mssql_field_seek().

----

mssql_fetch_object (msql)
fetch row as object

```
int mssql_fetch_object(int result);
```

This function returns an object with properties this correspond to the fetched row, or FALSE if there are no more rows.

mssql_fetch_object() is similar to mssql_fetch_array(), with one difference—an object is returned, not an array. Indirectly, this means that you can access the data only by the field names, and not by their offsets (numbers are illegal property names).

In terms of speed, the function is identical to mssql_fetch_array(), and almost as quick as mssql_fetch_row() (the difference is insignificant).

Refer to *www.php123.com* for on-line example.

See also mssql_fetch-array() and mssql_fetch-row().

----

mssql_fetch_row (msql)
get row as enumerated array

```
array mssql_fetch_row(int result);
```

This function returns an array that corresponds to the fetched row, or FALSE if there are no more rows.

mssql_fetch_row() fetches one row of data from the result associated with the specified result identifier. The row is returned as an array. Each result column is stored in an array offset, starting at offset 0.

A subsequent call to mssql_fetch_rows() would return the next row in the result set, or FALSE if there are no more rows.

Refer to *www.php123.com* for on-line example.

See also mssql_fetch_array(), mssql_fetch_object(), mssql_data_seek(), mssql_fetch_lengths(), and mssql_result().

---

mssql_field_seek (msql)
set field offset

```
int mssql_field_seek(int result, int field_offset);
```

This function seeks to the specified field offset. If the next call to mssql_fetch_field() does not include a field offset, this field would be returned.

Refer to *www.php123.com* for on-line example.

See also mssql_fetch_field().

---

mssql_free_result (msql)
free result memory

```
int mssql_free_result(int result);
```

mssql_free_result() should be called only if you are worried about using too much memory while your script is running. All result memory will automatically be freed when the script ends, but you may call mssql_free_result() with the result identifier as an argument. The associated result memory will be freed.

Refer to *www.php123.com* for on-line example.

---

mssql_num_fields (msql)
get number of fields in result

```
int mssql_num_fields(int result);
```

mssql_num_fields() returns the number of fields in a result set.

See also mssql_db_query(), mssql_query(), mssql_fetch_field(), mssql_num_rows().

---

mssql_num_rows (msql)
get number of rows in result

```
int mssql_num_rows(string result);
```

mssql_num_rows() returns the number of rows in a result set.

Refer to *www.php123.com* for on-line example.

See also mssql_db_query(), mssql_query(), and mssql_fetch_row().

---

mssql_pconnect (msql)
open persistent MS SQL connection

```
int mssql_pconnect(string servername, string username, string
password);
```

This function returns a positive MS SQL persistent link identifier on success, or FALSE on error.

mssql_pconnect() acts very much like mssql_connect() with two major differences:

First, when connecting, the function first tries to find a (persistent) link that's already open with the same host, username and password. If one is found, an identifier for it is returned instead of opening a new connection.

Second, the connection to the SQL server will not be closed when the execution of the script ends. Instead, the link will remain open for future use. (mssql_close() will not close links established by mssql_pconnect()). This is a persistent link.

Refer to *www.php123.com* for on-line example.

----

mssql_query (msql)
send MS SQL query

```
int mssql_query(string query, int link_identifier);
```

> This function returns a positive MS SQL result identifier on success, or FALSE on error.
>
> mssql_query() sends a query to the currently active database on the server that's associated with the specified link identifier. If the link identifier isn't specified, the last opened link is assumed. If no link is open, the function tries to establish a link as if mssql_connect() was called, and use it.

Refer to *www.php123.com* for on-line example.

See also mssql_db_query(), mssql_select_db(), and mssql_connect().

----

mssql_result (msql)
get result data

```
int mssql_result(int result, int i, mixed field);
```

> This function returns the contents of the cell at the row and offset in the specified MS SQL result set.
>
> mssql_result() returns the contents of one cell from a MS SQL result set. The field argument can be the field's offset, or the field's name, or the field's table dot field's name (fieldname.tablename). If the column name has been aliased ('select foo as bar from...'), use the alias instead of the column name.
>
> When working on large result sets, you should consider using one of the functions that fetch an entire row (specified below). As these functions return the contents of multiple cells in one function call, they're MUCH quicker than mssql_result(). Also, note that specifying a numeric offset for the field argument is much quicker than specifying a fieldname or tablename.fieldname argument.
>
> Recommended higher-performance alternatives are mssql_fetch_row(), mssql_fetch_array(), and mssql_fetch_object().

Refer to *www.php123.com* for on-line example.

----

mssql_select_db (msql)
select MS SQL database

```
int mssql_select_db(string database_name, int link_identifier);
```

> This function returns TRUE on success, FALSE on error.
>
> mssql_select_db() sets the current active database on the server associated with the specified link identifier. If no link identifier is specified, the last opened link is assumed. If no link is open, the function will try to establish a link as if mssql_connect() was called, and use it. Every subsequent call to mssql_query() is made on the active database.

Refer to *www.php123.com* for on-line example.

See also mssql_connect(), mssql_pconnect(), and mssql_query().

Sybase Functions (sybase)

sybase_affected_rows (sybase)
get number of affected rows in last query

```
int sybase_affected_rows(int [link_identifier] );
```

> sybase_affected_rows() returns the number of rows affected by the last INSERT, UPDATE, or DELETE query on the server associated with the specified link identifier. If the link identifier isn't specified, the last opened link is assumed.
>
> This command is not effective on SELECT statements, but only on statements that modify records. To retrieve the number of rows returned from a SELECT, use sybase_num_rows().

Refer to *www.php123.com* for on-line example.

----

sybase_close (sybase)
close Sybase connection

```
int sybase_close(int link_identifier);
```

sybase_close() closes the link to a Sybase database associated with the specified link identifier. It returns TRUE on success, FALSE on error. If the link identifier isn't specified, the last opened link is assumed.

Note that this isn't usually necessary, as non-persistent open links are automatically closed at the end of the script's execution.

sybase_close() will not close persistent links generated by sybase_pconnect().

Refer to *www.php123.com* for on-line example.

See also sybase_connect(), sybase_pconnect().

----

sybase_connect (sybase)
open Sybase server connection

```
int sybase_connect(string servername, string username, string
password);
```

This function returns a positive Sybase link identifier on success, or FALSE on error.

sybase_connect() establishes a connection to a Sybase server. The servername argument must be a valid servername defined in the "interfaces" file.

If a second call is made to sybase_connect() with the same arguments, no new link will be established but, instead, the link identifier of the already opened link will be returned.

The link to the server will be closed as soon as the execution of the script ends, unless it's closed earlier by explicitly calling sybase_close().

Refer to *www.php123.com* for on-line example.

See also sybase_pconnect(), sybase_close().

----

sybase_data_seek (sybase)
move internal row pointer

```
int sybase_data_seek(int result_identifier, int row_number);
```

> This function returns TRUE on success, FALSE on failure.
>
> sybase_data_seek() moves the internal row pointer of the Sybase result associated with the specified result identifier to point to the specified row number. The next call to sybase_fetch_row() would return that row.

Refer to *www.php123.com* for on-line example.

See also sybase_data_seek().

----

sybase_fetch_array (sybase)
fetch row as array

```
int sybase_fetch_array(int result);
```

> This function returns an array that corresponds to the fetched row, or FALSE if there are no more rows.
>
> sybase_fetch_array() is an extended version of sybase_fetch_row(). In addition to storing the data in the numeric indices of the result array, it also stores the data in associative indices, using the field names as keys.
>
> Note that using sybase_fetch_array() is NOT significantly slower than using sybase_fetch_row(), while it provides a significant added value.

Refer to *www.php123.com* for on-line example.

See also sybase_fetch_row().

----

sybase_fetch_field (sybase)
get field information

```
object sybase_fetch_field(int result, int field_offset);
```

> This function returns an object containing field information.
>
> sybase_fetch_field() can be used to obtain information about fields in a certain query result. If the field offset isn't specified, the next field not yet retrieved by sybase_fetch_field() is retrieved.
>
> The properties of the object are:
>
> **name**   column name. If the column is a result of a function, this property is set to computed#N, where #N is a serial number.

column_source	the table from which the column was taken
max_length	maximum length of the column
numeric	1 if the column is numeric

Refer to *www.php123.com* for on-line example.

See also sybase_field_seek().

----

sybase_fetch_object (sybase)
fetch row as object

```
int sybase_fetch_object(int result);
```

This function returns an object with properties that correspond to the fetched row, or FALSE if there are no more rows.

sybase_fetch_object() is similar to sybase_fetch_array(), with one difference—an object is returned, not an array. Indirectly, that means that you can access the data only by the field names, and not by their offsets (numbers are illegal property names).

In terms of speed, the function is identical to sybase_fetch_array(), and almost as quick as sybase_fetch_row() (the difference is insignificant).

Refer to *www.php123.com* for on-line example.

See also sybase_fetch-array() and sybase_fetch-row().

----

sybase_fetch_row (sybase)
get row as enumerated array

```
array sybase_fetch_row(int result);
```

This function returns an array that corresponds to the fetched row, or FALSE if there are no more rows.

sybase_fetch_row() fetches one row of data from the result associated with the specified result identifier. The row is returned as an array. Each result column is stored in an array offset, starting at offset 0.

Subsequent call to sybase_fetch_rows() return the next row in the result set, or FALSE if there are no more rows.

Refer to *www.php123.com* for on-line example.

See also sybase_fetch_array(), sybase_fetch_object(),data_seek(), sybase_fetch_
lengths(), and sybase_result().

---

sybase_field_seek (sybase)
set field offset

```
int sybase_field_seek(int result, int field_offset);
```

> This function seeks the specified field offset. If the next call to
> sybase_fetch_field() won't include a field offset, this field would be
> returned.

Refer to *www.php123.com* for on-line example.

See also sybase_fetch_field().

---

sybase_free_result (sybase)
free result memory

```
int sybase_free_result(int result);
```

> sybase_free_result() needs to be called only if you are worried about
> using too much memory while your script is running. All result
> memory will automatically be freed when the script ends, but you
> may call sybase_free_result() with the result identifier as an argument.
> The associated result memory will be freed.

Refer to *www.php123.com* for on-line example.

---

sybase_num_fields (sybase)
get number of fields in result

```
int sybase_num_fields(int result);
```

> sybase_num_fields() returns the number of fields in a result set.

Refer to *www.php123.com* for on-line example.

See also sybase_db_query(), sybase_query(), sybase_fetch_field(), and sybase_
num_rows().

---

sybase_num_rows (sybase)
get number of rows in result

```
int sybase_num_rows(string result);
```

> sybase_num_rows() returns the number of rows in a result set.

Refer to *www.php123.com* for on-line example.

See also sybase_db_query(), sybase_query(), and sybase_fetch_row().

---

sybase_pconnect (sybase)
open persistent Sybase connection

```
int sybase_pconnect(string servername, string username,
string password);
```

> This function returns a positive Sybase persistent link identifier on success, or FALSE on error.
>
> sybase_pconnect() acts very much like sybase_connect(), with two major differences: First, when connecting, the function first tries to find a (persistent) link that's already open with the same host, username, and password. If one is found, an identifier for it is returned instead of opening a new connection.
>
> Second, the connection to the SQL server is not closed when the execution of the script ends. Instead, the link remains open for future use (sybase_close() will not close links established by sybase_pconnect()). This is a persistent link.

Refer to *www.php123.com* for on-line example.

---

sybase_query (sybase)
send Sybase query

```
int sybase_query(string query, int link_identifier);
```

> This function returns a positive Sybase result identifier on success, or FALSE on error.

sybase_query() sends a query to the currently active database on the server associated with the specified link identifier. If the link identifier isn't specified, the last opened link is assumed. If no link is open, the function tries to establish a link as if sybase_connect() had been called, and use it.

Refer to *www.php123.com* for on-line example.

See also sybase_db_query(), sybase_select_db(), and sybase_connect().

----

sybase_result (sybase)
get result data

```
int sybase_result(int result, int i, mixed field);
```

This function returns the contents of the cell at the row and offset in the specified Sybase result set.

sybase_result() returns the contents of one cell from a Sybase result set. The field argument can be the field's offset, or the field's name, or the field's table dot field's name (fieldname.tablename). If the column name has been aliased ('select foo as bar from...'), use the alias instead of the column name.

When working on large result sets, you should consider using one of the functions that fetch an entire row (specified below). As these functions return the contents of multiple cells in one function call, they're MUCH quicker than sybase_result(). Also, note that specifying a numeric offset for the field argument is much quicker than specifying a fieldname or tablename.fieldname argument.

Recommended higher-performance alternatives are: sybase_fetch_row(), sybase_fetch_array(), and sybase_fetch_object().

Refer to *www.php123.com* for on-line example.

----

sybase_select_db (sybase)
select Sybase database

```
int sybase_select_db(string database_name, int
link_identifier);
```

This function returns: TRUE on success, FALSE on error.

sybase_select_db() sets the current active database on the server associated with the specified link identifier. If no link identifier is specified, the last opened link is assumed. If no link is open, the function will try to establish a link as if sybase_connect() had been called, and use it.

Every subsequent call to sybase_query() will be made on the active database.

Refer to *www.php123.com* for on-line example.

GRAPHICS-RELATED

getImageSize (image)
get size of GIF, JPG, or PNG image

```
array getimagesize (string filename);
```

The GetImageSize() function will determine the size of any GIF, JPG, or PNG image file and return the dimensions along with the file type and a height/width text string to be used inside a normal HTML IMG tag. It returns an array with the four elements below.

$array[0]	the width of the image in pixels.
$array[1]	the height of the image in pixels.
$array[2]	a flag indicating the type of the image, where 1 = GIF, 2 = JPG, and 3 = PNG.
$array[3]	a text string of the form "height=N width=N" that can be used directly in an <IMG> tag.

Example 1

Display some basic information about an image.

```
<?PHP
$image_type = array("invalid", "GIF image", "JPG image", "PNG
  image");
$size = GetImageSize("1.gif");
echo "Width: ".$size[0]."\n";
```

```
echo "Height: ".$size[1]."\n";
echo $image_type[$size[2]]."\n";
@Normal:echo $size[3]."\n";
?>
```

Output 1

```
Width: 100
Height: 67
GIF image
width="100" height="67"
```

Example 2

A more useful example of how to use GetImageSize().

```
<?PHP
$size = GetImageSize("1.gif");
echo '<IMG SRC="1.gif" '.$size[3].'>';
?>
```

Output 2

```
<IMG SRC="1.gif" width="100" height="67">
```

----

imageArc (image)
draw a partial ellipse

```
int imagearc(int img, int center_x, int center_y, int w,
int h, int s, int e, int col);
```

> This function draws a partial ellipse centered at *center_x*, *center_y* (where top left is 0,0) in the image represented by *img*. *w* and *h* specify the ellipse's width and height. The start and end points are specified in degrees indicated by the *s_degree* and *e_degree* arguments. Zero (0) degrees is 3 o'clock, and goes counterclockwise.

Example 1

The code below draws a circle 250 pixels in diameter centered in the image.

```
<?PHP
Header("Content-type: image/gif");
$img = ImageCreate(250, 250);
```

```
$black = ImageColorAllocate($img, 0, 0, 0);
$white = ImageColorAllocate($img, 255, 255, 255);
ImageFill($img, 0, 0, $black);
ImageArc($img, 125, 125, 250, 250, 0, 360, $white);
ImageGIF($img);
ImageDestroy($img);
?>
```

Output

---

imageChar (image)
draw a character horizontally

```
int imagechar(int img, int font, int x, int y, string c, int
color);
```

> This function draws the first character of the string *c* in the image
> identified by *img* at coordinates *x, y* (top left is 0,0) with the color
> *color*.
>
> Fonts 1, 2, 3, 4, and 5 are included with PHP, and increase in size as
> their respective number increases.

Example

The code below uses ImageChar() to place an 'A' in the top left corner, a 'B'
in the top right corner, a 'C' in the bottom left corner, and a 'D' in the bottom right corner of the image.

```
<?PHP
Header("Content-type: image/gif");
$img = ImageCreate(250, 250);
$black = ImageColorAllocate($img, 0, 0, 0);
```

```
$white = ImageColorAllocate($img, 255, 255, 255);
ImageFill($img, 100, 100, $black);
ImageChar($img, 5, 10, 10, "A", $white);
ImageChar($img, 5, 225, 10, "B", $white);
ImageChar($img, 5, 10, 225, "C", $white);
ImageChar($img, 5, 225, 225, "D", $white);
ImageGIF($img);
ImageDestroy($img);
?>
```

Output

See also imageloadfont().

----

imageCharUp (image)
draw a character vertically

```
int imagecharup(int img, int font, int x, int y, string c,
int color);
```

> This function draws the first character of the string *c* vertically in image *img* at coordinates (*x, y*), where top left is (0, 0), with the color *color*.
>
> Fonts 1, 2, 3, 4, and 5 are included with PHP, and increase in size as their respective number increases.

Example

The following code uses ImageChar() to place an 'A' in the top left corner, a 'B' in the top right corner, a 'C' in the bottom left corner, and a 'D' in the bottom right corner of the image. The four letters are all rotated 90 degress counterclockwise.

```php
<?PHP
Header("Content-type: image/gif");
$img = ImageCreate(250, 250);
$black = ImageColorAllocate($img, 0, 0, 0);
$white = ImageColorAllocate($img, 255, 255, 255);
ImageFill($img, 100, 100, $black);
ImageCharUp($img, 5, 20, 20, "A", $white);
ImageCharUp($img, 5, 215, 20, "B", $white);
ImageCharUp($img, 5, 20, 225, "C", $white);
ImageCharUp($img, 5, 215, 225, "D", $white);
ImageGIF($img);
ImageDestroy($img);
?>
```

Output

See also ImageChar() and imageloadfont().

----

imageColorAllocate (image)
allocate a color for an image

```
int imagecolorallocate(int img, int red, int green, int blue);
```

> This function returns a color identifier representing the color composed of the given red, green, and blue (RGB) components.
>
> The *img* argument is the return from the imagecreate() function.
>
> ImageColorAllocate must be called to create each color to be used in the image represented by *img*.

Example

The following code uses ImageColorAllocate() to make the image background black, the circle red, and fill the circle with green.

```
<?PHP
Header("Content-type: image/gif");
$img = ImageCreate(250, 250);
$black = ImageColorAllocate($img, 0, 0, 0);
$red = ImageColorAllocate($img, 255, 0, 0);
$green = ImageColorAllocate($img, 0, 255, 0);
ImageFill($img, 0, 0, $black);
ImageArc($img, 125, 125, 250, 250, 0, 360, $red);
ImageFill($img, 125, 125, $green);
ImageGIF($img);
ImageDestroy($img);
?>
```

Output

See also ImageColorTransparent().

----

imageColorTransparent (image)
define a color as transparent

```
int imagecolortransparent(int img, int color);
```

> This function sets the transparent color in the *img* image to *color*. *img*
> is the image identifier returned by imagecreate() and *color* is the color
> identifier returned by imagecolorallocate().

Example

The code below uses ImageColorTransparent() to make a part of the generated image "see-through."

```
<?PHP
Header("Content-type: image/gif");
$img = ImageCreate(250, 250);
```

```
$black = ImageColorAllocate($img, 0, 0, 0);
$white = ImageColorAllocate($img, 255, 255, 255);
$trans = ImageColorAllocate($img, 0, 255, 0);
ImageColorTransparent($img, $trans);
ImageFill($img, 0, 0, $black);
ImageArc($img, 125, 125, 250, 250, 0, 360, $white);
ImageFill($img, 125, 125, $trans);
ImageGIF($img);
ImageDestroy($img);
?>
```

Output

See also ImageColorAllocate().

----

imageCopyResized (image)
copy and resize part of an image

```
int imagecopyresized(int dst_img, int src_img, int dest_x,
int dest_y, int src_x, int src_y, int dest_w, int dest_h, int
src_w, int src_h);
```

This function copies a rectangular portion of one image to another image. *dst_img* is the destination image and *src_img* is the source image.

If the sizes of the source and destination differ, then the appropriate amount of stretching or shrinking of the copied image will be performed.

The coordinates (*dest_x*, *dest_y*, *src_x*, and *src_y*) refer to the upper left corners of the part of the image to copy or to copy to.

This function can be used to copy parts of an image within the same image (*dst_img* would equal *src_img*), but the two regions cannot overlap.

Example

The code below places an 'A' at (100, 100). Then ImageCopyResized() is used to make a copy of the letter, and to make it four times larger, at (200, 200).

```php
<?PHP
Header("Content-type: image/gif");
$img = ImageCreate(300, 300);
$black = ImageColorAllocate($img, 0, 0, 0);
$white = ImageColorAllocate($img, 255, 255, 255);
ImageFill($img, 0, 0, $black);
ImageChar($img, 5, 100, 100, "A", $white);
ImageCopyResized($img, $img, 200, 200, 100, 100, 100, 100, 25,
25);
ImageGIF($img);
ImageDestroy($img);
?>
```

Output

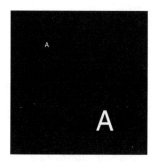

----

imageCreate (image)
GIF creation with PHP

```
int imagecreate (int x_size, int y_size);
```

> This function creates an empty image and returns a pointer to it.
>
> It uses the GD library, so PHP must already have been compiled with this library for it to work.

Example

The following code makes a solid black GIF image 50 pixels wide by 50 pixels high.

```
<?PHP
Header("Content-type: image/gif");
$img = ImageCreate(50, 50);
ImageFill($img, 0, 0, $black);
ImageGIF($img);
ImageDestroy($img);
?>
```

Output

See also ImageCreateFromGif() and ImageDestroy().

----

imageCreateFromGif (image)
create new image from file or URL

```
int imagecreatefromgif(string filename);
```

This function returns an image identifier representing the image obtained from the given filename. This contrasts with the ImageCreate() function which generates a blank image.

This function is useful for placing caption text on images and to create graphic buttons with dynamically generated text over 3D shaded buttons.

Example

The code below uses ImageCreateFromGif() to to initialize an image with the contents of 1.gif. Next, it places text on top of the image.

```
<?PHP
  $string = "Press Here";
  Header("Content-type: image/gif");
  $image = ImageCreateFromGIF("button1.gif");
  $yellow = ImageColorAllocate($image, 255, 255, 128);
```

```
$px = (imagesx($image) - ImageFontWidth(5) *
   strlen($string)) /2;
ImageString($image,5 ,$px ,9 , $string, $yellow);
ImageGif($image);
ImageDestroy($image);
?>
```

Press Here

See also ImageCreate().

----

imageDashedLine (image)
draw a dashed line

```
int imagedashedline(int img, int x1, int y1, int x2, int y2,
int color);
```

This function draws a dashed line from (x1, y1) to (x2, y2) (top left is 0,0) in image *img* of color *color*.

Example

The code below uses ImageDashedLine() to draw a dashed line.

```
<?PHP
Header("Content-type: image/gif");
$img = ImageCreate(250, 250);
$black = ImageColorAllocate($img, 0, 0, 0);
$white = ImageColorAllocate($img, 255, 255, 255);
ImageFill($img, 0, 0, $black);
ImageDashedLine($img, 0, 0, 250, 250, $white);
ImageGIF($img);
ImageDestroy($img);
?>
```

Output

See also ImageLine().

---

imageDestroy (image)
destroy an image

```
int imagedestroy(int img);
```

> This function frees any memory associated with image *img*. *img* is the image identifier returned by the ImageCreate() function.

Example

```
<?PHP
Header("Content-type: image/gif");
$img = ImageCreate(50, 50);
$black = ImageColorAllocate($img, 0, 0, 0);
ImageFill($img, 0, 0, $black);
ImageGIF($img);
ImageDestroy($img);
?>
```

See also ImageCreate().

---

imageFill (image)
flood fill

```
int imagefill(int img, int x, int y, int color);
```

> This function performs a flood fill starting at coordinate *x, y* (where top left is 0,0) with color *color* in the image *img*.

Example 1

The code below displays a GIF image 250 pixels high by 250 pixels wide. The function ImageFill() is used to make the entire image black.

```
<?PHP
Header("Content-type: image/gif");
$img = ImageCreate(250, 250);
$black = ImageColorAllocate($img, 0,0,0);
ImageFill($img, 100, 100, $black);
ImageGIF($img);
ImageDestroy($img);
?>
```

Output 1

Example 2

The code below displays a GIF image 250 pixels high by 250 pixels wide. First, the function ImageFill() is used to make the entire image black. Next, a white circle is drawn in the middle of the image, and ImageFill() is called to fill in the circle with white.

```
<?PHP
Header("Content-type: image/gif");
$img = ImageCreate(250, 250);
$black = ImageColorAllocate($img, 0,0,0);
$white = ImageColorAllocate($img, 255,255,255);
ImageFill($img, 100, 100, $black);
ImageArc($img, 125, 125, 250, 250, 0, 360, $white);
ImageFill($img, 125, 125, $white);
ImageGIF($img);
ImageDestroy($img);
?>
```

Output 2

imageFilledPolygon (image)
draw a filled polygon

```
int imagefilledpolygon(int img, array points, int num_points,
int color);
```

> This function creates a filled polygon in image *img* of color *color*. *points*
> is an array containing the polygon's vertices. The array is of the form
>
> points[0] = x0,
>
> points[1] = y0,
>
> points[2] = x1,
>
> points[3] = y1, etc.
>
> *num_points* is the total number of vertices in the array.

Example 1

The code below uses ImageFilledPolygon() to create a white square in
the image. The ImageFilledPolygon() function is equivalent to
ImageFilledRectangle($img, 10, 10, 240, 240, $white);.

```php
<?PHP
Header("Content-type: image/gif");
$img = ImageCreate(250, 250);
$black = ImageColorAllocate($img, 0, 0, 0);
$white = ImageColorAllocate($img, 255, 255, 255);
ImageFill($img, 0, 0, $black);
$a[0] = 10; $a[1] = 10;
$a[2] = 240; $a[3] = 10;
$a[4] = 240; $a[5] = 240;
$a[6] = 10; $a[7] = 240;
ImageFilledPolygon($img, $a, 4, $white);
ImageGIF($img);
ImageDestroy($img);
?>
```

Output 1

Example 2

The code below uses ImageFilledPolygon() to draw a stop sign.

```php
<?PHP
Header("Content-type: image/gif");
$img = ImageCreate(240, 240);
$trans = ImageColorAllocate($img, 0, 0, 0);
ImageColorTransparent($img, $trans);
$red = ImageColorAllocate($img, 255, 0, 0);
ImageFill($img, 0, 0, $black);
$a[0] = 0; $a[1] = 70;
$a[2] = 70; $a[3] = 0;
$a[4] = 170; $a[5] = 0;
$a[6] = 240; $a[7] = 70;
$a[8] = 240; $a[9] = 170;
$a[10] = 170; $a[11] = 240;
$a[12] = 70; $a[13] = 240;
$a[14] = 0; $a[15] = 170;
ImageFilledPolygon($img, $a, 8, $red);
$white = ImageColorAllocate($img, 255, 255, 255);
ImageString($img, 5, 100, 110, "STOP", $white);
ImageGIF($img);
ImageDestroy($img);
?>
```

Output 2

----

imageFilledRectangle (image)
draw a filled rectangle

```
int imagefilledrectangle(int img, int x1, int y1, int x2, int
y2, int color);
```

> This function creates a filled rectangle of color *col* in image *img* start-
> ing at upper left coordinates (*x1, y1*) and ending at bottom right coordi-
> nates (*x2, y2*), where (0, 0) is the top left corner of the image.

Example

The code below uses ImageFilledRectangle() to place a filled rectangle in the image.

```
<?PHP
Header("Content-type: image/gif");
$img = ImageCreate(250, 250);
$black = ImageColorAllocate($img, 0, 0, 0);
$white = ImageColorAllocate($img, 255, 255, 255);
ImageFill($img, 0, 0, $black);
ImageFilledRectangle($img, 10, 10, 240, 240, $white);
ImageGIF($img);
ImageDestroy($img);
?>
```

Output

----

imageFillToBorder (image)
flood fill with specific color

```
int imagefilltoborder(int img, int x, int y, int border, int
color);
```

> This function performs a flood fill with the specified color *color* begin-
> ning at the specified point (*x*, *y*) and stopping at a border color specified
> by *border*.
>
> To flood-fill an area defined by the color of the starting point, use
> ImageFill().

Example

The code below draws a white circle on a black background. ImageFillTo-
Border() is used to fill the top left corner of the image with green. The area
filled is between the edges of the image and the color white.

```
<?PHP
Header("Content-type: image/gif");
$img = ImageCreate(250, 250);
$black = ImageColorAllocate($img, 0, 0, 0);
$white = ImageColorAllocate($img, 255, 255, 255);
ImageFill($img, 0, 0, $black);
ImageArc($img, 125, 125, 250, 250, 0, 360, $white);
$green = ImageColorAllocate($img, 0, 255, 0);
ImageFillToBorder($img, 10, 10, $white, $green);
ImageGIF($img);
ImageDestroy($img);
?>
```

Output

See also ImageFill().

----

imageFontHeight (image)
get font height

```
int imagefontheight(int font);
```

> This function returns the height in pixels of a character in the specified font *font*.

Example

```
<?PHP
echo "Characters in font #1 are ".ImageFontHeight(1)." pixels
  high.\n";
echo "Characters in font #5 are ".ImageFontHeight(5)." pixels
  high.\n";
```

Output

```
Characters in font #1 are 8 pixels high.
Characters in font #5 are 15 pixels high.
```

See also ImageFontWidth() and ImageLoadFont().

----

imageFontWidth (image)
get font width

```
int imagefontwidth(int font);
```

> This function returns the width in pixels of a character in the specified font *font*.

Example

```php
<?PHP
echo "Characters in font #1 are ".ImageFontWidth(1)." pixels
  wide.\n";
echo "Characters in font #5 are ".ImageFontWidth(5)." pixels
  wide.\n";
?>
```

Output

```
Characters in font #1 are 5 pixels wide.
Characters in font #5 are 9 pixels wide.
```

See also ImageFontHeight() and ImageLoadFont().

----

imageGif (image)
output image to browser or file

```
int imagegif(int img, string filename);
```

> ImageGif creates a GIF image in *filename* from the image *img*.
>
> The image format will be GIF87a unless the image has been made transparent with ImageColorTransparent(), in which case the image format will be GIF89a.
>
> The *filename* argument is optional. If it is not present, the raw image date will be sent to standard output.

Example

The code below makes a solid black GIF image 50 pixels wide by 50 pixels high. The ImageGif() function is used to send the generated image out to the client in the GIF image format.

```php
<?PHP
Header("Content-type: image/gif");
$img = ImageCreate(50, 50);
ImageFill($img, 0, 0, $black);
ImageGIF($img);
ImageDestroy($img);
?>
```

Output

---

imageInterlace (image)
enable or disable interlace

```
int imageinterlace(int img, int interlace);
```

> This function determines whether the image will be stored linearly or interlaced. An interlaced image will appear to "fade-in" over several passes as it is being displayed. If *interlace* is 1, the *img* image will be interlaced, and if *interlace* is 0, then the image will not be interlaced.

Example
```
<?PHP
Header("Content-type: image/gif");
$img = ImageCreate(50, 50);
ImageFill($img, 0, 0, $black);
ImageInterlace($img, 1);
ImageGIF($img);
ImageDestroy($img);
?>
```

---

imageLine (image)
draw a line

```
int imageline(int img, int x1, int y1, int x2, int y2, int color);
```

> This function draws a line from (*x1,y1*) to (*x2,y2*) (where top left is 0,0) in image *img* of color *color*.

Example

The code below draws two white lines on the black background.

```php
<?PHP
 Header("Content-type: image/gif");
$img = ImageCreate(50, 50);
$black = ImageColorAllocate($img, 0, 0, 0);
$white = ImageColorAllocate($img, 255, 255, 255);
ImageFill($img, 0, 0, $black);
ImageLine($img, 0, 0, 50, 50, $white);
ImageLine($img, 50, 0, 0, 50, $white);
ImageGIF($img);
ImageDestroy($img);
?>
```

Output

See also ImageArc(), ImageCreate(), and ImageColorAllocate().

----

imageLoadFont (image)
load a new font

```
int imageloadfont(string file);
```

> ImageLoadFont loads a user-defined bitmap font and returns an identi-
> fier for the font (which is always greater than 5, so it will not conflict
> with the built-in fonts). The font file format is currently binary and
> architecture-dependent. This means you should generate the font files
> on the same type of CPU as the machine you are running PHP on.

Font file format

Byte position	C data type	Description
byte 0–3	int	number of characters in the font
byte 4–7	int	value of first character in the font (often 32 for space)
byte 8–11	int	pixel width of each character
byte 12–15	int	pixel height of each character
byte 16	char	array with character data, one byte per pixel in each character, for a total of (nchars*width*height) bytes.

See also ImageFontWidth() and ImageFontHeight().

---

imagePolygon (image)
draw a polygon

```
int imagepolygon(int img, int points, int num_points, int
color);
```

This function creates a polygon in image *img* of color *color*. *points* is an array containing the polygon's vertices. The array is of the form

points[0] = x0,

points[1] = y0,

points[2] = x1,

points[3] = y1, etc.

num_points is the total number of vertices in the array.

Example

The code below uses ImagePolygon() to create a white triangle in the image.

```
<?PHP
Header("Content-type: image/gif");
$img = ImageCreate(250, 250);
$black = ImageColorAllocate($img, 0, 0, 0);
$white = ImageColorAllocate($img, 255, 255, 255);
ImageFill($img, 0, 0, $black);
$a[0] = 125; $a[1] = 10;
```

```
$a[2] = 240; $a[3] = 240;
$a[4] = 10; $a[5] = 240;
ImagePolygon($img, $a, 3, $white);
ImageGIF($img);
ImageDestroy($img);
?>
```

Output

See also ImageFilledPolygon() and ImageCreate().

----

imageRectangle (image)
draw a rectangle

```
int imagerectangle(int img, int x1, int y1, int x2, int y2,
int color);
```

> This function creates a rectangle of color *color* in image *img* starting
> at upper left coordinate (*x1,y1*) and ending at bottom right coordinate
> (*x2, y2*), where (0,0) is the top left corner of the image.

Example

The code below draws a white rectangle in the image using ImageRectangle().

```
<?PHP
$img = ImageCreate(250, 250);
$black = ImageColorAllocate($img, 0, 0, 0);
$white = ImageColorAllocate($img, 255, 255, 255);
ImageFill($img, 0, 0, $black);
ImageRectangle($img, 10, 10, 240, 240, $white);
ImageGIF($img);
ImageDestroy($img);
?>
```

Output

See also ImageFilledRectangle().

---

imageSetPixel (image)
set a single pixel

```
int imagesetpixel(int img, int x, int y, int color);
```

> This draws a pixel at *x,y* (top left is 0,0) in image *img* of color *color*.

Example

The code below creates a filled square by calling ImageSetPixel() multiple times. It is equivalent to ImageFilledRectangle($img, 10, 10, 240, 240, $white);.

```php
<?PHP
Header("Content-type: image/gif");
$img = ImageCreate(250, 250);
$black = ImageColorAllocate($img, 0, 0, 0);
$white = ImageColorAllocate($img, 255, 255, 255);
ImageFill($img, 0, 0, $black);
for($x = 0;$x < 230;$x++)
  for($y = 0;$y < 230; $y++)
  ImageSetPixel($img, $x + 10, $y + 10, $white);
ImageGIF($img);
ImageDestroy($img);
?>
```

Output

See also ImageCreate() and ImageColorAllocate().

----

imageString (image)
draw a string horizontally

```
int imagestring(int img, int font, int x, int y, string s,
int color);
```

> This function draws the string *s* in the image *img* at coordinates (*x, y*), where (0,0) is the top left, in color *color*.
>
> Fonts 1, 2, 3, 4, and 5 are included with PHP, and increase in size as their respective number increases.
>
> To draw single characters in an image, use the ImageChar() function.

Example

The code below uses ImageString() to display a string.

```
<?PHP
Header("Content-type: image/gif");
$img = ImageCreate(250, 250);
$black = ImageColorAllocate($img, 0, 0, 0);
$white = ImageColorAllocate($img, 255, 255, 255);
ImageFill($img, 0, 0, $black);
ImageString($img, 5, 100, 100, "ABCabc", $white);
ImageGIF($img);
ImageDestroy($img);
?>
```

Output

See also ImageChar() and ImageLoadFont().

----

imageStringUp (image)
draw a string vertically

```
int imagestringup(int img, int font, int x, int y, string s,
int color);
```

> This function draws the string *s* vertically in the image *img* at coordinates (*x,y*), where top left is (0,0), in color *color*. Fonts 1, 2, 3, 4, and 5 are included with PHP, and increase in size as their respective number increases.

Example

The code below uses ImageStringUp() to display a string.

```
<?PHP
Header("Content-type: image/gif");
$img = ImageCreate(250, 250);
$black = ImageColorAllocate($img, 0, 0, 0);
$white = ImageColorAllocate($img, 255, 255, 255);
ImageFill($img, 0, 0, $black);
ImageStringUp($img, 5, 100, 100, "ABCabc", $white);
ImageGIF($img);
ImageDestroy($img);
?>
```

Output

See also ImageString() and ImageLoadFont().

----

imageSX (image)
get image width

```
int imagesx(int img);
```

This function returns the width in pixels of image *img*.

Example

```
<?PHP
$img = ImageCreate(250, 250);
echo "The just created image is ".ImageSX($img)." pixels
wide.\n";
?>
```

Output

```
The just created image is 250 pixels wide.
```

See also imagecreate() and imagesy().

----

imageSY (image)
get image height

```
int imagesy(int img);
```

This function returns the height in pixels of image *img*.

Example

```
<?PHP
$img = ImageCreate(250, 250);
echo "The just created image is ".ImageSY($img)." pixels
  high.\n";
?>
```

Output

```
The just created image is 250 pixels high.
```

See also imagecreate() and imagesx().

----

imageTTFBBox (image)
give bounding box of text using TrueType fonts

```
array ImageTTFBBox(int size, int angle, string fontfile,
string text);
```

This function calculates and returns the bounding box in pixels for a given *text*. *size* is the font size and *fontfile* is the name of the True-Type font file to use. *angle* is the degrees by which the text will be rotated. ImageTTFBBox() returns an array with eight elements representing four points making the bounding box of the text:

array[0]	lower left corner, X position
array[1]	lower left corner, Y position
array[2]	lower right corner, X position
array[3]	lower right corner, Y position
array[4]	upper right corner, X position
array[5]	upper right corner, Y position
array[6]	upper left corner, X position
array[7]	upper left corner, Y position

The points are relative to the text regardless of the angle, so "upper left" means in the top left-hand corner seeing the text horizontallty. This function requires both the GD library and the Freetype library.

Example

The following example uses the function ImageTTFBBox() to determine the size of the generated text so that ImageTTFText() can center the text both vertically and horizontally.

```
<?PHP
$text = "Welcome";
$width = 400;
$height = 300;
Header("Content-type: image/gif");
$img = ImageCreate($width, $height);
$black = ImageColorAllocate($img, 0,0,0);
$white = ImageColorAllocate($img, 225,225,255);
ImageFill($img, 1, 1, $white);
$box = ImageTTFBBox(50, 0, "arial.ttf", $text);
ImageTTFText($img, 50, 0, ($width - ($box[2] + $box[0])) / 2,
($height - ($box[7] + $box[1])) / 2, $black, "arial.ttf",
  $text);
ImageGIF($img);
ImageDestroy($img);
?>
```

Output

See also ImageTTFText().

---

imageTTFText (image)
write text to image using a TrueType font

```
array ImageTTFText(int img, int size, int angle, int x,
int y, int color, string fontfile, string text);
```

This function draws the string *text* in image *img*, starting at coordinates (*x, y*), where top left is (0,0), at an angle of *angle* in color *color*, using the TrueType font file *fontfile*.

The coordinates specified by (*x, y*) define the basepoint of the first character (roughly the lower-left corner of the character). This differs from ImageString(), where (*x, y*) define the upper-right corner of the first character. *angle* is in degrees, with 0 degrees being left-to-right-reading text (3 o'clock direction). Higher values represent a counter-clockwise rotation. For example, a value of 90 would result in bottom-to-top-reading text. *fontfile* is the path to the TrueType font to use. *text* is the text string, which may include UTF-8 character sequences (of the form: ©) to access characters in a font beyond the first 255. *col* is the color index. Using the negative of a color index has the effect of turning off antialiasing.

ImageTTFText() returns an array with eight elements representing four points making the bounding box of the text. See ImageTtfBBox() for an explanation of this array.

This function requires both the GD library and the Freetype library.

Example

The code below will create a GIF with a light blue background with the text "Welcome" in Arial 50 point. The text is near the bottom of the image and flush against the left edge.

```php
<?PHP
Header("Content-type: image/gif");
$img = ImageCreate(400, 300);
$black = ImageColorAllocate($img, 0,0,0);
$white = ImageColorAllocate($img, 225,225,255);
ImageFill($img, 1, 1, $white);
ImageTTFText($img, 50, 0, 0, 250, $black,
   "arial.ttf", "Welcome");
ImageGIF($img);
ImageDestroy($img);
?>
```

Output

See also ImageTTFBBox().

imageColorAt (image)
get index of color of a pixel

```
int imagecolorat(int img, int x, int y);
```

> This function returns the index of the color of the pixel at (x, y) in the image *img*.

Example

```php
<?PHP
$img = ImageCreate(250, 250);
$black = ImageColorAllocate($img, 0, 0, 0);
ImageFill($img, 0, 0, $black);
echo "The index of the color at (100,100) is ".
   ImageColorAt($img, 100, 100).".\n";
?>
```

Output

```
The index of the color at (100,100) is 0.
```

See also ImageColorSet() and ImageColorsforIndex().

----

imageColorClosest (image)
get index of the closest color to the specified color

```
int imagecolorclosest(int img, int red, int green, int blue);
```

> This function returns the index of the color in the palette of the image that is closest to the specified RGB value. Closeness is defined by the Euclidian distance in three-dimensional space between the colors.

Example

```php
<?PHP
$img = ImageCreate(250, 250);
$black = ImageColorAllocate($img, 0, 0, 0);
$white = ImageColorAllocate($img, 255, 255, 255);
echo "Closest color to 100,100,100 is
".ImageColorClosest($img, 100, 100, 100).".\n";
echo "Closest color to 200,200,200 is
".ImageColorClosest($img, 200, 200, 200).".\n";
?>
```

Output

```
Closest color to 100,100,100 is 0.
Closest color to 200,200,200 is 1.
```

See also imagecolorexact().

---

imageColorExact (image)
get index of the specified color

```
int imagecolorexact(int img, int red, int green, int blue);
```

> This function returns the index of the specified color in the palette
> of the image. If the color does not exist in the image's palette, −1 is
> returned.

Example

The code below allocates three colors to the palette, black, white, and red.
Then the function ImageColorExact() is called to check if the colors black,
red, and green exist in the palatte.

```php
<?PHP
$img = ImageCreate(250, 250);
$black = ImageColorAllocate($img, 0, 0, 0);
$white = ImageColorAllocate($img, 255, 255, 255);
$red = ImageColorAllocate($img, 255, 0, 0);
if(ImageColorExact($img, 0, 0, 0) >= 0)
  echo "yes";
else
  echo "no";
echo "\n";
if(ImageColorExact($img, 255, 0, 0) >= 0)
  echo "yes";
else
  echo "no";
echo "\n";
if(ImageColorExact($img, 0, 255, 0) >= 0)
  echo "yes";
else
  echo "no";
echo "\n";
?>
```

Output

```
yes
yes
no
```

See also imagecolorclosest().

----

imageColorResolve (image)
get the index of the specified color or its closest possible alternative

```
int imagecolorresolve(int img, int red, int green, int blue);
```

> This function returns a color index for a requested color. It returns
> either the exact color or the closest possible alternative, if the exact
> color can not be allocated.

Example

The code below uses the function ImageColorResolve() to allocate a palette
color that is either the one asked for or the closest available alternative.

```
<?PHP
Header("Content-type: image/gif");
$img = ImageCreate(50, 50);
$black = ImageColorResolve($img, 0, 0, 0);
ImageFill($img, 0, 0, $black);
ImageGIF($img);
ImageDestroy($img);
?>
```

See also imagecolorclosest().

----

imageColorSet (image)
set color for the specified palette index

```
bool imagecolorset(int img, int index, int red, int green,
int blue);
```

> This function sets the specified index in the palette to the specified
> color. This is useful for creating flood-fill-like effects in paletted
> images without the overhead of performing the actual flood-fill.

Example

The code below demonstrates how a color is allocated, and then the function ImageColorSet() is used to change its RGB values. Without the call to ImageColorSet(), the code below would be a black box. With it, it is a white box.

```
<?PHP
Header("Content-type: image/gif");
$img = ImageCreate(50, 50);
$black = ImageColorAllocate($img, 0, 0, 0);
ImageColorSet($img, $black, 255, 255, 255);
ImageFill($img, 0, 0, $black);
ImageGIF($img);
ImageDestroy($img);
?>
```

See also ImageColorAt().

----

imageColorsForIndex (image)
get the colors for an index

```
array imagecolorsforindex(int img, int index);
```

> This function returns an associative array with red, green, and blue keys that contain the appropriate values for the specified color index.

Example

The code below allocates the colors black, white, and red. Next it uses ImageColorsForIndex() to output the RGB values for the three colors.

```
<?PHP
$img = ImageCreate(50, 50);
$black = ImageColorAllocate($img, 0, 0, 0);
$white = ImageColorAllocate($img, 255, 255, 255);
$red = ImageColorAllocate($img, 255, 0, 0);
$rgb = ImageColorsForIndex($img, $black);
echo "RGB values
  ".$rgb[red].":".$rgb[blue].":".$rgb[green]."\n";
$rgb = ImageColorsForIndex($img, $white);
echo "RGB values
  ".$rgb[red].":".$rgb[blue].":".$rgb[green]."\n";
```

```
$rgb = ImageColorsForIndex($img, $red);
echo "RGB values
  ".$rgb[red].":".$rgb[blue].":".$rgb[green]."\n";
ImageDestroy($img);
?>
```

Output

```
RGB values 0:0:0
RGB values 255:255:255
RGB values 255:0:0
```

See also ImageColorAt() and ImageColorExact().

---

imageColorsTotal (image)
find out the number of colors in an image's palette

```
int imagecolorstotal(int img);
```

> This function returns the total number of colors in *img*'s palette.

Example

```
<?PHP
$img = ImageCreate(50, 50);
echo "# of colors in palette ".ImageColorsTotal($img)."\n";
$black = ImageColorAllocate($img, 0, 0, 0);
echo "# of colors in palette ".ImageColorsTotal($img)."\n";
$white = ImageColorAllocate($img, 255, 255, 255);
echo "# of colors in palette ".ImageColorsTotal($img)."\n";
$red = ImageColorAllocate($img, 255, 0, 0);
echo "# of colors in palette ".ImageColorsTotal($img)."\n";
ImageDestroy($img);
?>
```

Output

```
# of colors in palette 0
# of colors in palette 1
# of colors in palette 2
# of colors in palette 3
```

See also ImageColorAt() and ImageColorsForIndex().

---

imageColorsTotal (image)

find out the number of colors in an image's palette

```
int imagecolorstotal(int im);
```

This returns the number of colors in the specified image's palette.

See also imagecolorat() and imagecolorsforindex().

----

pdf_get_info (PDF)

returns a default info structure for a PDF document

```
info pdf_get_info(string filename);
```

This function will return a default info structure for the PDF document. This structure can be filled with data using functions provided with this library.

Example

```php
<?PHP
$info = PDF_get_info();
PDF_set_info_creator($info, "php123.com");
PDF_set_info_title($info, "PDF Example");
PDF_set_info_subject($info, "");
PDF_set_info_keywords($info, "PHP PHP3 PDF example");
PDF_set_info_author($info, "JSW");
?>
```

See also PDF_set_info_creator(), PDF_set_info_title(), PDF_set_info_subject(), PDF_set_info_keywords(), and PDF_set_info_author ().

----

pdf_set_info_creator (PDF)

set the creator field of the info structure

```
void pdf_set_info_creator(info info, string creator);
```

This function sets the creator of the PDF document. It must be called after PDF_get_info(), but before PDF_open().

Example

```
<?PHP
$info = PDF_get_info();
PDF_set_info_creator($info, "php123.com");
PDF_set_info_title($info, "PDF Example");
PDF_set_info_subject($info, "");
PDF_set_info_keywords($info, "PHP PHP3 PDF example");
PDF_set_info_author($info, "JSW");
?>
```

See also PDF_get_info(), PDF_set_info_title(), PDF_set_info_subject(), PDF_set_info_keywords(), and PDF_set_info_author().

----

pdf_set_info_title (PDF)
set the title field of the info structure

```
void pdf_set_info_title(info info, string creator);
```

> This function sets the title of the PDF document. It must be called after PDF_get_info(), but before PDF_open().

Example

```
<?PHP
$info = PDF_get_info();
PDF_set_info_creator($info, "php123.com");
PDF_set_info_title($info, "PDF Example");
PDF_set_info_subject($info, "");
PDF_set_info_keywords($info, "PHP PHP3 PDF example");
PDF_set_info_author($info, "JSW");
?>
```

See also PDF_get_info(), PDF_set_info_creator(), PDF_set_info_subject(), PDF_set_info_keywords(), and PDF_set_info_author().

----

pdf_set_info_subject (PDF)
set the subject field of the info structure

```
void pdf_set_info_subject(info info, string creator);
```

> This function sets the subject of the PDF document. It must be called after PDF_get_info(), but before PDF_open().

Example

```
<?PHP
$info = PDF_get_info();
PDF_set_info_creator($info, "php123.com");
PDF_set_info_title($info, "PDF Example");
PDF_set_info_subject($info, "");
PDF_set_info_keywords($info, "PHP PHP3 PDF example");
PDF_set_info_author($info, "JSW");
?>
```

See also PDF_get_info(), PDF_set_info_creator(), PDF_set_info_title(), PDF_set_info_keywords(), and PDF_set_info_author().

----

pdf_set_info_keywords (PDF)

set the keywords field of the info structure

```
void pdf_set_info_keywords(info info, string creator);
```

> This function sets the keywords of the PDF document. It must be called after PDF_get_info(), but before PDF_open().

Example

```
<?PHP
$info = PDF_get_info();
PDF_set_info_creator($info, "php123.com");
PDF_set_info_title($info, "PDF Example");
PDF_set_info_subject($info, "");
PDF_set_info_keywords($info, "PHP PHP3 PDF example");
PDF_set_info_author($info, "JSW");
?>
```

See also PDF_get_info(), PDF_set_info_creator(), PDF_set_info_title(), PDF_set_info_subject(), and PDF_set_info_author().

----

pdf_set_info_author (PDF)

set the author field of the info structure

```
void pdf_set_info_author(info info, string creator);
```

> This function sets the author of the PDF document. It must be called after PDF_get_info(), but before PDF_open().

Example

```
<?PHP
$info = PDF_get_info();
PDF_set_info_creator($info, "php123.com");
PDF_set_info_title($info, "PDF Example");
PDF_set_info_subject($info, "");
PDF_set_info_keywords($info, "PHP PHP3 PDF example");
PDF_set_info_author($info, "JSW");
?>
```

See also PDF_get_info(), PDF_set_info_creator(), PDF_set_info_title(), PDF_set_info_subject(), and PDF_set_info_keywords().

----

pdf_open (PDF)
open a new PDF document

```
int pdf_open(int descripterfile, int info);
```

> This function opens a new PDF document. *descripterfile* must be a valid file opened with fopen(). *info* is the structure returned from PDF_get_info(). The return value from this function is the first parameter in most of the PDF functions.

Example

The code below generates US letter-size page with the text "PHP3" near the top left.

```
<?PHP
$FONTNAME = "Helvetica";   $FONTSIZE = 24.0;
$CHARSET = "builtin";      $FILENAME = "/tmp/example.pdf";
$WIDTH = 612;  $HEIGHT = 792;  // US letter size
$info = PDF_get_info();
$pdf_fp = fopen($FILENAME, "w+");
$pdf = PDF_open($pdf_fp, $info);
PDF_begin_page($pdf, $WIDTH, $HEIGHT);
PDF_set_font($pdf, $FONTNAME, $FONTSIZE, $CHARSET);
PDF_set_text_pos($pdf, 50, 700);
PDF_show($pdf, "PHP3");
PDF_end_page($pdf);
PDF_close($pdf);
fclose($pdf_fp);
?>
```

See also PDF_close().

----

pdf_close (PDF)
close a PDF document

```
void pdf_close(int pdf_document);
```

> This function closes the PDF file pointed to by *pdf_document*.

Example

```
<?PHP
$FONTNAME = "Helvetica";   $FONTSIZE = 24.0;
$CHARSET = "builtin";      $FILENAME = "/tmp/example.pdf";
$WIDTH = 612;  $HEIGHT = 792;  // US letter size
$info = PDF_get_info();
$pdf_fp = fopen($FILENAME, "w+");
$pdf = PDF_open($pdf_fp, $info);
PDF_begin_page($pdf, $WIDTH, $HEIGHT);
PDF_set_font($pdf, $FONTNAME, $FONTSIZE, $CHARSET);
PDF_set_text_pos($pdf, 50, 700);
PDF_show($pdf, "PHP3");
PDF_end_page($pdf);
PDF_close($pdf);
fclose($pdf_fp);
?>
```

Output

```
1
```

See also PDF_open().

----

pdf_begin_page (PDF)
start a new page

```
void pdf_begin_page(int pdf document, double height, double
width);
```

This function starts a new page with height *height* and width *width*.

Common page sizes :

Size	Height	Width
A0	3368	2380
A1	2380	1684
A2	1684	2380
A3	1190	842
A4	842	595
A5	595	421
A6	421	297
B5	709	501
letter	792	612
legal	1008	612
ledger	792	1224
p11×17	1224	792

Example

```
<?PHP
$FONTNAME = "Helvetica";  $FONTSIZE = 24.0;
$CHARSET = "builtin";     $FILENAME = "/tmp/example.pdf";
$WIDTH = 612;  $HEIGHT = 792;  // US letter size
$info = PDF_get_info();
$pdf_fp = fopen($FILENAME, "w+");
$pdf = PDF_open($pdf_fp, $info);
PDF_begin_page($pdf, $WIDTH, $HEIGHT);
PDF_set_font($pdf, $FONTNAME, $FONTSIZE, $CHARSET);
PDF_set_text_pos($pdf, 50, 700);
PDF_show($pdf, "PHP3");
PDF_end_page($pdf);
PDF_close($pdf);
fclose($pdf_fp);
?>
```

Output

1

See also PDF_end_page().

----

pdf_end_page (PDF)
end a page

```
void pdf_end_page(int pdf document);
```

This function ends the current page.

Example

```php
<?PHP
$FONTNAME = "Helvetica";  $FONTSIZE = 24.0;
$CHARSET = "builtin";       $FILENAME = "/tmp/example.pdf";
$WIDTH = 612;  $HEIGHT = 792;  // US letter size
$info = PDF_get_info();
$pdf_fp = fopen($FILENAME, "w+");
$pdf = PDF_open($pdf_fp, $info);
PDF_begin_page($pdf, $WIDTH, $HEIGHT);
PDF_set_font($pdf, $FONTNAME, $FONTSIZE, $CHARSET);
PDF_set_text_pos($pdf, 50, 700);
PDF_show($pdf, "PHP3");
PDF_end_page($pdf);
PDF_close($pdf);
fclose($pdf_fp);
?>
```

Output

1

See also PHP_begin_page().

----

pdf_show (PDF)
output text at current position

```
void pdf_show(int pdf document, string text);
```

This function outputs the text *text* at the current position.

Example

The example below uses PDF_show() to display the text "PHP3".

```php
<?PHP
$FONTNAME = "Helvetica";  $FONTSIZE = 28.0;
```

```
$CHARSET = "builtin";      $FILENAME = "/tmp/example.pdf";
$WIDTH = 612;  $HEIGHT = 792;  // US letter size
$info = PDF_get_info();
$pdf_fp = fopen($FILENAME, "w+");
$pdf = PDF_open($pdf_fp, $info);
PDF_begin_page($pdf, $WIDTH, $HEIGHT);
PDF_set_font($pdf, $FONTNAME, $FONTSIZE, $CHARSET);
PDF_set_text_pos($pdf, 50, 700);
PDF_show($pdf, "PHP3");
PDF_end_page($pdf);
PDF_close($pdf);
fclose($pdf_fp);
?>
```

Output

1

See also PDF_show_xy() and PDF_set_text_pos().

----

pdf_show_xy (PDF)
output text at a specified position

```
void pdf_show_xy(int pdf document, string text, double
x-koor, double y-koor);
```

This function outputs the text *text* at the position (*x, y*).

Example

```
<?PHP
$FONTNAME = "Helvetica";  $FONTSIZE = 24.0;
$CHARSET = "builtin";      $FILENAME = "/tmp/example.pdf";
$WIDTH = 612;  $HEIGHT = 792;  // US letter size
$info = PDF_get_info();
$pdf_fp = fopen($FILENAME, "w+");
$pdf = PDF_open($pdf_fp, $info);
PDF_begin_page($pdf, $WIDTH, $HEIGHT);
PDF_set_font($pdf, $FONTNAME, $FONTSIZE, $CHARSET);
PDF_show_xy($pdf, "PHP3", 50, 700);
PDF_end_page($pdf);
PDF_close($pdf);
fclose($pdf_fp);
?>
```

Output

1

See also PDF_show().

----

pdf_set_font (PDF)
select the current font face and size

```
void pdf_set_font(int pdf document, string font name, double
size, string encoding);
```

> This function sets the current font face, font size, and encoding.
> PDF and Acrobat viewers support the following set of 14 core fonts:
> Courier, Courier Bold, Courier Oblique, Courier Bold Oblique, Hel-
> vetica, Helvetica Bold, Helvetica Oblique, Helvetica Bold Oblique,
> Times Roman, Times Bold, Times Italic, Times Bold Italic, Symbol,
> and Zapf Dingbats.

Example

The example below uses the function PDF_set_font() to print text in both
Helvetica and Courier fonts.

```php
<?PHP
$FONTNAME = "Helvetica";  $FONTSIZE = 24.0;
$CHARSET = "builtin";      $FILENAME = "/tmp/example.pdf";
$WIDTH = 612;  $HEIGHT = 792;  // US letter size
$info = PDF_get_info();
$pdf_fp = fopen($FILENAME, "w+");
$pdf = PDF_open($pdf_fp, $info);
PDF_begin_page($pdf, $WIDTH, $HEIGHT);
PDF_set_font($pdf, $FONTNAME, $FONTSIZE, $CHARSET);
PDF_set_text_pos($pdf, 50, 700);
PDF_show($pdf, "PHP3");
PDF_set_font($pdf, "Courier", $FONTSIZE, $CHARSET);
PDF_continue_text($pdf, "PHP3");
PDF_end_page($pdf);
PDF_close($pdf);
fclose($pdf_fp);
?>
```

Output

1

----

pdf_set_leading (PDF)
set distance between lines of text

```
void pdf_set leading(int pdf document, double distance);
```

> This function sets the spacing between lines of text. This value is used
> if the text is output with PDF_continue_text().

Example

The example below uses the function PDF_set_leading() to create double-spaced text.

```
<?PHP
$FONTNAME = "Helvetica";   $FONTSIZE = 24.0;
$CHARSET = "builtin";      $FILENAME = "/tmp/example.pdf";
$WIDTH = 612;  $HEIGHT = 792;  // US letter size
$info = PDF_get_info();
$pdf_fp = fopen($FILENAME, "w+");
$pdf = PDF_open($pdf_fp, $info);
PDF_begin_page($pdf, $WIDTH, $HEIGHT);
PDF_set_font($pdf, $FONTNAME, $FONTSIZE, $CHARSET);
PDF_set_leading($pdf, $FONTSIZE * 2);
PDF_show($pdf, "The quick brown fox");
PDF_continue_text($pdf, "The quick brown fox");
PDF_continue_text($pdf, "The quick brown fox");
PDF_end_page($pdf);
PDF_close($pdf);
fclose($pdf_fp);
?>
```

Output

1

See also pdf_set_word_spacing().

----

pdf_set_text_rendering (PDF)
change how text is rendered

```
void pdf_set_text_rendering(int pdf document, int mode);
```

This function sets the text rendering mode to *mode.* The valid modes are:

Mode	Description
0	fill text
1	stroke text
2	fill and stroke text
3	invisible text
4	fill text and add it to the clipping path
5	stroke text and add it to the clipping path
6	fill and stroke text and add it to the clipping path
7	add text to the clipping path

Refer to *www.php123.com* for on-line example.

----

pdf_set_horiz_scaling (PDF)
set horizontal scaling of text

```
void pdf_set_horiz_scaling(int pdf document, double scale);
```

This function sets the horizontal text scaling to *scale* percent. The default scale percentage is 100. For example, a scale value of 50 halves the horizontal width of the characters in the text.

----

pdf_set_text_rise (PDF)
sets the text rise

```
void pdf_set_text_rise(int pdf document, double rise);
```

This function sets the text rise to *rise.* The default text rise value is 0. The text rise amount is the number of text space units to move the text up or down. Positive values of rise move the text up, negative values of rise move the text down. This function is useful in creating superscripts or subscripts.

Refer to *www.php123.com* for on-line example.

----

pdf_set_text_matrix (PDF)
set the text matrix

```
void pdf_set_text_matrix(int pdf document, array matrix);
```

> This function sets a matrix that describes a transformation to be
> applied to the current font. Using this matrix, text can be translated
> (offset), skewed, scaled, or rotated.

Refer to *www.php123.com* for on-line example.

----

pdf_set_text_pos (PDF)
set text position

```
void pdf_set_text_pos(int pdf document, double x-koor, double
y-koor);
```

> This function sets the current text position to (*x*, *y*). The text output
> with the next call to PDF_show() will be at this new location.

Refer to *www.php123.com* for on-line example.

----

pdf_set_char_spacing (PDF)
set character spacing

```
void pdf_set_char_spacing(int pdf document, double space);
```

> This function sets the spacing between characters to *space*. In other
> words, it changes the horizontal distance between individual charac-
> ters in a string. The space is specified in text space units. It is reset to
> zero (default value) at the start of a new page. The space value can be
> either positive to make the characters further apart or negative to
> make them closer together.

Example

The following code prints three lines of double-spaced text. The first line
has the normal character spacing. The characters on the second line are so
close together that they overlap. The characters in the third line have extra
white space between them.

```php
<?PHP
$FONTNAME = "Helvetica";  $FONTSIZE = 24.0;
$CHARSET = "builtin";      $FILENAME = "/tmp/example.pdf";
$WIDTH = 612;  $HEIGHT = 792;  // US letter size
$info = PDF_get_info();
$pdf_fp = fopen($FILENAME, "w+");
$pdf = PDF_open($pdf_fp, $info);
PDF_begin_page($pdf, $WIDTH, $HEIGHT);
PDF_set_text_pos($pdf, 50, 700);
PDF_set_font($pdf, $FONTNAME, $FONTSIZE, $CHARSET);
PDF_set_leading($pdf, $FONTSIZE * 2);
PDF_show($pdf, "The quick brown fox");
PDF_set_char_spacing($pdf, -5);
PDF_continue_text($pdf, "The quick brown fox");
PDF_set_char_spacing($pdf, 5);
PDF_continue_text($pdf, "The quick brown fox");
PDF_end_page($pdf);
PDF_close($pdf);
fclose($pdf_fp);
?>
```

Output

1

---

pdf_set_word_spacing (PDF)
set spacing between words

```
void pdf_set_word_spacing(int pdf document, double space);
```

> This function sets the spacing between words to *space*. In other words,
> it changes the horizontal distance between individual words in a
> string. The space is defined in text space units. It is reset to zero
> (default value) at the start of a new page.

Example

The code below prints three lines of double-spaced text. The first line has
the normal word spacing. The words on the second line are closer together.
The words on the third line have extra white space between them.

```php
<?PHP
$FONTNAME = "Helvetica";  $FONTSIZE = 24.0;
$CHARSET = "builtin";      $FILENAME = "/tmp/example.pdf";
```

```php
$WIDTH = 612;  $HEIGHT = 792;  // US letter size
$info = PDF_get_info();
$pdf_fp = fopen($FILENAME, "w+");
$pdf = PDF_open($pdf_fp, $info);
PDF_begin_page($pdf, $WIDTH, $HEIGHT);
PDF_set_text_pos($pdf, 50, 700);
PDF_set_font($pdf, $FONTNAME, $FONTSIZE, $CHARSET);
PDF_set_leading($pdf, $FONTSIZE * 2);
PDF_show($pdf, "The quick brown fox");
PDF_set_word_spacing($pdf, -5);
PDF_continue_text($pdf, "The quick brown fox");
PDF_set_word_spacing($pdf, 5);
PDF_continue_text($pdf, "The quick brown fox");
PDF_end_page($pdf);
PDF_close($pdf);
fclose($pdf_fp);
?>
```

Output

1

----

pdf_continue_text (PDF)
output text on next line

```
void pdf_continue_text(int pdf document, string text);
```

This function outputs the text *text* on the next line. The spacing
between the lines is set with the PDF_set_leading() function.

Example

```php
<?PHP
$FONTNAME = "Helvetica";  $FONTSIZE = 24.0;
$CHARSET = "builtin";     $FILENAME = "/tmp/example.pdf";
$WIDTH = 612;  $HEIGHT = 792;  // US letter size
$info = PDF_get_info();
$pdf_fp = fopen($FILENAME, "w+");
$pdf = PDF_open($pdf_fp, $info);
PDF_begin_page($pdf, $WIDTH, $HEIGHT);
PDF_set_text_pos($pdf, 50, 700);
PDF_set_font($pdf, $FONTNAME, $FONTSIZE, $CHARSET);
PDF_show($pdf, "The quick brown fox");
PDF_continue_text($pdf, "The quick brown fox");
```

```
PDF_continue_text($pdf, "The quick brown fox");
PDF_end_page($pdf);
PDF_close($pdf);
fclose($pdf_fp);
?>
```

Output

1

See also PDF_set_leading().

----

pdf_stringwidth (PDF)
return width of a string in the current font in pixels

```
double pdf_stringwidth(int pdf document, string text);
```

> This function returns the width of string *text* in pixels. This function
> can be used to center text or to check the width a text to see if it will
> fit in a given space. PDF_set_font() must have been previously called.

Example

The code below uses the function PDF_stringwidth() to find the width of a
string. This width is used in a calculation to find the starting point of the
text in order to center it.

```
<?PHP
$FONTNAME = "Helvetica";   $FONTSIZE = 24.0;
$CHARSET = "builtin";       $FILENAME = "/tmp/example.pdf";
$WIDTH = 612; $HEIGHT = 792; // US letter size
$info = PDF_get_info();
$pdf_fp = fopen($FILENAME, "w+");
$pdf = PDF_open($pdf_fp, $info);
PDF_begin_page($pdf, $WIDTH, $HEIGHT);
PDF_set_font($pdf, $FONTNAME, $FONTSIZE, $CHARSET);
$text = "The quick brown fox";
PDF_show_xy($pdf, $text,    ($WIDTH / 2) - (PDF_stringwidth($pdf,
$text) / 2), 600);
PDF_end_page($pdf);
PDF_close($pdf);
fclose($pdf_fp);
?>
```

Output

1

See also PDF_show() and PDF_set_font().

----

pdf_save (PDF)
save current environment

```
void pdf_save(int pdf document);
```

> This function saves the current graphics state. Among other items, it saves the line caps, line joins, fill colors, stroke colors, character spacing, word spacing, text font, text size, and text rendering.

Refer to *www.php123.com* for on-line example.

See also PDF_restore().

----

pdf_restore (PDF)
restore a formerly saved environment

```
void pdf_restore(int pdf document);
```

> This function restores the most recently saved graphics state.

See also PDF_save().

----

pdf_translate (PDF)
set origin of coordinate system

```
void pdf_translate(int pdf document, double x-koor, double
y-koor);
```

> This function translates the origin of the coordinate system to (x, y).

Refer to *www.php123.com* for on-line example.

----

pdf_scale (PDF)

set scaling

```
void pdf_scale(int pdf document, double x-scale, double
y-scale);
```

This function scales the coordinate system by the factors *x* and *y*.

Example

The example below uses the function PDF_scale() to create two different text effects. The function can just as easily be used to modify the coordinate system for images, path, or any other object. It displays three lines of text. The first is normal. The second line uses a scale factor of (2,1) to create text that is twice as wide as normal. The third line uses a scale factor of (1,2) to create text that is twice as high as normal. Note: The x scale factor of 0.5 in the second call to PDF_scale() is used to "undo" the previous 2x scaling of the x axis.

```php
<?PHP
$FONTNAME = "Helvetica";   $FONTSIZE = 24.0;
$CHARSET = "builtin";      $FILENAME = "/tmp/example.pdf";
$WIDTH = 612;  $HEIGHT = 792;   // US letter size
$info = PDF_get_info();
$pdf_fp = fopen($FILENAME, "w+");
$pdf = PDF_open($pdf_fp, $info);
PDF_begin_page($pdf, $WIDTH, $HEIGHT);
PDF_set_font($pdf, $FONTNAME, $FONTSIZE, $CHARSET);
$text = "The quick brown fox";
PDF_show_xy($pdf, $text, 10, 600);
PDF_scale($pdf, 2, 1);
PDF_show_xy($pdf, $text, 10, 400);
PDF_scale($pdf, 0.5, 2);
PDF_show_xy($pdf, $text, 10, 100);
PDF_end_page($pdf);
PDF_close($pdf);
fclose($pdf_fp);
?>
```

Output

1

----

pdf_rotate (PDF)
set rotation

```
void pdf_rotate(int pdf document, double angle);
```

> This function rotates the coordinate system by *angle* degrees. Positive
> values represent counter-clockwise rotation, and negative values rep-
> resent clockwise rotation.

Example

The example below uses the function PDF_rotate() to display three lines of
text at varied angles. The second line of text is rotated 30 degrees counter-
clockwise. The third line is rotated a further 30 degrees.

```php
<?PHP
$FONTNAME = "Helvetica";  $FONTSIZE = 24.0;
$CHARSET = "builtin";     $FILENAME = "/tmp/example.pdf";
$WIDTH = 612;  $HEIGHT = 792;  // US letter size
$info = PDF_get_info();
$pdf_fp = fopen($FILENAME, "w+");
$pdf = PDF_open($pdf_fp, $info);
PDF_begin_page($pdf, $WIDTH, $HEIGHT);
PDF_set_font($pdf, $FONTNAME, $FONTSIZE, $CHARSET);
$text = "The quick brown fox";
PDF_show_xy($pdf, $text, 100, 10);
PDF_rotate($pdf, 30);
PDF_show_xy($pdf, $text, 100, 10);
PDF_rotate($pdf, 30);
PDF_show_xy($pdf, $text, 100, 10);
PDF_end_page($pdf);
PDF_close($pdf);
fclose($pdf_fp);
?>
```

Output

1

----

pdf_setflat (PDF)
set flatness

```
void pdf_setflat(int pdf document, double value);
```

> This function sets the flatness value to *value*. This value must be in the range between 0 and 100, inclusive. The default value is 0. Flatness is the maximum permitted distance in pixels between the correct path and an approximate path made up of straight line segments.

----

pdf_setlinejoin (PDF)
set the PDF linejoin parameter.

```
void pdf_setlinejoin(int pdf document, long value);
```

> This function specifies the shape to be used at the corners of stroked paths. Valid values for this parameter are:
>
> | linejoin | Type | Description |
> |----------|------|-------------|
> | 0 (default) | Miter joins | The outer edges of the strokes of the two segments are continued until they meet. |
> | 1 | Round joins | A circular arc with a diameter equal to the line width is drawn around the point where the two segments meet. This creates a rounded corner. |
> | 2 | Bevel joins | The two segments are drawn with butt end caps (see PDF_setlinecap()), and the resulting notch is filled in with a triangle. |

Example

The code below demonstrates how the three different line join styles look.

```php
<?PHP
$FILENAME = "/tmp/example.pdf";
$WIDTH = 612;  $HEIGHT = 792;  // US letter size
$info = PDF_get_info();
$pdf_fp = fopen($FILENAME, "w+");
$pdf = PDF_open($pdf_fp, $info);
PDF_begin_page($pdf, $WIDTH, $HEIGHT);

PDF_setlinewidth($pdf, 10);

PDF_setlinejoin($pdf, 0);
PDF_moveto($pdf, 25, 200);
PDF_lineto($pdf, $WIDTH - 25, 200);
```

```
PDF_lineto($pdf, $WIDTH - 150, 10);
PDF_stroke($pdf);

PDF_setlinejoin($pdf, 1);
PDF_moveto($pdf, 25, 400);
PDF_lineto($pdf, $WIDTH - 25, 400);
PDF_lineto($pdf, $WIDTH - 150, 210);
PDF_stroke($pdf);

PDF_setlinejoin($pdf, 2);
PDF_moveto($pdf, 25, 600);
PDF_lineto($pdf, $WIDTH - 25, 600);
PDF_lineto($pdf, $WIDTH - 150, 410);
PDF_stroke($pdf);

PDF_end_page($pdf);
PDF_close($pdf);
fclose($pdf_fp);
?>
```

Output

1

See also PDF_setlinecap() and PDF_lineto().

---

pdf_setlinecap (PDF)
set PDF linecap parameter

```
void pdf_setlinecap(int pdf document, int value);
```

This function specifies the shape to be used at the ends of stroked paths. Valid values for the linecap parameter are:

linecap	Type	Description
0 (default)	Butt end caps	The stroke is squared off at the end-point of the path.
1	Round end caps	A circle with a radius equal to the line width is drawn around the endpoint of the path.
2	Projecting square end caps	The stroke extends beyond the end of the path by a distance of half the line width.

Example

```php
<?PHP
$FILENAME = "/tmp/example.pdf";
$WIDTH = 612;  $HEIGHT = 792;  // US letter size
$info = PDF_get_info();
$pdf_fp = fopen($FILENAME, "w+");
$pdf = PDF_open($pdf_fp, $info);
PDF_begin_page($pdf, $WIDTH, $HEIGHT);

PDF_setlinewidth($pdf, 10);

PDF_setlinecap($pdf, 0);
PDF_moveto($pdf, 25, 200);
PDF_lineto($pdf, $WIDTH - 25, 200);
PDF_stroke($pdf);

PDF_setlinecap($pdf, 1);
PDF_moveto($pdf, 25, 400);
PDF_lineto($pdf, $WIDTH - 25, 400);
PDF_stroke($pdf);

PDF_setlinecap($pdf, 2);
PDF_moveto($pdf, 25, 600);
PDF_lineto($pdf, $WIDTH - 25, 600);
PDF_stroke($pdf);

PDF_end_page($pdf);
PDF_close($pdf);
fclose($pdf_fp);
?>
```

Output

1

See also PDF_setlinejoin() and PDF_lineto().

----

pdf_setmiterlimit (PDF)
set PDF miterlimit parameter

```
void pdf_setmiterlimit(int pdf document, double value);
```

This function sets the maximum thickness of the created joint between the two stroked paths. It is a ratio of the created joint to the line thickness. It can range from 1 to any number, and has a default value of 10. When two paths meet at a small angle with a miter join, the resulting thickness of the joint can be very large.

Example

In the example below, the joint between the two lines is a bevel rather than the default miter because of the call to PDF_setmiterlimit().

```
<?PHP
$FILENAME = "/tmp/example.pdf";
$WIDTH = 612;   $HEIGHT = 792;   // US letter size
$info = PDF_get_info();
$pdf_fp = fopen($FILENAME, "w+");
$pdf = PDF_open($pdf_fp, $info);
PDF_begin_page($pdf, $WIDTH, $HEIGHT);

PDF_setlinewidth($pdf, 2);

PDF_setmiterlimit($pdf, 2);
PDF_moveto($pdf, 25, 400);
PDF_lineto($pdf, $WIDTH - 25, 400);
PDF_lineto($pdf, 25, 200);
PDF_stroke($pdf);

PDF_end_page($pdf);
PDF_close($pdf);
fclose($pdf_fp);
```

Output

1

See also PDF_setlinejoin() and PDF_lineto().

----

pdf_setlinewidth (PDF)
set line width

```
void pdf_setlinewidth(int pdf document, double width);
```

> This function specifies the thickness of the line used to stroke a path, measured in pixels. A line width of 0 specifies the thinnest line that can be rendered with the given output device. The default line width is 1.

Example

The code below displays lines of varying widths.

```
<?PHP
$FILENAME = "/tmp/example.pdf";
$WIDTH = 612;   $HEIGHT = 792;   // US letter size
```

```
$info = PDF_get_info();
$pdf_fp = fopen($FILENAME, "w+");
$pdf = PDF_open($pdf_fp, $info);
PDF_begin_page($pdf, $WIDTH, $HEIGHT);

for($x = 100; $x < $HEIGHT; $x += 50) {
  PDF_setlinewidth($pdf, $x / 50);
  PDF_moveto($pdf, 25, $x);
  PDF_lineto($pdf, $WIDTH - 25, $x);
  PDF_stroke($pdf);
}

PDF_end_page($pdf);
PDF_close($pdf);
fclose($pdf_fp);
?>
```

Output

1

---

pdf_setdash (PDF)
set dash pattern

```
void pdf_setdash(int pdf document, double black, double
white);
```

Black	White	Line	Description of Pattern
0	0	#############	solid line
1	1	# # # # # # #	1 unit black then 1 unit white
3	3	### ### #	3 units black then 3 units white
3	1	### ### ### #	1 unit black then 3 units white

Example

The code below uses PDF_setdash() to display a series of lines with different 10-pixel-wide patterns of white and black space.

```
<?PHP
$FILENAME = "/tmp/example.pdf";
$WIDTH = 612;  $HEIGHT = 792;  // US letter size
$info = PDF_get_info();
$pdf_fp = fopen($FILENAME, "w+");
$pdf = PDF_open($pdf_fp, $info);
```

```
PDF_begin_page($pdf, $WIDTH, $HEIGHT);

PDF_setlinewidth($pdf, 10);
for($x = 1; $x < 10; $x++) {

   PDF_setdash($pdf, 10 - $x, $x);
   PDF_moveto($pdf, 25, $x * 50);
   PDF_lineto($pdf, $WIDTH - 25, $x * 50);
   PDF_stroke($pdf);

}

PDF_end_page($pdf);
PDF_close($pdf);
fclose($pdf_fp);
```

Output

1

See also PDF_lineto().

----

pdf_moveto (PDF)
set current point

```
void pdf_moveto(int pdf document, double x-koor, double
y-koor);
```

> This function sets the current point to the coordinates (*x*, *y*).

Example

```
<?PHP
$FILENAME = "/tmp/example.pdf";
$WIDTH = 612;   $HEIGHT = 792;   // US letter size
$info = PDF_get_info();
$pdf_fp = fopen($FILENAME, "w+");
$pdf = PDF_open($pdf_fp, $info);
PDF_begin_page($pdf, $WIDTH, $HEIGHT);

PDF_setlinewidth($pdf, 10);
PDF_moveto($pdf, 25, $x * 50);
PDF_lineto($pdf, $WIDTH - 25, $x * 50);
PDF_stroke($pdf);

PDF_end_page($pdf);
PDF_close($pdf);
fclose($pdf_fp);
?>
```

Output

1

----

pdf_curveto (PDF)
draw a curve

```
void pdf_curveto(int pdf document, double x1, double y1,
double x2, double y2, double x3, double y3);
```

> This function draws a cubic Bézier curve specified by the coordinates
> of four points. These four points control the position and shape of the
> Bézier curve. They are the two endpoints of the curve and two control
> points. The curve goes from current starting point to (x3, y3). The
> other two points control the shape of the curve.

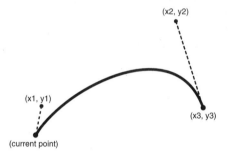

Example

```php
<?PHP
$FILENAME = "/tmp/example.pdf";
$WIDTH = 612;  $HEIGHT = 792;  // US letter size
$info = PDF_get_info();
$pdf_fp = fopen($FILENAME, "w+");
$pdf = PDF_open($pdf_fp, $info);
PDF_begin_page($pdf, $WIDTH, $HEIGHT);

PDF_moveto($pdf, 100, 100);
PDF_curveto($pdf, 110, 300, 290, 290, 400, 300);
PDF_stroke($pdf);

PDF_end_page($pdf);
PDF_close($pdf);
fclose($pdf_fp);
?>
```

Output

1

See also PDF_moveto().

----

pdf_lineto (PDF)
draw a line

```
void pdf_lineto(int pdf document, double x-koor, double
y-koor);
```

> This function draws a line from the current point to (x, y).

Example

```php
<?PHP
$FILENAME = "/tmp/example.pdf";
$WIDTH = 612;  $HEIGHT = 792;  // US letter size
$info = PDF_get_info();
$pdf_fp = fopen($FILENAME, "w+");
$pdf = PDF_open($pdf_fp, $info);
PDF_begin_page($pdf, $WIDTH, $HEIGHT);

PDF_setlinewidth($pdf, 10);
PDF_moveto($pdf, 25, $x * 50);
PDF_lineto($pdf, $WIDTH - 25, $x * 50);
PDF_stroke($pdf);

PDF_end_page($pdf);
PDF_close($pdf);
fclose($pdf_fp);
?>
```

Output

1

See also PDF_moveto().

----

pdf_circle (PDF)
draw a circle

```
void pdf_circle(int pdf document, double x-koor, double
y-koor, double radius);
```

> This function draws a circle centered at (x, y) with a radius of *radius*.

Example

The code below draws a 200-pixel-wide circle centered on the page.

```php
<?PHP
$FILENAME = "/tmp/example.pdf";
$WIDTH = 612;   $HEIGHT = 792;   // US letter size
$info = PDF_get_info();
$pdf_fp = fopen($FILENAME, "w+");
$pdf = PDF_open($pdf_fp, $info);
PDF_begin_page($pdf, $WIDTH, $HEIGHT);

PDF_circle($pdf, $WIDTH / 2, $HEIGHT / 2, 100);
PDF_stroke($pdf);

PDF_end_page($pdf);
PDF_close($pdf);
fclose($pdf_fp);
?>
```

Output

1

See also PDF_arc() and PDF_rectangle().

----

pdf_rectangle (PDF)
draw a rectangle

```
void pdf_rect(int pdf document, double x-koor, double y-koor,
double width, double height);
```

> This function draws a rectangle with a lower-left corner of (x, y) with
> the supplied *width* and *height*.

Example

The code below prints a border around the current page 25 pixels from the
edge.

```php
<?PHP
$FILENAME = "/tmp/example.pdf";
```

```
$WIDTH = 612;   $HEIGHT = 792;   // US letter size
$info = PDF_get_info();
$pdf_fp = fopen($FILENAME, "w+");
$pdf = PDF_open($pdf_fp, $info);
PDF_begin_page($pdf, $WIDTH, $HEIGHT);

PDF_rect($pdf, 25, 25, $WIDTH - 50, $HEIGHT - 50);
PDF_stroke($pdf);

PDF_end_page($pdf);
PDF_close($pdf);
fclose($pdf_fp);
?>
```

Output

1

See also PDF_circle().

----

pdf_closepath (PDF)
close path

```
void pdf_closepath(int pdf document);
```

> This function closes the current path. In other words, it draws a line
> from the current point to the starting point of the path.

Example

The code below creates two lines, and the PDF_closepath() function is used
to create a third line between the two endpoints. This creates a triangle.

```
<?PHP
$FILENAME = "/tmp/example.pdf";
$WIDTH = 612;   $HEIGHT = 792;   // US letter size
$info = PDF_get_info();
$pdf_fp = fopen($FILENAME, "w+");
$pdf = PDF_open($pdf_fp, $info);
PDF_begin_page($pdf, $WIDTH, $HEIGHT);

PDF_setlinewidth($pdf, 10);
PDF_moveto($pdf, 25, 25);
PDF_lineto($pdf, 25, $HEIGHT - 25);
PDF_lineto($pdf, $WIDTH - 25, $HEIGHT - 25);
PDF_closepath($pdf);
```

```
PDF_stroke($pdf);

PDF_end_page($pdf);
PDF_close($pdf);
fclose($pdf_fp);
?>
```

Output

1

See also PDF_stroke().

----

pdf_stroke (PDF)
draw line along path

```
void pdf_stroke(int pdf document);
```

> This function draws the current path with the current line width and
> current stroke color. It also clears the current path.

Example

```
<?PHP
$FILENAME = "/tmp/example.pdf";
$WIDTH = 612;  $HEIGHT = 792;  // US letter size
$info = PDF_get_info();
$pdf_fp = fopen($FILENAME, "w+");
$pdf = PDF_open($pdf_fp, $info);
PDF_begin_page($pdf, $WIDTH, $HEIGHT);

PDF_setlinewidth($pdf, 10);
PDF_moveto($pdf, 25, $x * 50);
PDF_lineto($pdf, $WIDTH - 25, $x * 50);
PDF_stroke($pdf);

PDF_end_page($pdf);
PDF_close($pdf);
fclose($pdf_fp);
?>
```

Output

1

See also PDF_closepath().

----

pdf_closepath_stroke (PDF)
close path and draw a line along path

```
void pdf_closepath_stroke(int pdf document);
```

> This function closes the current path and then strokes it. In other words, it draws a line from the current point to the starting point of the path and then does the equivalent of PDF_stroke().

Example

The code below draws two lines. The PDF_closepath_stroke() function creates a third line between the two endpoints. This creates a triangle.

```php
<?PHP
$FILENAME = "/tmp/example.pdf";
$WIDTH = 612;  $HEIGHT = 792;  // US letter size
$info = PDF_get_info();
$pdf_fp = fopen($FILENAME, "w+");
$pdf = PDF_open($pdf_fp, $info);
PDF_begin_page($pdf, $WIDTH, $HEIGHT);

PDF_setlinewidth($pdf, 10);
PDF_moveto($pdf, 25, 25);
PDF_lineto($pdf, 25, $HEIGHT - 25);
PDF_lineto($pdf, $WIDTH - 25, $HEIGHT - 25);
PDF_closepath_stroke($pdf);

PDF_end_page($pdf);
PDF_close($pdf);
fclose($pdf_fp);
?>
```

Output

1

See also PDF_stroke().

---

pdf_fill (PDF)
fill current path

```
void pdf_fill(int pdf document);
```

> This function fills the interior of the current path with the current fill color.

Example

The code below places a large filled rectangle on the page.

```
<?PHP
$FILENAME = "/tmp/example.pdf";
$WIDTH = 612;  $HEIGHT = 792;  // US letter size
$info = PDF_get_info();
$pdf_fp = fopen($FILENAME, "w+");
$pdf = PDF_open($pdf_fp, $info);
PDF_begin_page($pdf, $WIDTH, $HEIGHT);

PDF_rect($pdf, 25, 25, $WIDTH - 50, $HEIGHT - 50);
PDF_fill($pdf);
PDF_stroke($pdf);

PDF_end_page($pdf);
PDF_close($pdf);
fclose($pdf_fp);
?>
```

Output

1

See also PDF_stroke() and PDF_fill_stroke().

----

pdf_fill_stroke (PDF)
fill and stroke current path

```
void pdf_fill_stroke(int pdf document);
```

> This function strokes the current path and fills it. In other words, it
> draws a line from the current point to the starting point of the path,
> and then does the equivalent of PDF_fill().

Example

The code below places a large filled rectangle on the page.

```
<?PHP
$FILENAME = "/tmp/example.pdf";
$WIDTH = 612;  $HEIGHT = 792;  // US letter size
$info = PDF_get_info();
$pdf_fp = fopen($FILENAME, "w+");
$pdf = PDF_open($pdf_fp, $info);
PDF_begin_page($pdf, $WIDTH, $HEIGHT);
```

```
PDF_rect($pdf, 25, 25, $WIDTH - 50, $HEIGHT - 50);
PDF_fill_stroke($pdf);

PDF_end_page($pdf);
PDF_close($pdf);
fclose($pdf_fp);
?>
```

Output

1

See also PDF_stroke() and PDF_fill().

----

pdf_closepath_fill_stroke (PDF)
close, fill, and stroke current path

```
void pdf_closepath_fill_stroke(int pdf document);
```

> This function closes the current path, then strokes it, and finally fills
> it. In other words, it draws a line from the current point to the starting
> point of the path, then does the equivalent of PDF_fill(), and finally
> the equivalent to PDF_stroke().

Example

The code below draws two lines. The PDF_closepath_stroke() function creates
a third line between the two endpoints and fills. This creates a filled triangle.

```
<?PHP
$FILENAME = "/tmp/example.pdf";
$WIDTH = 612;  $HEIGHT = 792;  // US letter size
$info = PDF_get_info();
$pdf_fp = fopen($FILENAME, "w+");
$pdf = PDF_open($pdf_fp, $info);
PDF_begin_page($pdf, $WIDTH, $HEIGHT);

PDF_setlinewidth($pdf, 10);
PDF_moveto($pdf, 25, 25);
PDF_lineto($pdf, 25, $HEIGHT - 25);
PDF_lineto($pdf, $WIDTH - 25, $HEIGHT - 25);
PDF_closepath_fill_stroke($pdf);

PDF_end_page($pdf);
PDF_close($pdf);
fclose($pdf_fp);
?>
```

Output

1

See also PDF_fill_stroke(), PDF_stroke(), and PDF_fill().

----

pdf_endpath (PDF)
end current path

```
void pdf_endpath(int pdf document);
```

> This function ends the current path.

Example

The example below creates a blank page. The line (path) is not drawn, because it isn't stroked. Rather, it is deleted.

```
<?PHP
$FILENAME = "/tmp/example.pdf";
$WIDTH = 612;  $HEIGHT = 792;  // US letter size
$info = PDF_get_info();
$pdf_fp = fopen($FILENAME, "w+");
$pdf = PDF_open($pdf_fp, $info);
PDF_begin_page($pdf, $WIDTH, $HEIGHT);
PDF_moveto($pdf, 25, 25);
PDF_lineto($pdf, 25, $HEIGHT - 25);
PDF_endpath($pdf);

PDF_end_page($pdf);
PDF_close($pdf);
fclose($pdf_fp);
?>
```

Output

1

See also PDF_closepath().

----

pdf_clip (PDF)
clip to current path

```
void pdf_clip(int pdf document);
```

This function clips all drawing to the current path.

----

pdf_setgray_fill (PDF)
sets filling color to gray value

```
void pdf_setgray_fill(int pdf document, double value);
```

This function sets the current fill color. It is a value between 0 and 1, inclusive. 0 is black and 1 is white.

Example

The code below draws a triangle filled with light gray.

```php
<?PHP
$FILENAME = "/tmp/example.pdf";
$WIDTH = 612;  $HEIGHT = 792;  // US letter size
$info = PDF_get_info();
$pdf_fp = fopen($FILENAME, "w+");
$pdf = PDF_open($pdf_fp, $info);
PDF_begin_page($pdf, $WIDTH, $HEIGHT);

PDF_setgray_fill($pdf, 0.9);
PDF_setlinewidth($pdf, 10);
PDF_moveto($pdf, 25, 25);
PDF_lineto($pdf, 25, $HEIGHT - 25);
PDF_lineto($pdf, $WIDTH - 25, $HEIGHT - 25);
PDF_closepath_fill_stroke($pdf);

PDF_end_page($pdf);
PDF_close($pdf);
fclose($pdf_fp);
?>
```

Output

1

See also PDF_setgray() and PDF_setgray_stroke().

----

pdf_setgray_stroke (PDF)
set drawing color to gray value

```
void pdf_setgray_stroke(int pdf document, double gray value);
```

This function sets the current stroke color. It is a value between 0 and 1, inclusive. 0 is black and 1 is white.

Example

The code below draws a light gray triangle.

```php
<?PHP
$FILENAME = "/tmp/example.pdf";
$WIDTH = 612;  $HEIGHT = 792;  // US letter size
$info = PDF_get_info();
$pdf_fp = fopen($FILENAME, "w+");
$pdf = PDF_open($pdf_fp, $info);
PDF_begin_page($pdf, $WIDTH, $HEIGHT);

PDF_setgray_stroke($pdf, 0.9);
PDF_setlinewidth($pdf, 10);
PDF_moveto($pdf, 25, 25);
PDF_lineto($pdf, 25, $HEIGHT - 25);
PDF_lineto($pdf, $WIDTH - 25, $HEIGHT - 25);
PDF_closepath_stroke($pdf);

PDF_end_page($pdf);
PDF_close($pdf);
fclose($pdf_fp);
?>
```

Output

1

See also PDF_setgray() and PDF_setgray_fill().

----

pdf_setgray (PDF)
set drawing and filling color to gray value

```
void pdf_setgray(int pdf document, double gray value);
```

> This function sets the current stroke and fill colors. It is a value
> between 0 and 1, inclusive. 0 is black and 1 is white.

Example

The code below draws a light gray filled triangle.

```php
<?PHP
$FILENAME = "/tmp/example.pdf";
$WIDTH = 612;  $HEIGHT = 792;  // US letter size
$info = PDF_get_info();
$pdf_fp = fopen($FILENAME, "w+");
```

```
$pdf = PDF_open($pdf_fp, $info);
PDF_begin_page($pdf, $WIDTH, $HEIGHT);

PDF_setgray($pdf, 0.9);
PDF_setlinewidth($pdf, 10);
PDF_moveto($pdf, 25, 25);
PDF_lineto($pdf, 25, $HEIGHT - 25);
PDF_lineto($pdf, $WIDTH - 25, $HEIGHT - 25);
PDF_closepath_fill_stroke($pdf);

PDF_end_page($pdf);
PDF_close($pdf);
fclose($pdf_fp);
?>
```

Output

1

See also PDF_setgray_fill() and PDF_setgray_stroke().

----

pdf_setrgbcolor_fill (PDF)
set filling color to rgb value

```
void pdf_setrgbcolor_fill(int pdf document, double red value,
double green value, double blue value);
```

> This function sets the current fill color. Each color value is a number
> between 0 and 1, inclusive. 0 is the minimum intensity and 1 is the
> maximum intensity.

Example

The code below draws a triangle filled with yellow.

```
<?PHP
$FILENAME = "/tmp/example.pdf";
$WIDTH = 612;  $HEIGHT = 792;  // US letter size
$info = PDF_get_info();
$pdf_fp = fopen($FILENAME, "w+");
$pdf = PDF_open($pdf_fp, $info);
PDF_begin_page($pdf, $WIDTH, $HEIGHT);

PDF_setrgbcolor_fill($pdf, 1, 1, 0);
PDF_setlinewidth($pdf, 10);
PDF_moveto($pdf, 25, 25);
PDF_lineto($pdf, 25, $HEIGHT - 25);
PDF_lineto($pdf, $WIDTH - 25, $HEIGHT - 25);
```

```
PDF_closepath_fill_stroke($pdf);

PDF_end_page($pdf);
PDF_close($pdf);
fclose($pdf_fp);
?>
```

Output

1

----

pdf_set_rgbcolor_stroke (PDF)
set drawing color to rgb color value

```
void pdf_setrgbcolor_stroke(int pdf document, double red
value, double green value, double blue value);
```

> This function sets the current stroke color. Each color value is a num-
> ber between 0 and 1, inclusive. 0 is the minimum intensity and 1 is
> the maximum intensity.

Example

The code below draws a purple triangle.

```
<?PHP
$FILENAME = "/tmp/example.pdf";
$WIDTH = 612;  $HEIGHT = 792;  // US letter size
$info = PDF_get_info();
$pdf_fp = fopen($FILENAME, "w+");
$pdf = PDF_open($pdf_fp, $info);
PDF_begin_page($pdf, $WIDTH, $HEIGHT);

PDF_setrgbcolor_stroke($pdf, 1, 0, 1);
PDF_setlinewidth($pdf, 10);
PDF_moveto($pdf, 25, 25);
PDF_lineto($pdf, 25, $HEIGHT - 25);
PDF_lineto($pdf, $WIDTH - 25, $HEIGHT - 25);
PDF_closepath_stroke($pdf);

PDF_end_page($pdf);
PDF_close($pdf);
fclose($pdf_fp);
?>
```

Output

1

----

pdf_setrgbcolor (PDF)
set drawing and filling color to rgb color value

```
void pdf_setrgbcolor(int pdf document, double red value,
double green value, double blue value);
```

> This function sets the current fill and stroke color. Each color value is
> a number between 0 and 1, inclusive. 0 is the minimum intensity and
> 1 is the maximum intensity.

Example

The code below draws a filled red triangle.

```
<?PHP
$FILENAME = "/tmp/example.pdf";
$WIDTH = 612;  $HEIGHT = 792;  // US letter size
$info = PDF_get_info();
$pdf_fp = fopen($FILENAME, "w+");
$pdf = PDF_open($pdf_fp, $info);
PDF_begin_page($pdf, $WIDTH, $HEIGHT);

PDF_setrgbcolor($pdf, 1, 0, 0);
PDF_setlinewidth($pdf, 10);
PDF_moveto($pdf, 25, 25);
PDF_lineto($pdf, 25, $HEIGHT - 25);
PDF_lineto($pdf, $WIDTH - 25, $HEIGHT - 25);
PDF_closepath_fill_stroke($pdf);

PDF_end_page($pdf);
PDF_close($pdf);
fclose($pdf_fp);
?>
```

Output

```
1
```

FILE-RELATED

basename (file)
remove any leading directory components from a file name

```
string basename(string filename);
```

> Given a string containing a *filename*, this function returns a string
> containing the file with any leading directory components removed.

Example

```
<?PHP
$str = basename("/home/httpd/html/index.html");
echo $str;
?>
```

Output

```
index.html
```

See also dirname().

---

chdir (directory)
change directory

```
int chdir(string directory);
```

> This function changes PHP's current directory to the specified direc-
> tory. It returns FALSE if it is unable to change the directory, otherwise
> it returns TRUE.

Example.

The code below lists the files in /tmp, and then in /.

```
<?PHP
chdir("/tmp");
system("/bin/ls");
chdir("/");
system("/bin/ls");
?>
```

---

chmod (file)
change file mode

```
int chmod(string filename, int mode);
```

> This function attempts to change the access permissions of the file specified by *filename* to that given in *mode*. The mode is not automatically assumed to be an octal value, and therefore you need to prefix *mode* with a zero (0). It returns TRUE on success, otherwise it returns FALSE.

Example

The example below will change the mode of /tmp/test.html so that you can read it and write to it, and others can read it. It also changes the mode of /tmp/test2.html so that only the owner of the file can read and write it.

```
<?PHP
chmod("/tmp/test.html", 0644);
chmod("/tmp/test2.html", 0600);
?>
```

Output

```
ls -l /tmp/test.html /tmp/test2.html
-rw-r--r--   1 nobody   nobody          0 Jan 01 00:00 test.html
-rw-------   1 nobody   nobody          0 Jan 01 00:00 test2.html
```

See also chown() and chgrp().

----

chgrp (file)(x)
change file group

```
int chgrp(string filename, mixed group);
```

> This function attempts to change the group of the file *filename* to *group*. Only the superuser may change the group of a file arbitrarily. Other users may change the group of a file to any group of which that user is a member. It returns TRUE on success, otherwise it returns FALSE.

Refer to *www.php123.com* for on-line example.

See also chown() and chmod().

----

chown (file)
change the owner of a file

```
int chown(string filename, mixed user);
```

> This function attempts to change the owner of the file *filename* to user *user*. Only the superuser may change the owner of a file. It returns TRUE on success, otherwise it returns FALSE.

Refer to *www.php123.com* for on-line example.

See also chown() and chmod().

----

clearstatcache (file)
clear file stat cache

```
void clearstatcache(void);
```

> The stat() system call on many systems is very slow. Therefore, the result of the last call to any of the status functions (listed below) is stored for use on the next such call using the same filename. If you wish to force a new status check, for instance, if the file is being checked many times and may change or disappear, use this function to clear the results of the last call from memory.
>
> Affected functions include stat(), file_exists(), filectime(), fileatime(), filemtime(), fileinode(), filegroup(), fileowner(), filesize(), filetype(), and fileperms().

Example

In the example below, the modification time of /etc/hosts is checked twice. If for some reason the modification time could change between the two calls, then clearstatcache() must be called in order to guarantee that filemtime() does not return stale data.

```
<?PHP
$filename = "/etc/hosts";
$time = filemtime($filename);

// other code

Clearstatcache($filename);
$time = filemtime($filename);
?>
```

----

closedir (directory)
close directory handle

```
void closedir(int dir_handle);
```

> This function closes the directory stream indicated by dir_handle. The stream must have previously been opened by opendir().

Example

see opendir().

----

copy (file)(x)
copy a file

```
int copy(string source, string dest);
```

> This function will make a copy of a file. It returns TRUE if the copy succeeded, otherwise it returns FALSE.

Example

The code below will copy the file "/tmp/list" to "/tmp/list.bak".

```
<?PHP
if(!copy("/tmp/list", "/tmp/list.bak")) {
  echo "Copy failed!\n";
}
?>
```

See also rename().

----

dir (directory)
directory class

```
new dir(string directory);
```

> This is a pseudo-object-oriented mechanism for reading a directory. The given directory is opened. Two properties are available once directory has been opened. The handle property can be used with other directory functions such as readdir(), rewinddir(), and closedir(). The path property is set to path the directory that was opened. Three methods are available: read, rewind, and close.

Example

The below code is the equivalent of the UNIX command "ls /tmp".

```
<?PHP
$dir = dir("/tmp");
   while($file = $dir->read()) {
      echo "$file";
   }
   $dir->close();
?>
```

----

dirname (file)
return file name part of path

```
string dirname(string filename);
```

> Given a string containing a file name, this function will return a
> string containing the directory part of the file name.

Example

```
<?PHP
$str = dirname("/home/httpd/html/index.html");
echo $str;
?>
```

Output

```
/home/httpd/html
```

See also basename().

----

fclose (file)(x)
close an open file pointer

```
int fclose(int fp);
```

> The file pointed to by *fp* is closed. Any buffered output is flushed and
> any buffered input is discarded. It returns TRUE on success and FALSE
> on failure. The file pointer must be valid, and it must point to a file
> successfully opened by either fopen() or fsockopen().

Example

The program below opens /etc/hosts, displays the first line from it, and then uses fclose() to close the stream.

```
<?PHP
$fp = fopen("/etc/hosts", "r");
echo fgets($fp, 1024);
fclose($fp);
?>
```

Output

```
localhost
```

See also fopen().

----

feoF (file)
test for end-of-file on a file pointer

```
int feof(int fp);
```

> This function returns TRUE if the file pointer *fp* is at EOF (end of file) or an error occurs. Otherwise, it returns FALSE. The file pointer must be valid, and it must point to a file successfully opened by fopen(), popen(), or fsockopen().

Example

The program below will display the contents of the file /home/httpd/html/index.html. It uses feof() to determine when to stop reading from the file.

```
<?PHP
$index_fp = fopen("/home/httpd/html/index.html", "r");
do {
  $section = fgets($index_fp, 1024);
  echo $section;
} while(!feof($index_fp));
fclose($index_fp);
?>
```

----

fgetC (file)
get character from file pointer

```
string fgetc(int fp);
```

This function returns a string containing a single character read from the file pointed to by *fp*. It returns FALSE on EOF. The file pointer must be valid, and must point to a file successfully opened by fopen(), popen(), or fsockopen().

Example

The program below will display the contents of the file /home/httpd/html/index.html. It uses the function fgetc() to read a character at a time from the file.

```
<?PHP
$index_fp = fopen("/home/httpd/html/index.html", "r");
$section = fgetc($index_fp);
do {
  echo $section;
  $section = fgetc($index_fp);
} while(!feof($index_fp));
fclose($index_fp);
?>
```

See also fopen(), popen(), fsockopen(), and fgets().

---

fgetS (file)
get line from file pointer

```
string fgets(int fp, int length);
```

This functions returns a string of up to (*length* – 1) bytes read from the file pointed to by *fp*. Reading ends when (*length* – 1) bytes have been read, a newline is encountered, or on EOF, whichever comes first. If an error occurs, it returns FALSE. The file pointer must be valid and must point to a file successfully opened by fopen(), popen(), or fsockopen().

Example

Assume the file /home/httpd/html/index.html contained the code below:

```
<HTML>
<HEAD><TITLE>The Title</TITLE></HEAD>
<BODY>Welcome</BODY>
</HTML>
```

The code below uses fgets() to read a line at a time from the file.

```
<?PHP
$index_fp = fopen("/home/httpd/html/index.html", "r");
while(!feof($index_fp)) {
  $line = fgets($index_fp, 1024);
  echo $line;
}
fclose($index_fp);
?>
```

Output

```
<HTML>
<HEAD><TITLE>The Title</TITLE></HEAD>
<BODY>Welcome</BODY>
</HTMLL>
```

See also fgetss(), fopen(), popen(), fgetc(), and fsockopen().

---

fgetSS (file)
get line from file pointer and strip HTML tags

```
string fgetss(int fp, int length);
```

> This function is identical to fgets(), except that fgetss() attempts to strip any HTML and PHP tags from the text it reads.

Example

Assume the file /home/httpd/html/index.html contained the code below:

```
<HTML>
<HEAD><TITLE>The Title</TITLE></HEAD>
<BODY>Welcome</BODY>
</HTML>
```

The code

```
<?PHP
$index_fp = fopen("/home/httpd/html/index.html", "r");
while(!feof($index_fp)) {
  $line = fgetss($index_fp, 1024);
  echo $line;
}
```

```
fclose($index_fp);
?>
```

Output

```
The Title
Welcome
```

See also fgets(), fopen(), fsockopen(), and popen().

----

file (file)
read entire file into an array

```
array file(string filename);
```

> This function is identical to readfile(), except that file() returns the file
> specified by *filename* in an array. If suppression of error messages is
> desired, then this function should be called as @file().

Example 1

The code below is the equivalent to "cat /etc/hosts".

```
<?PHP
$hosts = file("/etc/hosts");
$x = 0;
while( $hosts[$x])
   echo $hosts[$x++];
?>
```

Output 1

(will vary depending on the contents of your /etc/hosts)

```
127.0.0.1  localhost localhost.localdomain
192.168.0.1  example.com
```

Example 2

```
<?PHP

$web_page = file("http://example.com/test.html");
$x = 0;
while( $web_page[$x])
   echo $web_page[$x++];

?>
```

Output 2

The contents of test.html will be displayed.

See also readfile(), fopen(), and popen().

----

file_Exists (file)
check whether a file exists

```
int file_exists(string filename);
```

> This function returns TRUE if the file specified by *filename* exists, otherwise it returns FALSE.

Example

```
<?PHP
$filename = "/etc/hosts";
if(file_exists($filename))
   echo $filename." exists\n";
else
   echo $filename." does not exist\n";

$filename = "/etc/hosts.abcdef";
if(file_exists($filename))
   echo $filename." exists\n";
else
   echo $filename." does not exist\n";
?>
```

Output

```
/etc/hosts exists
/etc/hosts.abcdef does not exist
```

See also clearstatcache().

----

fileAtime (file)
get last access time of file

```
int fileatime(string filename);
```

> This function returns the time the file was last accessed, or FALSE in case of an error. A classic example of the use of this function is to find temporary files to delete that have not been used in the past week.

Example

```
<?PHP
$filename = "/etc/hosts";
$time = fileatime($filename);
echo $filename . " was last accessed on ". gmdate(
  "M d Y H:i:s", $time);
?>
```

Output

```
/etc/hosts was last accessed on Jan 01 1999 00:00:00
```

See also filectime() and filemtime().

---

fileCtime (file)
get a file's inode modification time

```
int filectime(string filename);
```

> This function returns the last time a file's inode information was modified, or FALSE in case of an error. The inode contains a file's attributes, including its location.

Example

```
<?PHP
$filename = "/etc/hosts";
$time = filectime($filename);
echo $filename . " inode was last changed on ". gmdate(
  "M d Y H:i:s", $time);
?>
```

Output

```
/etc/hosts inode was last changed on Jan 01 1999 00:00:00
```

See also fileatime() and filemtime().

---

fileGroup (file)
get file group

```
int filegroup(string filename);
```

> This function returns the group ID of the owner of the file, or FALSE in case of an error.

Example

The file /etc/hosts is typically owned by the root group. The root group has a group id (GID) of 0.

```
<?PHP
$filename = "/etc/hosts";
$gid = filegroup($filename);
echo $filename . " is owned by group ". $gid;
?>
```

Output

```
/etc/hosts is owned by group 0
```

See also Fileowner().

----

fileiNode (file)
get file inode

```
int fileinode(string filename);
```

> This function returns the inode number of the specified file, or FALSE in case of an error.

Example

```
<?PHP
$filename = "/etc/hosts";
$inode = fileinode($filename);
echo $filename . " inode # is ". $inode;
?>
```

Output

```
/etc/hosts inode # is 12345
```

----

fileMtime (file)
get file modification time

```
int filemtime(string filename);
```

> This function returns the time the file was last modified, or FALSE in case of an error.

Example

```
<?PHP
$filename = "/etc/hosts";
$time = filemtime($filename);
echo $filename . " was last modified on ". gmdate(
  "M d Y H:i:s", $time);
?>
```

Output

```
/etc/hosts was last modified on Jan 01 1999 00:00:00
```

See also fileatime() and filectime().

----

fileOwner (file)
get file owner

```
int fileowner(string filename);
```

> This function returns the user ID of the owner of the file, or FALSE in case of an error.

Example

The file /etc/hosts is typically owned by root. root has a user ID (UID) of 0.

```
<?PHP
$filename = "/etc/hosts";
$uid = filegroup($filename);
echo $filename . " is owned by UID ". $uid;
?>
```

Output

```
/etc/hosts is owned by UID 0
```

See also Filegroup().

----

filePerms (file)
get file permissions

```
int fileperms(string filename);
```

> This function returns the permissions on the file, or FALSE in case of
> an error.

Example

The file /etc/hosts typically has permissions of rw-r--r--(644).

```
<?PHP
$filename = "/etc/hosts";
$perm = fileperms($filename);
printf("%o", $perm);
?>
```

Output

```
100644
```

----

fileSize (file)
get file size

```
int filesize(string filename);
```

> This function returns the size of the file, or FALSE in case of an error.

Example

```
<?PHP
$filename = "/etc/hosts";
$size = filesize($filename);
echo $filename . " is " . $size . " bytes";
?>
```

Output

```
/etc/hosts is 19212 bytes
```

----

fileType (file)
get file type

```
string filetype(string filename);
```

> This function returns the type of the specified file in a string. Possible values are:
>
> | Type | Description |
> |------|-------------|
> | fifo | pipe or FIFO |
> | char | character special file (device) |
> | dir | a directory |
> | block | block special file (device) |
> | link | symbolic link |
> | file | regular file |
> | unknown | ? |
>
> It returns FALSE if an error occurs.

Example

```php
<?PHP
$filename = "/etc/hosts";
$type = filetype($filename);
echo $filename . " is a " . $type;

$filename = "/etc";
$type = filetype($filename);
echo $filename . " is a " . $type;

$filename = "/dev/null";
$type = filetype($filename);
echo $filename . " is a " . $type;
?>
```

Output

```
/etc/hosts is a file
/etc is a dir
/dev/null is a char
```

See also stat().

----

fopen (file)
open file or URL

```
int fopen(string filename, string mode);
```

This function opens the file or URL specified by *filename*. The *mode* is a string containing one of the values below:

r   Open an existing file for reading. The stream is positioned at the beginning of the file.

r+   Open an existing file for reading and writing. The stream is positioned at the beginning of the file.

w   Truncate the file to 0 length or create a file for writing. The stream is positioned at the beginning of the file.

w+   Open a file for reading and writing. If the file does not exist, then it is created, otherwise it is truncated. The stream is positioned at the beginning of the file.

a   Open the file for writing. The file is created if it does not exist. The stream is positioned at the end of the file.

a+   Open the file for reading and writing. The file is created if it does not exist. The stream is positioned at the end of the file.

If *filename* begins with "http://" (case-insensitive), an HTTP 1.0 connection is opened to the specified server, and a file pointer is returned to the beginning of the text of the response. This function does not handle HTTP redirects, so you must include trailing slashes on directories. If *filename* begins with "ftp://" (case-insensitive), an ftp connection to the specified server is opened, and a pointer to the requested file is returned. The server specified must support passive-mode ftp, or the fopen call will fail. If *filename* begins with anything else, the file will be opened from the filesystem, and a file pointer to the file opened will be returned. The function returns FALSE if the open fails. If suppression of error messages is desired, then this function should be called as @file().

Example 1

The program below creates a file (or truncates it if it already exists), and outputs a string to the file. It then reads the string back, and displays it.

```
<?PHP
$fp = fopen("/tmp/test", "w+");
fputs($fp, "This string goes into the file.\n");
```

```
rewind($fp);
echo fgets($fp, 1024);
fclose($fp);
?>
```

Output 1

```
This string goes into the file.
```

Example 2

The program below outputs the first two lines from *http://www.example. com/*.

```
<?PHP
$fp = fopen("http://www.example.com/", "r");
echo fgets($fp, 1024);
echo fgets($fp, 1024);
fclose($fp);
?>
```

See also fclose(), fsockopen(), readfile(), and popen().

---

fpassThru (file)
output all remaining data on a file pointer

```
int fpassthru(int fp);
```

> This function reads on the specified file pointer *fp* until EOF is encountered, and writes the results to standard output. If an error occurs, fpassthru() returns FALSE. The file pointer must be valid, and must point to a file that was successfully opened by fopen(), popen(), or fsockopen(). The file is closed when fpassthru() finishes. After that, *fp* should is no longer valid.

Example

The program below will display the contents of the file /home/httpd/html/ index.html. It uses fpassthru() to display the entire contents of the file.

```
<?PHP
$index_fp = fopen("/home/httpd/html/index.html", "r");
fpassthru($index_fp);
fclose($index_fp);
?>
```

See also file().

---

fputs (file)
write to a file pointer

```
int fputs(int fp, string str, int length);
```

> This function writes the string *str* to *fp*, where *fp* is a pointer to a file opened with fopen(). If the optional parameter *length* is specified, it writes up to *length* characters. Otherwise, it writes the entire string. fputs() is simply an alias to fwrite().

Example

The program below creates a file (or truncates if it already exists), and outputs a string to the file using fputs(). It then reads the string back, and displays it.

```
<?PHP
$fp = fopen("/tmp/test", "w+");
fputs($fp, "This string goes into the file.\n");
rewind($fp);
echo fgets($fp, 1024);
fclose($fp);
?>
```

Output

```
This string goes into the file.
```

See also fwrite().

---

fread (file)
binary-safe file read

```
string fread(int fp, int length);
```

> This function reads up to *length* bytes from the file pointer *fp*. Reading stops when either *length* bytes have been read or when EOF is reached, whichever comes first.

Example

Assume the file /home/httpd/html/index.html contained the following code:

```
<HTML>
<HEAD><TITLE>The Title</TITLE></HEAD>
<BODY>Welcome</BODY>
</HTML>
```

The code below shows how to use fread() to read from a file in 10 byte chunks. In practice, you would normally want to read from the file in larger chunks to minimize the number of system calls.

```
<?PHP
$index_fp = fopen("/home/httpd/html/index.html", "r");
do {
  $section = fread($index_fp, 10);
  echo $section;
} while(!feof($index_fp));
fclose($index_fp);
?>
```

Output

```
<HTML>
<HEAD><TITLE>The Title</TITLE></HEAD>
<BODY>Welcome</BODY>
</HTML>
```

See also fwrite(), fopen(), fsockopen(), popen(), fgets(), fgetss(), file(), and fpassthru().

----

fseek (file)
seek on a file pointer

```
int fseek(int fp, int offset);
```

> This function sets the file position indicator for *fp* to *offset* bytes into the file. It is equivalent to the Unix C function *fseek(fp, offset, SEEK_SET)*. It returns 0 on success, otherwise it returns −1. Note: Seeking past the end of the file (EOF) is not considered an error. This function may not be used on file pointers returned by fopen() if they are of the form "http://" or "ftp://".

Example

Assume the file /tmp/test contains the code below:

ABCD

The program below uses fseek() to read and display the four characters from the file in reverse order.

```
<?PHP
$fp = fopen("/tmp/test", "r");
fseek($fp, 3);
echo fgetc($fp);
fseek($fp, 2);
echo fgetc($fp);
fseek($fp, 1);
echo fgetc($fp);
fseek($fp, 0);
echo fgetc($fp);
fclose($fp);
?>
```

Output

DCBA

See also ftell() and rewind().

----

ftell (file)
tell file pointer read/write position

```
int ftell(int fp);
```

> This function returns the position of the file position indicator for *fp*.
> If an error occurs, it returns FALSE. The file pointer must be valid and
> must point to a file successfully opened by fopen() or popen().

Example

The program below reads through the file /home/httpd/html/index.html. It uses ftell() to output the current position in the file after each line is read.

```
<?PHP
$fp = fopen("/home/httpd/html/index.html", "r");
fgets($fp, 1024);
echo ftell($fp)."\n";
fgets($fp, 1024);
echo ftell($fp)."\n";
fgets($fp, 1024);
echo ftell($fp)."\n";
```

```
fgets($fp, 1024);
echo ftell($fp)."\n";
fclose($fp);
?>
```

Output

```
56
63
71
138
```

See also fopen(), popen(), fseek() and rewind().

----

fwrite (file)
binary-safe file write

```
int fwrite(int fp, string string, int length);
```

> This function writes the string *str* to *fp*, where *fp* is a pointer to a file opened with fopen(). If the optional parameter *length* is given, writing stops after *length* bytes have been written or the end of the string is reached, whichever comes first.

Example

The program below creates a file (or truncates it if it already exists), and it outputs a string to the file using fwrite(). It then reads the string back, and displays it.

```
<?PHP
$fp = fopen("/tmp/test", "w+");
fwrite($fp, "This string goes into the file.\n");
rewind($fp);
echo fgets($fp, 1024);
fclose($fp);
?>
```

Output

```
This string goes into the file.
```

See also fputs(), fread(), fopen(), fsockopen(), popen(), and fputs().

----

gzclose (gz)
close an open gz-file pointer

```
int gzclose(int zp);
```

> The file pointed to by *zp* is closed. Any buffered output is flushed and any buffered input is discarded. It returns TRUE on success and FALSE on failure. This function is similar to fclose().

Example

```
<?PHP
$zp = gzopen("test.gz", "r");
while(!gzeof($zp)) {
   $character = gzgetc($zp);
   echo $character;
}
gzclose($zp);
?>
```

Output

```
The quick brown fox
```

See also fclose() and gzclose().

---

gzeof (gz)
test for end-of-file on a gz-file pointer

```
int gzeof(int zp);
```

> This function returns TRUE if the file pointer *zp* is at EOF (end of file) or an error occurs. Otherwise, it returns FALSE. This function is similar to feof().

Example

```
<?PHP
$zp = gzopen("test.gz", "r");
while(!gzeof($zp)) {
   $character = gzgetc($zp);
   echo $character;
```

```
}
gzclose($zp);
?>
```

Output

```
The quick brown fox
```

See also feof() and gzclose().

----

gzfile (gz)
read entire gz-file into an array

```
array gzfile(string filename);
```

> The function returns the file specified by *filename* in an array. This
> function is similar to file().

Example

```
<?PHP
$test = gzfile("test.gz");
$x = 0;
while( $test[$x])
  echo $test[$x++];
?>
```

Output

```
The quick brown fox
```

See also file() and gzclose().

----

gzgetc (gz)
get a character from gz-file pointer

```
int gzgetc(int zp);
```

> The function returns a single uncompressed character from the file
> pointed to by *zp*. It returns FALSE on EOF. This function is similar to
> fgetc().

Example

```
<?PHP
$zp = gzopen("test.gz", "r");
while(!gzeof($zp)) {
   $character = gzgetc($zp);
   echo $character;
}
gzclose($zp);
?>
```

Output

```
The quick brown fox
```

See also fgetc() and gzclose().

----

gzgets (gz)
get a line from gz-file pointer

```
int gzgets(int zp, int length);
```

> The function returns an uncompressed string of up to (*length* – 1) bytes read from the file pointed to by *zp*. Reading ends when (*length* – 1) bytes have been read, a newline is encountered, or on EOF, whichever comes first. If an error occurs, it returns FALSE. This function is similar to fgets().

Example

Assume the file test.gz contained the uncompressed data below:

```
<HTML>
<HEAD><TITLE>The Title</TITLE></HEAD>
<BODY>Welcome</BODY>
</HTML>
<?PHP
$zp = gzopen("test.gz", "r");
while(!gzeof($zp)) {
   $line = gzgetss($zp, 1024);
   echo $line;
}
gzclose($zp);
?>
```

Output

```
<HTML>
<HEAD><TITLE>The Title</TITLE></HEAD>
<BODY>Welcome</BODY>
</HTML>
```

See also fgets() and gzclose().

----

gzgetss (gz)
get a line from gz-file pointer and strip HTML tags

```
int gzgetss(int zp, int length);
```

> This function is identical to fgets(), except that fgetss() attempts to
> strip any HTML and PHP tags from the text it reads. This function is
> similar to fgetss().

Example

Assume the file test.gz contained this uncompressed data:

```
<HTML>
<HEAD><TITLE>The Title</TITLE></HEAD>
<BODY>Welcome</BODY>
</HTML>

<?PHP
$zp = gzopen("test.gz", "r");
while(!gzeof($zp)) {
   $line = gzgetss($zp, 1024);
   echo $line;
}
gzclose($zp);
?>
```

Output

```
The Title
Welcome
```

See also fgetss() and gzclose().

----

gzopen (gz)
open a gz-file

```
int gzopen(string filename, string mode);
```

> This function opens the file specified by *filename*. The mode parameter is the same as the one used in fopen(), with the addition of compression level (for example, "rb9"). Reads on files opened with gzopen() are transparently decompressed, and writes are transparently compressed. If gzopen() fails, then FALSE is returned. This function is similar to fopen().

Example

```
<?PHP
$zp = gzopen("test.gz", "rb");
gzpassthru($zp);
?>
```

Output

```
The quick brown fox
```

See also fopen() and gzclose().

----

gzpassthru (gz)
output all remaining data on a gz-file pointer

```
int gzpassthru(int zp);
```

> This function outputs all remaining uncompressed output on the file pointed to by *zp*. After this function completes, *zp* is closed. It returns the number of bytes output or FALSE in case of error. This function is similar to fpassthru().

Example

```
<?PHP
$zp = gzopen("test.gz", "rb");
gzpassthru($zp);
?>
```

Output

```
The quick brown fox
```

See also readfile(), gzfile(), and gzpassthru().

----

gzputs (gz)
write to a gz file pointer

```
int gzputs(int zp, string str, int [length]);
```

> This function is an alias to gzwrite().

Example

See gzwrite().

See also gzwrite().

----

gzread (gz)
binary-safe gz-file read

```
int gzread(int zp, int length);
```

> This function reads up to *length* bytes from the gz file pointer *zp*.
> Reading stops when *length* bytes have been read or EOF is reached,
> whichever comes first. This function is similar to fread().

Example
```
<?PHP
$zp = gzopen("test.gz", "rb");
echo gzread($zp, 1024);
?>
```

Output
```
The quick brown fox
```

See also fread(), gzopen() and gzclose().

----

gzrewind (gz)
rewind the position of a gz file pointer

```
int gzrewind(int zp);
```

> This function sets the file position indicator for *zp* to the beginning of
> the file. If an error occurs, it returns 0.

Example

```
<?PHP
$zp = gzopen("test.gz", "rb");
echo gzread($zp, 1024);
gzrewind($zp);
echo gzread($zp, 1024);
?>
```

Output

```
The quick brown fox
The quick brown fox
```

See also rewind(), gzopen(), and gzclose().

----

gzseek (gz)
seek on a gz file pointer

```
int gzseek(int zp, int offset);
```

This function sets the file position indicator for *zp* to *offset* bytes
into the file. It is equivalent to the Unix C function *fseek(fp, offset,
SEEK_SET)*. It returns 0 on success, otherwise it returns −1. This
function is similar to fseek() with a notable difference: If a file is
opened for writing, then only forward seeks are supported. The
"empty" part of the file that was skipped over is filled with zeros.

Example

```
<?PHP
$zp = gzopen("test.gz", "rb");
echo gzread($zp, 1024);
gzseek($zp, 10);
echo gzread($zp, 1024);
?>
```

Output

```
The quick brown fox brown fox
```

See also fseek(), gzopen(), and gzclose().

----

gztell (gz)
tell gz file pointer read/write position

```
int gztell(int zp);
```

> This function returns the position of the file indicator for *zp*. If an error occurs, FALSE is returned. This function is similar to ftell().

Example

```php
<?PHP
$zp = gzopen("test.gz", "rb");
echo "File position: ".gztell($zp)."\n";
echo "Character read: ".gzgetc($zp)."\n";
echo "File position: ".gztell($zp)."\n";
echo "Character read: ".gzgetc($zp)."\n";
echo "File position: ".gztell($zp)."\n";
echo "Character read: ".gzgetc($zp)."\n";
?>
```

Output

```
File position: 0
Character read: T
File position: 1
Character read: h
File position: 2
Character read: e
```

See also ftell(), gzopen(), and gzclose().

----

readgzfile (gz)
output a gz-file

```
int readgzfile(string filename);
```

> This function outputs the file *filename* to standard output. If the file is compressed, then this function decompresses it. This function is similar to readfile(), except that it adds the ability to read compressed files.

Example

```php
<?PHP
readgzfile("test.gz");
?>
```

Output

```
The quick brown fox
```

See also readfile(), gzfile(), and gzpassthru().

---

gzwrite (gz)
binary-safe gz-file write

```
int gzwrite(int zp, string string, int [length]);
```

> This function writes the compressed contents of *string* to *zp*. If the *length* argument is given, writing stops after *length* bytes have been written or the end of *string* is reached, whichever comes first. This function is similar to fwrite().

Example

```php
<?PHP
$zp = gzopen("/tmp/test.gz", "wb");
gzwrite($zp, "The quick brown fox");
gzclose($zp);
?>
```

See also fwrite(), gzfile(), and gzpassthru().

---

is_Dir (file)
tell whether the filename is a directory

```
bool is_dir(string filename);
```

> This function returns TRUE if the filename exists and is a directory, otherwise, it returns FALSE.

Example

```php
<?PHP
$yes_no = array("no", "yes");

$filename = "/etc/hosts";
$answer = is_dir($filename);
echo $yes_no[$answer];

$filename = "/etc";
$answer = is_dir($filename);
```

```
echo $yes_no[$answer];
?>
```

Output

```
no
yes
```

See also is_file() and is_link().

---

is_Executable (file)
tell whether the filename is executable

```
bool is_executable(string filename);
```

> This function returns TRUE if the filename exists and is executable, otherwise it returns FALSE.

Example

```
<?PHP
$yes_no = array("no", "yes");

$filename = "/etc/hosts";
$answer = is_executable($filename);
echo $yes_no[$answer];

$filename = "/bin/ls";
$answer = is_executable($filename);
echo $yes_no[$answer];
?>
```

Output

```
no
yes
```

See also is_file() and is_link().

---

is_File (file)
tell whether the filename is a regular file

```
bool is_file(string filename);
```

> This function returns TRUE if the filename exists and is a regular file, otherwise it returns FALSE.

Example

```
<?PHP
$yes_no = array("no", "yes");

$filename = "/dev/null";
$answer = is_file($filename);
echo $yes_no[$answer];

$filename = "/etc";
$answer = is_file($filename);
echo $yes_no[$answer];

$filename = "/etc/hosts";
$answer = is_file($filename);
echo $yes_no[$answer];
?>
```

Output

```
no
no
yes
```

See also is_dir() and is_link().

---

is_Link (file)
tell whether the filename is a symbolic link

```
bool is_link(string filename);
```

> This function returns TRUE if the filename exists and is a symbolic link, otherwise it returns FALSE.

Example

```
<?PHP
$yes_no = array("no", "yes");

$filename = "/etc/hosts";
$answer = is_link($filename);
echo $yes_no[$answer];

$filename = "/bin/ls";
$answer = is_link($filename);
echo $yes_no[$answer];
?>
```

Output

```
no
no
```

See also is_dir() and is_file().

----

is_Readable (file)
tell whether the filename is readable

```
bool is_readable(string filename);
```

> This function returns TRUE if the filename exists and is readable, oth-
> erwise it returns FALSE. Note: PHP may be accessing the file as the
> user ID the web server runs as (most likely 'nobody'). Also, safe mode
> limitations are not taken into account.

Example

```
<?PHP
$yes_no = array("no", "yes");

$filename = "/etc/hosts";
$answer = is_readable($filename);
echo $yes_no[$answer];

$filename = "/etc/shadow";
$answer = is_readable($filename);
echo $yes_no[$answer];
?>
```

Output

```
yes
no
```

See also is_writeable().

----

is_Writeable (file)
tell whether the filename is writeable

```
bool is_readable(string filename);
```

> The function returns TRUE if the filename exists and is writeable,
> otherwise it returns FALSE. Note: PHP may be accessing the file as
> the user ID the web server runs as (most likely 'nobody'). Also, safe
> mode limitations are not taken into account.

Example

```
<?PHP
$yes_no = array("no", "yes");

$filename = "/etc/hosts";
$answer = is_writeable($filename);
echo $yes_no[$answer];

$filename = "/bin/ls";
$answer = is_writeable($filename);
echo $yes_no[$answer];
?>
```

Output

```
no
no
```

See also is_readable().

----

link (file)(x)
create a hard link

```
int link(string target, string link);
```

> This function creates a hard link to *target* named *link*. If *link* already
> exists, then it will not be overwritten. It returns TRUE on success,
> and FALSE otherwise. This new name, *link*, can be used exactly as the
> old one for any use. Both names now refer to the same file, therefore
> they have the same permissions and ownership. It is impossible to tell
> which name was the original.

Example

The code below creates a file named /tmp/b and links /tmp/a to it. Any
change to a also changes b, because they are the same file.

```
<?PHP
$link = "/tmp/a";
$target = "/tmp/b";
touch($target, 0);
if(!link($target, $link))
  printf("Could not create link.\n");
?>
```

Output

The code above will create the output below in /tmp.

```
-rw-r--r--    2 nobody    nobody          0 Jan 01  1970 a
-rw-r--r--    2 nobody    nobody          0 Jan 01  1970 b
```

See also the symlink() to create soft links, and readlink() along with link-info().

----

linkInfo (file)
get information about a link

```
int linkinfo(string path);
```

> This function returns the first array element returned from the lstat() function. This function is used to verify if a link really exists. It returns −1 in case of error.

Example

```
<?PHP
if(linkinfo("/dev/null") == -1)
  printf("File not found\n");
else
  printf("File found\n");
if(linkinfo("/dev/does_not_exist") == -1)
  printf("File not found\n");
else
  printf("File found\n");
?>
```

Output

```
File found
File not found
```

See also lstat(), symlink(), link(), and readlink().

----

iStat (file)
give information about a file

```
array lstat(string filename);
```

> This function returns an array with information about *filename*. If *filename* specifies a symbolic link, lstat() returns information for the link, rather than for the target of the link. Otherwise, lstat() is identical to stat(). See stat() for a list of the returned array contents.

Example: See stat().

See also stat().

----

mkDir (file)
make directory

```
int mkdir(string pathname, int mode);
```

> This function attempts to create the directory specified by pathname. It returns TRUE on success and FALSE on failure.

Example

```php
<?PHP
$dir_name = "/tmp/test.dir";
if(!mkdir($dir_name, 0700))
   echo "Could not create directory " . $dir_name;

if(!rmdir($dir_name))
   echo "Could not remove directory " . $dir_name;
?>
```

See also rmdir().

----

opendir (directory)
open directory handle

```
int opendir(string path);
```

> This function returns a directory handle to be used in subsequent closedir(), readdir(), and rewinddir() calls.

Example

The following code is the equivalent of the UNIX command "ls /tmp" or the MS-DOS command "dir /b". It lists the files in the directory /tmp.

```
<?PHP
$handle = opendir("/tmp");
$file_name = readdir($handle);
while($file_name) {
  echo $file_name."\n";
  $file_name = readdir($handle);
}
closedir($handle);
?>
```

See also closedir(), readdir(), and rewinddir().

---

pclose (file)
close process file pointer

```
int pclose(int fp);
```

> This function closes a file pointer to a pipe that was previously opened
> by popen(). The file pointer must be valid, and must have been returned
> by a successful call to popen(). It returns the termination status of the
> process that was run.

Example: See popen().

See also popen().

---

popen (file)
open process file pointer

```
int popen(string command, string mode);
```

> This function opens a pipe to a process executed by forking the com-
> mand given by *command*.
>
> It returns a file pointer identical to that returned by fopen(), except
> that it is unidirectional (like all pipes, it may be used only for either
> reading or writing, not both) and it must be closed with pclose(). This
> pointer may be used with the functions fgets(), fgetss(), and fputs(). If
> an error occurs, this function returns FALSE.

Example

The code below opens a pipe to the command ls, and reads its output.

```php
<?PHP
$fp = popen("/bin/ls -la /dev", "r");
$str = fgets($fp, 1024);
while(!feof($fp)) {
  echo $str;
  $str = fgets($fp, 1024);
}
pclose($fp);
?>
```

Output

```
total 17
drwxrwxr-x   2 root        root           21504 May   1  02:54 .
drwxr-xr-x  32 root        root            1024 May   1  1994 ..
crw-rw—       1 root        uucp        5,  64 May   1  1994 cua0
crw-rw—       1 root        uucp        5,  65 May   1  1994 cua1
crw-rw—       1 root        uucp        5,  66 May   1  1994 cua2
crw-rw—       1 root        uucp        5,  67 May   1  1994 cua3
[and so on …]
```

See also pclose().

----

readdir (directory)
read entry from directory handle

```
string readdir(int dir_handle);
```

This function returns the filename of the next file from the directory. The filenames are returned in no particular order.

Example

See opendir().

----

readFile (file)
output a file to stdout

```
int readfile(string filename);
```

This function reads a file specified by *filename* and then writes it to standard output. It returns the number of bytes read from the file. If an error occurs, then FALSE is returned and an error message is printed. If *filename* begins with "http://" (case-insensitive), an HTTP 1.0 connection is opened to the specified server, and the text of the response is written to standard output. This function does not handle HTTP redirects, so you must include trailing slashes on directories. If *filename* begins with "ftp://" (case-insensitive), an ftp connection to the specified server is opened, and the requested file is written to standard output. The server specified must support passive mode ftp, or the readfile() call will fail. If *filename* begins with neither of these strings, the file is opened from the filesystem, and its contents written to standard output. If suppression of error messages is desired, then this function should be called as @readfile().

Example 1

Display the contents of /etc/hosts.

```
<?PHP
$filename="/etc/hosts";
readfile($filename);
?>
```

Example 2

Display the contents of *http://www.example.com/*.

```
<?PHP
$filename="http://www.example.com/";
readfile($filename);
?>
```

Example 3

The code below demonstrates how @readfile() is used when you do not want an error message printed. The program below will create no output.

```
<?PHP
$filename="/etc/does_not_exist";
@readfile($filename);
?>
```

See also fpassthru(), file(), and fopen().

----

readLink (file)
Return the target of a symbolic link

```
str readlink(string path);
```

This function returns the target of a symlink specified by *path*, or 0 in case of error.

Example

The code below creates a symlink named /tmp/null to /dev/null. It then uses readlink() to find the target of /tmp/null.

```
<?PHP
$link = "/tmp/null";
$target = "/dev/null";
if(!symlink($target, $link))
  printf("Could not create link.\n");
echo "Target of link ".$link." is ".readlink($link);
?>
```

Output

```
Target of link /tmp/null is /dev/null
```

See also symlink(), readlink(), and linkinfo().

----

rename (file)
rename a file

```
int rename(string oldname, string newname);
```

This function attempts to rename the file *oldname* to *newname*. It returns TRUE on success and FALSE on failure.

Example

The code below creates a file named /tmp/abc. It then uses rename() to rename the newly created file to /tmp/def.

```
<?
touch("/tmp/abc");
if(!rename("/tmp/abc", "/tmp/def"))
```

```
        echo "Could not rename file.\n";
    ?>
```

---

rewind (file)
rewind the position of a file pointer

```
int rewind(int fp);
```

> This function sets the file position indicator for *fp* to the beginning of
> the file stream. If an error occurs, it returns 0. It is the equivalent of
> calling fseek(*fp*, 0). The file pointer must be valid, and must point to a
> file successfully opened by fopen().

Example

The program below creates a file (or truncates it if it already exists), and it
outputs a string to the file. Next, it uses rewind() to return to the start of the
file. It then reads the string back and displays it.

```php
<?PHP
$fp = fopen("/tmp/test", "w+");
fputs($fp, "This string goes into the file.\n");
rewind($fp);
echo fgets($fp, 1024);
fclose($fp);
?>
```

Output

```
This string goes into the file.
```

See also fseek() and ftell().

---

rewindDir (directory)
rewind directory handle

```
void rewinddir(int dir_handle);
```

> The function resets the directory stream indicated by `dir_handle` to
> the beginning of the directory.

Example

See opendir().

---

rmDir (file)
remove directory

```
int rmdir(string dirname);
```

> This function attempts to remove the directory named by *dirname*.
> The directory must be empty, and the process must have the relevant
> permissions. If an error occurs, it returns 0.

Example

```
<?PHP
$dir_name = "/tmp/test.dir";
if(!mkdir($dir_name, 0700))
  echo "Could not create directory " . $dir_name;

if(!rmdir($dir_name))
  echo "Could not remove directory " . $dir_name;
?>
```

See also mkdir().

----

stat (file)
give information about a file

```
array stat(string filename);
```

> This function returns an array with information about *filename*. The
> array contains the following:
>
> | Element | Description |
> | --- | --- |
> | *array[0]* | device |
> | *array[1]* | inode # |
> | *array[2]* | file permissions (in octal) |
> | *array[3]* | number of links |
> | *array[4]* | user id of owner |
> | *array[5]* | group id owner |
> | *array[6]* | device type if inode device |
> | *array[7]* | size in bytes |

array[8]	time of last access
array[9]	time of last modification
array[10]	time of last change
array[11]	blocksize for filesystem I/O
array[12]	number of blocks allocated

Example

```
<?PHP
$info = stat("/etc/hosts");
echo "device: ".$info[0];
echo "inode: ".$info[1];
printf("permissions: %o", $info[2]);
echo "number of links: ".$info[3];
echo "UID: ".$info[4];
echo "GID: ".$info[5];
echo "device type: ".$info[6];
echo "size in bytes: ".$info[7];
echo "last access: ".gmdate("M d Y H:i:s",$info[8]);
echo "last modification: ".gmdate("M d Y H:i:s",$info[9]);
echo "last change: ".gmdate("M d Y H:i:s", $info[10]);
echo "blocksize: ".$info[11];
echo "number of blocks allocated: ".$info[12];
?>
```

Output

```
device: 2049
inode: 16396
permissions: 100644
number of links: 1
UID: 0
GID: 0
device type: 0
size in bytes: 212
last access: Apr 07 1999 08:01:42
last modification: Apr 07 1999 06:07:23
last change: Apr 07 1999 06:07:23
blocksize: 4096
number of blocks allocated: 2
```

See also lstat() to look up information on a symbolic link.

----

symLink (file)
create a symbolic link

```
int symlink(string target, string link);
```

> This function creates a symbolic link named *link* that points to *target*.
> On success, TRUE is returned, otherwise FALSE is returned.

Example

```
<?PHP
$link = "/tmp/null";
$target = "/dev/null";
if(!symlink($target, $link))
  printf("Could not create link.\n");
?>
```

Output

```
The above code will create the below link in /tmp.
lrwxrwxrwx   1 nobody    nobody          9 Jan 01 00:00
/tmp/null -> /dev/null
```

See also link() to create hard links, and readlink() along with linkinfo().

----

tempNam (file)
create unique file name

```
string tempnam(string dir, string prefix);
```

> The function generates a unique temporary filename using up to the
> first five characters of *prefix* in the directory *dir*. It returns the new
> temporary filename, or on failure it returns the null string. It is simi-
> lar to the UNIX C function tempnam().

Example

```
<?PHP
$temp_filename = tempnam("/tmp", "PHP.");
echo $temp_filename;

$temp_filename = tempnam("/tmp", "PHP.");
echo $temp_filename;
?>
```

Output

```
/tmp/PHP.00583daa
/tmp/PHP.00583eaa
```

----

touch (file)
set modification time of file

```
int touch(string filename, int time);
```

> This function attempts to set the modification time of the file named
> by *filename* to the value given by *time*. If the option *time* is not given,
> then the present time is used. If the file does not exist, then it is cre-
> ated. The function returns TRUE on success and FALSE otherwise.

Example

```php
<?PHP
$filename = "/tmp/touch_example";

touch($filename);
$time = filemtime($filename);
echo $filename . " was last modified on ". gmdate(
  "M d Y H:i:s", $time);

touch($filename, 0);
Clearstatcache($filename);
$time = filemtime($filename);
echo $filename . " was last modified on ". gmdate(
  "M d Y H:i:s", $time);

sleep(5);
touch($filename);
Clearstatcache($filename);
$time = filemtime($filename);
echo $filename . " was last modified on ". gmdate(
  "M d Y H:i:s", $time);

unlink($filename);
?>
```

Output

```
/tmp/touch_example was last modified on Jan 01 1999 00:00:00
/tmp/touch_example was last modified on Jan 01 1970 00:00:00
/tmp/touch_example was last modified on Jan 01 1999 00:00:05
```
----

umask (file)

change the current umask

```
int umask(int mask);
```

> This function sets PHP's umask to *mask* & 0777, and it returns the old umask. umask is used to set initial file permissions on newly created files. The high-bits in *mask* specify which permissions to turn off. When called without any arguments, it simply returns the current umask.

Example

```
<?PHP
touch("/tmp/abc");
umask(00000);
touch("/tmp/def");
umask(00066);
touch("/tmp/ghi");
?>
```

Output

The output of the command "ls –l /tmp" would look something like:

```
-rw-r--r--  1 nobody  nobody     0 Jan 01 00:00 /tmp/abc
-rw-rw-rw-  1 nobody  nobody     0 Jan 01 00:00 /tmp/def
-rw-------  1 nobody  nobody     0 Jan 01 00:00 /tmp/ghi
------------------------------------------------------------------------------
```

unlink (file)

delete a file

```
int unlink(string filename);
```

> This function deletes *filename*. It is similar to the Unix C unlink() function. It returns FALSE on an error. Note: The file is not actually deleted until its link count is 0 (there are no hard links to it) and no other process has the file open.

Example

```
<?PHP
$filename = "/tmp/unlink_example";
```

```
touch($filename);
unlink($filename);
?>
```

See also rmdir() for removing directories.

Appendix 1

Variables Provided to PHP3 Scripts

Environment variables are name/value pairs that exist within a particular user's session. For example, they are often defined on login to a UNIX system or on boot on a DOS system. When logging onto a UNIX system, variables for your home directory, execution search path, and terminal type are usually created. Programs executed later may use this information. For example, the TERM variable is consulted by many applications to determine if it is possible to create more advanced output tailored to your specific terminal type. Web servers use environment variables to pass information to programs that they execute to handle client requests.

PHP3 provides a few variables that it makes available to scripts on execution.

CGI Environment Variables

As defined by the Common Gateway Interface specification, web servers pass data to scripts and applications using environment variables. These are used to describe the HTTP request from a client to the script. Following is a list of all of the standard variables provided by a web server to a CGI application. Most of the variables are available to a PHP3 script during execution. For more information on CGI, see *http://www.w3.org/CGI/* or *http:// hoohoo.ncsa.uiuc.edu/cgi/*. For information specifically on these environment variables, see *http://hoohoo.ncsa.uiuc.edu/cgi/env.html*.

SERVER_SOFTWARE
This variable contains the name and version of the web server software in the format "name/version". This variable is set for all requests. Typically, it looks something like this:

```
Apache/1.3.9 (Unix)
```

SERVER_NAME

This variable contains the server's hostname, and it is set for all requests. For example:

```
www.php123.com
```

GATEWAY_INTERFACE

This variable contains the version of the CGI specification to which the server complies, and it is set for all requests. Typically, it looks like this:

```
CGI/1.1
```

SERVER_PROTOCOL

This variable contains the name and revision of the protocol by which the request was made. Typically, it will be one of these two values:

```
HTTP/1.0
HTTP/1.1
```

SERVER_PORT

This variable contains the port from which the client request was received. By default, it is port 80, but it can be changed.

REQUEST_METHOD

This variable contains the HTTP method by which the request was made. The three most common values are "GET", "HEAD", and "POST". An example value is:

```
GET
```

PATH_INFO

This variable contains the extra path information, as given by the client.

PATH_TRANSLATED

This variable contains a translated version of PATH_INFO.

SCRIPT_NAME

This variable contains the virtual path to the script being processed. For example, if the URL of the PHP3 script is:

```
http://www.php123.com/test/getenv.php3
```

then the SCRIPT_NAME environment variable would contain:

```
/test/getenv.php3
```

QUERY_STRING

This variable contains the URL-encoded search string. The value of this variable is the characters following the "?" character in the URL. The contents of this variable are passed untouched to CGI programs and to PHP3 scripts. In other words, the URL-encoded URL is not decoded. For example, if the URL was:

```
http://www.php123.com/test/application.php3?type=search&text
=new+cars
```

then, the QUERY_STRING would be:

```
type=search&text=new+cars
```

REMOTE_HOST

This variable contains the hostname of the client who made the request. If this information is not available to the server, then the server will set REMOTE_ADDR and leave this variable unset. An example value is:

```
ppp1.php123.com
```

REMOTE_ADDR

This variable contains the IP address of the host who made the request. An example value is:

```
192.168.0.24
```

AUTH_TYPE

This variable contains the authentication-method used to validate the user. For more information on the two main authentication schemes, see *RFC 2617: HTTP Authentication: Basic and Digest Access Authentication.* Currently, PHP3 only supports the Basic method. Example value is:

```
Basic
```

REMOTE_USER

The value of this variable is set to the authenticated user's name. If the AUTH_TYPE variable's value is "Basic," then the value for REMOTE_ USER will be the user's identification sent by the client. PHP3 scripts should check the $PHP_AUTH_USER variable for this information rather than consulting this environment variable. An example value is:

```
joeuser
```

REMOTE_IDENT

This variable contains the remote user's name as retrieved from the remote client if both the client and the HTTP server support it. The method of obtaining this information is defined in *RFC 913: Authentication Server*. It is recommended that this value be used only for logging or other noncritical purposes. This limitation is due to the fact that this value is controlled by the remote machine. If you do not trust the remote machine, then you should not trust this value. An example value is:

```
joeuser.ppp1.php123.com
```

CONTENT_TYPE

The value contains the media type of the attached entity from queries that have attached information, like HTTP POST and PUT. If there is no attached entity, then it is set to NULL. HTTP uses MIME Content-Types, which provide for an open method of data typing and date type negotiation. A common value is:

```
application/x-www-form-urlencoded
```

CONTENT_LENGTH

The length of the attached entity from the client.

HTTP_ Variables

The environment variables that begin with the string "HTTP_" contain HTTP header information supplied by the client. The web server provides these headers to CGI programs by placing them in environment variables. These values are also available to PHP3 scripts.

HTTP_ACCEPT

This environment variable contains the MIME Content-Types that the client will accept. A common value could be:

```
image/gif, image/x-xbitmap, image/jpeg, */*
```

HTTP_USER_AGENT

This variable contains the browser the client is using to send the request as it defines itself. It is of the form "Software/Version." A few examples are:

```
Mozilla/2.0 (compatible; MSIE 3.01; Windows 95)
Mozilla/2.02 (X11; I; Linux 1.2.2 i486)
Mozilla/4.04 (Macintosh; I; PPC)
Lynx/2-4-1  libwww/2.14
```

HTTP_REFERER

This variable contains the page that referred the client to the current page. This variable is often (mis)used as a way of protecting access to a page or script. This is not recommended, because this variable is defined by the client in its HTTP request. In other words, a malicious client could specify any referrer that they wish or a privacy-enhanced proxy server may always remove this information. Typically, this information should only be used to either determine the path a user takes through your site or to estimate the number of other sites that link to your own. Note that the word *referrer* is intentionally misspelled as *referer* in this context. An example value:

```
http://www.php123.com/test/application.php3
```

$PHP_ Variables

On execution, PHP3 provides several variables to PHP3 scripts.

$PHP_AUTH_USER

When PHP3 is running as an Apache module, it is possible to use HTTP Authentication with PHP3. When the client sends back login information, this variable contains the value the client entered in the "Username" prompt. An example value is:

```
joeuser
```

$PHP_AUTH_PW

When PHP3 is running as an Apache module, it is possible to use HTTP Authentication with PHP3. When the client sends back login information, this variable contains the value the client entered in the "Password" prompt. An example value is:

```
mypasswd123
```

$PHP_AUTH_TYPE

When PHP3 is running as an Apache module, it is possible to use HTTP Authentication with PHP3. When the client sends back login information, this variable contains the type of authentication used. Currently, only the "Basic" authentication method is supported. An example value is:

```
Basic
```

$PHP_SELF

This variable contains the path of the current script. It is useful in creating a form in a script with an action that points back to the same script. An example value is:

```
/test/getenv.php3
```

Example

Example PHP3 script to display the above environment variables and PHP3 provided variables follows.

```php
<?PHP

    printf("SERVER_SOFTWARE    : %s\n", getenv(server_software));
    printf("SERVER_NAME        : %s\n", getenv(server_name));
    printf("GATEWAY_INTERFACE  : %s\n", getenv(gateway_interface));
    printf("SERVER_PROTOCOL    : %s\n", getenv(server_protocol));
    printf("SERVER_PORT        : %s\n", getenv(server_port));
    printf("REQUEST_METHOD     : %s\n", getenv(request_method));
    printf("PATH_INFO          : %s\n", getenv(path_info));
    printf("PATH_TRANSLATED    : %s\n", getenv(path_translated));
    printf("SCRIPT_NAME        : %s\n", getenv(script_name));
    printf("QUERY_STRING       : %s\n", getenv(query_string));
    printf("REMOTE_HOST        : %s\n", getenv(remote_host));
    printf("REMOTE_ADDR        : %s\n", getenv(remote_addr));
    printf("AUTH_TYPE          : %s\n", getenv(auth_type));
    printf("REMOTE_USER        : %s\n", getenv(remote_user));
    printf("REMOTE_IDENT       : %s\n", getenv(remote_ident));
    printf("CONTENT_TYPE       : %s\n", getenv(content_type));
    printf("CONTENT_LENGTH     : %d\n", getenv(content_length));
    printf("HTTP_ACCEPT        : %s\n", getenv(http_accept));
    printf("HTTP_USER_AGENT    : %s\n", getenv(http_user_agent));
    printf("HTTP_REFERER       : %s\n", getenv(http_referer));
    printf("HTTP_HOST          : %s\n", getenv(http_host));
    printf("PHP_AUTH_USER      : %s\n", $PHP_AUTH_USER);
    printf("PHP_AUTH_PW        : %s\n", $PHP_AUTH_PW);
    printf("PHP_AUTH_TYPE      : %s\n", $PHP_AUTH_TYPE);
    printf("PHP_SELF           : %s\n", $PHP_SELF);
?>
```

Appendix 2

PostgreSQL and fsync()

Normally, PostgreSQL will call the system function fsync() after every completed transaction. This system function tells the operating system to copy all dirty file buffers in memory to disk. This guarantees that in the event of OS crash, database server crash, or power loss, all of your data is saved to disk. This mode of operation is very conservative, even more so than most other database systems. This mode of operation can be changed if performance is a more important requirement than reliability in the event of à crash.

When does the call to fsync() affect you? For example, when you do an UPDATE on a table, the command doesn't return (PHP waits) until the updated data is actually on the disk. Disabling the fsync() resulted in some of the author's PHP/PostgreSQL applications executing 5 to 20 times faster.

To disable the fsync() after each transaction, the command line option "-o –F" is used. On a UNIX system with a System V-style init system, PostgreSQL would be started on boot with a file named something like `/etc/rc.d/init.d/postgresql`. This option is added to the line where the postmaster process is started. It might look something like this:

```
su postgres -c '/usr/bin/postmaster -o -F -S -D/var/lib/
  pgsql -i'
```

The following table shows some timings (in seconds) of operations comparing PostgreSQL with fsync() (default) to PostgreSQL without fsync(), and to MySQL.

#	Description	PostgreSQL (default)	PostgreSQL (-o -F)	MySQL
1	A "null" timing, used to gauge the overhead" of the timing program.	0.000666	0.000666	0.000666
2	Connect	0.034303	0.034303	0.003105
3	Close	0.001097	0.001097	0.001099
4	1,000 inserts of two 50-character fields.	104.610781	5.230026	1.392756
5	100,000 inserts of two 50-character fields.	10606.060477	542.529195	243.724906
6	Delete of 1,000 records	0.678882	0.168635	0.08427
7	1 insert of two 50-character fields	0.148681	0.071726	0.00344
8	2 inserts of two 50-character fields	0.225288	0.079386	0.004734
9	Delete of 2 fields	0.141734	0.049482	0.003649
10	100 inserts of two 50-character fields	11.446849	0.579557	0.14569
11	Delete of 100 fields	0.173735	0.048706	0.003677
12	Vacuum on an empty db	4.027462	0.421858	N/A
13	Vacuum after 1,000 adds, then 1,000 deletes	4.099376	0.478491	N/A
14	SELECT on 1,000 records	0.241862	0.229982	0.049104
15	SELECT on 100,000 records	23.656851	23.656851	4.870907

A few notes on the timings: The execution times were computed using two calls to the PHP3 function microtime() both before and after the operation in question. The difference between the two times is shown in the table. The first time of about six microseconds measures the overhead of calling and saving the time with PHP3. These values should not be taken as absolutes, because the timings vary as much as a few milliseconds between runs due to factors outside of PHP3's control.

Conclusions

As we expected, reading from the database (using SELECT statements) is not affected by disabling the fsync() system call after each transaction. From looking at run #4, PosgreSQL is over 20 times faster writing data with fsync() disabled. This is a rather contrived test, because you typically wouldn't do 1,000 INSERT SQL statements in a single script execution. If you typically read data and rarely write data, then keeping the fsync() at its default is acceptable. If you write a good bit of data using INSERT, UPDATE, or DELETE, then disabling the fsync() could be a good trade-off. The individual sysadmin will have to balance the trade-offs, and make their own decision.

Reading List

Books

Advanced Programming in the UNIX Environment by W. Richard Stevens. Reading, MA: Addison-Wesley. 1992. 744 pages.

An Introduction to Database Systems by C. J. Date. (Systems Programming Series, Ed. 6). Reading, Mass.: Addison-Wesley. 1994. 839 pages.

Apache: The Definitive Guide by Ben Laurie and Peter Laurie. Sebastopol, Calif.: O'Reilly & Associates. 1999. 392 pages.

Code Complete: A Practical Handbook of Software Construction by Steve C. McConnell. Redmond, Washington: Microsoft Press. 1993. 857 pages.

HTML: The Definitive Guide, 3rd Ed., by Chuck Musciano and Bill Kennedy. Sebastopol, Calif.: O'Reilly & Associates. 1998. 608 pages.

The Art of Computer Programming: Fundamental Algorithms, Vol. 1, 3rd Ed., by Donald Ervin Knuth. Reading, Mass.: Addison Wesley Longman. 1997. 700 pages.

The Art of Computer Programming: Seminumerial Algorithms, Vol. 2, 3rd Ed., by Donald Ervin Knuth. Reading, Mass.: Addison Wesley Longman. 1997. 762 pages.

The Art of Computer Programming: Sorting and Searching (Art of Computer Programming, Vol. 3, 2nd Ed.) by Donald Ervin Knuth. Reading, Mass: Addison Wesley Longman. 1998. 780 pages.

Papers Available via the Web

Scripting: Higher Level Programming for the 21st Century, IEEE Computer magazine, March 1998, by John K. Ousterhout. Also available from *http://www.scriptics.com/people/john.ousterhout/scripting.html*.

The Cathedral and the Bazaar by Eric Steven Raymond. Available from *http://www.tuxedo.org/~esr/writings/cathedral-bazaar/*.

Open Source: Programming as if Quality Mattered by Eric Steven Raymond. Available from *http://www.intellectualcapital.com/issues/issue173/item1329.asp*.

The Linux Documentation Project. Available from *http://www.linuxdoc.org/*.

Important RFCs

RFC 1866: Hypertext Markup Language – 2.0
RFC 2068: Hypertext Transfer Protocol – HTTP/1.1
RFC 1725: Post Office Protocol, Version 3
RFC 822: Standard for the Format of ARPA Internet Text Messages
RFC 821: Simple Mail Transfer Protocol
RFC 1867: Form-Based File Upload in HTML

Other Important Standards

"HTML 3.2 Reference Specification"—available from *http://www.w3c.org/*.
"HTML 4.0 Specification"—available from *http://www.w3c.org/*.

Function Index

Index

Addison-Wesley Professional

How to Register Your Book

Register this Book

Visit: **http://www.aw.com/cseng/register**
Enter the ISBN*
Then you will receive:

- Notices and reminders about upcoming author appearances, tradeshows, and online chats with special guests
- Advanced notice of forthcoming editions of your book
- Book recommendations
- Notification about special contests and promotions throughout the year

*The ISBN can be found on the copyright page of the book

Visit our Web site

http://www.aw.com/cseng

When you think you've read enough, there's always more content for you at Addison-Wesley's web site. Our web site contains a directory of complete product information including:

- Chapters
- Exclusive author interviews
- Links to authors' pages
- Tables of contents
- Source code

You can also discover what tradeshows and conferences Addison-Wesley will be attending, read what others are saying about our titles, and find out where and when you can meet our authors and have them sign your book.

We encourage you to patronize the many fine retailers who stock Addison-Wesley titles. Visit our online directory to find stores near you.

Contact Us via Email

cepubprof@awl.com
Ask general questions about our books.
Sign up for our electronic mailing lists.
Submit corrections for our web site.

mikeh@awl.com
Submit a book proposal.
Send errata for a book.

cepubpublicity@awl.com
Request a review copy for a member of the media interested in reviewing new titles.

registration@awl.com
Request information about book registration.

Addison-Wesley Professional
One Jacob Way, Reading, Massachusetts 01867 USA
TEL 781-944-3700 • FAX 781-942-3076